AUSTRALIAN ECONOMIC DEVELOPMENT IN THE TWENTIETH CENTURY

Other Books for Students

INTERNATIONAL POLICY FOR THE WORLD ECONOMY
J. O. N. Perkins
University of Melbourne

THE ECONOMICS OF SOCIALISM
J. Wilczynski
Royal Military College, Duntroon

THE GROWTH OF THE INTERNATIONAL ECONOMY
A. E. Kenwood and A. L. Lougheed
University of Queensland

ACCEPTABLE INEQUALITIES
Ian Bowen
University of Western Australia

THE POLITICS OF NEW STATES
ed. R. D. Scott
Queen's University, Belfast, formerly University of Sydney

AUSTRALIAN ECONOMIC DEVELOPMENT IN THE TWENTIETH CENTURY

Essays by

W. A. SINCLAIR
N. CAIN
C. FORSTER
PAT BROWN and HELEN HUGHES
J. A. DOWIE
N. G. BUTLIN

edited by

C. FORSTER
Reader in Economic History
Australian National University

LONDON: GEORGE ALLEN & UNWIN LIMITED
SYDNEY: AUSTRALASIAN PUBLISHING COMPANY

FIRST PUBLISHED IN 1970

George Allen & Unwin ISBN 0 04 330171 1 *cased*
0 04 330172 x *paper*

Australasian Publishing Company, Sydney
SBN 900882 28 x *paper*

PRINTED IN GREAT BRITAIN
in 10 on 11 point Times Roman
BY BILLING & SONS LIMITED
GUILDFORD, SURREY

PREFACE

The purpose of this book is to analyse some aspects of Australian economic development in the twentieth century and place them in historical and international perspective. In Australia the nineteenth century has been studied much more intensively than the twentieth, and in this latter period the long-run examination of almost any economic topic must break new ground. The main economic histories of the period were written either before the Second World War or come close to general history. Earlier works have naturally dated, and little has been done to integrate the periods before and after the war.

This wide gap in the understanding of Australian development stems in part from the inadequate supply of small-scale studies, and in part from the fact that continuous and reliable statistical material may be only just beginning to emerge. These essays take a modest step towards an interpretation of the period. In their search for a natural starting point in time, most of the writers have chosen the break in development imposed by the depression at the beginning of the 1890s. All writers take their analysis into the 1960s and some are prepared to speculate on future developments. Their essays contain the results of recent research and, although the contributors have benefited from discussion and mutual criticism, each essay remains very firmly the work of its author. Contributors have retained virtual sovereignty in matters of interpretation and presentation. One aspect of this sovereignty is revealed in the level of presentation. It has been the intention of the writers to seek a fairly wide audience and present their work at a level appropriate to first and second year university students. To hit this target precisely has been a difficult task, and the reader must judge for himself how successfully it has been achieved.

Each essay is complete in its own right and it is inevitable and desirable that there be some overlap in content between them.

Various people have helped in the production of this book, but in particular I would like to thank Mrs Helen Bridge for invaluable editorial assistance.

COLIN FORSTER

CONTENTS

Chapter 1

CAPITAL FORMATION[1]

W. A. Sinclair

Capital formation usually plays a central role in economic life through its influence on economic growth and stability. At any particular time the level of investment, which is both an important item of expenditure in itself and also generates additional expenditure, is a major determinant of the level of economic activity. Over time, additions to the capital stock are an essential basis for increasing production. Of the two, it is the contribution to economic growth which is the more important, partly because in the long run economic growth makes a greater contribution to human welfare than economic stability, by providing the possibility of an overall rise in living standards. In addition, the primary aim of most investment is to secure a return, the influence on the level of economic activity being a side effect, so that it is unlikely that a high level of capital formation would be maintained if a satisfactory rate of growth of output was not being achieved, whereas the continuance of investment is much less dependent on stability in the past. In view of this, it would be reasonable to devote more attention to the relationship between capital formation and economic growth even if the complexity of the subject did not demand it in any case.

CAPITAL FORMATION AND ECONOMIC GROWTH

The extent to which capital formation generates economic growth will depend on its total amount and the fruitfulness of its components. Although these aspects are not completely unrelated, they can be kept separate for purposes of analysis. No such analysis would, however, be satisfactory without reference to the composition of newly created capital because both aspects of capital forma-

[1] Part of a grant from the Australian Research Grants Committee was used in the collection of material for this chapter.

tion are dependent on it. In the first place, total investment must largely be regarded as a composite outcome of the amounts of particular types of investment undertaken. Secondly, because the fruitfulness of different types of capital can differ, a given aggregate investment can vary in productivity according to its composition. For these reasons, in the discussion which follows, a central place is given to an extended treatment of the changing pattern of capital formation in twentieth-century Australia.

1. AGGREGATE CAPITAL FORMATION

One of the outstanding features of the Australian economy in the twentieth century, as indeed before that time, has been the large volume of investment which has taken place. In the 1960s, Australia occupied a very high position among countries ranked according to the proportion of gross domestic capital formation to gross domestic product. Only two countries, Norway and Iceland, appear to have exceeded it and it was approached among the advanced industrial nations only by West Germany.[2] Even before the Second World War it was higher than that currently attained by some developed economies.[3]

Fundamentally, high investment was a response to the multiplicity of opportunities for the development of a recent area of settlement well endowed with natural resources, and it is no coincidence that Canadian statistics suggest a rate of investment which is about the same as that of Australia.[4] At the stage of development which had been reached by the beginning of the twentieth century, Australia was a region in which there were latent possibilities of long-term expansion in both the primary and secondary divisions of industry. This in itself was an inducement to a high rate of capital formation but, in addition, the broad spectrum of investment opportunities could only be exploited with the aid of large injections of capital either to facilitate an eventual increase in output or to provide the

[2] The respective proportions may be stated as Norway about 29 per cent, Iceland about 24 per cent, Australia about 24 per cent and West Germany about 23 per cent. Based on statistics published in *Yearbook of National Account Statistics*, United Nations, New York.

[3] A calculation of about 18 per cent for Australia in the period 1900–30 was derived from statistical tables in N. G. Butlin, *Australian Domestic Product, Investment and Foreign Borrowing 1861–1938/39*, Cambridge University Press, London, 1962. This is about the same as the current French proportion and compares with USA, currently about 16 per cent, and UK about 15 per cent.

[4] *Yearbook of National Account Statistics.*

amenities which rising output made necessary. Several features of the region contributed to the volume of the required expenditure. Development involved a rapid increase in the population and, whether this came from overseas or was native born, it required the creation of capital equipment particularly in the form of means of shelter but also to provide for health, educational and other needs. The acceptance of high standards of housing by the community generally added to the importance of expenditure for this reason, as did also the fact that some of the population increase occurred in areas not formerly closely settled with little or no existing capital equipment for them to use. The obstacles of large distances and shortage of water were other aspects of development which could only be overcome by a large expenditure of funds.

If the general climate for investment was thus an expansive one, it is nevertheless not possible to explain the higher rate of investment after the Second World War in these terms, for the influences arising from the novelty of settlement in the area and from its natural characteristics were no stronger than previously. The important difference was the higher level of effective demand both at home and overseas. This had the immediate effect of creating a more favourable environment for investment on a broad front. It also meant that the scarcity of labour associated with the resultant high level of employment was an inducement to switch to more capital-intensive methods of production, a phenomenon which seems to have been most noticeable in agriculture.

During most of the period under consideration, then, and particularly after the Second World War, there was a high demand for capital, and this partly explains the high rate of investment. It might be thought that, to make this possible, the Australian rate of saving must also have been high. That, however, was not the case. The actual rate of investment could not have been achieved, given the level of consumption in Australia, without a significant inflow of funds from overseas. The periods when this occurred were for a few years before the First World War, in the 1920s and since the Second World War. In the first two of these, the main attraction of Australia for overseas investors was a rate of interest on government bonds which was higher than that obtainable in more developed countries and which was guaranteed by governments as stable as in those countries. After the Second World War, an element which was present in the 1920s supplanted these earlier attractions, namely, the opportunities for the profitable expansion of successful overseas companies into certain sectors of the Australian economy.

Funds were thus freely available at particular times to allow many of the investment opportunities available in Australia to be taken up and to ensure that capital formation in the aggregate was likely to make an important contribution to economic growth.

2. THE PATTERN OF CAPITAL FORMATION

Aggregate rates of investment tell us little about the role of capital formation in an economy unless they are broken down into specific categories to reveal a sectoral pattern. In the period with which we are concerned in Australia, the most meaningful way of doing this is in terms of the distinction between rural and urban investment. Looking at the period as a whole, one of the most conspicuous features of capital formaton has been the extent to which it has occurred in cities. The significance of this is not just that it reflects the high degree of urbanization in Australia. What makes it central to an understanding of the whole process of investment during the period concerned is that it has happened in spite of the fact that at the beginning of the century the governments of the Australian states, which were responsible for nearly half of the total capital formation of the next thirty years, were attempting to implement investment policies designed to create a quite different state of affairs. Their capital expenditure was directed to primary-producing regions with the explicit intention of generating additional investment there in order to facilitate the closer settlement of rural areas. This movement gathered momentum in the first half of the second decade of the century to take on the characteristics of a large-scale programme of rural development and it became an article of faith in the 1920s. Yet it is in that decade that the trend of capital formation becomes clearly set in favour of the cities.

The failure of governments to determine the pattern of investment even while they were still adhering to, and indeed stepping up, their efforts is a central paradox in the explanation of the composition of capital formation since the 1890s. The conflict was most intense in the period between the depressions of the 1890s and the 1930s. The reaction of the governments after that time was to lose much of their enthusiasm for creating a rural pattern of settlement and to play a much more passive role in general, responding to the pressures arising from private investment instead of attempting to take the initiative themselves. In the 1950s both state and Commonwealth governments increased their capital expenditure most rapidly on facilities to reduce congestion of various types in the cities. The rural construction they financed was largely intended to preserve a balance between town and country rather than create a new one. The tendency for public investment thus to be largely a combination of a laggard response to urban problems and a defensive operation in the country was a far cry from the circumstances at the commencement of the century. The state was no longer attempting to use its position as a large investor to influence to any great extent the behaviour of the private sector which must therefore be explained either in terms of forces internal to that sector or by other aspects of governmental policy. This significant change in the role of government in capital formation is an essential reference point for an understanding of the whole process of investment in the twentieth century.

The Setting for Twentieth-century Capital Formation

A marked change in the environment for investment which occurred in the 1890s provided the setting for capital formation in the twentieth century. For most of the second half of the nineteenth century the main inducements to invest had been an extreme housing shortage, an absence of effective transport links between main centres of population and the high profitability of wool growing.[5] The depression and subsequent drought between them made it evident that these inducements were no longer operative. Houses now stood unoccupied, the construction of a main trunk-line railway system was nearing completion in eastern Australia, and investment in wool growing had been carried far beyond the limits set by productive and market possibilities. As investible funds gradually became available again they would necessarily be used to produce a different pattern of capital formation from that in the past.

What that pattern would be was not immediately obvious, for the economy presented an opportunity for a choice of investment opportunities which had no parallel before that time. The pattern established in the thirty years before the depression of the 1890s was, at least initially, to a large extent an inescapable one. An inflow of population in the 1850s, of exceptional proportions on any standards, inevitably led to a marked emphasis on the provision of shelter in succeeding years. In addition, the wool industry was an obvious candidate for development and the necessity to provide means of transport difficult to ignore. All these activities required

[5] N. G. Butlin, *Investment in Australian Economic Development 1861-1900*, Cambridge University Press, London, 1964, Ch. 3.

large injections of capital and, given its scarcity, there was little left over for other uses. In the 1890s, on the other hand, the priorities were much less clear because more immediate pressures had now been met and the wool industry had lost its attraction.

The governments of the mainland states were not slow in reaching decisions to determine what the new pattern of capital formation would be and opted for the goal of the diversification of rural industry. In some respects, what had happened in the past seemed to point the way. The case for continuing with railway building was very strong if only because the construction of branch lines could make the existing system less uneconomic. More positively, a more closely-knit rail network would permit the development of newer rural industries, such as wheat growing, for which transport costs were crucial and proximity to a railway line essential. But the governments' resumption of their traditional role as railway builders was only a part of a whole new approach to rural development in which large-scale expenditure on irrigation and roads came to be seen as additional integral components. This in itself was, in a sense, an outcome of the previous pattern of capital formation in that the concentration on investment in the wool industry before 1890 was now clearly seen to have been excessive. Governmental action, that is, was essentially directed towards the correction of an imbalance which had developed in Australian economic growth.

Governmental Failure

In their attempts to restore balance to rural development, the state governments were motivated by the underlying aim of providing sevices which private investors could not or would not be prepared to undertake because of divergences between private and social costs. Their capital expenditure must therefore be judged not in terms of what proportion it constituted of total capital formation but of the extent to which it led to an overall pattern of investment which was consistent with the governments' intentions.

At first sight, the statistics suggest a more serious failure than was probably the case. Before 1890 the share of capital formation in primary industry was much larger than in manufacturing, whereas in the 1920s it fell below it (see Table 1·1). The period when the new governmental policy of rural development was put into operation thus coincided with a shift away from investment in the sector it was designed to encourage. However, the main reason for this change was that the period when the wool industry's basic equipment was constructed had come to an exaggerated end in the 1890s and that the equipment was more than adequate long into the twentieth century.

> In the second half of the nineteenth century Australian pastoralists constructed the equipment necessary to apply a new technology of wool production on an industry-wide basis; they built to the scale appropriate to 106 million sheep. Until the 1930s there was no sign of substantial alterations to that technology; and until 1930 the number of sheep remained below 106 million.[6]

What capital formation there was in the wool industry was mainly connected with protection against rabbits and with water supply and was largely associated with sub-division of large holdings as reconstruction went on in the industry.[7]

TABLE 1.1. *Shares in Gross Private Capital Formation 1880–1930* (per cent)

	Pastoral and Agricultural	Manufacturing
1881–90	37·7	7·7
1901–10	18·3	13·6
1921–30	16·1	19·3

Source: Butlin, *Australian Domestic Product*, pp. 20–1.

It need not follow, then, that the capital requirements of the newer primary industries which the governments were concerned to stimulate would be so great as to compensate for the demise of pastoral construction as a main form of capital formation. In point of fact, the technology on which the wheat industry's new surge of growth was based was mainly one of new breeds of wheat, use of fertilizers and fallowing, none of which necessitated much accompanying investment. The change in the ratio between investment in primary industry and in manufacturing is thus not incompatible with the aim of rural development. Given the provision of social overhead capital by the state, agricultural output was

[6] N. G. Butlin and A. Barnard, 'Pastoral Finance and Capital Requirements, 1860–1960', in A. Barnard, ed., *The Simple Fleece*, Melbourne University Press, Melbourne, 1962, p. 397.

[7] Ibid., pp. 397–8.

in a position to increase rapidly without much additional investment.

Nevertheless it is difficult to interpret the statistical evidence as pointing to the success of rural-development expenditure. As shown in Table 1.1, some of the shift away from investment in primary industry is located within the period under consideration and cannot therefore be ascribed to the changed position of the wool industry. Further, the long-term nature of the governments' investment plans might lead us to expect that the passage of time would tell in favour of a higher proportion of capital formation in primary industry whereas the reverse seems to have been the case.

It is possible that this does less than justice to private investment in rural areas through failing to take sufficient account of the value of improvements in the newer industries.[8] But it is by no means clear in cases where it is possible to associate particular items of public investment with the results accruing to them, that it can be shown that governments were significantly influencing the pattern of total capital formation. Thus there is a tendency in New South Wales for the volume of wheat carried on new railway lines completed during the First World War and soon afterwards to rise quickly at first but then fail to continue rising.[9] The initial response seems too quick to be an example of new settlement being stimulated and the subsequent stagnation suggests that there was little longer-term effect of this nature. A similar phenomenon was even more noticeable at the same time in Victoria where, outside the eastern Mallee and East Gippsland, it was often not just a question of stagnation but of actual decline in the value of freight carried. In both states only a little over half of the new mileage added between about 1900 and 1930 was associated with lines which could unequivocally be classed as wheat lines.[10] Many of the rest seem to have had little effect at all on investment in the areas they serviced. Irrigation expenditure in New South Wales is another case where it was admitted that in the first half of the 1920s public investment was not being followed by the expected response from the private sector, the number of new settlers not

[8] An attempt to estimate the value of improvements for the 1920s has been made by G. O. Gutman, 'Investment and Production in Australian Agriculture', *Review of Marketing and Agricultural Economics*, XXIII, 1955, pp. 237–310. However, the numerous problems involved cast doubt on the usefulness for our purposes of the results achieved.

[9] Based on figures of wheat carried from all stations presented annually in the Railway Commissioners' Reports, *NSW Parliamentary Papers*, 1920–9.

[10] Based on information given in the reports of Parliamentary Standing Committees, *NSWPP* and *Victorian Parliamentary Papers*, 1900–30.

coming up to the expectations on which expenditure had been based.[11] The balance of the evidence would thus seem to be that the respective proportions of investment in primary industry and in manufacturing after more than twenty years of governmental expenditure on rural development were not what the governments concerned had intended them to be.

If we turn to another major category of capital formation, residential construction, we find further support for this thesis for, in spite of the aims of public-investment policy, the pattern of house building was essentially a metropolitan one. In the first three decades of the twentieth century approximately 65 per cent of new houses built in Australia were located in the state capital cities, and for Victoria the proportion was more like three-quarters.[12] The failure of private investment in general to follow the lead of the public sector thus seems to be clear.

Inadequate Co-ordination of Public Expenditure

The unsuccessful outcome of the efforts of the state governments to promote rural development is not easily to be explained for there was a strong case for it on economic grounds. At the beginning of the twentieth century, land was still a plentiful factor of production in the sense that settlement was still sparse in many areas which were capable of more intensive development. We would expect capital formation to be primarily geared to exploiting this natural advantage and to be concentrated in land-using industries given that there was a market for primary products overseas. It would further seem a wise policy for governments to encourage a pattern of capital formation which took due account of the nature of resource endowment and capitalized on freely available natural resources.

An examination of governmental action between 1900 and 1930 strongly suggests that the fault lay less in the above analysis than in the manner in which the policy of developing natural resources was implemented. Two major defects were, firstly, that the various aspects of policy lacked sufficient co-ordination to lead to the expected results and secondly, that, even looked at in isolation, the projects undertaken were based on an inadequate appraisal of their economic consequences.

The charge of faulty co-ordination requires strong corroboration,

[11] *NSWPP*, 1924, IV, p. 265.

[12] These calculations are based on statistics given in Commonwealth censuses, 1901–33.

for at first sight there appears to have been a new appreciation in this period of the necessity for looking at public investment in rural areas as an integrated whole. Governments were no longer content, as in the nineteenth century, simply to link a region capable of development with a port by means of railway line. It was accepted that, in addition, roads must be built as feeders to the railway lines, dry areas must be irrigated in order to diversify primary production and permit more intensive use of the land, and the latter must be actively promoted by purchases of land and extension of credit to settlers. To make this possible, major administrative changes were made. There was a transfer of power during the period from local authorities which had neglected road building and from local water trusts whose attempts at irrigation had been primitive, to state governments. State instrumentalities were created to co-ordinate water conservation and make decisions as to the allocation of funds for this purpose. Subsequent to this, main roads boards were set up to spend funds on a state-wide basis with the help of expert advice as well as some financial assistance from the Commonwealth. Much of public capital formation in this period seems to have comprised an interrelated block of additions to productive capacity associated with a shift from local to more overall control based on a higher level of expertise.

Nevertheless, the apparently high degree of integration involved was to a large extent illusory and served to conceal the piecemeal nature of much governmental spending. In the first place, the timing of the various types of expenditure is not suggestive of a master plan. It was not until the 1920s that road building came to be taken seriously, by which time the long years of neglect had created a backlog of needs which was never made up in the period under consideration. The years of most vigorous road building, moreover, coincided with the period of disenchantment with irrigation, with the result that it was only in the first half of the 1920s that an approach to the full balanced development suggested earlier can be said to have occurred.

Secondly, the potential gains from interrelated public expenditure were far from fully realized because of poor co-ordination between the parts. There were obvious difficulties of overall planning inherent in the federal system and little attempt was made to overcome them by taking account of the fact that state boundaries did not necessarily mark off economic regions. Possibly more important was the high degree of independence of the intra-state instrumentalities. It would not be true to say that these authorities never took account of the relationship between their plans and what was being done in other directions. But the general pattern was one of piecemeal developments with co-ordination only occurring when one authority adjusted its plans to prior action on the part of another. New South Wales, where about 30 per cent of total public capital formation occurred, provided the most telling evidence of this. The co-ordination of authority in the irrigation settlements there has received favourable notice elsewhere[13] and thus the picture is not all black. However, looking at the state as a whole, there were major lacunae. It was New South Wales that the Commonwealth Transport Committee had mainly in mind when, right at the end of the 1920s, it was still drawing attention to the need for an authority to 'weld the transportation system into one unit, operating to the greatest advantage of the community and to ensure that all expenditure on the construction of new developmental works whether roads, railways, ports or irrigation should be mutually adjusted'.[14] The New South Wales Main Roads Board conceded this by complaining of lack of co-ordination and suggesting, a little late in the day in 1930, that 'it would be well to determine the whole programme of public works involved before entering upon any one of them'.[15] The authorities themselves were thus providing the evidence of their own shortcomings.

In Victoria, the next most important state with respect to public capital formation, the greater degree of co-operation which was achieved had its pitfalls, for in some important cases it had the effect of compounding errors of judgement on the part of one of the authorities and thus committing a larger volume of funds to basically unsound projects. Thus mistakes made in the choice of areas for closer settlement and irrigation were followed by the provision of roads and other services to these areas.[16] Another example is provided by the decision taken on very dubious economic grounds to build a railway line from Talangatta to Cudgewa which induced the Country Roads Board to build a number of roads in the region as the only way in which 'the new line would

[13] J. Andrews, 'The Emergence of the Wheat Belt in South-eastern Australia to 1930', in J. Andrews, ed., *Frontiers and Men*, Cheshire, Melbourne, 1966, p. 34.

[14] Report on Co-ordination of Transport by the Commonwealth Transport Committee, May 9, 1929, *Votes and Proceedings of the House of Representatives*, 1929, p. 111, as quoted in *NSWPP*, 1929–30, I, p. 1011.

[15] *NSWPP*, 1929–30, I, p. 1012.

[16] See below.

develop into a payable proposition in a reasonable time.[17] Although the Board was not always as explicit as this, the Talangatta–Cudgewa line was not an isolated example of unwise railway construction[18] and there must have been other cases where roads were built to complement uneconomic lines.

Early Laxity in Investment Criteria

Much of the above critique of rural development schemes implies a more fundamental weakness, namely, a failure to adopt satisfactory economic criteria in planning them. That this is no simple question is apparent from current difficulties in applying sophisticated techniques of cost-benefit analysis to actual situations. The main available ingredients for successful long-term investment in the early twentieth century were an act of faith and a lot of common sense. Nor were economic considerations the only ones which a government might be expected to take into account. Nevertheless, it was true of a large part of the governments' programmes that not sufficient account was taken of them to ensure that the objects of governmental policy were achieved. This either arose because no serious attempt was made to assess the costs and benefits of particular proposals or because the attempts that were made were too unrealistic.

The prevalence of such attitudes from an early stage in the new approach to rural development is most vividly exemplified by the manner in which the new enthusiasm for irrigation and closer settlement was translated into action. In 1916 a Royal Commission on closer settlement in irrigable districts in Victoria reported that 'from the commencement of the movement fundamental faults were committed all along the line of its development',[19] these being mainly concerned with the selection and purchase of the land which 'were conceived and carried out in a manner so crude as to be scarcely credible'.[20] The responsibility for these decisions lay with the first Chief Commissioner of the State Rivers and Water Supply Commission, who stated in a revealing sentence that the Commission 'did not go into the matter as a business proposition'.[21] The Royal Commission concluded that 'there was no evidence

[17] *VPP*, 1916, II, p. 594. A few years later the Board was making special mention of 'the construction of substantial road and bridge works between Corryong and the new railway terminus', *VPP*, 1923–4, II, p. 144.

[18] See the statement on the proportion of lines built for wheat growing in the state, p. 18, above.

[19] *VPP*, 1916, II, p. 564. [20] Ibid., p. 567. [21] Ibid., p. 503.

forthcoming that there had been any attempt to investigate the suitability of the land for intense cultivation'[22] and it was generally achnowledged that the Commission had not had available to it any expert advice.[23]

Similar aspersions can be cast on the activities of the Victorian Closer Settlement Board, the members of which admitted in 1915 that 'they had little time at their disposal for inspecting lands . . . as there were so many things demanding attention'.[24] A Royal Commission calculated that nearly two-thirds of the land so acquired was either unadaptable or 'more or less a failure'.[25] It concluded that 'the increased settlement under the Closer Settlement Acts does not justify the expenditure that has been incurred'.[26]

This particular chapter of errors has been cited firstly because, as has been suggested above,[27] on the choice of land for closer settlement depended much other public capital formation. Secondly, it was in Victoria that the greatest effort was made at this time to establish successful farming on small holdings and it is Victorian planning which has been singled out for special mention by other authorities.[28] It may therefore be significant that the nerve centre of the new governmental determination to encourage investment in rural areas with deliberative planning of public capital formation, little regard was taken of elementary economic determinants of the viability of the projects.

Public Investment Criteria after the First World War

If it is apparent that governmental spending on rural development was already strongly influenced by lack of prudence before 1914, this became much more the case in the 1920s. To some extent this was a consequence of the First World War. The pressure to settle returned soldiers on the land as quickly as possible was too strong to be ignored and there was a repetition of the sort of errors which had been so recently exposed in the Victorian Inquiries. Soldier settlement was said not to be 'solely a business proposition',[29] thus neatly echoing the words of the pre-war Chief Commissioner of the Victorian State Rivers and Water Supply Commission. The

[22] Ibid., p. 517.
[23] Ibid., p. 517–19, *passim.*
[24] *VPP*, 1915, II, p. 49.
[25] See table, ibid., p. 57.
[26] Ibid., p. 82.
[27] See p. 21, above.
[28] Andrews, *Frontiers and Men*, pp. 34–5, argues that close co-operation between the authorities concerned in Victoria took the place of formal co-ordination.
[29] *VPP*, 1925, II, p. 1087.

departmental machinery for handling soldier settlers was forced to breaking point[30] and in the circumstances, according to the Royal Commission which reported in 1925, 'it was suprising not that there had been so many mistakes but that there were so few'.[31] A basic weakness was again the choice of land for settlement as was also the case with the settlement of migrants as indicated by the Royal Commission of 1933 which found that 'the evidence showed that such investigations as had been made were not enough to justify confidence that either the soil or the rainfall would enable farming to be carried on successfully'.[32]

In a more general sense, the war and the subsequent vision of Empire Settlement created a climate of opinion in which the beneficial results of large-scale rural construction tended to be taken for granted. When the Prime Minister stated that Australia's resources, 'if brought to full development would probably solve most of the economic problems that face the world today',[33] he spoke for the nation. Such an atmosphere was not conducive to the careful estimation of costs and benefits.

The effect is perhaps most clearly seen on railway building. The resumption of construction after the depression of the 1890s was based on an awareness of the importance of the external economies of a transport system, but there was no adequate machinery for ensuring that these were assessed realistically by those who took the decisions on which new lines were to be built. The parliamentary sub-committees which considered proposals was neither equipped nor had the time to do so and they frequently overruled the rough-and-ready attempts at assessment on the part of railway officials as being too cautious, although these often actually proved too optimistic. As the Commonwealth Transport Commission put it, 'the methods adopted were insufficient to ensure that full consideration was given to the economic aspect'.[34] In these cirumstances, the determining factor in new approvals was the amount of finance available, the same vague justification being given for a whole block of new lines of varying potential productivity.

In New South Wales, the main railway-building state, each decade after 1900 saw a further erosion of economic criteria. In the early years of the century there was a concentration on filling in the Riverina network, where the case for railways was probably

[30] Ibid., p. 1068.
[31] Ibid., p. 1069.
[32] *VPP*, 1033, II, p. 955.
[33] S. M. Bruce, *Commonwealth Parliamentary Debates*, 113, 1926, p. 2462.
[34] *NSWPP*, 1929–30, I, p. 1011.

as strong as anywhere in Australia, although it would have been more economical to route the New South Wales produce of the region through Melbourne. With respect to proposals for lines to other areas, the Committees of Inquiry were at this time cautious. They became less so from about the beginning of the second decade of the century when increased loan funds became available to make possible a greatly expanded building programme. Some of the new lines approved were branches in good wheat-growing areas and of a type most easy to justify on economic grounds. But it is apparent that a multiplicity of lines were now being approved in a wide range of areas with little difference in the reasons given for approval. Some of these were lines which had been previously proposed and rejected.

The completion of the new batch of approvals was checked by the war, and it was not until the first half of the 1920s that there was scope for consideration of new proposals. When the Committees of Inquiry applied themselves to this task they did so in the expansive post-war climate of expectations to which reference has already been made. In tune with the spirit of the times there was a further liberalization of the criteria adopted. The minimum area of wheat land, which it was accepted that a line should service, was explicitly reduced[35] at a time when the coming of motorized transport would have justified a move in the opposite direction. The expected annual losses on new lines approved were much greater than had been countenanced previously.[36] Many long lines were approved despite a statement in one report that short lines were preferable because long lines increased the value of the land adjacent to them and thus made the intended closer settlement more difficult.[37]

A similar tendency for railway lines to be built with an increasingly nonchalant attitude to the limits of external economies is apparent in Western Australia[38] and Queensland. In the latter the Royal Commissions were frequently content with a recommendation from the Railway Commissioner that he was familiar with the route the line would follow. Queensland also provides the most conspicu-

[35] *NSWPP*, 1924, III, p. 629.

[36] The extreme case was the expected loss of £117,748 on the Guyra-Dorrigo line (*NSWPP*, 1926–7, II, p. 404). The pre-war high of £31,982 for the Dubbo-Werris Creek line (*NSWPP*, 1913, III, p. 625) was itself an exception for the period, argued partly on strategic grounds.

[37] *NSWPP*, 1912, III, p. 964.

[38] S. Glynn, 'Government Policy and Agricultural Development: Western Australia, 1900–1930', *Australian Economic History Review*, VII, 1967, pp. 115–41.

ous example, although New South Wales is also important in this respect, of lines being built on the principle that equality required that the whole state should be serviced rather than that there should be a concentration on areas of greatest economic potential. Some proposals for lines which seemed to have much to recommend them were refused on this ground.[39]

Victoria and South Australia differed in some respects from New South Wales, Western Australia and Queensland with regard to railway building. In neither state was there much scope left for extensive construction and in each case proposals for new lines were examined much more carefully. In South Australia many lines were rejected in the 1920s on the grounds that they would place an undue burden on the taxpayer.[40] Nevertheless, in Victoria at least, the closer scrutiny did not prevent many doubtful proposals from getting through the net. On the most generous estimate it would seem that about one-third of the new mileage added in the period as a whole was of dubious economic significance and the proportion was much higher than that after 1910.

Looking at the overall picture of railway building in Australia, the timing of the war seems to have contributed to the failure of public-investment policies. In the first twenty years of the twentieth century, the railway construction programme was at a stage where, given reasonable care in the selection of lines, additions to mileage were likely to enhance the value of the whole railway system. In three states at this time, the transition from a trunk-line to a branch-line system was being carried out. However, any subsequent development might be expected to have the opposite effect since it would involve extension of the rail system into areas which were less suited to the sort of primary production most dependent on transport facilities. Thus at a time when, in the normal course of events, there would have been a strong case for tapering railway building off sharply, a new stimulus to construction was felt in the form of the post-war vision of Empire Settlement. As a result, governments persisted with an innovation in transport which, even if the competitive force of the internal combustion engine had not been felt, would have been at the point of diminishing returns set by the pattern of natural resources.

[39] See, for example, the Report on the proposed line from Goologong to Wirrinya, *NSWPP*, 1924, III, p. 621 ff.

[40] *South Australian Parliamentary Papers*, 1925, II (p. 5 of the 13th General Report of the Parliamentary Standing Committee on Railways), for a clear statement to this effect.

Road Construction in the 1920s

If the third decade of the century, then, was a period when governments followed old paths to rural development with less regard to where they were leading, it was also one when an intensified approach was made towards a comprehensive transport system by the building of roads. It might be thought that this new departure would have helped to compensate for excesses in other directions. However, the evidence does not clearly point to this conclusion. There are, for a start, even greater difficulties in assessing the economic benefits of a road than of a railway line, even when the authorities concerned address themselves seriously to the question.[41] In the 1920s, economics seems to have played little part in the decisions of road-making instrumentalities. The New South Wales Main Roads Board had only just got around in 1930 to recognizing the need for 'a comprehensive study of the whole state to be undertaken with a view to selecting the roads which will result in the greatest development',[42] but it concluded plaintively that 'this would involve time and expense'.[43]

One important factor which could have been taken into account was the relationship between roads and the existing railway system. There was indeed a general recognition of the role which roads could play in complementing the railway system, particularly by acting as feeders to the lines in the wheat-growing areas, but little was done in this direction outside South Australia. In Victoria, where the most ambitious programme of road construction was undertaken and the most deliberate planning attempted, the principle received a low priority. A much higher one was given to the rebuilding of the existing arterial highways centring on Melbourne[44] and, as these ran alongside the main trunk railway lines, the construction of a system of improved roads in direct competition with the railways.

The other main guiding principle of the Victoria Country Roads Board was that roads should be built in areas which had previously lacked any effective transport and Gippsland was selected for special treatment. The consequence of this was to concentrate expenditure on remote areas which, with the exception of parts of

[41] Governmental attention has only recently been turned to the question of the economics of roads following the establishment of the Commonwealth Bureau of Roads.
[42] *NSWPP*, 1929–30, I, p. 1011.
[43] Ibid.
[44] First Annual Report of the Country Roads Board, *VPP*, 1914, II, p. 73 ff.

Gippsland suited to dairying, were not capable of intensive land use. Remote areas also received special attention in New South Wales and Queensland because of the policy of arbitrarily distributing a proportion of the funds available for road building to each section of the state. In Queensland, this principle was carried to the point that each of the major geographical regions received an equal share of the funds without allowance being made for differing population or other features.[45] In addition, in all states road building was a piecemeal affair because it still depended on the energy of local authorities.

Unintended Consequences of Rural Public Investment

There thus seems to be a good deal of evidence to show that much of the expenditure on rural development in the first thirty years of the twentieth century was ill conceived from the point of view of its economic return. It should not be inferred from this that it is part of our present purpose to pronounce judgement on the governments concerned. To do that would require taking many things into account. In particular, it may be argued that, at the time when the decisions were taken, their economic consequences were not as obvious as they later became. In addition, it is legitimate to point to the possible results which flowed from rural construction, particularly irrigation, after the end of the 1920s and also to the political difficulties of taking decisions on solely economic grounds. The point of the preceding discussion, however, has not been to weigh the governments in the balance but to indicate one reason for their failure to determine the pattern of capital formation. That is, that they seem to have proceeded on the assumption that the mere existence of public capital equipment would lead to complementary private investment. But the latter was dependent on the nature of the public assets created. The methods adopted by governments militated against the success of their policies.

If the injection of public funds thus did not provide as much stimulus to the rural economy as was intended, it also had some unexpected side effects in contributing to the importance of capital formation in the cities. In the first place, the nomadic nature of the large rural construction work force often made it more convenient for their dependents to live in the cities and thus add to the demand

[45] *NSWPP*, 1926, II, pp. 956–7. Note the comment of the Queensland Main Roads Board that 'this restraint demands caution in the gazettal of new roads in the Southern division, where the bulk of the population is concentrated'. *Queensland Parliamentary Papers*, 1926, II, p. 1256.

for urban facilities. Secondly, since the underlying purpose of rural development programmes was to make it possible for a larger population to live in Australia, capital expenditure in rural areas was linked with expenditure on assisting immigration. But it did not follow that the migrants would find their way into rural employment. They might well have a preference for city life and, given other factors favouring urban development, they might be able to realize it. If this were so, then the houses required for the new migrants, as well as for native-born Australians, would tend to find an ubran location and the work force involved in house building would be largely an urban work force. The resulting tendency for a snowballing growth of cities may have been encouraged by a special situation which existed as a result of the depression of the 1890s. The cheapness of urban labour following the end of the building boom, particularly in Melbourne, was probably one of the factors which induced manufacturers to shift to metropolitan locations in the early twentieth century.[46] This contributed to a growth of manufacturing industry based on the economies of concentration which was well under way when immigration resumed on a large scale in the second decade of the century. New immigrants at that time were faced with the prospect of expanding opportunities for employment in factories in Melbourne and Sydney.

A third aspect of the paradox of rural-development expenditure accelerating urban capital formation derives from the long-term nature of the investment involved. A great deal of it needs to be seen as one large investment project with a long gestation period between its commencement and its full completion. In the intervening period there was little incentive for investment in primary industry, whereas the opportunities for manufacturing investment gave the appearance of offering a quick return. This could have led to certain types of urban capital formation rising faster during the gestation period of rural investment than investment in primary industry, and this may have led in turn to the formation of urban vested interests which could continue, with the backing of governmental action, to lay claim to resources even after the point at which it may have become more economic to invest in rural industry. To some extent this must be qualified to allow for the delayed results of rural capital formation undertaken before 1890, but it is not obvious that the qualification is important enough to invali-

[46] Helen Hughes, 'Federation and Industrial Development', paper presented to Section G, Australian and New Zealand Association for the Advancement of Science, 1964, pp. 6–7.

date the point, for the railway system had not got far beyond the stage of trunk-line construction before 1890 and construction for purposes of irrigation was negligible up to that time.

The Favourable Climate for Urban Capital Formation

The shift of emphasis towards urban capital formation was by no means only an indirect consequence of public expenditure on rural development. There were other forces working in the same direction. To some extent these were inherent in the pattern of capital formation before 1890. For instance, the adoption of a fan system of trunk railway lines emanating from metropolitan centres in south-eastern Australia meant that the only practicable modification that could be made thereafter could not reverse the strong influence in favour of urban capital formation which was exerted by the highly centralized transport system. More generally, the process of urbanization set in train by this and other factors before 1890 had acquired a momentum of its own and was throwing up such hitherto neglected communal needs as sewerage and street improvement which would require heavy capital expenditure to satisfy them. Thus the claims of rural development for investible funds were already open to challenge in the cities at the beginning of the period under consideration. Had diversification of primary industry come sooner than it did, it is possible that the pattern of capital formation after 1900 might have been different, since the concentration on wool before the 1890s restricted opportunities for rural employment and hence helped to stimulate urban growth. By the time rural diversification did start to become significant, it was probably too late to reverse a trend towards urbanization which was backed by powerful vested interests.

Space does not permit an adequate discussion of new factors making for urbanization after 1900 even if enough were known about them. The adoption of a policy of tariff protection of manufacturing industry, for instance, by the Commonwealth government was a major step. But this is only one facet of the general influence of Australian social characteristics on the location of capital being translated into political action. Democratic forms of government and a balance between the major economic interest groups permitted the social preference for city life to be realized as a result of governmental measures which often insulated the community from the pull of economic forces. An existing pattern of urban living was thus perpetuated by legislation and regulation.

Nevertheless, urbanization was not without some economic

rationale. There were signs by the 1920s that Australia's natural advantage in exploiting its favourable land endowment was becoming less marked. The increased wheat output of the 1920s was a result of recourse being made to less suitable land than had previously been developed.[47] The basic argument for rural development was becoming less strong. However, a smooth transition to a more urbanized location of capital equipment could not be expected. It was difficult to change course at this time. The extension of the wheat belt before 1914 under favourable economic auspices built up a head of steam which was further fed by post-war plans for Empire Settlement. For governments to have exercised greater caution with respect to rural capital formation would have been to reverse a previously successful line of development and it took time for adjustment to be made to changing economic circumstances. The tendency for public and private investment to pull in opposite directions was thus partly a reflection of the stage which economic growth had reached in Australia. And the increasing tendency to protect manufacturing industry in the 1920s is to some extent indicative of an awareness of the reality of the situation. There is evidence from the mid-twenties at least that governments saw the tariff not just as politically expedient but also as an alternative to the policy of rural development. As has already been suggested, non-economic forces also exerted strong pressure in favour of urbanization and so exacerbated the apparent conflict in governmental policies. But the 1920s are an important decade because at that time economics was joining with other elements to sow the seeds of a new pattern of capital formation.

The Importance of Urban House Building

The type of capital formation most responsive to the forces making for urbanization was residential construction. Most of the first three decades of the twentieth century may be regarded as taking in one upward trend, for, although the level did not rise consistently throughout, the downturns which occurred can best be seen as interruptions to a long-term process of meeting the housing needs of a growing economy.[48] The fact that the upswing commenced as early as the very beginning of the century may seem suprising in view of the excess of the boom of the 1880s and the collapse and continued straitened circumstances of the building societies which

[47] Andrews, *Frontiers and Men*, pp. 21–6, 36–8 and 60.

[48] The course of residential construction is depicted in Chart 1.2.

had financed it. The explanation is to be found partly in the fact that housing is an industry in which excess capacity in one place does not inhibit new construction elsewhere. One reason for the generally high level of house building in Australia has been that new developments have often opened up new regions. Thus, at the beginning of the twentieth century the developments of Western Australia, following the gold discoveries of the 1890s, stimulated building there and this was soon added to by the effects of the extension of the wheat belt in New South Wales.[49] In any case, the worst excesses of speculative building had been concentrated in Melbourne and sufficient time had now elapsed in other centres for a modest recovery to get under way. This was encouraged by the consequences of the large emigration from Melbourne in the 1890s, since most of the migrants went to other states rather than overseas.

These accumulating pressures for a return to the days of a high level of building activity were strengthened at about the beginning of the second decade of the century by a resumption of heavy immigration to Australia and an age distribution of the native-born population which had become favourable to a bouyant market for houses.[50] The combined effect of these two influences, aided by improved lending facilities for housing,[51] set in train a strong building boom.

The gathering momentum of house building before the First World War is important to an understanding of the surge of construction to new levels in the 1920s. The war did more than create a backlog of housing needs by its effect in initiating an important downturn in building. It also cut short a boom which was underpinned by a strong groundswell of population pressure. Thus even before the main resumption of immigration after the war, new construction was proceeding at a rapid rate. The inflow of population which followed soon afterwards caught this wave and added considerably to the demand at a time when the post-war shortage of building materials was being alleviated by increased production. The continuance of immigration in the first half of the 1920s seems

[49] N. G. Butlin, 'Some Structural Features of Australian Capital Formation, 1861–1938/39', *Economic Record*, XXXV, 1959, pp. 400–1.

[50] A. R. Hall, 'Some Long Period Effects of the Kinked Age Distribution of the Population of Australia, 1861–1961', *Economic Record*, 39, 1963, Table 3, p. 50.

[51] Cf. Annual Report of the Modern Permanent Building Society for the year ended July 31, 1911: 'Having emancipated ourselves from the obligations to our former creditors, the question now arises as to whether we should continue an active building society business.' Australian National University Archives.

to have been important enough to prevent a significant narrowing of the gap between the demand for houses and the supply. The situation was described as one of shortage with houses as difficult to obtain as just before the war.[52] The boom was further fed by an improvement in the size and quality of houses.

From about half way through the decade the pressures for new houses began to ease. The backlog of past demand was now being made up and fears were expressed in Melbourne that speculative builders were building ahead of effective demand.[53] Immigration slackened and was not counter balanced by internal population pressures because there was now a low proportion of the population in the house-buying age group.[54] The marriage rate had been dropping steadily since the beginning of the decade and now stood well below the pre-war figure.[55] The boom was more strongly maintained in Sydney than Melbourne, the latter having some noticeable excess capacity in 1928[56] which was a record year for house building in Sydney.

In the light of earlier discussion, the increasing association between house building and urban growth is particularly significant. In the early years of the century, rural development such as that in the new wheat belt of New South Wales had an important influence on the location of new houses. But from the beginning of the second decade, the centre of interest swings unmistakeably to the cities. By that time Melbourne, worst hit in the depression of the 1890s, had thrown off its hangover as a result of population changes and the construction of tramlines which brought the outer suburbs within easy reach of the city. The serious shortage of housing became a matter of public comment. The *Argus*, with an eye for human interest, claimed that:

> . . . the appearance of a furniture van to the door of a house will attract to the scene a large number of house hunters like cows to a carcase, and . . . there will be a race to the agent for possession of the dwelling.[57]

From this time on it was developments in Melbourne and Sydney which dominated the housing market and, increasingly, urban house building was fed by a marked drift of population from the country.

[52] *Argus*, December 12, 1922.
[53] Ibid., July 30, 1924.
[54] Hall, *Economic Record*, 39.
[55] *Official Year Book of the Commonwealth of Australia*, Nos. 7 to 19.
[56] *Argus*, October 9, 1928.
[57] Ibid., June 3, 1914.

The Changing Role of Manufacturing Investment

Associated with the growing concentration on urban housing was an increasing tendency for additions to productive capacity to occur in factories rather than on farms. Initially the increase in manufacturing investment was not inconsistent with an emphasis on rural development. Of the few industries in which significant extensions of plant were made before the First World War, railway workshops and agricultural implements were directly connected with governmental attempts at closer settlement in the country. The investment which occurred in the building materials industries could be seen as a response to the associated increase in population as well as owing something to public construction, and part of the expansion of the food-processing industry was a consequence of an increased supply of primary products.

The sensitivity of the manufacturing sector at this time to developments elsewhere is indicated by the fact that factory investment was largely an extension of existing plant. No plant was laid down on any important scale for the production of new products with the exception of refrigerated foods, and there is little evidence of technical progress in the existing industries. Only in the metal-working industries was there a noticeable increase in the value of plant and machinery per employee and, since a large contribution was made to this by the erection of a wastefully planned iron and steel plant,[58] the significance of this apparent improvement must be qualified.

By the 1920s, however, manufacturing investment was in the process of becoming less an adjustment to the general pattern of capital formation and more an active determinant of the pattern, thus giving rise to conflict with governmental plans for rural development. The most significant step in this direction was taken before the war, when a start was made on the construction of plant to manufacture steel by the Broken Hill Proprietary Company of Newcastle in 1912. At the time it could be regarded as just another response to public construction in rural areas, the original motive for the investment being to compete in the local market for rails.[59] But steel has to be set apart from the earlier life, firstly because it was virtually a new Australian product and one in which Australia had an advantage over competing industrial countries. Secondly, it formed the basis for a whole complex of potential new industries. For this reason the Newcastle steel works must be regarded as the

[58] Helen Hughes, *The Australian Iron and Steel Industry 1848-1962*, Melbourne University Press, Melbourne, 1964, pp. 49–50.

[59] Ibid., p. 64.

first important sign of a new type of manufacturing investment which would be something other than just a response to developments elsewhere in the economy.

The war may have been another link in the transition to the more spontaneous manufacturing development of the 1920s. It was almost certainly connected causally with the slower expansion of capacity in the early years of hostilities. On the other hand, much of the investment which did occur under the stimulus of special wartime circumstances was in new manufacturing industries. The fillip given to steel was the most important such effect, for it came just after the industry had become operational and so broadened its horizons at a crucial stage of its existence. Steel sheets, structural steel and angle iron and plates were produced from a new plant which had not previously been envisaged. The war also spawned a new range of engineering activities, with the value of plant in the engineering industry being more than doubled, and the demand for uniforms induced expansion not only of clothing factories, but also of the as yet embryonic textile industries. The fall in manufacturing investment thus disguised the basis for a new diversified expansion resulting from the exceptional shortage of overseas goods and special demands.[60]

One indication that a rise in manufacturing investment in the 1920s was less dependent on other types of capital formation is provided by the appearance of major innovations. The motor car proved to be a new development with important effects on the pattern of investment from about 1920 onwards. In the manufacturing sector alone it led directly to the establishment of factories of motor-body building and car assembly and, in turn, stimulated some of the supplying industries, particularly rubber goods, to make similar extensions. The beginnings of a complex of capital equipment centred on the motor car were thus in evidence. Electricity played a similar, although less important, role as an innovation which led to the establishment of the electrical goods industries.

Another sign of spontaneity was the growth of a complex of industrial investment built around the nucleus of steel. A new blast furnace was erected by BHP in 1921 in anticipation of an increased demand,[61] and this, in conjunction with the wartime expansion, touched off the establishment of a group of iron and steel using

[60] For a fuller treatment of the effects of the war, see C. Forster, 'Australian Manufacturing and the War of 1914–18', *Economic Record*, XXIX, 1953, pp. 211–30.

[61] Hughes, *Australian Iron and Steel Industry*, p. 80.

industries at Newcastle. A wire and rod mill and wire-netting factory, and plant for the production of axles and wheels and galvanized iron, were among the most important developments.[62] To a large extent the resumption of the upswing in public capital formation and residential and commercial construction provided the rationale for these developments, but the secondary wave of investment in steel products consequent upon the creation of steel-making capacity suggested that industrial investment was acquiring a momentum of its own.

It would be easy to exaggerate the increased independence of manufacturing investment at this time. Other types of capital formation still frequently called the tune, particularly in the important example of the building-materials industries. The rise in residential and commercial construction and in expenditure on public works in the first half of the 1920s caught the latter unprepared. In 1920 the shortage of bricks, timber and cement was acute,[63] there not being enough of the last mentioned, it was said, to complete existing contracts.[64] The response to this situation was most marked in the cement industry, partly because the demand for the product rose most rapidly as a result of the new importance of reinforced concrete in construction,[65] and partly because of special conditions inherent in the nature of the structure of the industry.[66] The importance of the latter is indicated by the apparent emergence of excess capacity in cement-making plant in the mid-1920s[67] before the demand for cement began to decline.[68] In addition, the period of rising manufacturing investment was not long-lived. Most of the extension of heavy industry came at the very beginning of the decade.[69] Although other industries then took up the running, the second half of the 1920s saw a decline in total capital formation in

[62] Ibid., pp. 82–5.

[63] *Argus*, January 14, 1920 and April 23, 1920.

[64] Ibid., April 23, 1920. Current production had been affected by industrial unrest, but the claim by one company that this fully explained the shortage (ibid., August 27, 1920) must be treated with the usual caution reserved for statements by management about labour.

[65] C. Forster, *Industrial Development in Australia 1920–1930*, Australian National University, Canberra, 1964, p. 59.

[66] Ibid., pp. 66–7.

[67] Ibid.

[68] The building-material industries were also significantly assisted by governmental preference to Australians in the letting of tenders.

[69] The establishment of Australian Iron and Steel Ltd at Port Kembla in 1927 was an exception, but its immediate contribution to productive capacity was not great. Hughes, *Australian Iron and Steel Industry*, p. 107.

the manufacturing sector. Thus extensions to capacity were still to an important extent a response to the growth of other sectors, and their premature decline in the mid-twenties suggests that even economic growth was not sufficient to sustain them on its own.

On the other hand, however much it needs to be qualified, the thesis of manufacturing investment freeing itself from dependence on developments in other sectors is important to an understanding of the process of capital formation in the first three decades of the century. Just at about the time governmental plans rural for development should have been bearing fruit, there were new forces operating to swing the balance towards an urban pattern of capital formation. To an important extent they were governmentally induced, for the permeation of the effects of tariff protection were becoming increasingly widespread. But whatever the reasons, the pattern of manufacturing investment in the 1920s could no longer be said to be clearly compatible with the aims of public-investment policy.

The Urbanization of Public Capital Formation

The trend in favour of urban capital formation which was thus becoming apparent in the 1920s is reflected in the fact that a rising proportion of total investment was now taking place in metropolitan areas in response to the other developments going on there. One facet of this was that the twentieth century brought with it some major technical advances, the development of which required governmental action. This expenditure was predominantly city orientated either because of the existing urban pattern of settlement and market location or because the heavy overheads involved made them more economically feasible in large centres of population. A new source of light and power, electricity, and an associated innovation, the telephone, were absorbing about 15 per cent of public capital formation.[70] The direction of funds into these new channels became most apparent in the 1920s, particularly in the case of electricity and telephones. The major development was in Victoria, following the establishment of a semi-governmental authority, later to become known as the State Electricity Commission, in 1918. The installation of a generating plant at Yallourn may seem to suggest an exception to the rule that the new capital formation was largely urban, but the investment did more to develop Melbourne than Gippsland. In New South Wales the City of Sydney established an electrical undertaking as early as 1904 and it too expanded its

[70] Calculated from the estimates of Butlin, *Australian Domestic Product*, p. 27.

activities in the early 1920s, although there was much less co-ordination of municipal activities on a state basis than in Victoria. In the 1920s, also, the Commonwealth government accelerated its expenditure on the provision of telephone facilities.

Another element in the changing centre of gravity of public investment was initially a legacy of the nineteenth century. By the 1890s, the extreme shortage of housing dating from the 1850s had been reversed, but the resultant growth of large urban centres created a growing demand for communal facilities which would help to make suburban houses more pleasant places in which to live. Sewerage and street improvement were needs still awaiting satisfaction at the turn of the century. It was not until immediately prior to the renewal in public capital formation in the 1890s that authorities were set up for the purpose of effectively tackling the problem of sewerage in Sydney and Melbourne. Construction got away to a quicker start in Sydney, but in the first decade of the new century it became so rapid in Melbourne that by 1910 its leeway had been made up and practically the whole of Melbourne's inner suburbs had been connected with the sewerage system.[71] The next decade saw work being done in other capital cities with the aid of concrete piping for the first time.[72] By the 1920s, advance was on a broader front and a number of provincial towns became involved in rapid construction.

By the 1920s it was the continuing process of urbanization which was setting the pace for the accelerating provision of communal services. The backlog of meeting the sewerage requirements of the areas of settlement existing in Melbourne and Sydney at the beginning of the century had been substantially reduced and the further dispersal of the suburban population increasingly became the reason for further construction. There was, in addition, a general increase in expenditure on such urban necessities as water supply and street making, the former on the basis of standards which appear high in the light of more recent experience.

This increasing tendency for public expenditure to be related to city development was sharpened by institutional aspects of urbanization. One of the outstanding features of the 1920s is the substantial rise in the share of public capital formation financed by local authorities. As cities grew in size it followed that urban local authorities represented an increasing proportion of the population and for that reason alone more was spent on urban capital. In addition,

[71] *Victorian Year Book*, 1909–10, p. 277 ff.
[72] *NSWPP*, 1912, IV, p. 10.

local governments of city areas were often more powerful and had easier access to funds than their counterparts in the country. Further, the special semi-governmental authorities set up in city areas to be responsible for a particular type of expenditure over the whole area were especially well placed to raise loans and tended to be vigorous spenders. Institutional factors thus tended to make for even more urban capital formation than the general growth of cities might lead us to expect.

It may thus be seen that by the 1920s public authorities had become responsive to the bias in favour of the cities which was clearly asserting itself. The main thrust of the investment programmes of the state governments was still in rural areas, but local authorities were increasingly diverting funds to urban construction. (The rise in expenditure of local and semi-governmental authorities may be seen in Chart 1.1). The result was that public expenditure on capital equipment was not determining the overall pattern of capital formation as the state governments had intended, but was itself being determined by that pattern. A basis was thus laid at this time for the initiative in capital formation to be taken by private urban

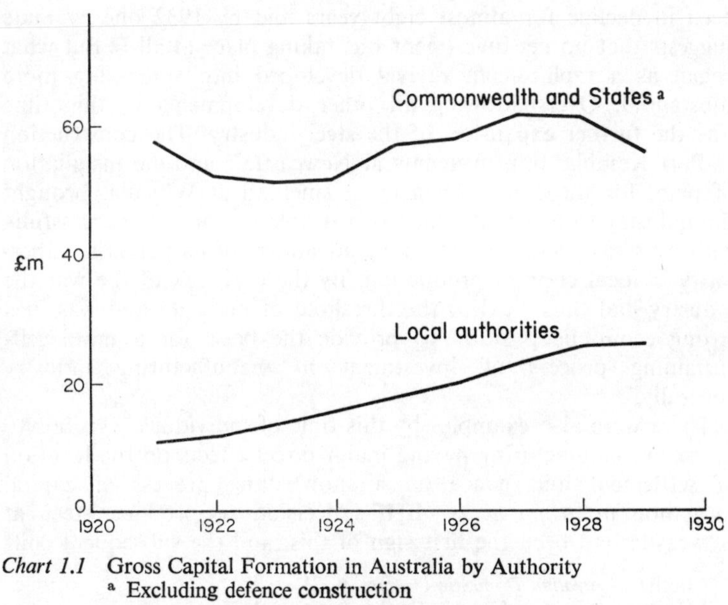

Chart 1.1 Gross Capital Formation in Australia by Authority
[a] Excluding defence construction

Source: Butlin, *Australian Domestic Product*, p. 17.

investors with public authorities either accepting their lead or attempting to do no more than contain the growth of metropolitan investment. In the years after the 1920s the goal of predominantly rural development faded and these portents of an acceptance of urbanization as a fact of life became a reality.

The Resumption of Manufacturing Investment after the 1920s

The key to the new terms of reference for the location of capital formation after the 1920s lay in the manufacturing sector. The emphasis on industrialization ensured that an increasing proportion of investible funds would be channelled into the cities. It also encouraged the tendency for manufacturers' investment plans to be influenced by those of other manufacturers, the beginnings of which were apparent in the 1920s. The more manufacturing industry developed a momentum of its own with the outputs of some sections being the inputs of others, the more would other types of capital formation be bent to fit the pattern of urban investment.

The rise in manufacturing investment in the 1930s was an important step on the path to this destination. The origins of the upswing are not difficult to identify for, when it began, manufacturing had been in decline for almost eight years and by 1932 one estimate suggests that no net investment was taking place at all.[73] But what began as a replacement revival developed into something more substantial. Overshadowing all other developments at this time was the further expansion of the steel industry. The construction at Port Kembla, improvements at Newcastle[74] and the installation of plant for the commencement of smelting at Whyalla, brought the industry to a size at which it was able to compete successfully with overseas producers by taking advantage of its potential superiority in local costs of production. By the outbreak of the war the industry had thus reached the threshold of maturity and was in a strong economic position to provide the basis for a more self-sustaining process of investment in manufacturing industry generally.[75]

There were also examples by this time of individual decisions to invest in manufacturing having major direct effects on the location of settlement and hence on a snowballing process of capital formation in urban areas. BHP's decision to produce steel at Newcastle had been the first sign of this, and the subsequent shift

[73] Butlin, *Australian Domestic Product*, p. 21.
[74] Hughes, *Australian Iron and Steel Industry*, p. 117.
[75] Hughes, 'Federation and Industrial Development', ANZAAS, 1964, p. 16.

of Australian Iron and Steel from Lithgow to Port Kembla in 1927, another. Possibly the choice of Geelong in 1926 as the main site for the assembly of Ford cars was a more crucial one, for the investment was in an industry not tied to mineral deposits.[76] But in the 1930s we have an example of a government, that of South Australia, itself being directly involved in this sort of decision-making process with its successful policy of encouraging the setting up of manufacturing establishments in that state.[77] A further stage in the adjustment of state governments to the failure of rural development had thus been reached before the Second World War.

The movement towards greater internal generation of investment in manufacturing industry received a check in the 1940s. Although the immediate effect of the Second World War was an unprecedented expansion in the metal and engineering industries and in explosives and chemicals, there was a subsequent decline in total manufacturing investment which continued into the immediate post-war period. Fears of a repetition of the slump after the First World War and shortages of labour and raw materials, particularly coal, were inhibiting investment plans at this time.

The failure of the expected depression to materialize and the long period of low investment in many industries made it almost inevitable that another upswing in capital formation should get under way in the 1940s. However, apart from the setting up of plant to manufacture Australian cars for the first time, there was little to distinguish expansion from what had gone on previously. The advance was not on an exceptionally broad front and it had a narrow base in the form of only a slow increase in the capital stock of the steel-making industry despite a rising demand for steel, a result of the reversal of the pre-war policy of BHP of creating capacity in advance of demand.

The Dynamism of Manufacturing Investment in the 1950s

It was in the decade of the 1950s that the most rapid advance was made towards manufacturing investment being a dominant force in the determination of the overall pattern of capital formation. In terms of the scale of expansion, its diversity and its significance for the Australian economy, nothing like it had been known before. There was scarcely a major industry which did not add to its capital

[76] Although it was tied to the coast; the major reason given for the selection of Geelong was its port facilities. *Argus*, March 31, 1925.

[77] T. J. Mitchell, 'J. W. Wainwright: The Industrialisation of South Australia 1935–40', *Australian Journal of Politics and History*, VIII, 1962, pp. 27–40.

equipment and a number of new industries quickly established large plants. The sharpness of the break with the past should not be exaggerated. The expansion of the 1950s depended on previous developments, for, although investors were faced by a particularly encouraging set of demand factors, and restrictions on overseas competition at the beginning of the decade, they would not have been able to exploit these opportunities to the extent that they did if sufficient plant had not been installed in the past to provide the basis for the advance to industrial maturity. Nevertheless, the 1950s do constitute a turning point in that the pace of diversification of capital equipment was considerably quickened at this time.

Basic to the acceleration of industrial investment was a more expansive attitude to the addition to steel-making capacity which led to the construction of a third blast-furnace at Port Kembla and various other important developments.[78] To some extent this resembled much of manufacturing investment in earlier decades in being a response to capital formation in other sectors of the economy.[79] However, it was increasingly the case that the city buildings and other urban facilities which absorbed much of the increased steel production themselves owed something to the development of manufacturing industry. In addition, a growing proportion of the increase in steel output was being stimulated by the demands of other manufacturing industries. The most important of these was the car industry, and associated with that industry was a major complex of industrial investment. The direct expenditure on plant for the manufacture of cars, which attracted a large quantity of both American and British funds, was itself considerable. In turn, the industry's demand for parts and materials sparked off a burst of other developments, particularly in rubber products.[80] The building of oil refineries, which was perhaps the most spectacular development of the first half of the 1950s, was another related development. The reasons for this sudden appearance of a major new industry were partly political and partly economic,[81] but underlying them was the growing Australian demand for petrol.

Motor cars were only the most important example of an industry

[78] Hughes, *Australian Iron and Steel Industry*, pp. 156–7.

[79] The considerable expansion of cement-making capacity at the time would be another important example of this.

[80] D. M. Hocking, 'The Contribution of Overseas Companies to Australia's Post-war Industrial Development', paper presented to Section G, ANZAAS, 1955.

[81] J. McB. Grant, 'The Petroleum Industry', in A. Hunter, ed., *The Economics of Australian Industry*, Melbourne University Press, Melbourne, 1965, p. 260.

providing the nucleus for a major complex of industrial investment which was independent of other types of capital formation. Electrical goods were the centre of another connected group of industries based to a large extent on want-creation rather than on a response to demands from other sectors of the economy. Similarly, the chemical industry ceased to be dependent for expansion on the agricultural and mining sectors and had become 'an industrial leader with the power to stimulate as well as satisfy demand'.[82]

The emergence of manufacturing investment as an important determinant of the pattern of capital formation, the origins of which lay in the 1920s, was thus apparent in the 1950s. Large blocs of capital equipment in city factories were unrelated or only partly related to rural construction, and a part of non-factory urban construction was a consequence of manufacturing development. Manufacturing investment could no longer be dismissed, as in the early years of the century, as an appendage of more dominant forms of capital formation; in large measure it now had a dynamic of its own and pulled some other types of capital formation along with it.

The Increasing Influence of Manufacturing Investment on House Building

One major category of capital formation which came increasingly under the influence of manufacturing investment was residential construction. There were specific demographic influences on the pattern of house building after the 1920s. The breaking of the boom at the end of that decade marked the end of the upswing dating from 1900 because it ushered in a period when, for the first time since the early part of the century, the number of houses exceeded real requirements. The strength of the recovery commencing in 1933 is at first sight suprising, particularly by contrast with the 1890s. To explain it we must take account of the fact that any pause in house building allows population growth to exert pressure for more construction. And, unlike the position in the 1880s, building in the 1920s had been closely geared to existing requirements. Also the age distribution of the population was probably more favourable to house building than before the depression for, although there was a marked deceleration in the growth of the 20–24 age group, the numbers in the more crucial 25–29 age group rose more quickly and the same was true of the 30–34 age group.[83] These changes, in addition to the tendency to postpone marriage in the

[82] A. Hunter and L. R. Webb, 'The Chemical Industry', in ibid., p. 290.
[83] Hall, *Economic Record*, 39.

depression years, led to a marked rise in the marriage rate in the second half of the 1930s. Further, the growth of new industrial centres at this time in New South Wales and South Australia contributed to the sharp rise in new construction. It may also have been the case, as has been argued for Britain in this decade,[84] that the depression was responsible for a shift in the distribution of income that was more favourable to home ownership.

A third upswing in residential construction began in the immediate post-war years, by which time the wartime pause had created a serious shortage of houses. With governmental encouragement, a very rapid rise in new houses built continued until the early 1950s, at which time the rate of increase declined until the second half of the decade. The influence of the post-war backlog was now much less strong and the proportion of the population in the house-buying age group was falling sharply.[85] The high level of building was being sustained by rapid immigration, rising living standards and a continued drift to the cities. For the first time there also occurred a significant rise in the proportion of residential construction consisting of flats.[86]

Underlying the demographic influences, however, was the growth of manufacturing industry. To an increasing extent new houses were located in the cities, and to an increasing extent urban employment was a consequence of industrialization. In addition to the direct housing needs of the manufacturing work force, a large part of the demand from those employed in service industries must be attributed to manufacturing investment. It has been estimated that the complementary employment in the mid-1950s was of the order of an additional 70 per cent to 80 per cent of the work force in manufacturing.[87] It is thus possible to see a large part of capital formation as being independent of other types of capital formation. Not only did such decisions make for a higher level of manufacturing investment than would have been the case if complete reliance had been placed on other forms of construction to provide the demand for manufactured goods, but also the decisions in their turn had major ramifications in determining the number of houses to be built and their location.

[84] H. W. Richardson, *Economic Recovery in Britain 1932–9*, Weidenfeld and Nicolson, London, 1967, Ch. 5.

[85] Hall, *Economic Record*, 39.

[86] A. R. Hall, 'Land and Building in the 1960s: The Requirements of Economic Growth', paper presented to Section G, ANZAAS, 1961, p. 3.

[87] B. Cameron, 'The Anatomy of High Employment', *Economic Record*, XXXVI, 1960, pp. 542–9.

The Growing Governmental Concentration on Urban Investment

The leadership of manufacturing investment not only helps to explain the increasingly urban concentration of house building but also the growing tendency for public capital formation to occur in the cities. There was no counterpart here to the grand design of rural development pursued before 1930. The situation was rather that the communal needs which were deemed by governments to have the highest priority after the Second World War were electricity supply, roads and education, and that although these services were important in both city and country areas, the pressure to supply them was greater in the latter. The more widespread supply of electricity to rural areas was a feature of the 1950s but the predominant demand factor behind the expansion of generating capacity was urban.[88] Educational buildings were inevitably related to the existing pattern of settlement and it was mainly in the suburbs of the capital cities that new schools were erected. The position with respec to roads was less clear in that 40 per cent of Commonwealth funds were eamarked for construction in the country and city road building fell far behind the demand. The problem was exacerbated in Melbourne by the fact that the authority of the Country Roads Board did not penetrate further into the metropolitan area than the outer suburbs and also by the distribution of Commonwealth government funds on a population and area basis. Even so, policy was inevitably influenced by a recognition of the urban transport problem, and in addition, funds spent on main highways, particularly between the capital cities, resulted in rapid communication between sections of manufacturing industry and their markets.

There were shifts in the importance of the major types of communal expenditure from the end of the Second World War, as shown in Table 1.2. Electricity occupied the centre of the stage in the late 1940s and early 1950s, when it was easily the most important single reason for public capital formation. The sharp rise in expenditure at this time reflects a recognition that the attempt to control post-war inflation by restraint of public investment had contributed to the appearance of major bottlenecks in the economy.[89] The stage

[88] W. Prest, 'The Electricity Supply Industry', in Hunter, ed., *The Economics of Australian Industry*, p. 114.

[89] Expenditure on electricity again became a casualty of anti-inflationary policy in 1952 as a result of a decision to reduce public expenditure to control rising prices. M. J. Artis and R. H. Wallace, 'Fiscal Policy in Post-War Australia', paper presented to Section G, ANZAAS, 1967, pp. 48–9 and 56–7, and Table 1.2.

was well set for expansion, for by the immediate post-war years all states except Western Australia had established a central co-ordinating electrical authority of some description. This, in addition to the commencement of the large-scale Snowy Hydro-electric Scheme by the Commonwealth government in 1949, provided a framework for rapidly increasing expenditure on generating plant and reticulation systems. The connection between these developments and urbanization was a close one. The Snowy Scheme, in particular, was primarily intended to meet the peak requirements of the industrial complexes of New South Wales and Victoria. However, the indirect role of manufacturing investment in capital expenditure for the supply of electricity may have been more important than its direct one, for the demand for immediate consumer use played the largest part in putting pressure on generating capacity.[90]

TABLE 1.2. *Components of Public Capital Formation 1948–60*

	1948–9		1952–3		1959–60	
	£m.	per cent	£m.	per cent	£m.	per cent
Power, fuel and light	22	15·5	104	26·8	117	20·4
Roads	28	19·7	57	14·7	130	22·7
Education	3	2·3	13	3·3	42	7·2
Water supply and sewerage	10	7·3	26	6·6	58	10·1
All other	78	55·2	189	48·6	228	39·6
Total	141	100·0	389	100·0	573	100·0

Source: Commonwealth Bureau of Census and Statistics, *Australian National Accounts, National Income and Expenditure, 1948–49 to 1959–60.*

From the early 1950s roads replaced electricity supply as the public utility on which governments were most willing to increase their expenditure, and by the end of the decade road building had become the most important category of public capital formation. Before this time a number of problems had so hindered the rise in road building expenditure that its share of total public capital formation fell back to the level of the 1920s. The authorities directly concerned failed to recognize the changed situation with respect to road use and were content to resume construction on

[90] Prest, 'The Electricity Supply Industry', in Hunter, ed., *The Economics of Australian Industry.*

the same basis as that laid down in the 1920s, the war being regarded as nothing more than an interruption of earlier plans. In looking to the future they made plans on the expectation that population would increase at the same rate as before the war.[91] The resulting population projection of the New South Wales Main Roads Board for Sydney in the year 2000 had been reached by 1960. Difficulties in obtaining funds were another problem, with the Commonwealth government showing a reluctance to accept a wider responsibility for roads. So, too, were shortages of construction materials and labour. In addition, the housing shortage was given as a reason for not proceeding more quickly with the widening of roads.[92]

In the 1950s these barriers to expansion weakened. The rapid rise in car ownership and the greatly increased use of road transport by manufacturing industry brought home forcefully the inadequacy of the existing system to public authorities. The Commonwealth government agreed to give increased assistance to the state governments for the purpose of improving it. The supply of construction materials increased with major extensions to manufacturing capacity and more capital-intensive methods of construction were adopted.

The construction of educational buildings, the other activity which absorbed a significantly higher proportion of the funds available for public investment, was mainly a function of the changing age distribution of the population. The sharp increase in the birth rate in the 1940s necessitated a progressive extension of buildings to accomodate the increased intake at succeeding levels of education. This was accentuated by a shift in the demand for such facilities towards outer suburban areas. As in the case of roads, the Commonwealth government speeded construction by making funds available for university buildings.

In addition to the city-orientated communal needs which became more important after the war, water supply and sewerage was another major reason for public expenditure in response to urban growth. The immediate pre-war decade had seen a rise in the importance of this type of capital formation. This was partly to be explained in terms of the lower total levels of expenditure in that decade, combined with the fact that expenditure on water supply and sewerage had gathered momentum in the later stages of the preceding upswing in public investment and was resumed more quickly than some other categories. However, there were new stimuli to construction such as the relocation of manufacturing industry at this time,

[91] *NSWPP*, 1945–6, I, p. 615.

[92] Ibid., 1947–8, II, p. 700.

particularly at Port Kembla, which necessitated the formulation of major new plans for the supply of water.[93] Similar developments after the war and rapid urban expansion led to greatly increased expenditure, but the extreme competition between various uses of public funds meant that the share of water and sewerage construction remained steady, taking the post-war period as a whole.

The Laggard Governmental Response to Urban Needs

The extent to which private urban investment determined the pattern of public investment is only partly conveyed by the emphasis on the provision of facilities mainly intended to meet city needs. More significant is the way in which governmental expenditure was a laggard response to previous developments in the private sector. There was no overall programme of urban development based on formal governmental planning to set the conditions for industrial expansion. It was rather the case that the latter set up needs for communal expenditure and governments went some of the way towards meeting them in a piecemeal fashion. Governments thus opted out of decisions on the location of capital formation as far as their investment policy was concerned, leaving these decisions to private individuals.[94]

The lag in the response to communal urban needs is evident in the case of most of the main types of expenditure. Although education became a more important object of public capital formation, buildings were not constructed rapidly enough to keep pace with the demands made by the growing urban population. The imbalance between private and public investment in urban areas was most obviously apparent with respect to roads, the inadequacy of which, although intensified by the fixed proportion of Commonwealth funds spent in rural areas, was fundamentally a reflection of governmental failure to match the activities of private investors in the car industry. Sewerage is another example of a major facility being provided more slowly than the corresponding private investment in house building. Over 20 per cent of the houses in Melbourne were unsewered throughout the 1950s and over 30 per cent of those in Sydney.[95]

An exception to the rule of passive governmental response to

[93] Ibid., 1940, III, p. 461.

[94] The powers of state governments over town planning were not exercised in such a way as to invalidate this statement.

[95] R. Mathews, *Public Investment in Australia*, Cheshire, Melbourne, 1967, p. 251.

pressures for communal services is provided by the Snowy Mountains Scheme which resembled some of the ambitious investment of the earlier period when rural development was the keynote of much public expenditure, although there was no precedent for the amount spent on one project or for the technical expertise involved. Despite the fact that the decision to set up the Snowy Mountain Authority was partly provoked by difficulty in meeting the urban demands for electricity, it did involve an element of formal planning not evident in other types of public expenditure to meet city needs. As such it demonstrated the traditional dislike by Australian governments of precise economic calculation as to the likely cost and benefits of large-scale investment. This laid it open to criticism on the grounds of both high operating costs in comparison with alternative schemes and of the large capital costs of the Snowy Scheme.[96] These, however, did not establish clearly that, whatever the weaknesses of the original calculation by the public authority concerned, the decision to set up the Snowy Mountain Authority was an uneconomic one in the event.[97] What does seem evident is that the Snowy Scheme was a special case of forward planning for urban needs in a general environment of belated governmental reaction to pressures resulting from problems which had already arisen and were often acute. In the main, private urban investors were making the running.

The Changed Attitude to Rural Development

A further reason for seeing public capital formation in the period since the Second World War as an adjustment to the driving force of urban private investment is the change in governmental attitudes to expenditure on rural development. Not only did it decline in importance compared with the period before 1930, but it also became more piecemeal and more cautious. In addition, there were instances of the pattern of extra-metropolitan settlement being determined as a by-product of public investment to meet the needs of the larger urban centres.

In place of the massive assault on the vast open spaces which characterized an earlier period came a greater governmental concern with individual projects. In cases where responsibility was accepted

[96] B. J. McFarlane, 'Investment Policy in the Electric Power Sector', paper presented to Section G, ANZAAS, 1961, and 'The Snowy—An Appraisal', *Current Affairs Bulletin*, No. 31, Sydney, 1963.

[97] For a detailed discussion of this question see Mathews, *Public Investment in Australia*, pp. 183–91.

for a co-ordinated block of additions to the sort of social capital which would encourage private rural investment, as was true of some expenditure in the northern part of Australia, the area involved was small.[98] More important were the efforts of governments to increase output in the existing settled areas, and here they concentrated on one main type of expenditure, irrigation. In so doing, they showed a greater concern for the consequences of their actions than had previously been the case. Although modern techniques of evaluating irrigation projects by calculation of expected costs and benefits had not yet come into use and the projects that were undertaken were open to attack on economic grounds, there was a greater consciousness of technical problems and, although still only uncertainly, a great tendency to temper the continuing preoccupation with engineering aspects of the projects with other relevant considerations.

Irrigation also provides an example, in the form of the Snowy Scheme, of encouragement of non-metropolitan development as an outgrowth of expenditure primarily intended to service the cities. The diversion of the waters of the Snowy River into the Murray basin would not have been carried out had not the decision to develop them as a source of hydro-electric power been taken. Electricity supply, mainly for Melbourne, based on the deposits of brown coal in Gippsland, was also the major reason for the acceleration in the growth of population settled in that area.

The secondary role of public investors in the determination of the pattern of total capital formation is again illustrated by the case of rural transport improvement. Railway construction, the major item in the earlier programme of rural development, declined greatly in importance. What expenditure was incurred was mainly on standardization of gauges which was intended to link the capital cities. As has been seen,[99] an important part of the increasing expenditure on roads was for a similar purpose. For the rest, the insistence that some road funds be earmarked for expenditure in rural areas, although it reduced the construction of capital equipment in the cities and thus constituted an exception to the general pattern of the period, was in itself evidence of the essentially defensive nature of public investment in the period since the Second World War. It was not an active attempt to encourage rural development

[98] For further details of rural development schemes, see ibid., Ch. 8, and E. S. Hoffman, 'Agricultural Development Projects', in D. B. Williams, ed., *Agriculture in the Australian Economy*, Sydney University Press, Sydney, 1967, Ch. 12.

[99] See pp. 16–28 above.

but reflected a desire to avoid an excessively urban allocation of resources.

The Paradox of the Investment Boom in Primary Industry

It is a paradox of the years following the Second World War that the period which saw urbanization come into the open as the major force in the regional pattern of capital formation and in which governments abandoned their formerly aggressive approach to rural development, also was one in which there occurred an investment boom in primary industry which had no parallel in the twentieth century up to that time. The key to this lies in the technical advances which became available to farmers or which farmers now had the funds to adopt. Although it is not uncommon for new techniques to permit rises in agricultural output without much investment, this was not generally the case in Australia in this period.[100] Even myxomatosis, the outstanding example of a divorce between technology and investment of capital, resulted in the provision of extra facilities to take advantage of the improved pasture growth it caused. In addition, basic activities like clearing became much more mechanical at this time.[101] New techniques thus help to explain the high level of investment, compared wtith the past, and to show how investment could rise rapidly without a great deal of complementary public investment. In addition, much of the investment took place in already settled areas where public facilities had already been provided in the past.

Looked at in more detail, the fact that the rise in agricultural investment was most marked in the early 1950s is partly a reflection of the influence of the Second World War. The war brought the unimpressive rise in agricultural investment of the previous forty years to an end. Marketing difficulties, followed by shortage of labour and materials, so inhibited capital formation that expenditure on machinery fell to very low levels and numbers of livestock sharply declined, the latter partly being caused by the drought of the mid-forties.[102] To some extent the subsequent development was a reaction to this severe check to expansion. Even in relation to the moderate claims which investment in primary industry made on resources,

[100] K. O. Campbell, 'Some Reflections on Agricultural Investment', *Australian Journal of Agricultural Economics*, II, 1958, pp. 93–103.

[101] C. M. Donald, 'Innovation in Agriculture', in Williams, ed., *Agriculture in the Australian Economy*, p. 66.

[102] F. H. Gruen, 'Capital Formation in Australian Agriculture', *Australian Journal of Agricultural Economics*, I, 1957, p. 97.

shortages during the war created a backlog of demand. Imports of machinery and equipment were cut off and domestic production fell sharply. There was no marked improvement in this respect until the late 1940s,[103] which is the time of most rapid increase in agricultural investment.

The significance of technical progress is indicated by the fact that easily the largest part of the increased capital expenditure was on machinery. In the second half of the 1950s there was considerable competition between sellers which resulted in progressive improvement in the quality of machinery for sale.[104] But even before this time, increasing purchases were instrumental in introducing better techniques into farming. In particular, they extended the range of mechanized primary industry because the post-war period saw an extension to pastoral industry of the process of mechanization in the wheat industry dating from before the war. The practice of mounting implements on tractors was one example of this, equipment for fodder conservation being another.[105] Tractors were also increasingly being used for clearing and large-scale mechanical equipment was applied to the sinking of dams.[106] Horticulture and dairying were other industries where certain operations were mechanized for the first time with the use of tractors.[107] On wheat farms a cumulative process of mechanization was in progress on a much larger scale than before the war. More powerful tractors were introduced to pull bigger machines and this in turn necessitated the replacement of many smaller machines. Replacement generally went on at a rapid rate because, in the period of post-war shortage of agricultural machinery, farmers were not always able to obtain the model they wanted.[108]

Not all of the greatly increased expenditure on machines can be attributed to autonomous technical progress. Another important influence was the post-1945 change in the relative prices of capital and labour. The desire to replace labour in farming operations had been a motive for mechanization before the war, but in the

[103] E. A. Saxon, 'Equipment and Materials Essential for Rural Production', *Quarterly Review of Agricultural Economics*, V, 1952, p. 60.

[104] M. Bernasek and Z. M. Kubinski, 'Agricultural Machinery and Implements,' in Hunter, ed., *The Economics of Australian Industry*, p. 470.

[105] F. O. Grogan and A. Bollen, 'Farm Machinery in Australia', *Quarterly Review of Agricultural Economics*, V, 1952, p. 146.

[106] Ibid.

[107] E. A. Saxon, 'Tractors on Australian Farms', *Quarterly Review of Agricultural Economics*, VI, 1953, p. 11.

[108] Grogan and Bollen, *Quarterly Review of Agricultural Economics*, V, p. 146.

new context of full employment the incentive became very much stronger and was not checked by a marked rise in the price of agricultural machinery in the late 1940s and early 1950s.[109] Additional reasons for mechanization are more nebulous but may nevertheless have been of some importance. The depreciation allowance of 20 per cent per annum for income-tax purposes introduced in 1951 may have helped to sustain the high level of purchase after that time.[110] A desire for conspicuous consumption has also been noted,[111] and it is by no means irrelevant in this context to mention the fascination, which is not confined to farmers, of power-driven machinery.

The shift in emphasis towards urban capital formation thus did not occur against a background of rural stagnation. There were forces in operation which permitted a rise in private investment in primary industry that was not dependent on a simultaneous expenditure of public investible funds and which generated major investment booms in both city and country areas. Indeed, there was a connection between the two, for the rapid introduction of machinery on to farms can either be seen as freeing labour to live in the cities or as a response to the shortage of hands resulting from the buoyant labour market there. If, as is likely, the latter was the stronger influence, then much of the investment which occurred in the country can be regarded as a further consequence of the initiative of private urban investors.

Conclusion

The foregoing discussion points to two major changes which have occurred in the structure of capital formation in Australia since 1900. Firstly, investment in manufacturing industry, which in the early years of the century played second fiddle to other types of construction, emerged as a driving force in determining the pattern of capital formation. On the other hand, the role of public capital formation has become less one of pace-setter and more one of following the lead of the private sector.

The two changes were not unrelated. The more the forces making

[109] Bernasek and Kubinski, 'Agricultural Machinery and Implements', in Hunter, ed., *The Economics of Australian Industry*, pp. 470–2.

[110] Campbell casts doubt on the importance of this factor, *Australian Journal of Agricultural Economics*, II, p. 102.

[111] Bernasek and Kubinski, 'Agricultural Machinery and Implements', in Hunter, ed., *The Economics of Australian Industry*, p. 470.

for industrialization asserted themselves, the more governments had to switch their attention from positive policies of development in rural areas to meeting the demands for the expenditure of public funds on the amenities of life in the cities where the new factories were located. This implies some degree of failure with respect to the governments' earlier policies, for if they had been successful in their aim of rural development they would have created a different regional pattern of capital formation. The failure was partly of their own making in that their expenditure in rural areas was not planned carefully enough to justify the hopes held for it. But it was also a consequence of a conflict between the pull of natural resources, which favoured the application of scarce capital to freely available land, and other influences making for urbanization and growth of secondary industry. The seeds of the conflict had already been planted at the beginning of the period and subsequent events sharpened it further. By the second half of the century it had been largely resolved in favour of urban development, although echoes of it still persisted, particularly in some aspects of governmental spending in rural areas and a failure to tackle seriously the problems thrown up by the growth of cities.

The crucial decade in the transition seems to have been the 1920s. Until that time, manufacturing investment had given little cause for comment as a counterweight to the main rural thrust of governmental policies. It is in the 1920s that there can be seen the first signs of investment being undertaken in secondary industry which was independent of other forms of investment and which itself gave rise to investment in other sectors. This was also the time when public investment clearly swung towards an increasing emphasis on urban development, although the effort to encourage investment in primary industry also became more determined. The importance of the 1920s in this respect is brought out clearly by the composition of public investment after that time. There is a tendency to regard the Second World War as the appropriate benchmark for more recent developments in the public sector. The post-war period has seen much higher levels of public investment than ever before, but only in a very limited sense can the war be seen as a meaningful break in the pattern of investment. All but one of the categories of investment which became more important in the recovery of the 1930s continued to do so after the war and all were largely associated with urban development. All the major shifts in the importance of categories of public investment of the 1920s, with the exception of the increased importance of expenditure on telephone facilities, became established trends from the 1930s to the 1950s.

A further significant feature of the 1920s is that the rise in private investment in primary industry which occurred in that decade was not very important from the perspective of later developments. This is contrary to what might be expected of an economy in a stage of growth in which the main emphasis was on the exploitation of abundant land. It is, on the other hand, consistent with the interpretation of the 1920s as a crucial phase in the eventual supremacy of an urban way of life.

To sum up, in the early years of the twentieth century, Australian governments adopted a broad strategy of economic growth in their investment policies, the keynote of which was the closer settlement of rural areas. They eventually abandoned this in favour of contenting themselves with responding to the course set by private investors who did not share their vision of rural development, and the governments' change of policy was in part a belated recognition that this was the case.

3. THE PRODUCTIVITY OF CAPITAL

The significance of the pattern of capital formation is not just that it is basic to an explanation of the movement of total investment but also that it has an important bearing on the productivity of capital. The developments of the first three decades of the twentieth century point to a significant reduction in the extent to which aggregate capital formation gave rise to increased production. In the first place, the increased emphasis on urban construction, coming at a time when pastoral construction ceased to be important, was associated with a change in the composition of capital formation in favour of a higher component of virtually unproductive investment.[112] Types of investment which may be so described seem to have contributed about 35 per cent of the total in the 1880s but by the end of the 1920s were more than half of all investment. The major element in the new position of unproductive outlays

[112] The crudity of the term 'unproductive investment' has no other justification than the importance of distinguishing types of investment from one another on the basis of their contribution to gross national product as conventionally estimated. The components of capital formation which are taken to belong to the 'unproductive' category are residential construction, telegraph, water and sewerage, public buildings, defence construction and local-government expenditure.

was the increased spending by local and semi-governmental authorities on the provision of urban amenities.

A second relevant feature of the pattern of capital formation in the period between the depression of the 1890s and the 1930s arises from the governmental policy of rural development which resulted in total additions to capital having a higher social-overhead content. If we distinguish investment, which directly made for an increase in output, from certain categories of public investment, which were only indirectly productive in that they required further private investment before their economic potenital could be realized,[113] then the latter increases in importance as compared with the 1880s while the former drops sharply. It has already been suggested that the gains from the increasingly important public construction in rural areas were limited by faulty planning and a failure to integrate it with investment in the private sector.[114] It is therefore probable that the shift towards less directly productive investment in this period was also a shift to investment which was ultimately less productive in general. There would appear to have been a major swing away from more productive types of capital formation towards less productive ones in the first thirty years of the century and a tendency for capital formation increasingly to become more an outcome of past economic growth than a stimulus to new growth.

The tendency for capital formation to become increasingly divorced from the generation of output is most noticeable in the 1920s. Until that time only directly productive investment became less important, but afterwards the more rapid rise of unproductive outlays was at the expense of both directly and indirectly productive investment. It is also likely that rural construction by public authorities was carried out more strictly in accordance with economic criteria before 1914 than in the 1920s.

To some extent this situation arose because economic growth, as usually understood today, was not the dominant influence on investment at the time. A desire to provide for an increasing population, rather than increasing output per head, seems to have been a major *raison d'être* for capital formation. A high rate of migration in the second and third decades of the century stimulated house building and other types of unproductive investment, and this

[113] The main types of expenditure regarded for this purpose as indirectly productive are railways, roads and bridges, electricity and irrigation.

[114] See pp. 16–28 above.

coincided with a lagged effect of high migration in earlier periods, which produced an age composition of the population which was conducive to a high demand for houses. Another lagged response to previous population growth was reflected in the increased expenditure on previously neglected urban facilities. This, then, was a period when current pressures to provide for a growing population were compounded with accumulated ones. In addition, inasmuch as rural construction by public authorities had an explicit objective, it was to settle more people on the land. This was what was normally meant by the word 'development' when used in connection with public expenditure and, although it may have been taken to imply an increase in output per head, it may not have done so in practice. A large part of capital formation was in fact taken to need no other justification than that it would enable the land to support a higher population.[115] Even manufacturing investment was to a large extent a function, directly or indirectly, of population increase. We have seen that the demand of the construction industries for materials was an important influence at this time on extensions to manufacturing capacity which were ultimately stimulated by population increase. There was a large element of simple duplication of the capital stock in adding to manufacturing equipment, and to a large extent this can be regarded as capital being created to keep step with the increase of the population. In general, then, in the first thirty years of the twentieth century it was a desire to add to the number of people in Australia which set the pace for capital formation. Although this made for a higher level of investment than would otherwise have been the case, the incremental use of funds was not of a type likely to lead to substantial increases in output.

After the 1920s there were changes in the composition of capital formation of a type likely to raise its overall productivity. By the beginning of the 1960s, directly productive investment had risen to approach one half of the total, whereas the importance of unproductive investment fell sharply from a similar position at the commencement of the period. Indirectly productive also seems to have made up a smaller share of the total than in the previous period.[116] To a large extent the latter two changes are a reflection of the

[115] Or even more negatively, that it had kept many settlers on their farms who would otherwise have abandoned them. Report of the Committee of Public Accounts on roads in South Gippsland, *VPP*, 1931, p. 638.

[116] Based on statistics published in Butlin, *Australian Domestic Product*, pp. 19 and 25, and in *National Income and Expenditure 1947–48 to 1959–60.*

acceptance of a new role by governments in capital formation after the depression of the 1930s. This first affected the importance of types of expenditure which we have classified as indirectly productive, partly because of the failure of rural construction schemes to come up to expectations, and the consequent difficulty of discovering new lines of expenditure in rural areas which could not be branded as wasteful. A more important reason, however, was probably the reduced availability of overseas funds for public investment after the depression, rural investment being more affected than urban because the former had been more dependent on overseas loans. After the Second World War, public capital formation was hampered generally by shortage of funds and this helped further to swing the balance back in the direction of emphasizing investment which was more immediately productive. The marked increase in the supply of overseas funds for manufacturing investment accentuated the shift still more.

Nevertheless, more than a changed composition of capital formation was required to raise its overall productivity to the highest international standards. Australia does not appear to have invested an exceptionally large proportion of its funds in the capital-intensive industries in the 1950s when compared with such countries as the United States of America, West Germany, France, Italy and the United Kingdom.[117] It would therefore appear that the change in the pattern of capital formation since the 1920s has, in this respect, brought Australia more into line with the advanced industrial countries. If, as seems to be indicated by a comparison of growth rates with total investment, the productivity of Australian capital remains lower than in these countries,[118] it thus seems that this has arisen more within particular sectors than from an emphasis on less fruitful sectors. Further, as there is no reason for supposing that there has been any deterioration within sectors since the 1920s, it is a corollary of this that the composition of capital formation between 1900 and 1930 was only one obstacle to the achievement of a high productivity of capital at that time.

Although, in view of the large amount of research which still needs to be done, it would be premature to attempt a full explanation of the productivity of seperate types of capital formation, the relevance of some of the issues already discussed is worth noting. The failure, to which attention has been drawn, of public and private

[117] See Table II in J. W. Nevile, 'How Productive is Australian Capital?', *Economic Record*, 43, 1967, p. 409.

[118] Ibid., Table I, p. 407.

investment to mesh together may be regarded as a constraint on the productivity of capital. The reluctance of the private sector to conform to governmental attempts to promote rural development prevented a significant amount of capital from being put to effective use. The subsequent failure of governments to plan for urban development may well also have restricted the gains to be made from private investment.

However, this emphasis on the importance of the way in which Australia's capital stock evolved over time should not be allowed to obscure the underlying significance of other factors. Of these, the smallness of Australia's population and the sparsity of settlement between the metropolitan centres seem especially relevant in the present context. Virtually all the countries whose productivity of capital was much higher than Australia's in the 1950s also had much larger populations. In comparison with them, the Australian experience of a restricted home market and limitation of economies of scale for locally produced goods and services goes some of the way towards explaining a lower return of investment. This may have been fortified by the wide spread of the Australian tariff which may have militated against the emergence of more highly productive export industries in the manufacturing sector.

To see the smallness of the Australian population as an important barrier to improving the productivity of capital is to highlight the complexity of the relationship between capital formation and economic growth. It has been argued that the high priority given to population growth as an influence on Australian investment between 1900 and 1930 was not necessarily consistent with increasing output per head. To some extent, the shift towards a more productive composition of capital after 1930 may have resulted from a recognition of this. That shift, however, did not raise Australia out of the international ruck in terms of the productivity of its capital, partly because its population was still small. It would thus seem that while the path to the improvement of productivity lies in the direction of a larger population, the pursuit of this as an objective has in the past been associated with a less immediately productive compostion of capital. Whether there need be a short-term conflict between population increase and improved capital productivity is a question which requires a more extended treatment than space will here permit. However, the possibility of such conflict is too central a theme of twentieth-century Australian history to be omitted altogether.

4. CONCLUSION

The changing pattern of capital formation is an essential key to an understanding of the relationship between capital formation and economic growth in Australia after 1900. During that time there were two main periods of economic growth: firstly, from the early years of the century until the late 1920s, with an interruption for the First World War, and secondly, from the end of the Second World War. In the first, there seems to have been a marked deceleration in the rate of growth in relation to that of the period from about the beginning of the 1860s to the 1890s.[119] There does not, however, seem to have been a fall in the amount of investment expressed as a proportion of gross domestic product in the first three decades of the twentieth century.[120] Virtually the whole of the deceleration must therefore be attributed to what must have been a marked deterioration in the productivity of capital after 1900. No explanation of this would be complete without reference to the greatly reduced significance of investment in the wool industry compared with the second half of the nineteenth century. However, another major element was the change in the composition of capital during the period up to the end of the 1920s, involving both a substantial rise in the proportion of unproductive investment consequent on the process of urbanization, and also a determined governmental attempt to promote rural development through large-scale construction which did not yield the expected return. The simultaneous emphasis on both urbanization and rural development thus made for a much less fruitful stock of capital than in the second half of the nineteenth century.

In the period since 1945, there has been a return to a more rapid rate of economic growth in Australia.[121] Much of this can be attributed to a marked increase in aggregate investment measured as a proportion of gross national product. Although there has also been a change in the composition of capital formation giving greater weight to directly productive investment, the productivity of capital

[119] The fall was of the order of from 5 per cent per annum between 1860 and 1890 to 3 per cent per annum between 1900 and 1930, using Butlin's estimate of gross domestic product at constant prices in *Australian Domestic Product*, pp. 460–1.

[120] Over the period as a whole the proportion seems to have been about 18 per cent, which is about the same as that for the period 1860–90. Calculated from Butlin, *Australian Domestic Product*, pp. 10–11 and 16–17.

[121] The estimate published in the Vernon Report suggests a growth rate of the order of 4 per cent per annum. See Commonwealth of Australia, *Report of the Committee of Economic Enquiry*, Canberra, 1965, II, p. 467.

is still not high on international standards. The emergence of manufacturing investment as a more dominant form of capital formation has not had as great an effect on output per head as in some other countries, partly because the Australian population is very small in comparison with theirs. It would thus appear that during the twentieth century as a whole, the contribution made by capital formation to Australian economic growth has derived much more from its high aggregate level than from the fruitfulness of its components.

CAPITAL FORMATION AND ECONOMIC STABILITY

If there are doubts about the contribution made by capital formation to economic growth, its relationship with economic stability is much less complicated. With the exception of the two world wars there was only one major downturn, from 1928–9 to 1931–2 in the aggregate level after a slump in the first few years of the twentieth century. Apart from a slight drop in 1952–3, in the periods intervening between wars and depression, annual figures are always an advance on the previous year. There can be little doubt that, although there were important exceptions, capital formation was, generally speaking, an important stabilizing influence on the economy.

The explanation of the steadiness of the upswings in investment is not to any large extent to be found in divergent movements in public and private investment cancelling each other out, as tended to happen in the second half of the nineteenth century.[122] As can be seen from Chart 1.2, public investment does not often play the role of compensating for fluctuation in the private sector, the two types of investment moving generally together over the whole period. The important exceptions to this occur in 1907–08 and 1908–09 when a fall in private investment was outweighed by rising public expenditure and in 1921–2 and 1922–3 when a boom in private investment was associated with declining public investment. It is unlikely that there was anything systematic in these two cases of divergent movements. In the first, a general deterioration in economic conditions coincided with the implementation of a more vigorous policy of public expenditure. The second was the result of competi-

[122] See N. G. Butlin, *Private Capital Formation in Australia*, Australian National University, Canberra, 1955, pp. 17–23 and *Investment in Australian Economic Development*, pp. 370–90.

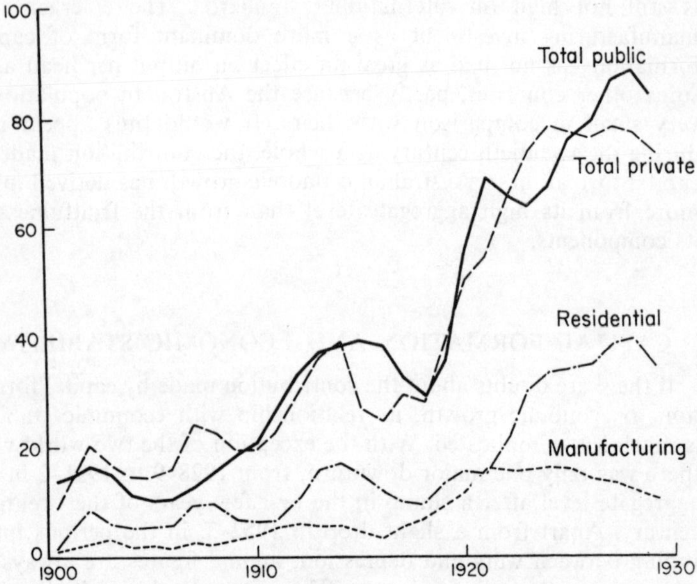

Chart 1.2 Categories of Capital Formation in Australia, 1900–01 to 1928–29

Source: Butlin, *Australian Domestic Product*, pp. 16–19.

tion for labour and construction materials between the two sectors and of governmental difficulties in raising loan funds.

The marked tendency towards parallel fluctuation in public and private investment suggests that each must have been characterized by a high degree of stability. In the case of private investment, this was to some extent the outcome of divergent short-term movements of residential construction and manufacturing investment. As shown in Chart 1.2, the strongest upswing in manufacturing investment before the First World War, between 1909 and 1912, coincided with a falling level of house building, whereas with the onset of the pre-war house-building boom manufacturing began to drop. Again, a fall in residential construction at the beginning of the 1920s occurred simultaneously with a sharp increase in manufacturing investment, but when the later strong upswing in house building got under way, manufacturing investment reached a plateau and then declined. This inversity was probably almost entirely accidental. The timing of inducements to invest in the two areas before the war was different, with demographic pressures making themselves felt in the housing market later than the rise in demand for manufactured products. By the time the house-building boom started, manufacturing capacity had already been enlarged considerably, given the size of the market. Immediately after the war, house building was more sensitive to high interest rates than manufacturing investment, much of which was financed by wartime profits, and shortages of materials were a further inhibiting factor. By the time these difficulties had been overcome the upswing in manufacturing investment had lost much of its steam. The only obvious connection between the two types of investment was that the shortage of building materials in the early 1920s contributed to the sharpness of the rise in manufacturing investment, but this was only one of the influences on manufacturers at the time.

The stability of public capital formation in this period resulted from the long-term nature of the construction undertaken as part of a conscious policy of development and from the steady availability of funds, particularly from overseas, for most of the time. In the ten years before the war considerable steadiness was imparted to total public investment by the regular unbroken rise in expenditure on railway buildings. The 1920s saw expenditure by local and semi-governmental authorities emerge as an even more important steadying influence than railway buildings.[123]

Looking at the first three decades of the twentieth century as a whole, it can be seen that, as in the case of the relationship between capital formation and economic growth, demographic factors have a special relevance to economic stability. Immigration and the changing age composition of the population imparted an underlying long-term stimulus to investment after the first decade which influenced the course of public expenditure in rural areas, residential construction and expenditure on other urban facilities. Whatever the results of this on the fruitfulness of capital, it rendered it less liable to violent fluctuation.

After the 1920s the general absence of downward movements in investment for most of the 1920s, the late 1940s and the 1950s, require a different explanation. Before the Second World War there was a return to more normal levels of investment after the depression, with new growth factors superimposed in later years perhaps at about the time when the recovery might have been expected to peter out. In the post-war period the situation was one mainly of investment giving rise to potential instability in an upward direction. Excessive claims were often made on resources in relation

[123] See Chart 1.1.

to their availability, and governmental policy was framed to control these tendencies and maintain economic stability.

Little can be said here of the major exception to the stability of capital formation, the precipitous fall in the late 1920s and early 1930s. That it was a major element in the depression of the 1930s almost goes without saying, but an assessment of the causation of the collapse of investment would require much more space than is available here. What can be said is that the question is almost certainly a more complicated one than is sometimes thought. The peak in total investment precedes the 1929 Stock Exchange crash by at least a year, and the statistics of the seperate types of capital formation suggest that the origins of the downturn went back much earlier than that. Manufacturing investment was never as high again in the 1920s as it had been in 1923–4. The continued rise in total investment for the following four years was largely in public investment and residential construction. The importance of population increase in sustaining the level of activity is particularly noticeable in those years. How much the eventual downturn in public investment is to be explained in terms of the reduced availability of overseas capital is not revealed by the coincidence between overseas financial difficulties and the accelerated fall in public spending. Opportunities for railway building were declining before this time and expenditure in this direction reached its peak in 1926–7. The switch of emphasis towards road building did not fully compensate for the decline in railway building. It is therefore likely that a crisis had been reached in public investment before depressing overseas influences were felt, and this may be further indicated by the failure of public investment to play as important a role after the depression, associated as this was with a shrinkage in railway construction. There is thus evidence, with respect to both manufacturing investment and public capital formation, that the forces of expansion were waning before the end of the 1920s, and it is evident also that the population pressures which had sustained house building at a high level during most of the decade were about to moderate. The downturn in investment which reached its trough in 1931–2 thus seems to have been a good deal more than the outcome of an external shock, although the world depression made a major contribution to it. It seems to have signalized the end of an era in Australian capital formation with origins dating back to the previous major depression in the 1890s. Some of the many differences between capital formation in the two main upswings of the twentieth century which have been referred to in these pages, would almost certainly have been apparent even if there had been no world depression in the 1930s; the changed pattern after the 1920s was in an important sense inherent in the nature of Australian economic development.

Chapter 2

TRADE AND ECONOMIC STRUCTURE AT THE PERIPHERY: THE AUSTRALIAN BALANCE OF PAYMENTS, 1890–1965[1]

Neville Cain

I INTRODUCTION

That Australia's economic advance has always been closely associated with the international movement of goods, services and factors of production should be well known. The roles of trade in the getting and spending of her income, and of labour and capital immigration in the augmenting of her resource base, are illustrated below by graphs for the period since 1880. It may be useful to offer, as context for the Australian story, one or two generalizations about the evolution of the international economy as it has affected 'Western' countries of recent settlement, and to follow this with a perspective of Australian trade and payments since the late nineteeth century.

1. THE INTERNATIONAL ECONOMY

It should be stressed that what follows *is* a series of generalisations, merely descriptive and necessarily rather loose. Readers should remain alert to divergencies of experience by nation and commodity, to debate about the reliability of particular time-series (such as the secular net barter terms of trade), and to elements of continuity between periods which are hereunder distinguished.[2]

[1] I am very grateful to Noel Butlin and Alan Hall for helpful comment upon a draft of this paper, and to other colleagues in the Research School for descending upon surviving ambiguities.

[2] Useful references are: S. Kuznets, *Modern Economic Growth*, Yale University Press, New Haven, 1966, Ch. 6; A. Maizels, *Industrial Growth and World*

In the fifty or so years preceding World War I, trade and factor migration joined vigorously to lift—with a force and timing which varied among participating countries—economic performance at both the industrial 'centre' and agricultural 'periphery' of the Western world. This economic universe, pivoting on Britain, was an expanding one in which trade rose strongly with production; in which regional specialization flourished as labour and capital moved from the centre to exploit the comparative land advantage of the periphery; and in which the net barter terms of trade between industrial and primary products—between, broadly, centre and periphery—appear to have moved inversely with their relative export volumes. The momentum of primary export development in countries such as Australia was related not merely to population and income growth in, and factor migration from, countries such as Britain, but also to structural change within the latter away from those land-intensive activities in which they were at a disadvantage. And economic intercourse accomplished more than the export development of newer countries; it helped also to modify their resource endowments and (in conjunction with other influences) so to extend their domestic markets that by 1913 most had developed substantial non-primary sectors of their own. This progress, however, was often of an unsophisticated sort, and before World War I only the United States among newer countries was able to join Germany in industrial confrontation of Britain.

After 1918 the rate of growth of production, and of international goods and factors flows, fell sharply away. Before that, tariffs in certain regions appear to have modified only slightly the process by which production and trade had reinforced each other; but now many countries sought to expand domestic production almost entirely at the expense of imports. Soaring agricultural and industrial

---

Trade, Cambridge University Press, Cambridge, 1963, Parts I and II; G. M. Meier, *International Trade and Development*, Harper and Row, New York, 1963; I. Svennilson, *Growth and Stagnation in the European Economy*, United Nations, Geneva, 1954; W. A. Lewis, *Economic Survey 1919–1939*, Allen and Unwin, London, 1950; W. K. Hancock, *Survey of British Commonwealth Affairs*, Vol. II, *Problems of Economic Policy 1918–1939*, Part I, Oxford University Press, London, 1940; H. W. Arndt, *The Economic Lessons of the Nineteen-Thirties*, Oxford University Press, London, 1944; R. Nurkse, *International Currency Experience*, League of Nations, Geneva, 1944 and *Patterns of Trade and Development*, Blackwell, Oxford, 1962; A. K. Cairncross, *Factors in Economic Development*, Allen and Unwin, London, 1963, Chs 12 and 13; and A. C. L. Day, *Outline of Monetary Economics*, Oxford University Press, Oxford, 1960, Chs 27 and 38.

tariffs at centre and periphery respectively signalled the end of a once-easy reciprocity: between the beginning of the first war and the close of the second the volume of world trade, after recovering to its 1913 level in the mid-twenties, then merely fluctuated about it. Yet the level of production fared little better, and unemployment mounted as these efforts to turn the emphasis of development inward met with only limited success. The fortunes of individual countries varied with the extent to which they were traders, with the types of good they exported and imported, and with the trading groups (if any) to which they belonged. Industrial nations, for example, were better off according as they exported machinery rather than textiles; primary producers, for example, were better off according as they exported wool rather than wheat; and Britain, for example, was better off—we are not saying well off—according as she exported her unemployed (which, for example, had its corollary in Australia's migration and high-tariff policy of the twenties). If, as some argue, economic eclipse had loomed for Britain late in the nineteenth century, in the twenties (with her export industries in disarray and many overseas assets liquidated in prosecution of the war) it certainly arrived.

In the thirties collapse, misery and beggar-my-neighbour policies became universal; unemployment, already formidable by the later twenties in many countries, climbed to unprecedented heights. But ideological shock, 'innovation' in monetary thinking and the conspicuous successes of government economic management during World War II, combined to ease the passage of a new dispensation. After that war, Western governments joined in disowning the economic philosophies of the thirties and proclaiming, in white papers and trade charters, the consistency of high employment with high trade. Even with a hangover of substantial tariffs trade resumed the surge which had been interrupted by World War I. This was associated first with some retreat from the high but costly degree of self-sufficiency achieved during war, and then with rapid economic growth among the countries concerned—in what measure spontaneous and in what contrived we shall not essay, observing merely that domestic activity outpaced reviving trade: the bias of growth (now at high employment) was clearly inward. If international commerce had been a significant condition of movements in production over the seventy years before World War II, now (very broadly speaking) it seemed more their by-product.

The flow of capital picked up markedly, but while its real annual value exceeded that of pre-World War I its proportion of investment and income in debtor and creditor countries alike was much lower.

Besides being largely American, much of the increase in capital movement (in contrast with American outflow to Europe during the twenties) was governmental and directed toward underdeveloped countries. Private American capital continued, as in the twenties, to be discriminating, seeking its due in Europe, Canada, the Middle East and Australia. At the close of our period, Britain, further diminished in economic and political stature, languished barefoot at Europe's door as others hastened to fill her shoes in South-east Asia and the Antipodes. But Britain's post-war misfortunes helped to sustain flows of labour and capital to regions (such as Australasia) which, whatever the arithmetic of their lessened dependence, remained avid for them.

Until the 1950s it had been usual for the net barter terms of trade between primary products and manufacturers to vary inversely with their relative trade volumes. For much of the period 1895–1913 (which also saw an upswing in the general price level) they favoured primary products; for much of that between the wars (as the general price level receded after inflation in World War I), they favoured manufactures. From World War II onward inflation of the general price level was continuous, but after the early fifties, when the post-boom in primary prices had passed away, a relatively more buoyant trade in manufactures was accompanied not by a worsening but an improvement in their relative value. Associated with that, in turn, was a switch in the nature of specialization and exchange—a larger proportion of it represented trade among manufacturing countries, the selective exchange of manufactures for manufactures. In part this phenomenon was intra-European, the product of swiftly rising living standards, and anticipation (by mutual tariff concessions) of full commitment to the Common Market. Whether over the *long* period—whatever the short-term fluctuations—the terms of trade tended to move in favour of industrial activity, it would be hazardous to guess.

Through those seemingly felicitous gold-standard years of expansion and interchange before World War I, trading countries could afford to tolerate, if at times with unease, the balance of payments mechanism by which international fluctuations ramified; in the moribund, insecure world of 1919–39 they could not, and sought to export their problems while excluding the problems of others. These efforts were not very successful, indeed were largely self-defeating. The gold standard, suspended during the war and reinstated during the twenties, survived uneasily in now uncongenial circumstances before collapsing in depression. If it was not as efficacious a mechanism of international settlements before the war as legend would have, it was much less so afterward. Since World War II, although armed with institutions, techniques and a degree of international consultation (co-operation may be too strong a word) unknown in other days, policy-makers have found the reconciliation of internal and external balance a major anxiety. For in the inflationary environment of growth at high employment, this reconciliation, threatened continually by demand 'spill-over' and ratcheting costs, has proved elusive. Some countries (Australia among them) have managed the problem with smaller degrees of unemployment than others. We live, it would seem, a much modified gold-standard existence in which exchange rates are pegged but not fixed (the understanding—if not always the practice—being that variations should be made only for 'fundamental' reasons such as productivity lag or steady deterioration in terms of trade); in which exchange reserves are used to buffer fluctuations in external receipts; in which comparable rates of inflation among trading countries is the policy rule-of-thumb; but in which gold, if banished from domestic circulation, exercises a formidable sway over international liquidity.

2. AUSTRALIA AND THE INTERNATIONAL ECONOMY

Australia always relied considerably upon production for export. But the degree of this reliance varied, and from the 1860s—with which recent estimates begin—the ratio of exports to national income moved in a wave-like fashion. There was, as well, a suggestion of downward *trend* in the ratio after World War I, when lessened 'dependence' upon primary production and exports—lessened participation in the international economy—became the unmistakable bias of national economic policy. But a suggestion only: the contrived reallocation of resources did not make any substantial headway between the wars, while the outcome of the dramatic resource shift which occurred in and immediately after World War II was, for a time, obscured by an extraordinary rise in Australia's terms of trade. By the late fifties, however, when these terms had receded, the momentum of growth was more clearly indigenous. Yet the low export ratio of that time was not unprecedented; and at the end of our period, in the mid-sixties, a momentous export development in minerals promised to lift the ratio substantially.

Traditionally, Australia drew upon the labour, capital and 'know-how' of other countries (especially Britain) to extend her resource base. But while labour immigration maintained its importance in this respect, capital immigration did not. From the 1880s the ratio of net capital inflow to investment fell continuously away: domestic savings financed a rising share of additions to the capital stock. Yet our long period closed with signs of a reversal in this trend too, as minerals beckoned foreign capital on a large scale; and in the 1970s the export and capital inflow ratios may well rise together, returning Australia to a level of involvement with the world economy which would hardly have been guessed at in 1960.

The nature and geographical emphasis of Australia's transactions with the rest of the world varied through the years. Rapid population and capital growth did not—until very recently, anyway—modify the land-bias of her resource endowment sufficiently to allow non-primary output any significant *direct* participation in commodity exports; but within that constraint exports displayed a certain flexibility. This was the product of influences—discovery of new resources and changing use of old in response to relative profitabilities—which were weakest between the wars. But if there were variations, they were upon a familiar theme—the importance of wool and mining in Australian growth. Among commodity imports producers' equipment and materials were conspicuous from the beginning, reflecting the needs of a manufacturing advance which, already considerable by World War I, afterwards became increasingly 'artificial' and sophisticated. Variations in the composition of invisible trade were accounted for largely by gold production in the case of receipts, and debt service in that of payments. Inflation was instrumental in both, and diminishing reliance upon foreign savings in the second. Finally, the nature and uses of capital inflow were transformed. Through the twenty years after 1870 the public and private sectors vied for foreign money; the former offered fixed-interest terms and the latter largely so; and rural-cum-export development was the major use of borrowed money. In contrast, through the fifteen years after 1950 overseas borrowing was almost entirely private, of an equity description, and employed largely in manufacturing-cum-import replacement. In certain of these respects the twenties were a watershed. Accompanying all these changes in the nature of goods and factor flows were others in their geographical distribution. In the later nineteenth century, when Australia served so neatly the requirements of an international specialization centred upon Britain, her external transactions were oriented accordingly. But by the 1960s Britain was rivalled by Japan as a market for Australia's exports, by America as a source of imports and capital, and by southern Europe as a provider of people. Again the twenties were a watershed.

The step from a relatively straightforward overview of Australia's external transactions to an historical examination of her balance of payments as such, is somewhat awkward. Certainly we are obliged to simplify in order to penetrate a complex system of relationships. Here the 'capacity to import' seems a useful device: whatever the interrelations of its constitutents—export volume, the terms of trade and net capital inflow—over the long period, their separate consideration will carry us a certain distance behind the balance of payments—behind, that is, the simple financial summary of Australia's transactions with the rest of the world. Given the nature of her comparative advantage, it paid Australia to export primary products in exchange for the manufacturers and materials essential to her growth and diversification. But the capacity to import these things varied greatly. Thus the sturdy advance of import volume up to 1913 was followed by several fluctuations—severe falls in, and recoveries from, war, depression and war—before resuming in the late forties and carrying on (if with some hesitation during the fifties) into the present day. These variations will be discussed below. Of course reliance upon the capacity to import was modified over the years: net import substitution occurred. This process was much less spontaneous after World War I than before: comprehensive industrial protection in varying guise—the tariff, war, and import controls—made for a more (but not entirely) artificial expansion of manufacturing activity. It is notable, here, that the attempt to turn development inward was least successful between the wars but very successful during the fifties, when comprehensive import controls prevailed in the contrasting context of rapid growth at full employment.

The 'capacity to import' device serves yet another purpose. It leads fairly naturally (via implicit comparison with the 'propensity to import') into an examination of balance of payments disequilibrium—an examination not merely of sudden falls in external receipts which interrupted growth (for example—war and drought—aside—the early nineties and early thirties) but also those alternations of tension and ease between external receipts and local expenditure upon imports which characterized growth itself. Such alternations, needless to add, were the joint products of 'internal' and 'external' influences. This distinction should not be carried too far; but among the 'internal' influences, anyway, was the intensity with which development (population) policy was pursued. The economy's response to external imbalance varied over time with policy attitudes and the institutional arrangements to which they gave rise; and here what distinguished the post-1945 period from the half century preceding it was a resolve to eschew unemployment as a remedy for external deficit. Naturally the means to balance affected the nature of subsequent economic change: we are returned, full circle, to the structural issues with which we began. For example, had exchange depreciation rather than import controls been the response to balance of payments pressure in the 1950s, what would the export ratio have been late in that decade?

The essay which follows is an introductory traverse of a vast subject seeking to raise questions rather than answer them. Even then it attempts too much, but will have achieved its purpose if others are provoked to more elaborate effort. It will be convenient to tackle the Australian story in an order somewhat different to that of its summary above. We shall begin by despatching a certain amount of information about external transactions (Section II), move on then to a two-pronged examination of the balance of payments (III and IV), and conclude with an assessment of the extent to which Australia has varied its participation in the international economy (V).

II THE LEVEL, NATURE AND DIRECTION OF EXTERNAL TRANSACTIONS

The following description of Australia's transactions with the rest of the world will require some patience of the reader, but it provides the backdrop for issues raised in Sections III to V. We shall discuss the level, nature and direction first of transactions on current account ('visible' and 'invisible'), and then of transactions on capital account.

1. TRANSACTIONS ON CURRENT ACCOUNT[3]

As Chart 2.1 reveals there were two surges in the value of *visible* (commodity) exports and imports, from about 1900 into the mid-twenties and following World War II, and prolonged stagnation—

[3] The sources of these current account figures are as follows: to 1900, N. G. Butlin, *Australian Domestic Product, Investment and Foreign Borrowing, 1869–1938/39*, Cambridge University Press, Cambridge, 1963; and since 1900, I. McLean, 'The Australian Balance of Payments on Current Account, 1901 to 1964/65', *Australian Economic Papers*, 7, 1968, pp. 77–90, adjusted for 1941/45 to 1923/4 along lines suggested by P. Swan, ibid., pp. 91–103, and for 1901–

even, at one stage, collapse—between the mid-twenties and mid-forties. The only notable divergence of the two visible series occurred between 1930 and 1945 when restrained importing was compelled by the extreme exigencies of depression and war. Some idea of the relative contributions of volume and price changes in the value of visible trade is given by certain of our Charts; but because these and other variations will have our attention below we shall not pursue them here. The *balance of visible trade* (Chart 2.2) was usually favourable, although this was truer of the period following 1930; calamitous drought at the turn of the century caused the major exception before then, but there was also a marked weakening of the visible balance in the later twenties, preluding economic collapse. It was strong after that, although the odd deficit did occur during the modern era of high employment and expenditure 'spill-over" into substantial foreign reserves.

The swings of *invisible* exports and imports were not as mutual as those of their visible counterparts. They diverged markedly between 1900 and 1930, converged between then and 1945, but after that parted company again. Invisible *exports* rose quickly into the early 1900s, when gold production and exports reached their zenith, receded a little into the twenties, and then recovered in the thirties. The comparative stability of the series into the late twenties is somewhat misleading, a long decline in gold production being almost compensated by growth in transport receipts and income from the accumulating London assets of the banking system. The subsequent recovery of gold to a value peak in 1940/41 roughly equivalent to that of 1903 was—as a corollary of currency devaluation through the thirties—only partly a volume phenomenon. Then, as war and post-war inflation rendered its production unprofitable, this source of invisible income fell sharply away. Total invisible credits were sustained, for a time, by allied war expenditure in Australia, but not until the mid-fifties had they fully recovered from post-war relapse. In contrast with the comparative stagnation of invisible exports through the first thirty years of this century, invisible *imports* climbed strongly. Service of a growing external debt was the major

---

27/8 to cover items on invisible account which seem to have been overlooked. The latter adjustments depended in part upon a 'London funds' series kindly provided by Alan Hall. For the sake of consistency with modern practice gold is classified as 'invisible', and the invisible figures, in turn, are on a 'produced gold' basis; but for those who might prefer it certain of the charts offer for comparison the 'traded gold' basis through 1890–1913, the major gold-standard interval in our period.

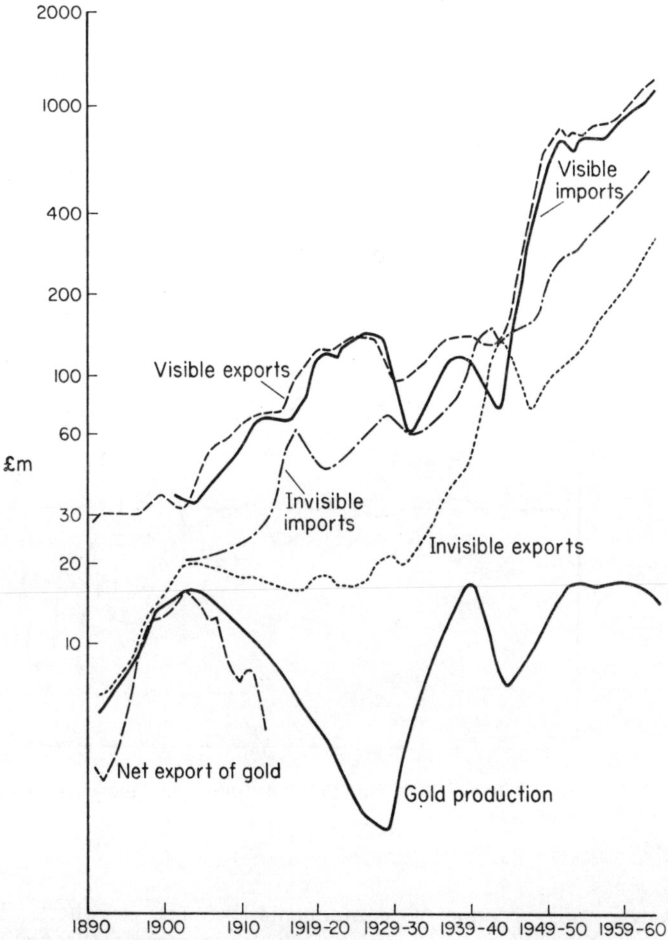

Chart 2.1 Balance of Payments Components 1891 to 1963–64 (three-year moving averages, current prices)

Source: See p. 73, n.3. No breakdown of imports into visible and invisible has been attempted for the nineties.

influence into the thirties, but after the second war, as inflation eroded old fixed-interest indebtedness, and capital inflow contributed far less to the creation of Australian assets, other items began to dominate the series, carrying it strongly forward without relapse.

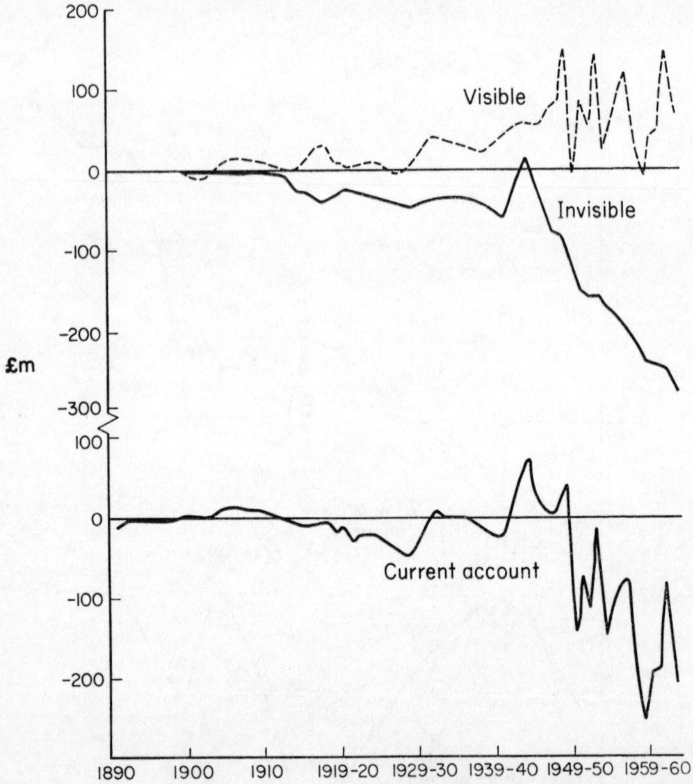

Chart 2.2 Trade Balances 1891 to 1963–64 (three-year moving averages, current prices)

Source: See p. 73, n.3.

However, this account of components belongs elsewhere. The *balance of invisible trade* was heavily unfavourable throughout, with the exception of that brief interval at the close of World War II, when invisible exports soared.

For much of the long period the deficit on invisible account outweighed the surplus on visible: the *current account balance* was typically unfavourable. On four occasions, however—the crises of the early nineties and early thirties, the mentioned interval at the close of World War II, and the years 1904–11—it was favourable. The latter was the only *sustained* exception to payments deficit: Australia was normally a net importer of capital. She was also, as we shall see, normally a net importer of labour; and indeed a broad directional correspondence between labour and capital flows, both inward and outward prevailed.

So much, then, for the level of transactions on current account. What of their nature and direction? We may begin with visible trade. Table 2.1 gives a breakdown, by commodity, of visible exports.

TABLE 2.1. *Major Rural 'Commodities', Per Cent of Visible Exports 1910–1963/64*
(annual averages)

	1910 –13	1924/5 –27/8	1935/6 –38/9	1950/1 –53/4	1960/1 –63/4
Wool (greasy and scoured)	38·6	45·0	38·0	57·0	35·5
Hides and skins	6·4	5·9	4·4	2·5	3·0
All meats	7·7	4·2	8·2	5·7	9·0
Pastoral	52·7	55·1	50·6	65·2	47·5
Wheat and flour	14·3	16·2	15·7	10·4	13·8
Barley, oats, sugar, fruit	0·8	5·0	7·2	7·2	9·2
Dairy products	5·7	6·3	9·0	3·6	3·4
Major rural commodities	73·5	82·6	82·5	86·4	73·9
Other	26·5	17·4	17·5	13·6	26·1
Total	100	100	100	100	100

Source: Commonwealth Bureau of Census and Statistics, *Overseas Trade* for individual export values; p. 73, n. 3 for value of total visible exports.

'Others' include minerals, finished manufactures and miscellaneous rural commodities. Primary (that is, rural and mineral) activity dominated export income throughout; although if manufactures were negligible in the sizeable 'other' of 1910–13, they carried far more weight in the equally sizeable 'other' of 1960/1–63/4, contributing 12 per cent of total visible export value in the final year. That contribution—composed of such items as iron and steel, vehicles and parts, drugs and chemicals—was to rise even further. But from the standpoint of our chosen period this was a very recent phenomenon. As for primary exports, the 1910–13 column gives the end-result of a major diversification originating in the early nineties. In

TABLE 2.2. *Visible Imports by 'Economic Class' Per Cent of Total Value*

	1913	1920/1	1929/30	1938/9	1948/9	1959/60	1963/4
I PRODUCER GOODS							
(a) *Materials*							
1. Blg. and cons.	8·9	8·3	7·1	4·1	3·4	3·5	3·2
2. Rural inds.	1·3	0·8	1·5	1·8	0·9	0·9	1·4
3. Mfg.	35·4	43·4	38·3	38·1	39·0	39·6	38·1
	45·6	52·5	46·9	44·0	43·3	44·0	42·7
(b) *Fuels and Lubricants*	1·8	4·5	8·1	7·8	8·8	2·8	2·4
(c) *Auxiliary aids to prod.*[a]	2·7	3·7	4·1	4·5	6·4	3·1	3·0
(d) *Capital equipt.*							
1. Farm	1·6	1·0	1·0	0·6	0·5	2·1	2·5
2. Commerce	8·9	7·5	7·7	11·1	9·3	15·8	17·4
	10·5	8·5	8·7	11·7	9·8	17·9	19·9
(e) *Transport equipt.*							
1. Completed road vehicles	4·5	4·2	7·8	9·5	12·2	9·9	11·2
2. Rly. equipt.	0·2	0·1	0·2	0·1	0·1	0·2	0·2
3. Vessels	2·1	1·0	0·1	0·7	0·2	0·4	0·3
4. Aircraft	—	—	—	0·4	0·8	2·5	1·2
	6·9	5·3	8·1	10·8	13·3	13·0	12·9
Total Producer Goods	67·6	74·5	75·9	78·8	81·9	81·0	80·9
II FINISHED CONSUMER GOODS[b]	28·1	24·9	23·7	19·8	17·4	17·7	17·9
III MUNITIONS & WAR STORES	4·3	0·6	0·4	1·4	0·7	1·3	1·2
	100	100	100	100	100	100	100

[a] Includes, among other things, advertising matter and containers.

[b] Includes food, beverages, tobacco, clothing and accessories, household equipment, jewellery, pharmaceutical and medical goods, books and other printed matter, and recreational equipment.

Source: Calculated from material supplied by Commonwealth Bureau of Census and Statistics.

Note: The official figures employ a sub-classification by degree of 'transformation'. Thus capital equipment, transport equipment and munitions and war stores are 'more elaborately transformed'; but producer materials and finished consumer goods embrace an array of 'crude', 'simply transformed' and 'more elaborately transformed' commodities.

the late eighties wool accounted for almost twice its 1910–13 share of visible export income. After 1890 frozen beef and mutton, meat preserved in cans, tallow, skins and so on joined wool in 'pastoral' earnings; agricultural products such as wheat and flour, butter, cheese and timber made themselves felt as exports; and minerals (tin, copper, lead, zinc and coal) were considerable in sum. Even if—given the altered circumstances of Australian wool growing, butting against its grazing frontier in the mid-nineties—we regard the arrival of non-wool pastoral exports as substituting for wool exports, a contrast between the total pastoral share of export income in the late eighties and 1910–13 remains. Only once in this century (the early 1950s) did wool even approach its later nineteenth-century pre-eminence. By World War I, indeed, the primary production and export pattern of the next half century was established. Diversification did not cease: it merely became an ebb and flow of emphasis—according to relative profitabilities—among the constituents of the 1910–13 product array. Apart from exports as a whole, to be examined later, there is not the space to discuss the price and volume behaviour of these constituents separately over the long period.[4] Nor shall we, in this same context, be discussing the influence of

[4] But the following figures for the recent period are of interest:

Exports of Rural Origin:
Average Annual Rates of Growth 1949/50–1963/64
(per cent)

Product	Quantum	Value (f.o.b.)
Wool (greasy equivalent)	2·7	−0·1
Wheat and flour	5·7	3·9
Beef and veal	10·5	21·2
Mutton	15·1	24·6
Lamb	−1·8	1·6
Canned meats	−5·7	−4·8
All meats	5·4	10·7
Butter	6·0	3·9

continued at foot of next page

trade treaties upon the fortunes of individual commodities. Suffice it to observe, here, that Australia's trading achievement was conditioned by her ability to vary the direction as well as composition of exports—indeed, the two often went together. A brief statement of major changes in the direction of *total* visible trade will be given subsequently.

If manufactures represent a loosening of the tie between farm production and exports about which it may be possible to enthuse, contemporary mineral exploitation seems even more likely to justify Australian hopes. Vast deposits yielded by highly capitalized prospecting promise to lift export performance handsomely. In Australia then, 'land' has proved to be quite other than a diminishing or, at best, fixed resource. Not that, like the Magic Pudding, it replenishes with every bite (some of the bites have in fact been irreparable); it is rather that we do not know how big the pudding is. For a country whose population may for some time remain small in relation to its 'expanding' resources, one prospect is that any tendency to lessened participation in the international economy will be arrested. Another —related—prospect is that primary export flexibility (now of kind rather than degree) will give the lie to gloomy prognoses about Australia's terms of trade.

If official figures are often inscrutable, those in Table 2.2—of visible *imports* by 'economic class'—are more than usually so, and we shall not take their analysis far.

The first thing to observe is that we have no details of any changes in classification which occurred; but these would have been more relevant within rather than between the major categories (I, II and III). Whatever the limitations of the figures, it is clear that a high proportion of imports were manufactured producer goods for use in the non-primary sector. Evidently 'finished consumer goods' never included passenger cars; indeed, had it done so—had an appropriate proportion of the producer goods sub-category 'completed road vehicles' been so allocated—its diminishing tendency

All dairy products	3·2	3·0
Sugar	8·9	10·7
Apples (fresh)	6·3	8·8
Dried vine fruits	3·2	8·5
Canned fruits	4·7	6·1
All exports of rural orgin	4·0	2·3

Source: Commonwealth of Australia, *Report of the Committee of Economic Enquiry*, Canberra, 1965, Vol. I, p. 310.

may have been substantially modified. Within item I, the drop in 'fuels and lubricants' after 1948/9 was related to the development of local refining capacity: the proportion of these goods now arriving less expensively 'in the crude' rose markedly, and was accommodated by item I(a).

So much, then, for the composition of visible trade. What of its direction? Tables 2.3(a) and 2.3(b) indicate the major changes:

TABLE 2.3(a). *Direction of Visible Trade 1902–1938/9*
(annual averages, per cent)

	1902–6		1923/4–1927/8		1934/5–1938/9	
	Exps	Imps	Exps	Imps	Exps	Imps
United Kingdom	46·1	58·3	38·7	43·3	52·3	42·5
Other British countries	25·1	13·6	11·1	13·2	12·3	16·4
Western Europe	19·5	11·0	28·2	7·8	16·5	7·8
Other foreign countries	9·3	17·1	22·0	35·7	18·9	33·3
Total	100	100	100	100	100	100
USA	4·7	12·6	7·9	24·5	4·0	15·7
Canada	0·3	0·7	0·5	2·6	1·5	7·0
Japan	1·1	1·0	8·1	2·8	8·1	5·3

Source: Official Year Book of the Commonwealth of Australia. First two intervals include bullion and specie. The USA and Japan appear in 'Other foreign' but are here shown separately as well (along with Canada from 'Other British countries') to allow comparison with the period after World War II. 'Other British countries' includes, for example, Canada, New Zealand, Cape Colony, India and Ceylon. 'Western Europe' consists of Australia's major trading partners there, essentially Germany, Belgium, France, Italy and the Netherlands.

The changes between 1902 and 1927/8 reflect in part the establishment of direct shipping links with customer countries and the decline of Britain merely as an entrepôt for Australian trade. Probably, however, the greater part of this transformation was accomplished by 1902, after which—whatever the remaining exaggeration of relaxation in the British connection—the direction of change is entirely consistent with what we know of the period, especially the emergence of America on the world trading scene. By the late twenties the United Kingdom share of imports had fallen far more heavily than that of exports, and here the American contribution to imports—despite Imperial Preference—was particularly impressive. Britain, compromised by the product-mix of her exports, lagging productivity and a return to gold at pre-war parity, was especially vulnerable at the periphery to American competition in equipment and the new consumer durables. It is worth noting, in connection with equipment imports, that the twenties saw the first considerable wave of American direct investment in Australia. This decade also witnessed the arrival of Japan as a significant market for Australian exports. In the thirties, by virtue of the Ottawa Agreement, tardy devaluation of the dollar, and later Australia's trade diversion policy—to which America took such strong exception—Britain managed merely to maintain her share of imports. But her share of exports rose. Ottawa again was an influence, and it is not surprising that the proportion of Australian export income accounted for by meat and dairy products—for which, in contrast with wool and wheat, the British market was determining—should have risen compared with the twenties.

For the more recent period a different classification of Australia's trading partners becomes necessary, (see Table 2.3(b)).

The shift in the destination of exports is pronounced; as the British market took a rapidly diminishing share, first Japan and later other Asian countries increased theirs. Western Europe, however, was as responsible as Asia for absorbing the drop in Britain's contribution in the early fifties. Analysis of these trends would be a subject on its own, covering the rates of growth of customer countries; their income-elasticities of demand for wool, wheat and minerals; international commodity agreement; and the formation of trading blocs such as the Common Market.[5] On the side of imports the most notable change was the sharp drop in the North American share between the late thirties and early fifties and its strong recovery into the early sixties. There again many influences were at work. Among those accounting for the initial drop were dollar shortage and then devaluation of the Australian and British pounds against the dollar in 1949. We cannot examine here the conditions responsible for the subsequent advance to a level similar to that of the late twenties, except to observe (because it will interest us in another context) that it was accompanied, as in the twenties, by a rising American contribution to direct foreign investment in Australia.

[5] The interested reader should begin with J. G. Crawford, *Australian Trade Policy 1942–1966*, ANUP, Canberra, 1968.

TABLE 2.3(b). *Direction of Visible Trade 1937/8–1964/5*
(annual averages, per cent)

	1937/8		1950/1–1954/5		1960/1–1964/5	
	Exps	Imps	Exps	Imps	Exps	Imps
United Kingdom	54·8	40·6	35·7	45·6	19·8	29·2
Western Europe	16·7	9·6	24·4	14·3	17·5	16·1
Total	71·5	50·2	60·1	59·5	37·3	45·3
Asia and Pacific						
USA and Canada	8·3	22·6	10·9	13·9	11·6	25·6
NZ and Pacific Is.	6·2	4·6	6·1	20·	9·4	2·7
Japan	3·7	4·7	7·5	2·3	16·8	6·6
China (Mainland)	1·2	0·6	1·3	0·5	5·9	0·6
India, Pakistan, and S.E. Asian countries	4·1	11·3	7·4	12·7	8·5	9·2
Total	23·5	43·8	33·2	31·4	52·2	44·7
All other markets	5·0	6·0	6·7	8·7	10·5	10·0
Total	100	100	100	100	100	100

Source: J. G. Crawford, *Australian Trade Policy 1942–1966*, ANUP, Canberra, 1968, pp. 568–9.

It remains for us to consider the nature and direction of *invisible* trade. We will then have rounded out our description of transactions on current account. As inspection of Chart 2.1 reveals, invisible imports were a higher proportion of *total* imports than invisible exports were of *total* exports. The major influence in this was debt service: the discrepancy largely reflected Australia's role as a net borrower overseas.

Table 2.4 illustrates the changing composition of invisible exports and imports. The more conspicuous movements therein have already been touched upon. If, in 1910–13, we were to substitute gold exports for gold production in invisible exports (to put matters on a traded-gold basis during the main gold-standard interval) the item would fall from 59 to 53 per cent. Either way, so significant was the development in gold coming out of the nineties depression that in 1903 it directly rivalled wool as a source of external income—but (in contrast with the gold boom of the mid-nineteenth century) drought had much to do with that. Lacking figures for the *direction* of invisible trade we must rely upon inference from other information. On the side of imports, for example, our knowledge of the external debt leads us to

TABLE 2.4. *Composition of Invisible Trade 1910-1963/4* (annual averages, per cent)

	1910–13		1924/5 –27/8		1935/6 –38/9		1950/1 –53/4		1960/1 –63/4	
	Creds	Debs	Creds	Debs	Creds	Debs	Creds	Debs	Creds	Debs
Gold production	59·0	—	14·4		32·4		13·8		6·1	
Transportation	19·9	24·0	41·0	26·0	30·7	20·7	40·7	41·4	42·1	36·8
Travel	5·1	7·2	6·0	6·0	4·6	6·6	4·4	5·8	7·0	8·7
Property income	8·0	63·6	24·1	64·7	10·3	57·5	12·3	29·8	15·0	33·6
Government	—	—	—	—	2·4	3·3	7·2	7·2	9·4	3·7
Transfers	8·0	2·4	14·5	1·9	10·2	4·7	15·7	9·7	13·9	11·9
Miscellaneous	—	2·8	—	1·4	9·4	7·2	7·2	6·1	6·4	5·3
	100	100	100	100	100	100	100	100	100	100

Source: see p. 73, n. 3.

suppose that for much of the period a high proportion of property payments would have been to Britain; but that from the twenties onward America needs to be considered. As for transportation, did or did not Australian use of British shipping move *pari passu* with Australian reliance upon British trade?

2. TRANSACTIONS ON CAPITAL ACCOUNT

It was found—using the indirect measure of net capital flow, the balance on current account—that Australia was normally a net importer of capital. But as we shall see below (Section V (a)) this reliance upon foreign savings to finance investment diminished over the years. We shall see, too, that the public sector was a net borrower overseas between the two depressions and a net lender for much of the period remaining. What, then, of the private sector? The two periods of interest here are 1904–28/9 and the years following 1948/9. For the latter we have official direct estimates of private capital flow; for the former an approximation is necessary, combining with the current account balance information about changes in the public external debt, the net London assets of the banking system, and other items, to arrive at a somewhat rough 'residual' estimate.

In the decade following the crisis of 1893, withdrawal of British capital from banking, pastoral and other enterprises was, in several years, more than offset by new British inflow on mining account; but in 1904 there began a sustained net outflow which only ceased some eight years later. The eyes of British investors had turned unambiguously away. Yet there was more to capital export through these years than merely British withdrawal. For the period of outflow (1904–11) the public sector, if a net borrower, was but a small one (£3·5m.): a relative cheapening of local money and a diversion of domestic savings towards the public sector after the crisis had been influential in this, and the local content of the public debt rose accordingly. On private account a novel development (originating around the turn of the century) was the accumulation of 'London funds': in contrast with the later nineteenth century the London assets of the Australian banking system now exceeded its liabilities. This was the outcome of strong growth in London assets, and again was consistent with the movement in relative rates of interest. The expansion of net London assets, together with some minor items,[6] yielded a capital outflow of £14·5m. Subtracting the £3·8m. of public *inflow* we get £10·7m. Now the cumulating (positive) current account balance for the period was £60m. and the increase in the stock of monetary gold £22m. We arrive, then, at a cumulative residual of £27·3m. for 1904–11, which, aside from errors and omissions, includes municipal authority transactions. These, however, appear to have been negligible. Now in what measure did this approximation to private 'long-term' (that is non-banking) net capital outflow represent the acquisition of titles to Australian assets as British investors unloaded, and in what measure purchases by Australians of titles to *foreign* assets (for example in Britain, New Zealand and Malaya)? Presumably the former influence was the weightier, but until better information is available it would be unwise to dismiss the second as insubstantial. Extending the period to the eve of World War I, the cumulative residual slips a little to £24·8m.

What is curious about the war-cum-post-war interval (1914/15–1919/20) is that while an overall net capital inflow occurred, the private sector (both banking and non-banking, as before the war) seems to have gone on exporting capital. The public sector borrowed heavily (£131m.). But the movement of London funds was upward. This increase, together with a small rise in the stock of monetary gold and so on, brings apparent borrowing back to £96·7m. More-

[6] Increases in Western Australian Sinking Fund and Australian holdings of New Zealand public debt.

over, the cumulative (now negative) current account balance was only £73m.; that is, a residual long-term private outflow of £24m. results. What sort of titles did Australians acquire? Their own? Was this all part of that familiar British wartime phenomenon—liquidation of overseas assets to help finance the war? Or did Australians invest directly, say, in the British war effort?

Moving into the first decade of high-tariff protection (1920/1–1928/9) we find a transformation. Public overseas borrowing rose by £220m. and the net outcome of the other directly calculated movements (in London funds, gold stock and so on) was negligible: apparent borrowing remained at about £220m. But the cumulative (still negative) current account balance for this decade was £317m., so yielding a private 'long-term' net inflow of £97m., or nearly one-third of total net inflow. This immediately raises questions about the role of private foreign capital in sheltered Australian industrial development at this time. After all, the £97m. amounts to 15 per cent of total gross private capital formation for the period. Making rough allowances for other uses, 25 per cent would not be an unreasonable estimate of the foreign contribution to private *industrial-commercial* investment in the twenties. This contribution was substantial, and it appears to have taken direct more often than portfolio form.

For the period after 1948/9 the official direct estimates yield the net flows shown in Table 2.5.

TABLE 2.5. *1948/9–1966/7* (£*m*.)

Short-term net capital inflow	391
Long-term net capital inflow	2,958
Total net capital inflow	3,349

Source: Commonwealth Bureau of Census and Statistics, *Balance of Payments*.

Long-term borrowing was overwhelmingly private.[7] The last four years of the nineteen accounted for 72 per cent of net long-term inflow, and inflation had only a little to do with it: in the sixties a substantial rise in the level of *real* inflow occurred.

What of the character of private borrowing and the uses to which

[7] At the level of *gross* flows private outflow was negligible. *Portfolio* investment overseas was in fact *negative*; Australians sold up their foreign securities in order to invest at home.

it was put? In the nineteenth century private borrowing had been largely of the fixed-interest type. A transition to the equity (profit-taking) type occurred in the twenties, and this was consummated after World War II. The twenties, moreover, saw a marked acceleration of direct equity borrowing; and for the period after 1948/9, when first import controls and later the tariff held sway, gross foreign equity investment was composed as in Table 2.6.

TABLE 2.6. *Composition of Foreign Equity Investment in Australia 1948/9–1963/4 (per cent)*

Portfolio	12·5
Direct	87·5[a]
Gross investment in companies	100·0[b]

[a] Direct investment consisted of 37 per cent undistributed profits and 63 per cent new inflow.

[b] Gross foreign investment in companies accounted for about 20 per cent of gross private investment in companies (about 25 per cent in the early sixties).

Source: Calculated from data in Commonwealth of Australia, 'Private Overseas Investment in Australia', *Supplement to the Treasury Information Bulletin*, Canberra, 1965.

In the nineteenth century private inflow had been employed largely in rural-cum-export development. In the twenties the emphasis moved toward manufacturing-cum-import replacement and associated activities, and this continued to be the case after 1948/9. Thus 60 per cent of direct private inflow during the early sixties went into manufacturing and 32 per cent into 'commerce'. Oil and petrol distribution were significant in the latter. We cannot dwell upon the investment attractions of urban Australia for the foreigner in the twenties and following World War II, except to observe that barriers which limited the access of his goods to a relatively prosperous and politically stable environment were instrumental in attracting his capital. And given the role of manufacturing in more recent Australian growth, it may be seen that overseas capital and its accompanying know-how were far more significant in that growth than the ratio of total net inflow to total investment would convey.

This discussion of transactions on capital account may be concluded by inquiring how much American money found its way to Australia after 1920. The public sector was the larger external borrower in the twenties and began to make substantial use of American capital then: 22 per cent of its foreign long-term funds was raised in New York. As for private borrowing, if the only available estimate of direct American investment in Australia has any credence perhaps 20 per cent of net private inflow during the twenties was thus accounted for.[8] While it may be the case, then, that Australia's technological links with Britain aggravated the unfavourable productivity outcome of industrialization in the twenties, at least those links had begun to weaken. For the period after World War II the official figures in Table 2.7 are eloquent enough.

TABLE 2.7. *Inflow of Private Foreign Investment in Companies 1947/8–1963/4 (per cent)*

United Kingdom	54·4
United States and Canada	34·3
Other	11·3
	100·0

Source: 'Private Overseas Investment in Australia', *Supplement to the Treasury Information Bulletin*, 1965.

III THE CAPACITY TO IMPORT

We have gathered much information about Australia's external transactions without really getting behind the balance of payments as such. That task will be tackled now, in two stages. In the first (Part III) the 'capacity to import' will be examined, and in the second (Part IV) 'payments equilibrium'. Our present concern, then, is with the capacity to import, which, despite some tendency to lessened dependence upon trade, was always crucial in Australian growth.

[8] D. T. Brash, *American Investment in Australian Industry*, ANUP, Canberra, 1966, pp. 22–5, and using A£ 1 = US $4·80 to translate his dollar estimates into a rough Australian equivalent. For the origins of *public* overseas money, see *Finance Bulletin*, No. 24, p. 36.

Of course its constituents—export volume, the net barter terms of trade and net (real) capital inflow—were interrelated through time, but their separate study will be of considerable value. The section concludes with an assessment of their joint outcome in terms of import volume, and with a query about the extent to which Australia did manage to reduce its *relative* reliance upon the capacity to import.

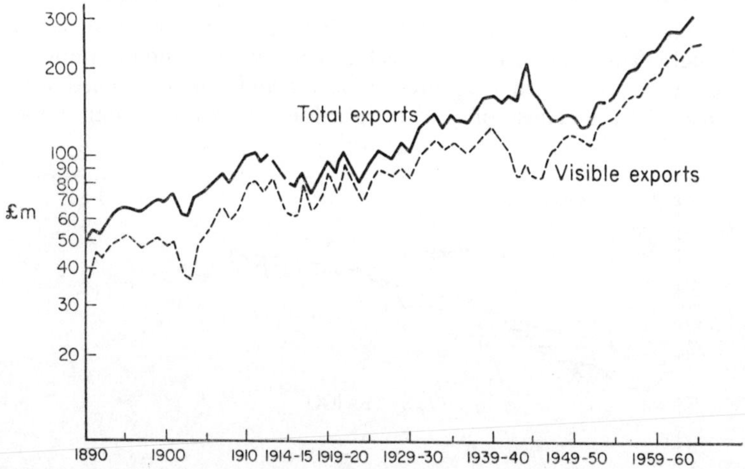

Chart 2.3 'Real' exports 1890 to 1964–65 (annual series)

Source: See p. 73, n.3 for export values; deflated by export price index based at 1938–39.

1. EXPORT VOLUME

In Chart 2.3 a perspective of total export volume for the entire period 1890–1965 is presented. Its upward progression was far from smooth. Rapid increase before World War I was followed by collapse and recovery, and only in the thirties did a *substantial* advance over the immediately pre-war level occur. Another trough ensued between the late thirties and mid-fifties (although interrupted by a swelling of invisible income at the close of the war), after which exports climbed swiftly into the present day.

At times the total and visible export series moved discrepantly. Gold was largely responsible before World War II and other invisible income at its end. As we have seen, until very late in the period visible income was overwhelmingly rural in origin. The importance of gold at the turn of the century may be indicated readily enough: it transforms what would have been a total exports series trending downward during the great drought of 1895–1902, into one trending upward; and even for a time after that, although less conspicuous, it continued to enjoy a status as overseas earner which it was never to retrieve. From 1903, however, it was a prodigious expansion of rural production, incipient in the drought, which dominated export volume. This was associated with a diversification of land use which has been described. But after hesitating in the early 1910s, exports plummeted into the war interval, which was inaugurated by severe drought. Through the twenties visible export volume did not improve greatly on its immediately pre-war level; and this, combined with (*inter alia*) the eclipse of gold production, made for a total export

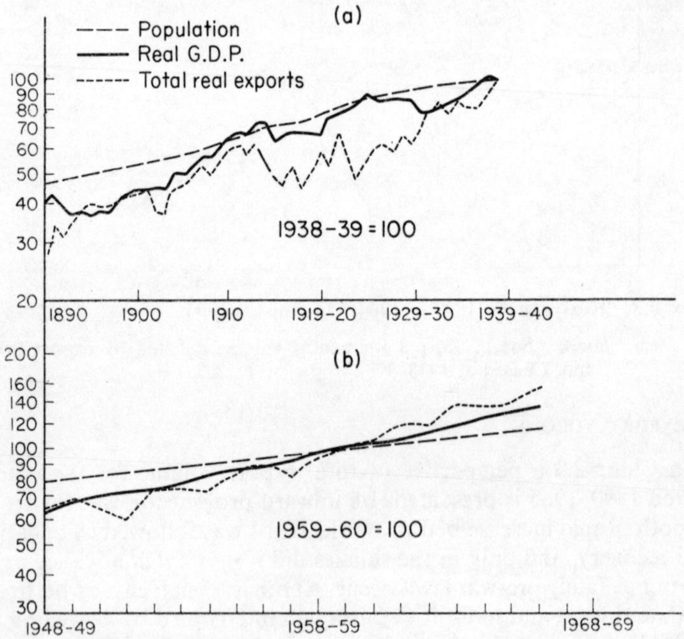

Chart 2.4 Selected 'Real' Indexes 1890 to 1938–39, 1948–49 to 1966–67

Source: (a) For population, see Commonwealth Bureau of Census and Statistics, *Demography Bulletin;* for real G.D.P. at 1938–39 prices I am grateful to Noel Butlin for an unpublished series; and for real exports, see Chart 2.3.
(b) *Demography Bulletin*; and for real exports and G.D.P. at 1959–60, prices, Commonwealth Bureau of Census and Statistics, *National Income and Expenditure.*

performance which—whatever the limitations of our figures[9]—was at least unremarkable in a decade noted for schemes of rural settlement. In the thirties, however, visible export volume rose strongly, while the recovery of gold production helped to offset a decline in other invisible earnings. In contrast with the period preceding it, the interwar period had been less flexible in its pattern of land use. Given the marked shift of resources out of primary activity which occurred during World War II, it is hardly surprising that there was then a relatively deeper dip in commodity exports than in World War I. But just as the first war began with a severe drought, so did the second conclude with one; and just as the decade following the first war accomplished little more than a recovery from wartime shortfall in export volume, so did the decade following the second. From then on expansion was swift. It proceeded—in the context of rapid population growth and high employment—with some flexibility of land use and a loosening of the tie between farm production and exports. Chart 2.4 compares the rate of growth of total volume with that of population and real gross domestic product for two major sub-periods.

Which influences bore significantly upon export volume over the long period? This cannot be taken far, and comment will be limited mainly to *rural* exports.

These exports were the difference between rural production and local absorption of same. Absorption we put to one side.[10] Production depended, of course, upon the size of the rural work force and its productivity. Rural employment climbed from the nineties to an absolute peak in the later thirties (without even a dip in the trough

[9] It is probable that our series understates commodity export volume somewhat in the second half of the twenties; but any allowance for this would make little difference to the picture we have drawn of a weak export performance between 1913 and the late twenties. An index by Wilson shows, for 1924/5–1928/9, an improvement in average annual export volume (excluding gold) over 1911–13, but virtually none in export volume including gold. R. Wilson, 'London Funds and the Australian Economy', *Economic Record,* XI (1935), pp. 97–121.

[10] Readers might themselves reflect upon the growth in local demand for foodstuffs, raw materials and fodder as the human and livestock populations grew. But a brief word about foodstuffs, anyway. It is easy to exaggerate the effect of local population growth upon foodstuff exports, but shortly after World War II they were being taken quite seriously. It is worth observing, in this context, that between 1860 and 1890 (when the Australian population grew very swiftly) the ratio of rural production to total production fell much less than the ratio of export production to total production Between the early nineties and 1910 this situation was reversed, and so on. In only one case since 1890 has strong population pressure coincided with strong export growth, namely, the quite remarkable period from the mid-fifties into the present day.

of the depression), fell sharply in the war, recovered about half that drop by 1953/4, only to recede again until, in 1961, it was virtually the same as in 1910. What of average labour productivity? Clearly if we compare, say, 1961 with 1910, there was a great increase: a much greater output was produced by a comparable work force. Now the statistical notion of labour productivity through time compounds a variety of influences—investment, technology, the weather, product and location mix—which cannot be considered at length. All we can do is examine briefly the three intervals of substantial net advance in rural export volume: 1890–1910, the 1930s, and 1955–65. In each of these productivity rose, most rapidly in the last and (if we ignore the drought of 1895–1902) about equally less rapidly in the other two. Let us consider them chronologically.

Looking at time-series of wheat yields and fleece weights, we cannot fail to be impressed by the increases achieved between 1890 and World War I. What did technical change (such as new varieties, fertilizers and machinery improvements in wheat, and breeding practices in wool) contribute to these? Take wheat. How much of the statistical advance in yield is to be explained simply by the changing geographical emphasis of a swiftly growing acreage? Through this period a substantial proportion of the increase in wheat acreage was sown in New South Wales, on ertswhile pastoral land. In so far as this colony offered a higher productivity in wheat than older areas like South Australia, the location-mix factor alone would have lifted the Australian yield per acre. Take wool, for instance. How much of the rise in fleece weight was due to the culling effect of prolonged drought and the marked shift in flock composition toward the heavier-woolled and more palatable cross-bred through the same period? In short, to what extent do the per acre and per sheep statistics reflect, for this interval especially, merely alternative ways of using the same resources in response to the usual incentives; that is, to what extent do they reflect the rural diversification that was going on? Now the rural capital stock may have grown about comparably with the rural work force over these years. The economic history of farm mechanization at the turn of the century has yet to be written; that other major aspect of rural change in this period—the export of frozen meat—imposed a capital requirement in the form of freezing and chilling works which is easily overlooked; and of course the public sector was active in the provision of a rural infra-structure. In short, we might suggest that the handsome rise in rural output and exports before World War I was *largely* the outcome of an *extensive* development using additional labour, capital and land, but that an increase in labour productivity occurred which perhaps owed as much to location and product-mix as to technical change. The entire rural transformation had its origin in the late eighties, when a reorientation of the economy towards primary activity began; it occurred, for the most part, in a favourable price environment; and it was muted for a time by severe drought.

It some measure the expansion of rural output, exports and labour productivity in the thirties was the lagged consequence of (largely public) investment in the twenties; but to some extent, as well, it was the outcome of an unhappy 'grow-more-wheat' campaign at the beginning of the decade, a fine run of seasons, the familiar supply response to falling farm incomes, and (related to that) the 'flogging' of land and equipment. In short, it is difficult to establish just how 'tenable' the higher level of rural production was in the highly unfavourable price environment of that time. As observed elsewhere, the rural export achievement in the twenties was unimpressive; productivity improvement was negligible. There was more to this than the gestation period of railway and irrigation schemes; but we cannot pursue the matter, involving as it would (for example) the spread of activity into inferior land (the location-mix factor now being negative), the slower pace of mechanization and technical change as compared with pre-World War I, and government rural policies which inhibited optimal resource use.

Following the early fifties, Australia's export performance became remarkably strong. As the rural work force stagnated, investment and technical change combined to lift labour productivity at a very rapid rate. Broadly, in contrast with 1890–1910 development was highly *intensive*, substituting capital for labour and land; and if (relatedly) the public sector was not *very* active in the provision of rural infra-structure (though beef roads, port facilities and some railway modernization testified to a continuing interest and commitment in this regard), it was *extremely* active in subsidizing the rural sector,[11] in promoting its technology through such agencies as the CSIRO, and in conducting trade negotiations on its behalf. Among the more significant technical developments were rapid mechanization, much higher-yielding wheat varieties, trace elements, selective breeding, pasture improvement and myxamatosis (both of which

[11] Perhaps the most significant and eagerly accepted subsidy of all being the cheapening of capital for rural investment. Thus, when speculating about the capital costs of recent improvements in manufacturing productivity (see below, Section V, 2) we should not be blind to those associated with parallel improvements in rural efficiency.

boosted sheep-carrying capacity and with it the outlays to accommodate the additional sheep).[12] So notable had the achievement been as export prices weakened, that in 1966 a Treasury publication could insouciantly declare:

> '. . . despite the fears voiced from time to time about the future of Australia's exports of primary products, results so far seem to show that increases in production can more than offset the effect on export proceeds of falling prices. Whereas the future of export prices is problematical, experience in Australia and elsewhere suggests that the upward trend in productivity in the main primary industries can continue.'[13]

The contrasts with 1890–1910 were fairly plain: among them were the price situation, the highly intensive nature of development, the greater role of relatively 'disembodied' technical change, and the omnipresence of government. As already observed, the recent period also witnessed a substantial augmenting of rural exports with exports of manufactures (a development in which, we might add, government promotion again was influential).

Before turning aside from export volume, we may briefly extend the discussion of rural exports to primary exports as a whole, with a remark or two about minerals. Today's *boom* had only begun when our period ended: certainly mineral export volume had doubled since 1954, but it had done so from a small base. Indeed, taking the entire period, by far the most significant mineral had been gold. That the incentive to produce it should have increased in both depression decades will not surprise the economist. Its price fixed in terms of national currencies, the real value of gold rose as dramatically as commodity prices fell. But the two depression experiences were in other ways distinctive. During the second, most major currencies were themselves depreciated against gold in a cycle of devaluation which did not end until the later thirties, by when they bore roughly the same relationship to each other as at the beginning but a worsened relationship to gold. On the other hand, the thirties

[12] After a long expansion Australian sheep grazing encountered its frontier in the mid-nineties. Then the sheep population fluctuated, and not until the late twenties did it begin to edge above its nineteenth-century maximum. But the significant easing of physical constraint came only with extensive pasture improvement after 1950. By the mid-sixties there were 60 per cent more sheep in Australia than in the later thirties, and rising fleece weights bore less of the burden in expanding wool production than they had before 1950.

[13] Commonwealth of Australia, 'The Australian Balance of Payments', *Supplement to the Treasury Information Bulletin*, Canberra, 1966, p. 23.

did not see the discoveries of rich deposits and advances in mining technology which the nineties did. The latter phenomenon may even have given gold a relative cost as well as relative price advantage over other activities in the nineties.[14]

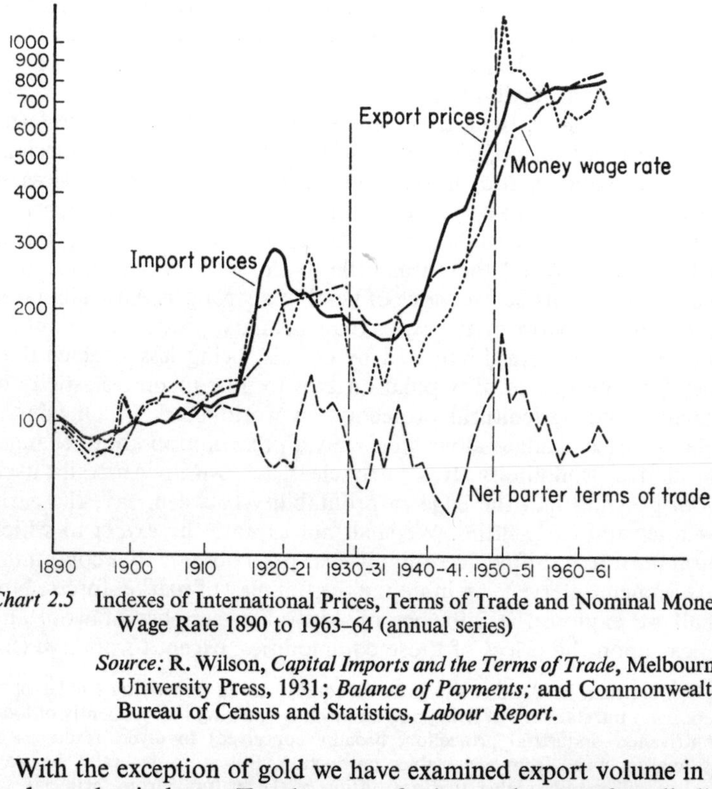

Chart 2.5 Indexes of International Prices, Terms of Trade and Nominal Money Wage Rate 1890 to 1963–64 (annual series)

Source: R. Wilson, *Capital Imports and the Terms of Trade*, Melbourne University Press, 1931; *Balance of Payments;* and Commonwealth Bureau of Census and Statistics, *Labour Report*.

With the exception of gold we have examined export volume in a fairly mechanical way. To what sort of prices and costs, after all, did the export sector respond? The arrangement of our discussion—along 'capacity to import' lines—is such that we must handle (or rather dismiss) that question within the broader one: what happened to Australia's terms of trade between 1890 and 1965?

[14] But the capital costs of gold mining in the nineties should not be underestimated. Exploration was expensive and technical developments other than cyaniding (which has held the limelight) required substantial outlays (for example, the gold dredge and the mechanical drill). British money may have paid for these things, but that had a balance of payments corollary. See G. Blainey, 'Technology in Australian History', *Business Archives and History*, IV, 1964, pp. 117–37.

2. THE NET BARTER TERMS OF TRADE

Australia experienced wide fluctuations in the terms on which she traded with the rest of the world (Chart 2.5). Was there, as well, a secular deterioration of these terms?[15] Until we have figures adequate to the task[16] we cannot know. Whatever the answer, we can reasonably say that the terms would have been lower (higher) had Australia been less (more) flexible in the direction and composition of her trade—but that flexibility has been discussed.

Let us consider, then, the *fluctuations* which occurred. The terms of trade reversals occasioned by war and depression are especially notable. Notable, too, is the great instability of *export* prices in peacetime. These, in turn, were dominated by wool. A comparison of wool and wheat unit export values is instructive (Chart 2.6). Before World War I there was little to choose between them; after that, odd years aside, the price of wool was stronger. Australia fared rather better between the wars than primary producing countries whose exports were dominated by cereals, being less affected than they by slower rates of population growth, low income elasticity of demand and agricultural protection in world markets. Of course, relative price changes alone yield only a presumption about changes in relative profitability. It is fairly clear that within Australia itself wool growing had the edge in profitability between, say, the early twenties and early fifties. We shall not explore the *extent* to which rural resources shifted accordingly, except to observe that continuing government intervention inhibited the full play of market forces. Nor shall we explore the influence of Australian supplies of wool and wheat upon the prices of those commodities, except to observe (for

[15] If so, then here (other things being equal) was an underlying secular pressure upon the standard of living and an incentive (arising independently of local contrivance—industrial protection, broadly conceived) to divert resources at the margin away from exportables production. But more generally, anyway, readers will readily gather that any sifting of the 'natural' from 'artificial' influences upon industrial structure and so export volume would be a complex task. It will not be hazarded here.

[16] Until, that is, we have indexes of export and import prices devised especially for the long period, accommodating invisible trade and comprehending, as far as possible, all significant changes in quality (which may well have favoured Australia) and product-mix. It is surprising that in an economy as 'open' as the Australian, the government statistician has yet to produce—even for relatively short periods—national income series adjusted for the terms of trade. Despite our reservations about the usefulness of linked commodity price indexes for exports and imports in the secular terms of trade context, we have not been able to avoid using them in another; they provide the only means of arriving swiftly at unbroken long-run series of export and import volume.

example) that Australia's share of world wool production was 25–30 per cent, and of exports 40–46 per cent, over the half century following 1910.

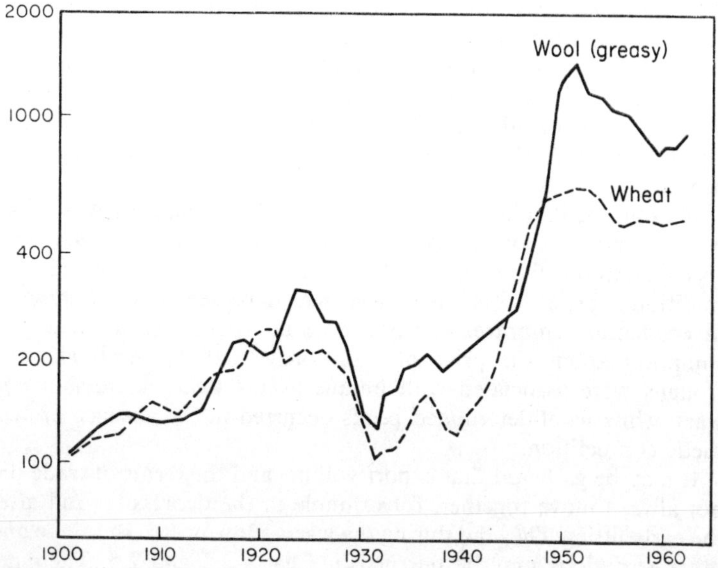

Chart 2.6 Indexes of Unit Export Values 1901 to 1962–63 (three-year moving averages 1901 = 100)

Source: Overseas Trade.

Taking the export sector *as a whole*, it was the 'internal' (or intersectoral) net barter terms of trade which influenced the incentive to produce, for these comprehended the 'net burden' imposed upon the sector by local development policy. We shall touch upon that burden elsewhere, in the context of relative resource shift between sectors. But to measure it all precisely through time would be awkward, and a brief reference to more recent history must suffice. It is clear that the internal terms of trade were less favourable between 1955 and 1965 than they had been between 1945 and 1955; yet rural production and export volume rose very rapidly. This was *partly* the lagged outcome of farm programmes initiated in better days, but more so of ongoing investment and technical change which boosted labour productivity. But the measure in which price-cost squeeze was offset would have depended upon how expensive the process had been in terms of capital—in short, upon *total* factor productivity in the export sector. We may risk the judgement, here, that despite heavy rural investment it had increased more rapidly than at any other time since 1890. This bears, of course, upon Australia's *factoral* terms of trade (or, to put it broadly, upon any contribution which the export sector may have made to improvement of Australia's relative cost situation in the trading world). But these waters are deep, and we simply observe that in the concluding decade of our period, when both the external and internal net barter terms worsened, the corresponding factoral terms may have improved.

It would be injudicious to guess at the likely course of Australia's net barter terms over, say, the next twenty years. Readers may speculate about the supply and demand elasticities of not only our traditional exports but also those which present and prospective diversification embrace. The past does not yield even a vague presumption about the price of traditional (that is, rural) exports: troughs were associated with unique events (war, depression and war), while wool-determined peaks occurred in the absence of synthetic competition.

It may be gathered that export volume and the terms of trade did not always move together, for example in the depression and after the early fifties. They did during the wars—downward. But these and other variations may be pursued in Charts 2.3 and 2.5. Their net outcome was the 'export-based' capacity to import, which varied from *total* capacity by the amount of real capital flow.

3. NET CAPITAL INFLOW

Because capital movement has already been touched upon, three observations will be enough to despatch the subject here. First, we need to remind ourselves that while Australia normally borrowed overseas (so augmenting the export-based capacity to import), between 1904 and 1911 especially she was a net lender. Secondly, the rate of capital inflow varied greatly; so did the terms of trade; and the result was a volatility of total capacity to import which (as we shall see) had certain implications for the stability of domestic activity (the two most dramatic examples—despite a degree of offset from rising export volume—being the depressions of the early nineties and early thirties). And thirdly, a comparison of the major periods of capital inflow reveals that the average annual level of real (as opposed to money) inflow was similar in the 1880s and 1920s, and perhaps one-third higher in the fifteen years concluding our long period—which, however, was entirely consistent with a diminishing *share* of foreign investment in local capital formation.[17]

4. TOTAL CAPACITY TO IMPORT

What, then, was the joint outcome of changes in the three constituents of Australia's capacity to import between 1890 and 1965? Chart 2.7 presents the import volume story; and the role of each constituent in the movements which occurred[18] may be broadly inferred from the charts preceding it. The absolute impact of war and depression upon import volume is evident enough, and the result was that sustained growth prior to 1914 was followed by a long interval of marked fluctuation before resuming in the late forties.

The question naturally occurs: to what extent did Australia manage to *substitute* for the capacity to import? Reliable estimates of *net* import replacement over the long period have yet to appear. Some figures for 1913–59 have been elicited from Maizels by Corden, but we must avoid giving them a currency they have yet to earn.[19] What does seem fairly clear is that the most extensive—and sophisticated—achievement occurred after 1950. The period before 1913 is barren of even intelligent guesses about replacement, but there is reason to believe that it may have been substantial then. Among shorter intervals only the later thirties seem worthy of notice. Industrial protection in the twenties appears to have accomplished little.[20]

[17] See below, Section V, 1. Real capital inflow has been calculated only roughly by deflating total net capital inflow with an import price index based at 1938/39. Annual real inflow was markedly higher in the first half of the sixties than in the fifties.

[18] That is, in a 'statistical' sense. As already observed the longer the period the greater the degree of interaction between the three. Even in fairly short intervals this interaction may be considerable. For example, the decline of capital inflow after 1890 was not unrelated, on the supply side, to the course of Australia's terms of trade.

[19] W. M. Corden, 'Industrialisation and Trade: Review Article', *Australian Economic Papers*, 3, 1964, pp. 113–23. Corden rightly has reservations about the figures, which purport to measure the relationship between imports of manufacturers and total consumption of manufactures between 1913 and 1959.

[20] For pre-1913, see below Section IV, 1. Bryan Haig's examination of Australian expenditure reveals a marked contrast between the twenties and fifties in the degree to which local manufacturers met the demand for investment goods. B. D. Haig and Jennifer Finlayson, 'Consumption Expenditure and Living Standards, 1920/21 to 1965/66', in preparation.

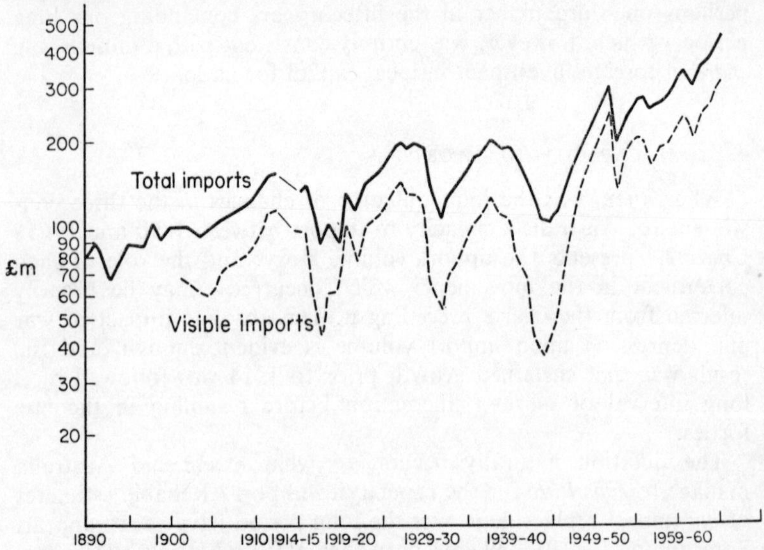

Chart 2.7 'Real' Imports 1890 to 1964–65 (annual series)

Source: See p. 73, n.3 for import values; deflated by an import price index based at 1938–39.

IV PAYMENTS 'EQUILIBRIUM'

The capacity to import did not always accommodate the desire to import. Certainly the balance of payments always balanced; Australia always paid her way. But at times the price was high; too high, certainly, for us to regard 'balance' and 'equilibrium' as synonyms.

Disequilibrium occurred most dramatically when the capacity to import was completely undermined, as in the early nineties and early thirties. In each case severe unemployment was a major characteristic of the adjustment process by which the demand for imports was brought into line with the capacity to pay for them. Yet there were other occasions of tension in the balance of payments when the adjustments required were relative rather than absolute, were part of growth rather than its reversals.

Our concern, in the end, is with *general* equilibrium. External and internal equilibrium are not really separable; we cannot have one without the other. Over the long period before World War II the most conspicuous symptom of general disequilibrium was substantial unemployment: external balance was often achieved at the expense of domestic activity. But after the war such a 'policy' ceased to be acceptable, and the Commonwealth government intervened continually to secure an appropriate distribution of national expenditure between home and foreign goods at 'full' employment.

1. 1880–1913

Through the eighties, aggregate economic growth at high employment, nourished by heavy inflows of labour and capital, was vigorous. The course, composition and *per capita* outcome of activity at this time have been well established and described elsewhere,[21] and we shall not retell what should be a familiar story. One or two observations about the balance of payments must suffice. In the second half of the eighties the Australian capacity to import evened out; rising export volume was offset by lower terms of trade and capital inflow steadied; the corollary was stability of total debits. Apparently it was not until after 1890 that any inconsistency between the behaviour of local expenditure and the capacity to import emerged. Gold flows were unexceptional; there was not even a drift of the exchange rate towards the gold export point; and we have, as yet, no evidence of abnormal unemployment before 1891 which might have rendered such phenomena consistent with disequilibrium. In short, the balance of payments—in contrast with its behaviour before 1929—appears to have adjusted smoothly to changes occurring within and without the the Australian economy at this time. But the collapse of capital inflow in 1891 was so great and sudden a shock that smooth adaptation was impossible. Although the terms of trade deteriorated even further, they were offset by a surge in export volume: export proceeds stabilized. It is an interesting sidelight on the mechanism of gold-standard adjustment at the periphery that heavy unemployment[22] and not gold flows brought the level of local expenditure (and with it absorption of imports) abruptly into line with a suddenly constricted capacity to import; and, in time, the money-wage rate more into line with the course of import prices. We need to recall, here, that capital ebbs and flows which were marginal to Britain were far more than that at the periphery: in the eighties,

[21] N. G. Butlin, *Investment in Australian Economic Development 1861–1900*, Cambridge University Press, Cambridge, 1964, Part A; A. R. Hall, *The Stock Exchange of Melbourne and the Victorian Economy 1852–1900*, ANUP, Canberra, 1968, Ch. 4.

[22] Wood estimated that in Victoria and New South Wales unemployment reached 26·5 per cent among factory workers. G. L. Wood, *Borrowing and Business in Australia*, Oxford University Press, Oxford, 1930, p. 99.

after all, the ratio of capital inflow to Australian fixed capital formation had been about 50 per cent.

Two other points of interest emerge from the depression interval 1891–4. First, we can only speculate about the extent to which general institutional collapse resulted in a modification of that formidable fixed-interest transfer problem which was a legacy of heavy overseas borrowing in the eighties—a modification, that is, beyond what the market may have achieved in the absence of financial reconstruction. The question is complex, but upon its answer depends, in turn, the extent to which the pressure upon local employment (to reduce imports and release foreign exchange) was eased thereby. Secondly, there was a marked revival of the ratio of exports to national income: its long decline since the sixties, arrested in the late eighties, was now reversed. Initially the structural bias of unemployment was very influential in this, but as urban employment recovered from 1894 onward, the ratio continued to rise: export volume (if on account of gold through the drought period) and the terms of trade accompanied each other upward. And just as the emphasis of rural activity was changing, so was that of secondary activity—from construction to manufacturing.[23]

Associated with this redirection was a substantial fall in the prices of labour and—when the liquidity crisis of 1893 had passed—capital. Indeed, thanks largely to unemployment relatively far heavier than in Britain, Australia seems to have emerged from the early nineties with a relative cost improvement which poses questions about the nature of her manufacturing progress before World War I. How much of it was import-competitive rather than of a merely 'processing' or 'service' sort linked to rural development? Coghlan referred to a 'fair number of industries of a more complex character' (by which he appears to have meant import-competitive types) being

[23] This was all part of what Coghlan has described: 'The redirection of attention towards productive industry, from which it had been diverted during the land boom, was noticeable about 1891 and greatly increased after the crisis'. T. Coghlan, *Labour and Industry in Australia*, Vol. 4, Oxford University Press, London, 1918, p. 1941. The redirection may have become 'noticeable' in 1891 but it seems to have begun in the late eighties. For details of the Australian economy's reorientation in and after the nineties see Butlin, *Investment in Australian Economic Development*, Part D; W. A. Sinclair, *Economic Recovery in Victoria 1894–1899*, ANUP, Canberra, 1956 and 'Aspects of Economic Growth 1900–1930', Ch. 6 in A. Boxer, ed., *Aspects of the Australian Economy*, Melbourne University Press, Melbourne, 1965; and A. Hall, *The London Capital Market and Australia 1870–1914*, ANUP, Canberra, 1963, Chs 5–8, and *Stock Exchange of Melbourne*, Ch. 6.

'firmly established' by 1900.[24] Looking backward from about 1907, how many such industries had derived impetus from a major relative cost adjustment in the mid-nineties which gave them a larger share of markets growing swiftly in and beyond the phase of economic recovery? We say 1907 because (if the ratio of local wages to import prices has any meaning in this context) the relative cost advantage may have gone by then. It is notable, here, that the Lyne tariff of 1908 was the first of the *explicitly* protective Commonwealth tariffs;[25] and that manufacturing progress after 1910 seems to have depended less on import competition than the linkage effects of a major construction boom.

The impression, then, is one of export-led recovery from the nineties depression and a possibly substantial advance in import replacement. The multiplier and liquidity effects of rising export income ramified through the economy, assisted by a relative cost adjustment which restrained expenditure leakage into imports; and after 1900, as urban activity accelerated, the export ratio receded. However, balance of payments strength did not dissipate *altogether* in local expansion. It was used partly to export capital, and one concomitant was a rate of unemployment which, while fairly low, still exceeded that in Britain. Despite such unemployment, by 1910 real income per head of population had recovered to about its level of the late eighties, and this without the underpinning of capital inflow —indeed the opposite. Had the drought of 1895–1902 not occurred it is likely (on any reasonable assumptions) that much more would have been achieved. The rural sector would have been better placed to exploit high export prices, the demand for labour and capital would have been more buoyant, and net capital inflow may have resumed well before 1912—all this, again, with clear implications for aggregative and *per capita* performance. Certainly the following of depression by prolonged drought rendered alternative overseas investments all the rosier in British eyes. A comparison with, for example, the Canadian case through these years might be instructive: more stable weather and a less experimental export development (which together allowed full exploitation of the upswing in commodity prices from the mid-nineties) would be among the features distinguishing it from the Australian. Yet Australia's achievement was impressive enough in the circumstances. The economy displayed

[24] T. A. Coghlan, *A Statistical Account of the Seven Colonies of Australasia*, 1899–1900, No. 8, Government Printer, Sydney, 1900, p. 597.

[25] We may, of course, allow that earlier, less comprehensive tariffs had some influence upon the fortunes of particular industries.

considerable resilience after a long and balmy expansion had ended in complete collapse. There was some good luck in it (Western Australian gold), and some bad (drought and rabbits). And if the impact of indigenous technical progress in the export sector can be overestimated, that progress was nevertheless real.

We move forward now to that unhappy interwar period of stagnation and relapse, a period of laggardly *per capita* performance due to mounting unemployment and (the early thirties aside) a degree of relative work-force shift from higher to lower productivity occupations.

2. 1919–1939[26]

In the aftermath of war, national policy aimed at the provision of job opportunities on a broad front for a work force increasing rapidly with immigration. The rural sector was expected, by and large, to take up where it had left off in 1913; but the urban sector, it was realized, would need assistance. Thus the tariff of 1920/1 was expected not merely to consolidate manufacturing achievement but to provide room for more.

How successfully was this vision implemented? Did employment keep pace with work-force growth? Let us examine the indicators. National income peaked in the mid-twenties, and investment (after tapering for a while) in 1926/7—by which time the private sector had surrendered much of the burden of capital formation to governments. All this was associated with a levelling out of the capacity to import: total import volume stabilized and its commodity component even receded somewhat, instrumental in which—and reflecting the demise of local expansion—was a rise in the rate of unemployment after mid-1927. Evidently, then, the economy was in some difficulty well before the calamity of 1929/30, and forces were at work to bring

[26] Useful references are Butlin, *Gross Domestic Product;* M. Keating, 'Australian Workforce and Employment 1910/11 to 1960/61', *Australian Economic History Review*, VII, 1967, pp. 150–71, and 'Employment and the Growth of Australian Gross Domestic Product', *Economic Record*, 45, 1969, pp. 27–47; Hancock, *Survey;* D. B. Copland, ed., *An Economic Survey of Australia*, Annals of the American Academy of Political and Social Science, 158, 1931; C. Forster, *Industrial Development in Australia* 1920–1930, ANU, Canberra, 1964, Parts 1 and 3; W. R. Maclaurin, *Economic Planning in Australia 1929-1936*, King, London, 1937; L. F. Giblin, *The Growth of a Central Bank*, Melbourne University Press, Melbourne, 1951, and Commonwealth of Australia, *Report of the Royal Commission appointed to inquire into the Monetary and Banking Systems at present in operation in Australia*, 1937.

local expenditure into line with a recalcitrant capacity to import. The year 1926/7 provided the turning point. Apart from the phenomena already observed, it was notable for a significant drop in London funds, deterioration of the exchange rate, heavy gold outflow, a peak rate of immigration when expansion was spent, and finally cessation of decline in the export sector's share of employment. In 1928 the rate of unemployment came to resemble that of 1921, when international recession had prevailed.

The predicament of manufacturing as a provider of additional jobs in the later twenties was plain enough—a stagnant market, shared with overseas competitors; a tariff which seems merely to have kept pace with falling import prices;[27] and a rising wage level which tended to offset any improvement in manufacturing productivity. It is hardly surprising, then, that total manufacturing employment should have receded after 1926/7.

As for the export sector in the later twenties, it was not the expansionary force of other days, and overseas earnings advanced less than commensurately with Australian needs. Converging price and cost movements, unaccompanied by significant productivity improvement, now compromised the diversification which had been carried through by 1913; despite a degree of retreat towards wool, primary activity came to know distress.[28]

We have observed how, from mid-1927, a rise in the rate of unemployment eased pressure upon the balance of payments and so upon London funds. Until then (apart from a sharp lift in the mid-twenties) the tendency of the rate had been downward since the crisis of 1921. Now if the economy had moved unsteadily *towards* equilibrium, how close had it actually got when the mentioned reversal occurred? In late 1926 and early 1927, certainly, the rate approximated what seems to have been then regarded as its 'normal' level. Whether this level might have been achieved more quickly, and

[27] Recent work suggests that the decline of import prices in the twenties may have been steeper than previously thought. Susan Bambrick, 'Indexes of Australian Import Prices, 1900 to 1927/28', *Australian Economic History Review*, VIII, 1968, pp. 62–9.

[28] Wool was less prone than other primary exports to mounting domestic cost pressures, and more importantly its price (in contrast with other primary prices) had risen very strongly into 1924/5. By that time, sheep numbers had returned to their level of 1910. As they moved beyond, wool prices fell, but grazing remained profitable; more profitable, certainly, than sugar and butter production (which began to receive assistance in the twenties), wheat growing and gold mining (which did not). Gold, its price fixed, suffered very severely after 1913 as unit production costs climbed.

whether, indeed, it was itself reducible in *some* degree—reducible, that is, in terms of the economic thinking of *that* day rather than this—are matters for conjecture. In connection with the former we may speculate whether, for example, the exchange crisis of 1924/5 was 'avoidable'; in connection with the latter, whether, for example, a relative cost adjustment might have been managed, with a distribution of emphasis among exchange devaluation, tariff increases and wage restraint appropriate to circumstances then prevailing. Here we may wonder if a policy of return to gold at pre-war parity comprehended certain implications of the development task which Australia had set herself, especially the effect of contrived structural change upon the economy's productivity performance and so its relative cost situation. Perhaps, then, *some* of the unemployment which prevailed was the price of currency 'soundness', as then construed.

But enough of what might have been. After all, a certain pragmatism is called for. The rate of unemployment did not compare unfavourably with rates overseas; and that Australia's industrial development got as far as it did when (in contrast with the pre-war period) import prices were falling, was in a way notable.

If the Australian economy was in difficulty by the later twenties, it was soon to know far worse. In 1929/30 the terms of trade plummeted, long-term capital inflow dried up and export volume fell: in short, the capacity to import shrank catastrophically. As in the early nineties, the problem of meeting fixed-interest charges upon the external debt became acute. Gold stocks and London funds were decimated, the gold standard was abandoned, the tariff was lifted high and certain import controls were introduced. Commodity imports, sticky in 1929/30, tumbled in the following year, but the cause was less restriction of trade and a drifting exchange rate than massive unemployment which slashed the level of national expenditure (Chart 2.8). Although export volume now was rising strongly, it failed to offset the fall in export prices: in contrast with the nineties (when it was dynamic in recovery) export income fell, and it was not to retrieve its late-twenties level until 1936/7.

Deflation, then, was largely responsible for bringing the demand for imports into line with the capacity to import. The Premiers' Plan promulgated in 1931, played its part in this by contriving reductions of government expenditure. Relative cost adjustment was essayed as well. We have mentioned the tariff. The Arbitration Court decreed a reduction of the money wage and the Premiers' Plan a reduction of the rate of interest. To what extent these moves led

Chart 2.8 Unemployment 1906 to 1964 (annual average)

Source: Labour Report (percentage of trade unionists, to 1950); *Report of the Committee of Economic Enquiry* (registered unemployed as percentage of estimated work force, 1950 onwards).

the market it is hard to say; but they may have, in *some* degree anyway, rendered factor prices more flexible than otherwise. More importantly, through 1930 the exchange on sterling had drifted in the open market until, in February 1931, endeavouring to regulate what they could not supress, the banks were offering £A130 for £Stg100. The rate became 125:100 soon afterward (and was to remain that into the late sixties). Thus, when sterling itself depreciated in 1932, Australia moved even further from gold. The extent to which a relative cost improvement was achieved—the extent to which demand was switched inward—again is difficult to guage. Some import replacement occurred in the later thirties, but the import-content of recovery still was high: certainly there had been an improvement in the capacity to import, but substantial unemployment lingered to balance the external accounts. It is notable that while the money wage had been brought into line with import prices early in the decade, it then strayed away again. Moreover, the expansion of manufacturing in the later thirties may have been at least partly at the expense of exports. Although the tariff had been adjusted downward in allowance for the protective effect of exchange depreciation, the adjustment took time and even then was possibly incomplete. The export sector appears to have been worse off in relation to industrial protection at the end of the thirties than it had been at the end of the twenties, immediately before the tariff soared in defence of the balance of payments.

We might sum up by saying that on the eve of World War II external balance still was being achieved at the expense of internal: unemployment had fallen greatly but the economy was not yet in equilibrium—although its rate of recovery had compared well with rates overseas. The contrasts between the early thirties and early nineties are numerous—the heavy outflow of gold; the presence of net London assets in the banking system to cushion (however inadequately in a major crisis) the drop in external income; the greater relative importance of decline in the terms of trade; the abandonment of the gold standard and depreciation of the exchange rate; the drop in export income and the lethargic export ratio; the tinkering with the domestic economy and internal debtor-creditor contracts but not contracts to pay interest overseas; and so on.

3. 1940–1965

The Australian economic experience of World War II differed significantly from that of World War I. Of course, there were similarities too, among them severe falls in export volume and the terms of trade. But whereas through the first conflict Australia remained a net borrower overseas (partially offsetting the collapse in her export-based capacity to import) in the later stages of the second she became a net lender (in this case accumulating foreign exchange). Again, through 1914–18 the economic commitment to war was incomplete and the industrial response to import shortage ambiguous: some forms of manufacturing flourished and others languished for (among other reasons) want of essential imports. The economy as well reacted adversely to disruption of its export trade. One outcome of these troubles was a marked lift in the rate of unemployment.

Through 1939–45, in contrast, the economic commitment to war became total: full employment was contrived and resources directed as the war effort required; rural employment was greatly reduced and import substitution promoted with a sophisticated emphasis, instrumental in which was a crash programme of work-force education.[29] In short Australia, thrown upon her own resources, coped well with the exigency and elaborated her industrial base in the process. She emerged from depression and war with a heightened sense of isolation, some loss of faith in rural development, and a determination to avoid the wastes and misery of unemployment. Immediate policy symptons were a White Paper on full employment and legislation to extend into peacetime government influence over the banking system; while circumstance—import shortage at a time of strong local demand for goods of all descriptions—accommodated the urge for further industrialization and carried the work-force share of manufacturing to a level which has not been significantly exceeded since.

Yet commodity import volume recovered strongly enough from its wartime trough, in the late forties passing its level of the late thirties and reflecting an improvement in the capacity to import, which was due as much to buoyant terms of trade as to reviving export volume. Late in the forties, too, the traditional task of migrant absorption was resumed on a grand scale, now with an emphatically urban-industrial bias. Wool prices, and with them the terms of trade, climbed even higher to their remarkable peak of 1950/1, so meeting even further the import requirements of a development programme now in full swing. As already observed, it was somewhat ironical that a policy founded at least partly in apprehensions about the terms of trade should be accommodated by an improvement in them. But trouble was in store.

It must be assumed that the reader is acquainted with Australia's economic history since 1950[30]—the strong aggregative and *per*

[29] D. P. Mellor, *The Role of Science and Industry*, Vol. V in Series 4, Civil, *Australia in the War of 1939–1945*, Australian War Memorial, Canberra, 1958. It should be observed that in 1949 a mild recession occured, and that this may have influenced the decision to devalue against the dollar.

[30] In contrast with other periods the post-war literature is voluminous, but among the essential references are: *Report of the Committee of Economic Enquiry*, 2 vols, Canberra, 1965; R. Mathews, *Public Investment in Australia*, Cheshire, Melbourne, 1967; A. Hunter, ed., *The Economics of Australian Industry*, Melbourne University Press, Melbourne, 1963; Brash, *American Investment in Australian Industry;* B. Cameron, *Federal Economic Policy*, Cheshire, Melbourne, 1968; W. M. Corden, *Australian Economic Policy Discussion: A Survey*, Melbourne University Press, Melbourne, 1968, which includes useful bibliographies; G. D. McColl, *The Australian Balance of Payments. A Study of Post-war Developments*, Melbourne University Press, Melbourne, 1965, and Commonwealth of Australia, 'Private Overseas Investment in Australia' and 'The Australian Balance of Payments', *Supplement to the Treasury Information Bulletin*, Canberra, 1965 and Canberra, 1966, respectively. Aside from the many relevant articles in the

capita performance as compared with the interwar years, the parts played in this by high employment and marked improvements in labour productivity, problems associated with the achievement (such as inflationary pressures and the height of the investment ratio) and the far greater role of government in economic management as compared with other days. We confine ourselves, here, to the balance of payments story.

In 1951/2 wool prices and the terms of trade fell sharply away, but import volume continued to rise strongly: a heavy drain on foreign reserves resulted, and in March 1952 quantitative import restrictions were imposed. These—although eased progressively after 1956—were not removed until 1960. Through this period, then, the balance of payments was in varying degrees of disequilibrium. The removal of controls did not necessarily mean that equilibrium had been achieved; but more of that later.

In the mid-fifties it seemed that export volume and capital inflow were unlikely, in the foreseeable future, to compensate for lower terms of trade, and that the economy had yet to adjust to this drop in its capacity to import. Thus, even had the authorities been entirely successful (as they had not) in removing those inflationary pressures attending rapid development and the expenditure- switching effect of import controls, a substantial excess demand for imports would probably have remained. In short, a relative cost disability had apparently emerged. There was more to this than the ratchet effect on costs of the spectacular wool boom; indeed, the tenets of policy themselves seemed at issue. Could Australia go on pursuing the full-employment ideal as literally as she had since 1945 without her rate of inflation exceeding rates overseas? Should she ease up, as well, on her extremely vigorous migration-industrialization programme? This—even aside from its inflationary impact in the circumstances of the day—seemed to be emasculating comparative advantage unduly and opening up the prospect of sluggish productivity advance and continuing relative cost adjustment with the rest

---

Economic Record, the following should be consulted: T. W. Swan, 'Longer-Run Problems of the Balance of Payments', paper presented to Section G, ANZAAS, Melbourne, 1955; M. J. Artis and R. H. Wallace, 'Fiscal Policy in Post-war Australia', ANZAAS, Melbourne, 1967; P. H. Karmel, 'The Economic Effects of Immigration', in *Australia and the Migrant*, Angus and Robertson, Sydney, 1953, pp. 88–103; and J. Perkins, 'Some Fallacies about Overseas Borrowing', *Australian Quarterly*, 32, 1960, pp. 74–88. The Swan and Karmel papers are reprinted in H. W. Arndt and W. M. Corden, eds, *The Australian Economy: A Volume of Readings*, Cheshire, Melbourne, 1963, which also includes other useful pieces, chiefly from the *Economic Record*.

of the world. It is interesting, here, that reviving import volume in the later fifties (as controls were eased) was associated not only with increases in export volume and capital inflow, but also lower immigration targets and a higher rate of unemployment.

Yet inflation persisted, and early in 1960, as one part of a comprehensive policy of disinflation, import controls were substantially removed. Despite further restrictions on domestic spending in the subsequent Commonwealth budget, imports continued to increase. London funds dipped steeply: they had apparently been inadequate to the exercise of controlling domestic demand partly through import competition. But only apparently, because when even further remedial action was taken in November 1960 (the now-infamous credit squeeze, which precipitated a sharp rise in unemployment) there were signs that the original measures were bearing fruit. So short-term external balance was secured, if somewhat more abruptly than expected; and it was indicative of transformed attitudes that a degree of unemployment which would have gone unnoticed in the twenties (let alone the thirties) almost unseated the government. The weakness of policy had been less in overestimating the capacity to import and the competitiveness of Australian industry, than in failing to recognize the existence of lags in the economic system.

After the balance of payments 'crisis' of 1960/1 the capacity to import moved strongly upward. There was a leap in long-term capital inflow, the export sector was resilient in response to price-cost squeeze, and (as if to confirm its coming of-age) the manufacturing sector now moved beyond import replacement to become a significant direct contributor to external income. Partly through good fortune and partly through good economic management (in which skilful monetary policy has been conspicuous), since the early sixties fluctuations in the level of activity have been relatively small; the difficulties associated with short-term surges in the demand for imports have been overcome.

In February 1963 the government appointed a 'Committee of Enquiry'[31] to assess development strategy. The Committee reported in 1965. Its tone was circumspect, and where in 1929 the Brigden Report had been ignored by force of circumstance, in 1965 the Vernon Report was ignored by choice. Soon afterward two Informations Bulletins[32] embodying the 'Treasury view' appeared, dealing

[31] *Report of the Committee of Economic Enquiry.*

[32] Commonwealth of Australia, 'Private Overseas Investment' and 'Australian Balance of Payments', *Supplement to the Treasury Information Bulletin*, Canberra, 1965 and Canberra, 1966, respectively.

optimistically with aspects of the balance of payments which the Vernon Report had accorded somewhat gloomy notice. Whatever the merits of the Treasury analysis, subsequent events—particularly large mineral and natural-gas discoveries and exploitation—conspired to vindicate its mood. Today, in contrast with the mid-fifties, chronic balance of payments difficulty seems far away: the expansion of export volume is apparently taken for granted[33] and the attention of commentators is focused upon the political costs of a swelling private capital inflow. Within the government a division of opinion has emerged about whether the tariff—which returned to effective working life when import controls were lifted—should be made a more discriminating instrument of industrial protection than it has traditionally been. Broadly speaking, a greater concern for the ownership and allocation of Australia's resources, and not merely their full employment, has become evident in recent years.

Nevertheless, Australia cannot afford to be complacent about the balance of payments. Even with the techniques and experience now available to policy-makers, the maintenance of an appropriate balance of expenditure between domestic and foreign goods is inevitably a delicate one in full employment growth. And perhaps the most important lesson of the history we have delved is that capital inflow—which at this time is productive of an extraordinary ease in our external accounts—tends to be highly volatile. In the longer term, the price-cost situation of the export sector will require an unrelaxing vigilance.

V DEGREE OF INVOLVEMENT WITH THE WORLD ECONOMY

So far in this discussion of Australia's involvement with the international economy, we have merely alluded, here and there, to a matter which will now be treated explicitly—namely, changes in the *degree* of that involvement over time. Did Australia reduce her reliance upon factor inflow; and did exports provide a diminishing proportion of national income?

[33] It is only fair to point out that the Treasury's apparent readiness, in one place, to regard the farmer's incentive to invest as somehow independent of the (net) price he receives, was subsequently qualified. See Commonwealth of Australia, 'Australian Balance of Payments', *Supplement to the Treasury Information Bulletin*, Canberra, 1966, p. 37. It is interesting, here, that the good luck being experienced by Australian wheat growers (sales to China) at the time of the Treasury pronouncement, has since turned bad: the international grains agreement has apparently been undermined by chronic oversupply.

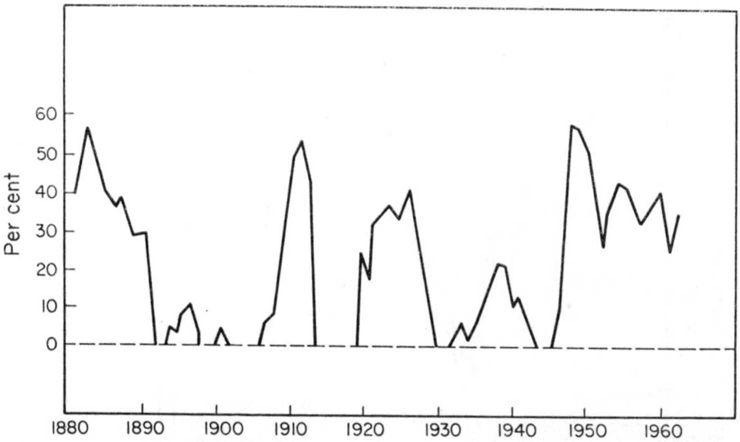

Chart 2.9 Ratio of Positive Net Migration to Population Increase 1880 to 1962 (annual series)

Source: Demography Bulletin.

1. FACTOR MIGRATION AND THE RESOURCE BASE

Australia's reliance upon net immigration as a source of population growth was maintained roughly at later nineteenth century levels[34] (Chart 2.9), but the contribution of overseas savings to local capital formation fell continuously away (Chart 2.10).

After 1891 some alternation of net immigration between inflow and outflow occurred, but in 1907 sustained inflow resumed, taking the ratio of net immigration to population increase to heights (in 1911–13) comparable with those of the early eighties. Wartime interruption was followed by another wave of arrivals in the twenties: this peaked in 1927, before subsiding once more into depression and net outflow. Recovery of the ratio in the later thirties was again abbreviated by war, but then huge inflows in 1949 and 1950 swiftly restored it to early-eighties pre-eminence. After that it resembled rather more its level of the twenties. But this is deceiving, because in one respect its economic impact was distinctive. It has been estimated[35] that the contribution of migration to the Australian work force (as distinct from population) was 73 per cent between 1947 and 1961—the outcome of a depression birth rate which undermined the local contri-

[34] But note that the rate of growth of total population was considerably higher in the eighties than in any subsequent decade of heavy migration.

[35] M. Keating, 'Trends in the Australian Workforce', unpublished seminar paper, Australian National University, November 28, 1966, Table 7.

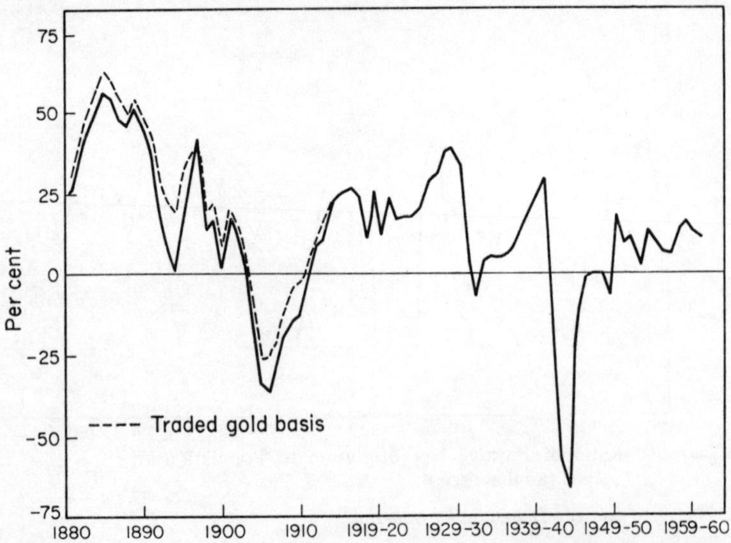

Chart 2.10 Ratio of Net Capital Inflow to Gross Capital Formation 1881 to 1961–62 (three-year moving averages, current prices)

Source: See p. 73, n.3 for net capital inflow; Butlin, *Australian Domestic Product*, and *National Income and Expenditure*, for gross capital formation.

bution to work-force growth after World War II. It was 42 per cent between 1921 and 1928, and 61 per cent between 1911 and 1914. There may have been echoes of the 1890s depression in the 1911–14 figure. Needless to say, such estimates throw light upon the performance of the Australian economy in different periods. So would an examination of the occupational composition of migration over the years. But these matters cannot be our concern. All we need observe of the long period is that Australia's endeavour to augment her stock of human capital in the cheapest possible way met with considerable success—except, perhaps, during the 1920s, when substantial unemployment prevailed.

Comparing the three periods of heavy capital inflow—the eighties, the twenties and the fifteen years after 1950—a decline is observable in the ratio of capital inflow to gross capital formation from 50 per cent to 25 per cent to 12 per cent. The latter figure probably understates the contribution of foreign capital to recent Australian growth. We have in mind here not merely its assistance in lifting the overall investment ratio to an all-time high, but also accompanying

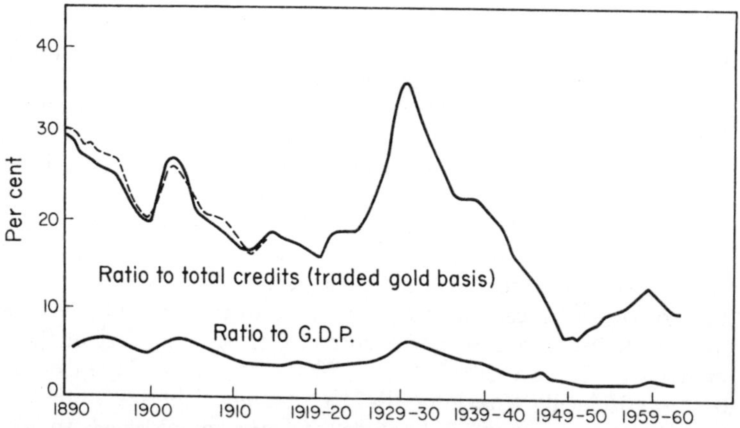

Chart 2.11 Ratio of Net Property Payments to Total Credits and G.D.P. 1891 to 1963–64 (three-year moving averages, current prices)

Source: See p. 73, n.3 for net property payments and total credits; Butlin, *Australian Domestic Product*, and *National Income and Expenditure*, for gross domestic product.

technical and managerial know-how which were strategic in post-war manufacturing progress. But whatever the qualifications we make, the rising share of local savings in investment is unmistakable. Take, for example, the public sector. Certainly it was a net borrower overseas between the two depressions, but the period witnessed, as well, a very substantial advance in the local content of the public debt. This content, negligible in the mid-nineties, was about 50 per cent in the mid-twenties. Between the early thirties and 1950 it was a net *lender* overseas; a certain (not very large) amount of the external debt was repatriated, while resort was made to the Australian loan market to carry public outlays forward in war and peace. Through this interval the domestic share of the public debt rose strongly, interest payments upon it increasing from 42–50 per cent of total payments in the thirties, to 77 per cent in 1950.[36] After that Australian governments turned to the international loan market, but on a very modest scale: overseas borrowing was overwhelmingly private. Public investment outlays continued to be financed locally, but with a new twist—now 'forced' local savings (the product of a fixed

[36] Commonwealth of Australia. *The Australian Balance of Payments 1928/29 to 1949/50*, No. 2, Government Printer, Canberra, 1952, p. 53. See also p. 75, Table XI, for repatriation of public overseas debt through the years 1936/37–1949/50.

schedule of progressive marginal income-tax rates in circumstances of inflation) joined the profits and amortization funds of public business undertakings to reduce reliance on the loan market.

This would seem the appropriate place in which to consider the ratios of external debt service payments to total export receipts, and to gross domestic product. Chart 2.11 is not offered in the 'benefits and costs' context of foreign borrowing—that is a complex question—but simply as illustrative of forces at work in Australian development. The tendency of the two ratios therein is downward. But this was the outcome of more than a receding foreign contribution to Australian capital formation and growth. Within the general movement two broad swings occurred. Consider the first of these, between 1890 and 1930/1. As at 1890 the emphasis of the external debt was decidedly 'fixed interest'. That of public debt was entirely so; that of private (debentures, bank deposits and so on) largely so. The general movement of the debt service ratios down to about 1912 is therefore hardly surprising—after the mid-nineties economic recovery, debt repatriation, accumulation of overseas assets, and the modification—even writing off—of certain private commitments during the banking and other reconstruction schemes of the nineties all lowered the debt service ratios (although the effects of drought, and perhaps remittances on account of British mining investment, can be seen in the early 1900s). During the war, public overseas borrowing became heavy, but universal wartime inflation and (in some degree) the continuing export of capital on banking and private account prevented any marked change of the ratios. Through the twenties, however, the movement of both was upward, strongly so in their second half and more strongly for the ratio to exports than the ratio to national income. Several influences were at work. Both the public and private sectors were heavy net borrowers; the rate of interest on public overseas borrowing tended to rise (affecting, of course, not merely new borrowings but conversions too); and export receipts receded and national income stagnated after the middle of the decade. Much of private inflow in the twenties probably was of an equity description, and to the extent that it entered industries whose growth outlasted that of the economy as a whole would have boosted the ratios somewhat in the second half of the twenties. On the other hand, this equity characteristic of private borrowing would have helped in a small way to ease the problem of debt service in the depression.

The first swing terminated, as it began, in depression. The ratio of service payments to export receipts reached an extraordinary height, while their ratio to national income returned to its level of the mid-nineties. The bulk of external debt was at fixed interest and the consequence—an immense transfer problem as external income shrank—exercised the minds (and the patience) of contemporaries. In contrast with 1893, most of this fixed-interest commitment was governmental, and despite Lang's fulminations Australian governments declined to do what many financial institutions had done in 1893—unfix the fixed.

As the recovery of national income and external receipts proceeded, so the ratios fell. A negotiated suspension of war debt payments to Britain, and some minor debt repatriation and conversion loans at lower rates of interest by the public sector, also helped the ratios downward. Then, in World War II and the quinquennium following, world-wide inflation (far greater than in and after World War I) took its toll of old fixed-interest indebtedness. Between war's end and 1950 the ratio of service payments to exports fell at a greater rate than that to national income, because of discrepant rates of advance in export and local prices; but after that export prices receded as local prices continued to rise (if rather less quickly than before). Thus the ratio of service payments to exports climbed as export income stagnated and private oversea investors shared in a vigorous local expansion. If the ratios are rather less than in other days, discussion of debt service has been rather more; and the equity characteristic of capital inflow since the war has given rise, in some quarters, to anxiety about foreign ownership of Australian industry.

But these matters are not our immediate concern. Certainly, however, should any significant interruption to growth occur the 'burden' of debt service is likely to prove more flexible than in other days. But how likely *are* such interruptions? In modern society inflation seems 'built-in'. It is possible, indeed, that if our economic objectives had been achievable with a lesser rate of inflation, the debt service ratio to national income would be even lower than it is. For where a rising price level was once an irregular boon to fixed-interest borrowers such as Australia, now—because of its supposed tendency to exaggerate the share of profits in national income, and because of the changed nature of Australian borrowing—it may have kept the ratio somewhat higher than it would otherwise have been.

But this possibility should not be exaggerated. More substantial ones, perhaps, are a rising share of private foreign capital in Australian investment and its increasing concentration in industries which are both capital-intensive and in the van of growth. Such influences would swell the ratio—which need not be a 'bad thing' provided that local gains from oversea investment are pressed to some optimum (by policy as well as natural means). It can be argued, of course, that the borrowing is partly unnecessary anyway, that (assuming we wish to maintain current rates of investment) measures could be taken to raise the local propensity to save. But political unwillingness to restrain consumption standards would seem even further from our concerns than the preceding few paragraphs have been.

2. DEPENDENCE UPON EXPORT INCOME: THE EXPORT RATIO

Longish swings of the current-price ratio of total exports (total current account credits) to national income were not unusual. It fell from about 26 per cent in the 1860s to 16 per cent in the eighties, recovered to 26 per cent in the first decade of this century and receded to about 17 per cent at the turn of the thirties. Then it fluctuated, in 1950 approximating its high level of half a century before, in 1960 its low level of the late twenties (Chart 2.12). Such shifts of emphasis

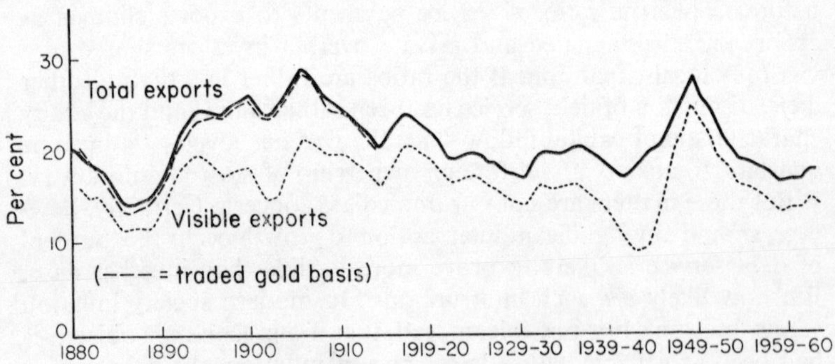

Chart 2.12 Ratios to G.D.P. 1881 to 1963–64 (three-year moving averages, current prices)

Source: See p. 73, n.3 for export values; Butlin, *Australian Domestic Product*, and *National Income and Expenditure*, for gross domestic product.

between export and domestic activity according to their relative profitabilities (shifts *away* from export production usually being associated with heavy factor inflow) have not, of course, gone unnoticed in the literature; but more attention has been given to the later nineteenth century than the twentieth; and more to the relative decline of the export sector before 1890 than to its robust progress afterward.[37] We have discussed that progress already. All that concerns us here is that its diminuendo into World War I was not especially distinctive; it was largely in keeping with the nineteenth-century pattern.

After the war, however, policy and circumstance each tugged at the ratio. Additions to the work force and capital stock through the twenties favoured non-export activity; but this was not an altogether spontaneous development. Although early colonial and Commonwealth 'revenue' tariffs may have been more protective than is sometimes supposed, they did not compare with the 'high protection'—and an accommodating change of emphasis in public investment—which sustained the relative profitability of import substitution after World War I. One distinctive concomitant was a flow of private capital from abroad into the urban-industrial sector. Yet the twenties saw no *dramatic* shift in the pattern of resource allocation. The high, wide-ranging industrial tariff should perhaps be judged in terms of what might have been: that the share of import-competitive activity advanced *at all*, and in the way that it did, in a context of swiftly falling import prices and aggressive international trading was impressive enough. It might be argued that the presence of substantial urban unemployment through the twenties 'exaggerated' the share of the primary-cum-export activity in total activity and understated that of import replacement. Yet unemployment was perhaps one index of the degree of success attending the policy of 'inward' development. Here it is notable that despite Australia's industrial ambition at the beginning of the twenties, subsequent upward revisions of the tariff seem to have been increasingly defensive in character. From the mid-twenties, as import prices continued to recede, the tariff provided little or no room for manufacturing expansion; and the interesting question becomes, not 'why high protection? but 'why not higher protection?'—which, after all, is the question to which the Brigden Enquiry[38] addressed itself late in the decade.

Whatever the industrial achievement, it was arrested in the late twenties and even reversed in the early thirties when the structural bias of now-extreme unemployment lifted the export sector's share of employment and real output sharply. In contrast with the nineties the current-price export ratio (despite the mentioned bias, exchange

[37] Butlin, *Investment in Australian Economic Development*, Parts A and D; and Hall, *The London Capital Market and Australia*, Chs 5, 7 and 8.

[38] J. B. Brigden and others, *The Australian Tariff. An Economic Enquiry*, Melbourne University Press, Melbourne, 1929.

depreciation and excellent seasons) did not advance commensurately. After the mid-thirties relative industrial expansion resumed, but it was not until the era of total industrial protection—the import shortages of the war and early post-war years—that a dramatic resource shift (now at full employment) occurred: the primary-cum-export work force shrank not only relatively but absolutely, and with it the sector's share of real output.

After the war, however, the outcome of this structural break was for a time obscured by sharply rising terms of trade: the current-price export ratio soared to a peak rivalling that of the early 1900s. But as the terms of trade receded, so did the structural break—now consolidated by economic policy—reveal itself, and by the late fifties the ratio was quite low. By and large, Australian policy-makers had endorsed the changes forced upon the economy by war, and where rural settlement had once played a part in the population programme, that programme resumed in the late forties with an overwhelmingly industrial emphasis. It was perhaps symptomatic that chronic balance of payments pressure during the early fifties should issue not in exchange depreciation but import controls. These controls were accompanied by a substantial achievement in net import replacement, as notable for its range as its amount; and when they were lifted in 1960 the tariff was left to resume the burden of industrial protection.

Looking at the period from World War I into the late fifties, we can reasonably say (after allowing for offsetting rural assistance) that policy had imposed a net burden upon the primary sector:[39] the Australian export ratio and real income per head were lower, and population higher, than would have been the case without industrial protection. This, of course, is *not* to say that manufacturing would not have advanced at all after 1920 without protection, but merely that it would have advanced less and in a different way. Certainly the erosion of comparative advantage (to absorb, in urban-industrial activity, a population increasing rapidly with immigration) could be taken quite far in an economy as sophisticated and well endowed as the Australian. Yet even in the late twenties, when her living standards well exceeded those in most of the western world, Australia still found it judicious to count the economic costs of a contrived

[39] It would be easy to exaggerate that burden. The operative word is 'net': farmers received a variety of countervailing subsidies—indirect as well as direct—the importance of which should not be underestimated. And whatever the net burden, it did not of course, account wholly for relative resource shift. But this opens up too large a subject.

lessening of dependence: 'Our surplus resources available to subsidize industry are limited and will not stand any greater strain than imposed by the present tariff'.[40]

By the mid-fifties it seemed that the justification for another counting had arrived. Given current levels of capital inflow and the terms of trade, much appeared to hinge upon the resilience of the rural export sector. Could it cope with burdens imposed by population and high-employment policies and finance the imports needed for development at the same time? It seemed unlikely: commodity export volume—then only struggling past its level of 1938/9—would lag and Australia would be forced into less and less efficient forms of import replacement, to the detriment of a standard of living which was no longer unique.

But by the mid-sixties—following a remarkable surge in export volume, a jump in the level of real capital inflow, a marked improvement in manufacturing labour productivity and even the appearance of some fairly sophisticated industrial products among exports—a transformation had occurred. From the turn of the sixties export volume had begun to outpace real national income; the real export ratio, emasculated since the thirties, had risen. Moreover, the prospect was that the current-price export ratio might accompany it upward once the exploitation of vast new mineral wealth was properly under way. But whether, given the possible relative growth of non-traded activities[41] and the ongoing pursuit of import replacement, these ratios would know the heights of old, was another matter. It is sufficient to observe that for some time Australia's participation in the international economy was likely to grow rather than diminish: the lucky country had been lucky once more.

And what of manufacturing exports? The Australian manufacturing sector emerged from the fifties—the era of import controls—with a handsome achievement in net import replacement to its credit. Not merely the amount, but the variety of replacement undertaken suggested that the sector had matured. To the extent that this development was accompanied by a significant advance in manufacturing productivity, the costs of industrial protection apparently were the less: no longer, it seemed, would the shifting of resources towards manufacturing significantly depress *overall* productivity

[40] Brigden, *The Australian Tariff*, p. 87.

[41] Until fairly late in our long period there does not appear to have been any marked *relative* growth of that group of activities which might be regarded as strictly non-traded. In trend terms, stagnant real income per head and the decline of domestic service apparently were responsible.

performance. Had the policy inaugurated in the twenties, and given a fillip by war, at last borne fruit?

But we need to ask another question first: which 'productivity' are we talking about? As it happens, *labour* productivity. What of total factor productivity—or more specifically, how expensive was the manufacturing achievement in terms of capital? Apparently quite expensive; the costs of protection may have been higher than at first appears. Until we know fairly accurately how the manufacturing capital stock moved we can only guess at the size of the productivity 'residual' in the mid-sixties.

If the input requirements of Australian manufacturing over time have been relatively high per unit of output compared with other industrial countries (so leaving less room for the residual), is this because technological change has pushed upward the minimum scale of plants, so compromising producers in small (albeit rapidly growing) markets such as the Australian? Or is it because, regardless of economies which are potentially realizable, Australians have preferred a high degree of 'competition' in their product markets?

Yet it is impressive that in the early sixties, when the tariff was probably less protective than the import controls it replaced, the industrial sector seems to have been inconvenienced little by import competition. Tariff adjustment was piecemeal. And ever since, of course, manufactured exports have gone on rising. It may well be, then, that the productivity residual is sizeable. The bearing of past protection upon factors subsumed by this residual (such as scale, and the technological and managerial expertise accompanying *foreign* investment in particular) is again a matter for guesswork.

Chapter 3

ECONOMIES OF SCALE AND AUSTRALIAN MANUFACTURING[1]

Colin Forster

The growth of manufacturing has been the outstanding structural change in the Australian economy in this century. Australia has joined the ranks of the highly industrialized countries, and the efficiency of its manufacturing sector is basic to its prosperity. The first part of this chapter is an attempt to outline, mainly through statistics, the growth and changes in manufacturing output, and to compare the performance with that of other countries. The second and main part of this chapter concentrates on a particular problem of development. The successful establishment of a mature manufacturing sector was not accomplished overnight, nor without considerable difficulties: the period covered here encompasses two world wars and a world depression. But external events aside, within the economy the industrialization process had to surmount substantial obstacles. It will be argued below that the main problem resulted from the small size of the market for manufactured goods, which limited the economies, internal and external, obtainable from large-scale production. Viewed in this way, it is thought that a better understanding is obtained of the process of Australian industrialization.

I

MANUFACTURING AS A SECTOR IN THE ECONOMY

At the beginning of this century, manufacturing was of limited importance in the Australian economy. Factory output made up only some 12–13 per cent of gross domestic product, and generally it was of less value than pastoral production. For the next forty years its expansion within the economy was not rapid: in current prices it averaged 14–15 per cent in the 1920s, and about 16 per cent in the

[1] I wish to thank Mrs Helen Bridge for research assistance.

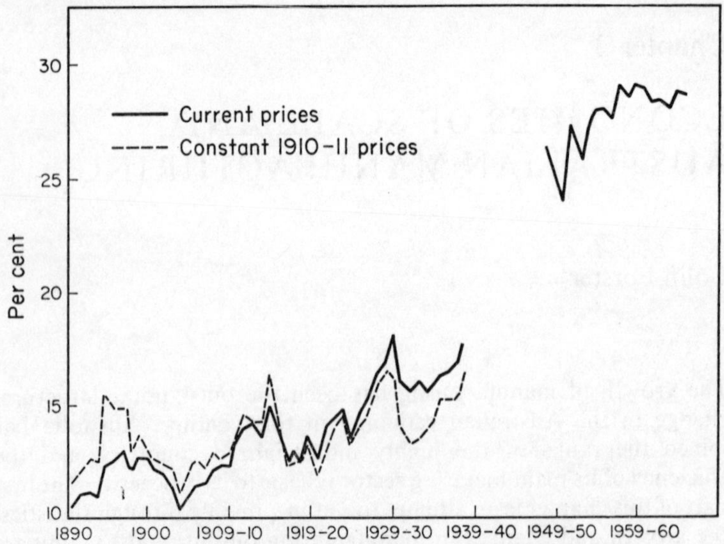

Chart 3.1 Australia: Manufacturing as Percentage of G.D.P.

Source: For current price figures see N. G. Butlin, *Australian Domestic Product*, pp. 12–13, and Commonwealth Bureau of Statistics and Census, *Australian National Accounts, 1948–49 to 1962–63* and 1953–54 to 1966–67.
For constant price figures see Butlin, op. cit., pp. 460–1.

1930s. A sharp break in this slow upward trend came, however, with the war: at the end of the forties it averaged around 25 per cent, and since the mid-1950s has settled at about 28 per cent (see Chart 3.1).

This picture must be slightly qualified if manufacturing is not limited to factories: a factory being defined by the Commonwealth Statistician as 'an industrial establishment in which four or more hands are employed, or in which power other than hand is used'. Although there are employment estimates for manufacturing broadly defined, little is known about the non-factory output, and workers in this category would generally be part-time and/or of low productivity. This situation is not confined to Australia: most countries limit their production censuses in a similar fashion, and apart from the discussion immediately below, this chapter relates to manufacturing carried on in factories. Fortunately, in Australia the difference between the two has not been large over the last sixty years: manufacturing employment exceeded factory employment by about 13 per cent in 1910–11; this difference had halved by the late twenties, and was insignificant by the late forties when both settled at about 28–29 per cent of total employment.[2] This figure of about 30 per cent is fairly typical of a mature industrial economy, and seems unlikely to change in the near future. It could rise if manufactured exports rose substantially, but there is an underlying tendency for it to decline through the relative expansion of 'service' industries.

OUTPUT

The growing importance of the manufacturing sector has involved a very substantial increase in manufacturing output (see Table 3.1). The precise contours of this growth remain to be charted, but it is felt that although published estimates of output are not sufficiently

TABLE 3.1. *Australia: Manufacturing Output*

Index (1911–13 = 100)

1900	1911–13	1927–8/ 29–30	1936–7/ 38–9	1947–8/ 49–50	1963–4
58	100	159	221	345	870

Average Annual Rate of Growth	Per cent
1900 to 1911–13	4·6
1911–13 to 1927–8/29–30	2·8
1927–8/29–30 to 1936–7/38–9	3·7
1936–7/38–9 to 1947–8/49–50	4·1
1949–50 to 1963–4	6·2
1900 to 1963–4	4·3

Source: Estimates to 1913; Butlin, *Australian Domestic Product*, p. 461. Estimates 1911–13 to 1953–4; A. Maizels, 'Trends in Production and Labour Productivity in Australian Manufacturing Industries', *Economic Record*, XXXIII, 1957, p. 166. Estimates from 1949–50; Commonwealth Bureau of Census and Statistics, *Indexes of Factory Production, 1948–50 to 1966–67.* Note that Butlin's and official estimates are given as annual figures, while Maizels' are for the periods shown in the table.

[2] N. G. Butlin and J. A. Dowie, 'Estimates of Australian Workforce and Employment 1861–1961', *Australian Economic History Review*, IX, 1969, and *Official Year Book of the Commonwealth of Australia*, Nos. 1 to 50.

accurate to lend themselves to detailed analysis, in broad outline they convey an impression which is unlikely to be greatly altered by later research.

Overall, the Australian rate of growth of manufacturing output appears to be very high when compared with the main economies of Western Europe. It is, however, roughly the same as that of the United States and two other countries in similar stages of development, Canada and Argentina (see Table 3.2). Growth in Japan was substantially higher.

TABLE 3.2. *Total Manufacturing Production, 1901–57*

	1957 Index 1901 = 100	Average annual rate of growth Per cent
Australia	1,006	4·2
France	356	2·3
West Germany (excl. Saar)	505	2·9
United Kingdom	371	2·4
United States	903	4·0
Canada[a]	968	4·0
Argentina[a]	1,217	4·4

[a] For Canada and Argentina, 1899 = 100

Source: Canada, Australia, Argentina: Organization for European Economic Co-operation, *Industrial Statistics, 1900–1957*, Paris, 1958, p. 11. France, Germany, UK, US: A. Maizels, *Industrial Growth and World Trade*, Cambridge University Press, London, 1963, p. 535.

Although the growth rate of Australian manufacturing output was high on international standards, it was by no means constant over the whole period. Interpretation is limited by the dates for which estimates of output are available, and perhaps too much reliance should not be placed on the periods before 1949. Table 3.1 indicates a markedly lower-than-average rate of growth between 1911–13 and 1936–7/38–9; a time span containing two set-backs to growth—the First World War and the depression of the thirties. These estimates also reflect a much higher growth rate since the late forties compared with that of the preceeding half century.

PRODUCTIVITY

Once again the available material does not permit very precise or sophisticated calculations. The best that can be done at this stage is to consider the performance of manufacturing in terms of labour productivity.

TABLE 3.3. *Australia: Average Annual Rate of Growth of Manufacturing Output*

	Per cent	
	Per Employee	Per Employee-hour[a]
1903–04 to 1911–13	1·0	1·0
1911–13 to 1927–8/29–30	1·0	1·4
1927–8/29–30 to 1936–7/38–9	1·3	1·5
1936–7/38–9 to 1947–8/49–50	–0·3	0·6
1949–50 to 1963–4	4·1	4·1

[a] Assumes no change in number of hours worked 1903–04 to 1911–13, and 1949–50 to 1963–4. See Maizels, *Economic Record*, XXXIII, p. 171.

Source: Butlin, *Australian Domestic Product*, p. 461, and *Year Book*, Nos. 1 and 8. Maizels, *Economic Record*, XXXIII, pp. 168 and 172. *Indexes of Factory Production, 1949–50 to 1966–67*, and *Year Book*, Nos. 39 and 53.

Table 3.3 shows the rate of growth of manufacturing output per man to have been low between 1903–04 and 1947–8/49–50; it was actually negative on the average over the last eleven-year period. However, in historical terms, the growth rate has been very high since 1949–50; in fact the break with the past is so great as to suggest a turning point in manufacturing development. When a comparison is made between this measure and output per man-hour, it can be seen that a portion of the poor performance in output per man between 1911–13 and 1947–8/49–50 was the result of a significant decline in hours of work, a decline of almost one-fifth. Nevertheless, the marked contrast with the post 1949–50 period remains. How does this Australian growth compare with that of other countries? Some rough comparisons can be made with the United Kingdom, United States and Canada, and although these must be regarded simply as approximations they are adequate for the purpose in hand (see Table 3.4).

TABLE 3.4. *Manufacturing: Average Annual Rate of Growth of Output per Man-hour*

Per cent

	1907 to 1935	1935 to 1949	1950 to 1960
United Kingdom	2·0[a]	2·0[a]	2·6
United States	3·2	1·4	3·2
	1911–13 to 1936/9	1936/9 to 1947/50	
Canada	2·6	1·7 (to 1950)	3·0
Australia	1·4	0·6	4·0

[a] Output per operative-hour. Output per man-hour would be slightly lower.

Source: For first two periods; UK: K. S. Lomax, 'Production and Productivity Movements in the United Kingdom Since 1900', *Journal of the Royal Statistical Society*, Series A, 122, 1959, p. 203; US: J. W. Kendrick, *Productivity Trends in the United States*, Princeton, Princeton University Press, 1961, Table D–II; Canada and Australia: Maizels, *Economic Record*, XXXIII, p. 166. For the third period; G. Bannock, 'Productivity in Manufacturing pre-war to 1960', *Productivity Measurement Review*, No. 31, 1962; Australia: *Indexes of Factory Production, 1949–50 to 1966–67*.

These estimates help to confirm the impression that the Australian productivity performance to the end of the forties was a mediocre one, but since then it has been at least comparable with these three countries.

COMPOSITION OF OUTPUT

Along with the growth of output and productivity have gone substantial changes in the composition of output. For a variety of reasons—the large number of industries, inadequate statistics, index number problems—no single measure of changing output composition is satisfactory. It has been necessary therefore to adopt several types of approach to the problem, which when considered together, at least appear to highlight the main features. In particular, attention is directed to the stage of development of manufacturing about 1900, the changes that have since taken place, and the question whether these changes have led to a pattern of output appropriate to a developed economy.

At the beginning of the century, manufacturing was strongly resource oriented. T. A. Coghlan considered that 'the greater portion of the manufactories of Australasia may be classified as domestic industries—that is to say, industries naturally arising from the circumstances of the population, or connected with the treatment of perishable products . . .'.[3] These were contrasted with 'industries the production from which comes into competition with imported goods'.[4] The relative importance of these three groups, as estimated by Coghlan, can be seen in Table 3.5.

TABLE 3.5. *Australia: Employment in Factories, 1903*

	Domestic industries for the treatment of perishable products for immediate use:	Industries dependent upon the natural resources of the country	Industries the production from which comes into competition with imported goods:
Number	10,627	99,513	86,284
Per cent	5·4	50·7	43·9

Source: T. A. Coghlan, *A Statistical Account of Australia and New Zealand, 1903–4,* Government Printer, Sydney, 1904, p. 996. Factory production includes gas and electricity.

Coghlan does not give details of industries within each group, and it is useful to turn to an examination of the main industries, and to product rather than employment. These details are available for Australia from 1908 (see Table 3.6).

Although this list of principal industries is influenced by the industry definition adopted by the Commonwealth Statistician, it bears out Coghlan's general impressions. Industries based on the processing of domestic resources—metals, timber, wheat and meat—are clearly important, and these had developed considerable exports. Others were local industries like printing, or industries heavily protected by freight, like bricks. The high ranking of the railway and engineering industries is perhaps surprising, but preference in government contracts was very important, especially in the first, whilst engineering

[3] T. A. Coghlan, *A Statistical Account of the Seven Colonies of Australasia, 1899–1900,* Government Printer, Sydney, 1900, p. 597.

[4] Ibid., p. 598.

TABLE 3.6. *Australia: Value Added in Principal Manufacturing Industries, Average 1908–10*[a]

Industry	£000	Per cent
Electrotyping, stereotyping, printing and binding	3,191	8·0
Engineering, ironworks and foundries	2,837	7·1
Smelting	2,794	7·0
Clothing (tailoring and slop)	2,182	5·5
Sawmills	2,165	5·4
Railway carriages, railway and tramway workshops	1,836	4·6
Breweries	1,768	4·4
Boots and shoes	1,316	3·3
Flour mills	1,025	2·6
Bricks, tiles, pottery and earthenware	1,024	2·6
Meat and fish preserving, ice and refrigerating	933	2·3
Other	18,752	47·1
Total manufacturing	39,823	100·0

[a] Tasmania is not included in 1908.

Source: Commonwealth Bureau of Census and Statistics, *Production Bulletin*, Nos. 3, 4 and 5.

covered a very broad range of industries. In both, repair and assembly work were common.[5]

This pattern of production suggests that manufacturing was at a fairly simple level of development. Can this conclusion be supported by contrasting the Australian output with that of a more mature industrial economy, the United States? The method adopted in Table 3.7 is the common one of a classification which emphasizes levels of development: in a typical process of change in the twentieth century the importance of two industry groups, food, etc. and textiles, has declined, while metal products and chemicals have grown.

[5] In 1903 T. A. Coghlan observed that 'the employment afforded in railway workshops is chiefly in the nature of repairs . . .'. *A Statistical Account of Australia and New Zealand, 1903–4*, p. 981. In 1916 the Inter-state Commission could still refer to the engineering industry in these terms: 'there are a large number of works whose output is of a general and very varied character. This, no doubt, is incidental to a new country opening up its industries. . . .' *Tariff Investigation. Machinery: Engines and Boilers, and Machinery Generally, Report*, 1916, p. 7.

Countries in the forefront of industrialization thus tend to emphasize the fast growing industries. It must be noted however, that there are substantial difficulties in inter-country comparisons. Here, the broad nature of the conclusions depends on the relations between the prices of the commodity groups being similar within both countries.

TABLE 3.7. *Value Added in Manufacturing by Industrial Groups, 1909*[a]

	Per cent	
	United States	Australia
Food, beverages and tobacco (20–22)	18	24
Textiles (23)	8	3
Basic metals (34)	6	8
Metal products (including transport equipment) (35–38)	22	19
Chemicals (31–32)	6	4
Miscellaneous (24–30, 33, 39)	40	42
Total manufacturing	100	100

[a] Numbers after each industry group refer to the International Standard Industrial Classification.

Source: US: Bureau of the Census, *Thirteenth Census of the United States*, 1910, Vol. VIII, Manufactures, 1909. Australia: *Production Bulletin*, No. 4.

The only industry comparison which clearly suggests a lower stage of industrial development is food, etc. In fact, however, these industrial groupings in this instance conceal the essential contrasts. We have seen that metal products reach their position in Australia only through a good deal of repair work, and there is also disproportionate reliance on the old industry of coaches and wagons. Basic metals do not indicate a developed metal industry in Australia, but rather processing for export. Again, chemicals in Australia are very different from those in the United States, and emphasize such industries as soap, candles, and tallow refining; the position confirms Maizels' comment that 'less-developed countries . . . tend to have a relatively high chemicals output . . . but the output pattern is very different from that of the chemical industries in the economically advanced countries'.[6] Finally, the small proportion of output in

[6] Maizels, *Industrial Growth*, pp. 53–4.

textiles in Australia indicates a pre-modern rather than a modern pattern. The textile industry was virtually non-existent, and the figure reaches 3 per cent only because of wool scouring for export. In the Australian situation, future industrial development meant the relative expansion of textiles. Thus the classification of output into these industrial groups brings out little of the essential characteristics of the Australian manufacturing pattern. It should be supplemented by what is probably a more revealing approach—a more direct consideration of the absence of certain industries. These turn out to be those which would have been considered basic to a developed industrial structure at that time, and include the textile industry in the form of spinning and weaving, hosiery and knitted goods; steel, either in the primary production or secondary rolling; machinery and equipment (except over a limited range); and finally modern chemicals. There were also almost no signs of development in the new industries of motor vehicles and electrical equipment.

All these industries have been established in this century, but only by a gradual process. Motor vehicle production commenced at the beginning of the 1920s with body production and vehicle assembly, and then gradually included parts and accessories, so that by the end of the thirties it was estimated that typically about half the factory cost of cars consisted of Australian labour and materials.[7] The first extension of production to include the engine and chassis was made at the end of the forties, and a decade later a large proportion of motor vehicles had at least 90 per cent Australian content. In steel, large-scale production began in 1915, but production of a full range of products on a scale sufficient to meet Australian demand was not accomplished until the end of the 1950s.[8] Again, the modern chemicals industry was initially closely tied to demands from mining and farming, especially for explosives and superphosphate, and the main product was sulphuric acid. In the thirties a large alkali plant was built, and during the war this range of products was substantially increased. But the main growth of the chemical industry (and its development as an integrated whole) has taken place since about the middle of the 1950s and has been associated with the production of petro-chemicals based on expansion of oil refining. Finally, in the traditional textile industries of woollen and worsted cloth and hosiery

[7] *Tariff Board's Report on Motor Vehicles*, 1938, p. 11.

[8] In terms of ingot equivalent, imports met about 60 per cent of the demand for steel products in the 1920s, fell to about 15 per cent at the end of the 1930s, rose sharply in the 1950s, but then became negligible by the end of that decade. The industry is discussed in more detail later in the chapter.

and knitted goods, the Australian producers obtained the greater part of the market by the end of the 1920s; in cotton textiles, production began in coarse cloth late in the twenties, but expansion was much slower than in wool.

As a result of this expansion in the range of industries, imports of manufactures appear to have declined markedly as a percentage of total manufacturing supplies (see Table 3.8).

TABLE 3.8. *Australia: Import-content of Supplies*[a] *of Manufactured Goods (1955 prices)*

	1913	1929	1937	1950	1955	1957	1959
Per cent	39	37	25	25	21	15	15

[a] ' "Supplies" are defined as gross value of production of non-food manufactures, free of duplication, *plus* c.i.f. value of imports of "finished" manufactures.'

Source: Maizels, *Industrial Growth*, p. 136.

Given these developments, it might be expected that the pattern of Australian manufacturing production would resemble that of a mature industrial economy. A comparison is made in Table 3.9 with the United States for 1958.

TABLE 3.9. *Value Added in Manufacturing by Industrial Groups*

Per cent

	US (1958)	Aust. (1958–9)
Food, beverages and tobacco	13	13
Textiles	4	6
Basic metals	8	9
Metal products	35	33
Chemicals	11	9
Miscellaneous	29	30
Total manufacturing	100	100

Source: United Nations Statistical Office, *The Growth of World Industry – National Tables, 1938–61*, New York, 1963, pp. 32 and 813.

Too close a parallel cannot be expected between countries, in part because of their natural resources and their involvement in exports.

Nevertheless, the American and Australian profiles are remarkably similar, and there is nothing in the composition of output in other industrialized countries to suggest that Australian does not have a range of industries appropriate to an advanced industrial country. As will be shown later, certain manufacturing industries have been established on a limited scale only, but this does not compare with the almost entire absence of whole technical processes before the First World War. In other words, in the short space of some forty to fifty years, the industrial profile was transformed to that of a mature economy.

II

THE MARKET FOR AUSTRALIAN MANUFACTURES

One basic feature which distinguishes Australian manufacturing during the twentieth century from that in other countries which have successfully industrialized is the size of the market. The market has been limited not by income per head in Australia, which has been high on international standards, but by the small size of the population. Although it has grown rapidly, population amounted to a mere 3·8 million in 1900 and was still only 11·6 million in 1966. Not merely has the internal market been small, but this has been virtually the only market for Australian manufactures. Only a very minor part of

TABLE 3.10. *Share of Manufactures*[a] *in Total Exports, 1899–1959*

Per cent

	1899	1913	1929	1955	1959
Australia	n.a.	12	7	11	12
Belgium–Luxembourg	46	45	73	80	83
Netherlands	n.a.	n.a.	38	48	52
Sweden	30	41	43	53	63
Switzerland	75	77	84	92	92

[a] Defined as those goods included in the United Nations' *Standard International Trade Classification*, Section 5 to 8. These include metals and engineering, chemicals, textiles and clothing and other manufactures.

Source: Australia: *Overseas Trade*, Nos. 26 and 12; and United Nations, *Yearbook of International Trade Statistics*, 1957 (Vol. 2) and 1962. For other countries: Maizels, *Industrial Growth*, p. 58.

output has been exported, consisting mainly, especially until recently, of simply processed food and materials. Outside this category, manufactured products have been of small importance in relation to total exports. Other countries with a comparably small population have industrialized successfully, but they appear to have specialized more narrowly within manufacturing and developed a large volume of exports. Leading examples are Belgium, the Netherlands, Sweden and Switzerland,[9] and in each case the dependence on manufactured exports extends well into the past. In Table 3.10 a contrast is drawn between the experience of Australia and these countries. It must be borne in mind that the actual figures depend on how manufactured exports are defined, but whatever the definition the essential contrast remains.

Not only do manufactures make up a very important part of the total value of exports in these countries but, like Australia, these countries are heavily involved in international trade, so that exports are large in relation to national product.[10] The concentration of exports in certain fields of manufacturing can be seen clearly in the experience of Switzerland (see Table 3.11).

TABLE 3.11. *Switzerland: Manufacturing Exports*

	Per cent of output 1955	Per cent of total exports 1956
Machines and precision instruments	70	28·5
Watches	95	19·9
Chemicals	60	16·3
Textiles	45	12·1

Source: W. A. Jöhr and F. Kneschaurek, 'Study of the Efficiency of a Small Nation: Switzerland', Ch. 4 in E. A. G. Robinson, ed., *Economic Consequences of the Size of Nations,* Macmillan, London, 1960, pp. 63 and 74.

[9] The populations of these countries have grown between 1899 and 1966 thus: Belgium–Luxembourg 6·9m. to 9·9m.; Netherlands 5·1m. to 12·5m.; Sweden 5·1m. to 7·8m.; Switzerland 3·3m. to 6·1m.

[10] At the end of the 1950s these countries in fact had much larger export ratios than Australia. Average commodity exports 1957–9 in proportion to GNP were: Australia 14·7 per cent, Belgium–Luxembourg 27·7 per cent, Netherlands 35·0 per cent, Sweden 20·2 per cent and Switzerland 21·4 per cent. S. Kuznets, 'Quantitative Aspects of the Economic Growth of Nations: IX, Level and Structure of Foreign Trade: Comparisons for Recent Years', *Economic Development and Cultural Change*, XIII, 1964, p. 93.

The reasons for Australia's small involvement in exporting manufactures should become apparent in the course of this chapter. One, however, is worth noting here. The proximity of the countries mentioned above to the large European market was very important in promoting their international trade, whereas Australia is in a peculiarly isolated position.

Yet another market different is of great importance. Transport costs within Australia break up the population to an unusual extent into a number of separate markets. Although the population has been heavily concentrated in half a dozen metropolitan centres, these centres are themselves a considerable distance apart. The two largest cities by far, Melbourne and Sydney, are some 590 miles apart by rail and 580 miles by sea. Each held in 1901 only 13 per cent of the population, although they had risen to 18 per cent and 21 per cent respectively of the greatly expanded population of 1961.[11] The problem of distance was not improved by efficient transport. Shipping, for example, has been a high-cost industry in Australia, and since the beginning of the century manufacturers have complained that freight rates between Europe and Australia are often lower than those between Australian ports. In terms of concentration of population in an accessible market, there is thus a marked contrast between Australia and the European countries already discussed, all of which are small in area.

The size of the market could affect the performance of manufacturing in two principal ways: through economies of scale and through the degree of competition. The second of these is the subject of Chapter 4: the first will be examined here. Failure to achieve the economies of large-scale production simply means higher costs, which may in turn be sufficient to preclude the establishment of certain industries. Since the Australian market has been small, has manufacturing performance been restricted in this manner and to a significant degree? Clearly the question opens a wide area of inquiry, and it would be surprising if very precise or quantitative conclusions could be reached. Nevertheless, the problem is important, and is one in which there has been a resurgence of interest in the last fifteen years. It is worth repeating E. A. G. Robinson's views at an international conference on general aspects of size and productivity:

> . . . in a broad sense we were engaged in returning to the great issues with which Adam Smith was concerned. It is paradoxical that in the hundred and eighty years since his book [*An Inquiry*

[11] The implications of this growth in the size of the cities will be discussed later.

into the Nature and Causes of the Wealth of Nations] was first published the relation of the size of nations to their economic prosperity and to their level of income per head has received comparatively little academic discussion . . . many of us had a feeling of incredulity when we failed to discover a volume of antecedent literature such as the subject seemed to have deserved.[12]

THE MEANING OF ECONOMIES OF SCALE

Economies of scale refer to the reduction in unit costs brought about by the increase in output of the plant (or firm), industry or economy. They are usually regarded from the point of view of the plant (or firm), and can thus be either internal or external: internal if the plant (or firm) expands, external if the industry or economy expands. In a similar way diseconomies of scale result if expansion raises average costs, while constant returns occur if there is no effect on average costs.

The concept of internal economies of scale was effectively developed by Alfred Marshall. He considered that 'the advantages of production on a large scale are best shown in manufacture', and they consist of 'economy of skill, economy of machinery and economy of materials: but the last of these is rapidly losing importance relatively to the other two'.[13] Basically they are the economies that spring from the fuller use of indivisible men and machines, and they operate in a variety of ways.[14] Marshall defined external economies as 'those dependent on the general development of the industry', which arose especially through 'the concentration of many small businesses of a similar character in particular localities: or, as is commonly said, by the localization of industry'.[15] How these external economies operate has been summarized concisely by Benham:

> It may then pay other firms to specialize more in catering for the needs of the industry. Special banking and insurance facilities

[12] *Economic Consequences*, p. xiii.

[13] A. Marshall, *Principles of Economics*, 8th edn, Macmillan, London, 1947, p. 278.

[14] For discussion of the main forms that internal economies take, see C. Pratten and R. M. Dean, *The Economies of Large-scale Production in British Industry*, Cambridge University Press, London, 1965, pp. 17–18; B. Balassa, *The Theory of Economic Integration*, Irwin, Illinois, 1961, pp. 121–2; and generally E. A. G. Robinson, *The Structure of Competitive Industry*, Cambridge University Press, London, 1958.

[15] Marshall, *Principles of Economics*, p. 266.

> may be made available; a trade journal may be started; transport rates may be reduced owing to the greater volume of traffic; 'repair shops' for its machines may be set up in the district, somebody may find it worth while to purchase from the firms in the industry by-products which were previously wasted; additional labour can be obtained when required from young people and others in the district who may have acquired, from living there, some knowledge of the customs of the industry. These and similar advantages may largely resolve themselves, upon analysis into 'internal economies' to some firm outside the industry.[16]

Over the succeeding twenty to thirty years Marshall observed that the importance of his original concept of external economies, depending on localization, was being eroded. These, he thought, had been the most important sort of economies in the past, but at least by the start of the twentieth century the position had changed:

> . . . with the growth of capital, the development of machinery, and the improvement of the means of communication, the importance of internal economies has increased steadily and fast; whilst some of the old external economies have declined in importance; *and many of those which have risen in their place are national, or even cosmopolitan, rather than local.*[17]

It was this last point that was developed by Allyn Young in 1928.[18] Moving from Marshall's partial equilibrium analysis, he extended the concept of external economies to the whole economy, so that the growth of external economies through the growth of total production (and the market) in a self-reinforcing fashion becomes a major explanation of that growth. As Young says: 'the division of labour depends upon the extent of the [whole] market, but the extent of the market also depends upon the division of labour'.[19]

In its turn Young's approach was extended by economists in the 1940s and 1950s looking at the problem of underdeveloped countries. Arndt summarizes the position:

[16] F. Benham, *Economics*, Pitman, London, 1945, p. 248.

[17] A. Marshall, *Industry and Trade*, Macmillan, London, 1923, p. 167 (italics added).

[18] A. Young, 'Increasing Returns and Economic Progress', *Economic Journal*, XXXVIII, 1928, pp. 527–42.

[19] Ibid., p. 539.

> The emphasis now is on the effect of external economies, not so much in reducing costs, as in stimulating investment; and the significance of external (as contrasted with internal) economies is that they cause divergence between private and social marginal product. They are thus advanced as a major explanation of the paradox that private investment does not appear to be attracted by the investment opportunities offered by capital-poor underdeveloped countries where the marginal productivity of capital might be expected to be high . . .
>
> While 'external economies' here still seems to mean the same as to Allyn Young, a new interpretation has really crept in. The difference is not merely that Allyn Young used the concept to explain the actual process of cumulative progress in the advanced and still growing economies, while here it is used to account for the failure of this cumulative process to get under way in the relatively stagnant underdeveloped aeras. The more important change lies in the new emphasis on the significance of external economies for the inducement to invest. In place of increasing returns, in the sense of falling costs with increasing output, we are now concerned with mutual support between acts of investment in different fields, . . . and external economies, instead of covering those cases of increasing returns which occur independently of the output of individual firms (or industries), now cover those cases where the favourable repercussions of investment do not (fully) accrue to the investor in a given field.[20]

Economies of scale can thus be interpreted in a variety of ways; and, in particular, the concept of external economies has been greatly extended to explain processes of growth. In what follows all these aspects of scale will be used to discuss the problem arising in the relation between Australian manufacturing and the size of its market.

ECONOMIES OF SCALE IN OPERATION

Although almost no studies have been done on Australia, there is a considerable volume of work overseas suggesting that significant economies can be obtained from production on a large scale.[21] It has already been suggested that small industrialized countries have

[20] H. W. Arndt, 'External Economies in Economic Growth', *Economic Record*, XXXI, 1955, pp. 196–7.

[21] B. Balassa, *The Theory of Economic Integration*, Part II, has made a general survey of the literature. There is additional material cited in E. F. Denison, *Why*

specialized in particular lines of manufactures for export. As Robinson observes: 'Switzerland has managed to secure the necessary economies of scale in her chief manufacturing industries by a very heavy reliance on export markets'.[22] Moreover, in Switzerland, the 'export industries lead in productivity, whereas branches working mostly for the home market have a lower productivity, especially if they are . . . protected by tariffs or quantitative restrictions'.[23] It would also seem that some small high-income countries, such as Norway, Denmark and New Zealand, have been limited in the development of their manufacturing partly through an inability to obtain sufficient economies of scale. Similarly, it has been strongly argued that it is the absence of broad external economies of scale which is an important part of the explanation for the failure of underdeveloped countries to establish efficient manufacturing industries.

How do these considerations apply to conditions in Australia in the twentieth century? Much of the work attempting to measure the size of economies of scale deals with industries serving medium or large markets: comparisons are made between Britain and the United States; advantages of European union are examined. Perhaps it is regarded as self-evident that countries with small markets face immense difficulties. Denison remarks that: 'Other things being equal, the larger the size of existing markets the smaller, presumably, are gains from economies of scale as markets expand.'[24] Nevertheless, he was prepared to guess that in the United States between 1929 and 1957 economies resulting from the expansion of the national market accounted for 10 per cent of the increase in total output—or 41 per cent of the increase in output per unit of input.[25] If Denison is right, the smaller the country the greater the gains from market expansion, so that Australian growth should have been severely handicapped over the last seventy years, but at the same time should have obtained significant benefits as the market expanded. Before turning to consider directly this aspect, the evidence for the influence

---

Growth Rates Differ, Brookings Institution, Washington, 1967, pp. 226–8. The emphasis in these references and in this chapter is on plant rather than firm economies.

[22] *Economic Consequences*, p. xvi.

[23] Jöhr and Kneschaurek, 'Study of the Efficiency of a Small Nation', ibid., pp. 63–4.

[24] *Why Growth Rates Differ*, p. 228.

[25] E. F. Denison, *The Sources of Economic Growth in the United States and the Alternatives Before Us*, Committee for Economic Development, New York, 1962, p. 266.

of economies of scale in Australian manufacturing will be considered from three other points of view: (a) the size of factories; (b) the location of industry; and (c) the composition of output.

(a) *Size of Factories*

It is commonly suggested that if internal economies of scale are important, then over a long period a growth in the average size of factories can be expected. On the other hand, J. Jewkes finds that in the period up to 1939 there is no 'country where the figures of the average size of factory measured in terms of wage earners suggest any significant trend either upwards or downwards'; and his conclusion is much the same even if the period is extended to the mid-1950s.[26] While Australian experience supports this conclusion, the average is not a very useful measure, because it is so influenced by the existence of large numbers of very small factories.[27] Of more relevance would be the proportion of employment in large factories. Here the only long-run measure is of factories employing more than 100, and these show a marked increase in importance (see Table 3.12).

TABLE 3.12.
Per cent of Manufacturing Employment in Factories Employing over 100 Persons

1906	35·5
1931	40·8
1920–21	42·9
1938–39	47·5
1949–50	49·0
1965–66	52·7

Source: Year Book.

Over the same period the average size of the plant employing more than 100 persons also rose—from 207 persons in 1906 to 326 in 1965–6.

However, the use of size of factories, especially as measured by employment, to suggest the influence of economies of scale over

[26] J. Jewkes, 'Are The Economies of Scale Unlimited?', Ch. 6 in Robinson, ed., *Economic Consequences*, pp. 98 and 99. Robinson himself agrees: 'There was little evidence . . . that, as measured by numbers of employees, units of production are getting significantly larger'. Ibid., p. xvii.

[27] In Australia in 1965–6, 40 per cent of the 'factories' employed less than four persons and accounted for only 3·5 per cent of employment. *Year Book*, No. 53, pp. 1111–2.

time is most unsatisfactory for a number of reasons. Output is a better measure of size, and since it is known that output per head has increased substantially, then employment figures significantly understate the increase in size. Changes in the average size of factories have also been affected by changes in the composition of output, and this has been substantial. More important, and more generally, while economies of scale may lead to an increase in size of plants, they may also, through more narrow specialization, decrease size. Specialization may be vertical, leading to the 'disintegration' of the production process. This was the aspect emphasized by Allyn Young in 1928: 'With the extension of the division of labour among industries the representative firm, like the industry of which it is a part, loses its identity. Its internal economies dissolve into the internal and external economies of the more highly specialized undertakings which are its successors, and are supplemented by new economies.'[28] Advantages, he suggests, stem from management specialization and less compromise in location, but especially from the 'economies of capitalistic or roundabout methods of production'.[29] Size may also be reduced through lateral specialization—by more narrow concentration on a particular, undifferentiated product. It is, for example, often claimed that this is one of the great advantages of American production,[30] and a comparison of Canadian and American manufacturing plants found that 'one is struck not so much by the relatively greater size of the United States production units—although United States plants usually are somewhat larger—but by the fact that the Canadian plant in practically all cases produces a much greater variety of products for its size'.[31] Undoubtedly the expansion of the market has permitted greater specialization by Australian factories, but the degree and effect of this specialization on size have hardly been noticed. In the wool textile industry, however, M. Dedman observed that 'as the industry has developed, specialization has advanced as against both lateral and vertical integration . . .'.[32] By 1959 nearly half the firms in the industry specialized in one major process and they provided 22 per cent of the employment. Overall, there was 'a clear increase in the average size of the firms as the

[28] *Economic Journal*, XXXVIII, p. 538.

[29] Ibid., p. 539.

[30] M. Frankel, *British and American Productivity. A Comparison and Interpretation*, University of Illinois, Urbana, 1957, pp. 72–80.

[31] D. H. Fullerton and H. A. Hampson, *Canadian Secondary Manufacturing Industry*, Royal Commission on Canada's Economic Prospects, 1957, p. 73.

[32] M. Dedman, 'Integration in the Australian Wool Textile Industry', *Economic Record*, XXIV, 1948, p. 116.

number of processes performed grows larger'.[33] In this industry at least, growth has permitted the emergence of smaller, more specialized firms.

(b) *Location of Industry*

If important economies of scale can be obtained, they might be expected to show, as Marshall suggested, in the location of industry and the movement of commodities. What was the position at the beginning of the century? Allowing a number of years for the effects of free trade between the states to be felt, the share of manufacturing in each state reflected fairly closely their share of population (see Table 3.13).

TABLE 3.13. *Australia: State Shares of Population, Factory Employment and Value Added, 1909*

	NSW	Vic.	Qld	SA	WA	Tas.	Cth
Per cent of population	37·3	29·5	13·4	9·1	6·1	4·5	99·9
Per cent factory value added	37·1	31·3	12·2	9·3	5·9	4·3	100·1
Per cent factory employment.	34·4	36·5	11·1	9·7	4·8	3·5	100·0

Source: Year Book, No. 4, pp. 125, 555, 567.

There is no evidence of a concentration of industry such as existed in the United States some sixty years earlier, where, according to North, 75 per cent of manufacturing employment was in the north-east,[34] which had only 37 per cent of the population. The Australian statistics could be interpreted as a *prima facie* case against the importance of economies of scale. Of course, it is not as simple as that, and in part they reflect the fact, already mentioned, that transport costs were substantial between the main centres in each state; but more important, a very large part of factory output consisted of such locally tied industries as those based on food and raw materials (including saw milling and smelting), some building materials,

[33] G. C. Harcourt and D. H. Whitehead, 'The Wool Textile Industry', Ch. 13 in A. Hunter, ed., *The Economics of Australian Industry*, Melbourne University Press, Melbourne, 1965, p. 427.

[34] D. C. North, *The Economic Growth of the United States 1790–1860*, Prentice-Hall, New Jersey, 1961, p. 159.

repair work, printing, electricity and gas. In industries not so tied there was a good deal of concentration in a particular state. Using the very rough industrial divisions of the *Production Bulletin*, and considering only those industries employing more than 1,000 in Australia, we will regard an industry as localized if a state's share of that industry's employment is at least one-third larger than its share of population. Using these criteria no industries were localized in NSW, but the position was different in Victoria, whose share of population was 29·5 per cent in 1909 (see Table 3.14).

TABLE 3.14. *Manufacturing Employment: Share of Victoria in Selected Industries, 1909*

Industry	Total Commonwealth employment	Per cent of employment in Victoria
Glass (inc. bottles)	1,403	44·8
Agricultural implements	4,081	46·4
Brass and copper	1,115	64·1
Biscuits	3,026	39·3
Confectionery	3,223	44·2
Tobacco, cigars, etc.	3,991	61·4
Woollen, cotton, tweed mills	2,965	57·9
Boots and shoes (inc. repair)	14,023	4·9
Tanneries	2,980	50·4
Dressmaking and millinery	16,323	57·1
Hats and caps	3,361	50·2
Shirts, ties, scarfs	9,366	65·3
Rope, cordage, bags, flax	1,275	68·1
Bedding, flock, upholstery	1,375	44·1
Chemicals, drugs, medicine	1,813	54·4
Jewellery	1,492	45·4

Source: Production Bulletin, No. 4, pp. 72–7.

Thus Victoria, with about 30 per cent of the Australian population, provided about 50 per cent of the employment in these industries, which themselves made up about one-quarter of total factory employment.

Two conclusions can be drawn from the location by states of Australian manufacturing in 1909. First, the greater part of manufacturing employment was in what are generally regarded as local industries. Their location throws no light on the influence of economies of scale. Second, other industries were concentrated to a striking extent in Victoria, and, in fact, in Melbourne. Whatever the original cause of this localization—no doubt the Victorian tariff was very important—it would seem that a major reason for its continuation, with free trade between the states, must have been external economies of scale of the Marshallian type.[35]

The localization of industry in Victoria stands out also in the quantity and direction of interstate trade in manufactures. For instance, Victorian exports of manufactures interstate in 1909 of £6·4m. were roughly double those of NSW.[36] Between 1900 (the last year of colonial tariffs) and 1909 Victorian manufactured exports for interstate rose from £1·7m. to £6·4m. (including a small amount of re-exports in 1909), and these amounted to 8 per cent of the value of Victorian factory output in 1900, and a very substantial 19 per cent in 1909. The great variety of manufactures in Victorian exports is impressive and, in particular, the expansion is headed by the products of the clothing industries, so that apparel and attire, woollen goods, hats and caps, and boots and shoes rise from 12·5 per cent of these exports in 1900 to 27·2 per cent in 1909.

The question of location of industry is a complex one, but some further aspects related to scale are worth noting. Within states

TABLE 3.15. *Sydney Metropolitan District as Per Cent of NSW*[a]

Date	Factory work force	Population
1901	64	36
1911	71	38
1921	74	43
1933	79	48
1947	76	50
1954	75	54
1961	74	56

[a] The metropolitan district grew over this period as the city expanded.

Source: NSW Statistical Register.

[35] The economies of scale were probably not internal, because the number of factories ranged from 4 in biscuits to 548 in dressmaking and millinery.

[36] *Overseas Trade*, 1909. Figures used include exports of processed foodstuffs.

manufacturing has been heavily concentrated in metropolitan centres. The position in NSW is set out in Table 3.15.

Factory employment in NSW has been heavily concentrated during this century in Sydney, growing from 64 per cent of the total in 1901 to about 80 per cent in the 1930s. Since then there has been a decline, reflecting the growth of the Newcastle and Wollongong–Port Kembla areas. This concentration of factory employment in Sydney has been much stronger than that of population, but the ratio between the two has fallen from 1·9 in 1911 to 1·3 in 1961, presumably because of the growth of factories elsewhere and the increase in service occupations in Sydney. Even early in the century manufacturing in the country tended to be in tied industries, while mobile industries settled in Sydney. In 1903, for example, perhaps the most striking contrast is that the industry of clothing and textile fabrics employed 30 per cent of Sydney's factory employees but only 10 per cent of the factory employees outside Sydney. Industries which were relatively more important in the country were mainly resource oriented: saw mills, food processing and smelting.[37]

A number of reasons can be advanced to account for the concentration of NSW industries in Sydney, but there is a pervasive theme of a search for the economies of scale—internal and external—which can only be obtained in a centre of some size.[38] The argument can be illustrated by the experience of the woollen textile mills in country towns during the 1920s. These were established in a burst of enthusiasm for this industry after the war, but they found survival very difficult. Basically, their problems were those of scale, especially in the training and maintenance of an efficient work force; but more generally, as one mill complained, there were 'the many vexatious delays and difficulties' stemming from their location.[39] These difficulties were not sufficient to locate the primary steel industry in Sydney: the pull of resource location was stronger. But since the original establishment of this industry, both Newcastle and Wollongong–Port Kembla have obtained economies of scale of their own.

(c) *Composition of Output*

Another method of observing the effects of economies of scale is

[37] *NSW Statistical Register*, 1903, pp. 390–3.

[38] The reasons for manufacturing being concentrated in metropolitan centres are discussed by G. J. R. Linge, 'The Location of Manufacturing in Australia', Ch. 2 in Hunter, ed., *The Economics of Australian Industry*, especially pp. 56–7. In the main, they boil down to aspects of economies of scale.

[39] C. Forster, *Industrial Development in Australia 1920–1930*, ANU, Canberra, 1964, pp. 89–90.

to examine the composition of industries that make up Australian manufacturing. In the first years of this century Australian manufacturing consisted almost entirely of the fairly 'simple' industries such as the production of foodstuffs, clothing, building materials, printing, furniture and metal working, including repairs. There was a large range of industries in which production was not attempted at all, or else output was very small and confined to the simpler aspects. These included textiles, iron and steel, a very wide range of engineering industries, ship building and chemicals. To a very large extent these industries did not exist because of problems relating to economies of scale, and one of the enduring difficulties of the Australian economy has been to cope with these problems and to establish these industries. Their number has increased with innovations in the twentieth century through the addition of electrical equipment, motor vehicles and aircraft. Since 1900 all these industries have been established in Australia (though some may still not produce the complete range of products normally associated with them), and always with a considerable time lag after their development in large industrialized countries. Heavy protective duties have been necessary to ensure their establishment, and in many instances heavy duties have been necessary to maintain them.

At first consideration it may not be obvious that the main obstacles to the establishment of these industries centred around scale. Consider, then, an industry which would seem relatively easy to operate, in which the size of the production unit was relatively small, and which already existed to a limited degree—woollen textiles.

Just before the First World War there were twenty-two woollen mills in Australia employing 3,090 workers. These mills supplied almost the entire local market in flannels and blankets, with production averaging about £0·5 m. per annum in the three years 1911–13. In the production of 'tweed and cloth', however, the value of local output averaged only some £300,000, compared with annual imports of approximately £3m.[40] In this field, then, Australian producers had made almost no impression on the market. At the Royal Commission inquiring into tariffs for the industry during 1905–06, manufacturers complained of the many difficulties they faced in competing with English imports, difficulties such as higher wage rates and local prejudice. But it is clear that a basic disadvantage centred around the small size of the market, which reduced the ability of the Australian manufacturer to obtain long runs of a standardized product.

[40] Forster, *Industrial Development*, p. 73.

This difficulty was much more pronounced in the production of 'tweed and cloth' than in flannels and blankets.

Some observers of the industry thought that the solution to the problem of the mills producing 'anything and everthing' was for the mills to specialize.[41] With the example of Britain before them, 'the individual mills should take up the manufacture of special lines of goods, confine themselves to that . . .'.[42] When asked if the market was too small for such a practice, an English importer thought that that the market was limited only 'for the class of goods they are making', whereas there would be an expanded market (presumably through price reductions) 'if they confined themselves to special cloths'.[43]

To the manufacturer himself it was not so obvious that specialization was a possibility. The size of the market definitely prohibited the manufacture of some lines. The foreman of the Ballarat Woollen and Worsted Co. Ltd commented:

> . . . I would point out that if we manufactured that class of goods we should have to make a speciality of it; and after we had acquired the necessary machinery, we could turn out enough in one month to satisfy the requirements of Australia for twenty years. The same remark is applicable to the broadcloth which is made in the West of England. If we started to manufacture that, we should need to make a speciality of it; and when our machinery was in proper running order we could supply more in one year than Australia would use in ten years.[44]

In fact the Ballarat mill produced a great variety of products—worsted coatings, serges, trousers and suitings, woollen flannels, military clothing, rugs and shawls. But the manager felt that 'if we did not vary our manufacture, we should very soon land ourselves in difficulties'.[45]

The same view was taken by the representative of the Sydney mill, John Vicars and Company, who examined the problem of specialization more closely:

[41] Royal Commission on Customs and Excise Tariffs, 1906, Minutes of Evidence, Supplement to Vols II, III, IV, Division V—Apparel and Textiles, p. 52.

[41] Ibid., p. 55.

[43] Ibid., p. 54.

[44] Royal Commission on Customs and Excise Tariffs, 1906, Minutes of Evidence, Vol. III, Division V—Apparel and Textiles, p. 1317.

[45] Ibid., p. 1285.

> [Specialization] would mean greater perfection, and decrease in our cost of production. At the present time, in order to fill up our works, we have to make blankets, travelling rugs, tweeds, serges and everything else . . . It is not working to advantage to make various kinds of goods in one mill. We cover the large field which we do merely to obtain sufficient work to keep going.[46]

Moreover, 'if we cut down our lines by one half, we could not double our out-put in the other lines'.[47] Thus when he was asked whether the great number of patterns and qualities the firm produced was the reason for its failure to obtain large orders, he thought this was a reversal of cause and effect: 'No. We put forward a multiplicity of patterns in the hope of being able to catch a little of anything.'[48]

It is clear that although some form of specialization was highly desirable, it did not seem practicable to Australian manufacturers. Given the size of the market and the great variety in demand (raised on a wide selection of British imports), there seems no reason to doubt their judgement. The problem of specialization for Australian mills was not simply one of end product. Usually, within a single mill all stages of production were performed, and given the scale of operations and limited supplies of skilled labour, considerable inefficiency must have resulted.

The small size of the industry would have made it difficult to obtain supplies of highly qualified labour. The representative of the Ballarat mill made light of this problem:

> The difficulties in connexion with labour have been gradually overcome. They constituted a very serious problem in days gone by. We could not secure a continuous supply of labour for sufficiently long to enable us to insure proficiency, but we have altered all that. For example, if a foreman's position in our factory becomes vacant, we never dream of importing a man, but promote to the position someone whom we have trained ourselves.[49]

Especially as applied to a mill isolated in the small town of Ballarat, it is very hard to accept these views. More real seems the experience of the South Australian Woollen Co. Ltd, where the labour supply was unsatisfactory because of 'want of opportunities for learning and training. Very frequently if we lose an operator we have to educate another to take his place.'[50] In fact, both mills have taken a

[46] Ibid., p. 1398.
[47] Ibid., p. 1408.
[48] Ibid.
[49] Ibid., p. 1282.
[50] Ibid., p. 1421.

narrow view of labour supplies. To obtain skilled labour and also to prevent standards declining compared with those overseas, a much larger industry was needed than that existing in Australia, where it was also dispersed between several centres. The necessity to rely on skilled labour from overseas became obvious in the 1920s, when the industry expanded and improved the quality of production assisted by a high tariff.[51] Two other instances of diseconomies felt by the industry will be mentioned. First, capital equipment had to be imported from England so raising its cost and making it difficult to service and repair (relatively to England). Second, the industry was not large enough to provide the waste materials to enable the manufacture of cheap or 'shoddy' products.[52]

THE IMPORTANCE OF ECONOMIES OF SCALE

A rigorous assessment of the changing importance of economies of scale in Australian manufacturing in this century requires detailed studies of the main industries, written with an eye to this concept. These do not exist; but fortunately the development of the steel industry, in which economies of scale are known to be significant, has been examined from various points of view. In the absence then of the ideal material, the method adopted in this section is to approach the problem in the following fashion: (a) Assess in a general way the importance of internal economies of scale in the first decade of this century, and then in the 1960s. (b) In similar manner examine external economies of scale. (c) Take the development of the steel industry as an example of the way in which economies of scale, themselves changing over time with changes in technology, can affect the costs of an industry which itself is expanding both in size and in range of output.

(a) *Internal Economies of Scale*

It has been shown that Australia possessed a range of fairly simple industries around the period 1900–10, and it seems probable that in a large proportion of these something like full internal economies were obtained. More important for growth was the position in a whole range of industries, especially those making producer and consumer durables, where it seems doubtful if Australia's small and dispersed population could provide a sufficient market for even one

[51] Forster, *Industrial Development*, pp. 86–7.

[52] Royal Commission on Customs and Excise Tariffs, 1907, Progress Report No. 21, blankets, woollen piece goods, p. 14.

plant of efficient size. These industries include the broad fields of steel, engineering (including machinery, electrical manufactures, motor vehicles, ships, agricultural implements) and chemicals. Clearly some particular products would have to be excepted from such wide categories, but products from other industries such as paper could also be included.

By the 1960s the growth of population, swiftly changing technology, the greater range of production, and economic policy had produced a more complex situation. Even though discussion must necessarily be brief, it is worth distinguishing three situations where important internal economies of scale are still not obtained.

(i) It is not as easy as it was sixty years ago to name such large industry groups in which a single plant could not obtain maximum internal economies of scale. Nevertheless, broad categories of industry are still heavily disadvantaged even at the one plant level, including such fields as aircraft, ships and chemicals. Take the examples of chemicals which were examined by the Tariff Board as late as 1966. The Board found that 'for most of the chemicals produced in Australia the domestic market . . . is small by world standards'.[53] This has meant that the choice of production process has been restricted, so that the methods adopted, while being best suited to a market of Australia's size, are much less economical than those used overseas.[54] More generally, capital costs are often the main cost in the product and in complex plants these rise far less than proportionately to plant size, and since 'Australian chemical plants are small by world standards'[55] costs are substantially higher; large plants also make possible economies in power and labour, and permit recovery of more by-products. While the Australian market as a whole may permit an optimum-sized plant, its division because of transport costs may not. Thus, in oil refining, where economies of scale are important, 'the Australian market for petroleum products must be treated as five or more separate areas. Within each of these marketing areas the demand for petroleum products at present is insufficient to support one refinery which would be taking full advantage of the economies of large-scale production . . . '.[56]

Examples can easily be extended through particular products such as glass sheets, aluminium foil and ball bearings. In aluminium

[53] *Tariff Board's Report on Industrial Chemicals and Synthetic Resins*, 1966, p. 17.

[54] Ibid., pp. 18–19.

[55] Ibid., p. 14.

[56] J. McB. Grant, 'The Petroleum Industry', Ch. 8 in Hunter, ed., *The Economics of Australian Industry*, pp. 283–4. The comment applies to the early 1960s.

foil the one producer found that 'even for the major selling varieties, orders in Australia are generally small and have to be custom made because of varying user requirements . . .'.[57] Again, the one Australian producer of ball bearings, although concentrating on a limited range only, suffered severely from 'relatively small scale operations and small production runs for the limited Australian market . . . Evidence submitted on behalf of two overseas producers indicated that their yearly throughput was about 15 times that of [the Australian Company].'[58]

(ii) The fact that the Australian market is too small for even one optimum-sized plant is still very important, but in many industries the growth of the market by the 1960s had changed the situation. Although the size of the market has warranted at least one plant, the typical response has been the establishment of more than the optimum number of plants so that none achieves full economies of scale. The situation arises in the main where the optimum number of plants is small and there is protection from overseas competition through the tariff and/or transport costs.[59] It is most obvious in the production of consumer durables such as motor vehicles, refrigerators, and television sets. Perhaps the leading example is the motor-car industry. Here, in the mid-1960s, five international companies producing a dozen models competed for a passenger vehicle market of about 350,000 a year. Although the market was highly protected, these companies were beginning to feel the impact of Japanese competition. This is an industry in which economies of scale are known to be important, although detailed quantitative evidence is limited: much depends on such factors as the extent of the producer's integration and the number and life of the models. Maxcy's conservative estimate for a British firm in the mid-1960s is worth noting:

> Something like a 40 per cent reduction in costs can be expected as production increases from 1,000 to 50,000 units per annum. Doubling volume to 100,000 units should lower costs by 15 per cent; while a further doubling to 200,000 should achieve another 10 per cent in savings. The jump to 400,000 yields an additional 5 per cent and expansion beyond this point results in progressively

[57] *Tariff Board's Report on Aluminium Foil*, 1964, p. 11.

[58] *Tariff Board's Report on Precision Ground Ball Bearings*, 1964, p. 9.

[59] The comparable situation in Canada has recently been studied by H. C. Eastman and S. Styholt, *The Tariff and Competition in Canada*, Macmillan, Toronto, 1967.

smaller savings for each additional 100,000, the gains tapering off at a level of about 1,000,000.[60]

(iii) Complicating and overlapping the preceeding two categories of small plant size in Australia, is the problem of specialization within plants. Optimum plant size cannot be judged in relation to the broad output of an industry. Within that range of output specialization can be narrowed to an even greater degree than, for example, to woollen cloth or steel pipe. Pratten and Dean conclude that here lies the greatest scope for economies.

> Substantial economies usually relate to the scale of output of individual products, and where scale is increased by widening the range of products technical economies may be small. . . . Our estimates show that there are often substantial economies to be achieved by standardizing production, by increasing the output of particular products, and by extending production runs. These conclusions may seem obvious, but the extent to which there is in practice a lack of standardization and concentration of production suggests that they are worth stressing.[61]

The same view is echoed by Robinson: 'Not a little of the success of the American economy would seem to derive from the concentration of all efforts of a concern on mastering the problems of design and production of a quite narrow range of products'.[62] It was this aspect that was emphasized in explanation of differences in productivity between American and Canadian manufacturing; steel, rubber products, wire, even bricks are cited as examples where American plants of similar size to Canadian produce a much narrower range of output.[63]

The situation in Australia shows in a variety of ways. An American manufacturer operating a branch in Australia complained that 'where the US company can set up a machine in eight hours to run for weeks, we take the same time to set it up but only run it for two hours'.[64] The problem is often met by the use of multi-purpose machinery: 'where we use an ordinary turret lathe, the UK company

[60] G. Maxcy, 'The Motor Industry', Ch. 15 in Hunter, ed., *The Economics of Australian Industry*, p. 497.

[61] *Economies of Large-scale Production*, p. 103.

[62] *Economic Consequences*, p. xviii.

[63] Fullerton and Hampson, *Canadian Secondary Manufacturing*, pp. 72–3.

[64] D. T. Brash, *American Investment in Australian Industry*, ANUP, Canberra, 1966, p. 158.

uses a multi-station loading lathe, and the US company uses a twelve spindle machine which performs twelve operations simultaneously'.[65] In the production of steel tubes, Tubemakers of Australia Ltd 'stated that because of the comparatively small Australian market and the wide variety of types and sizes of tube required, it had installed general purpose rather than specialized plants'.[66] Further, 'to some extent unused capacity is taken up by general engineering work although tube manufacture remains the principal activity. An unusual feature of this field of production is the fact that, in order to save costs, expensive items of plant . . . can be moved from factory to factory as required.'[67] It is salutary to consider the production methods adopted by the company producing heat-resisting glassware. It had a twenty-five ton capacity furnace which it could not operate continuously because of insufficient demand; the furnace was used to produce both clear and opal pyrex alternately, 'thus increasing production costs, accelerating depreciation and creating inventory problems'; and its range of products was said to exceed that of a great American company.[68]

Illustrations could be continued, but their over-all extent is difficult to measure. Partly because of Australia's relative isolation, international contrasts in degree of specialization are often overlooked in assessing relative efficiency. But in Canada, with the example of the United States nearby, differences in specialization are more obvious, and it has been shown above that they are regarded as critical. It is hard to believe that they would be any less important in Australia. Certainly Robinson was prepared to guess that in this connection 'the differences between the United States, on the one hand, and France or the United Kingdom on the other hand, seemed as significant as those between the latter and some of the nations of 10–15 million, though here again the differences were important'.[69]

(b) *External Economies of Scale*

The question of whether the size of the market justifies the existence of an optimum-sized plant cannot be looked at simply in terms of conditions within the plant. The plant operates in an environment which affects the cost of establishing and running it.

[65] Ibid.

[66] *Tariff Board's Report on Hollow Bars, Tubes and Pipes of Iron or Steel*, 1965, p. 5.

[67] Ibid., p. 7.

[68] *Tariff Board's Report on Glassware*, 1965, pp. 5 and 7.

[69] *Economic Consequences*, p. xviii.

The economy as a whole provides the external economies to the plant, and the inability of the Australian economy to provide these to a satisfactory degree was perhaps the main difficulty that faced development of manufacturing in the early years of the century.

Since Young wrote it has been clear that a major source of rising real income is in the external economies obtained simply as an economy expands. In other words, the larger the economy the greater the external economies that are available. In this general way the small size of the Australian economy at the beginning of the century limited external economies in manufacturing. But the problem was deeper and more specific. The narrow and unsophisticated base in Australian manufacturing meant that the problems of expansion in that sector were like those general growth problems of underdeveloped countries which are so emphasized today—problems relating to the interdependence of industries. The provision of overhead capital was satisfactory in a general way, but within manufacturing, expansion meant breaking out of the existing confined circle of industries and moving into industries more characteristic of a modern industrial structure. These industries were import competing, and the lack of a number of significant external economies made investment in them unattractive.

One of the main difficulties centred around external economies was the provision of finance for manufacturing. The economy had an agriculture-commerce bias and lacked the institutional channels to direct savings into manufacturing. Banks were not interested, and stock exchanges hardly began to handle manufacturing securities until the 1920s. The main source of finance was retained earnings, which tended to be directed along the established lines of service and processing industries.[70] Foreign capital, which in this period meant British capital, was traditionally not interested in Australian manufacturing. It favoured government bonds and pastoral, banking and mining companies as fields of investment, and English manufacturing companies establishing branches would have been competing against their own exports. In fact it was not until the 1920s that foreign investment became of some importance as a source of funds.

Another problem was the supply of labour. A disciplined factory work force with a generally satisfactory level of education existed, but very often it did not possess the specific skills necessary for new industries. Training was not easily obtained in technical schools, and expensive training on the job would have been necessary. In fact, as new industries were established in the 1920s, there was reli-

[70] Forster, *Industrial Development*, Ch. VIII.

ance on skilled migrants.[71] Much the same comment can be made about management, which would have been unfamiliar with the processes of production in new industries. Australia was a technological backwater: building up knowledge and skills is a dynamic process and had not begun in groups of related industries. It was this problem of the interdependence of industries that was so important in this period. When moving into a new field, probably the main problem is to find supply, service and market industries.[72] Their absence can be overcome in part by increasing the size of the investment and engaging in a variety of activities, but the size of the investment may deter potential investors, and the spread of activities reduces the advantages of specialization. To some extent imports may be used to meet supply problems, but there are still the difficulties based on differing specifications, maintaining stocks, etc. especially given Australia's distance from its main suppliers. This problem of interdependence will be looked at more specifically in relation to the unusual circumstances which permitted BHP's successful breakthrough into steel.

By the 1960s many of these external diseconomies had undoubtedly been eliminated, although it must be emphasized that in some circumstances growth may not automatically give external economies. In the usual industrialization process, income per head rises in part because of the higher productivity of the manufacturing sector and the cumulative effect of external economies. However, apart from New Zealand, Australia is the only country in the world where output per head in primary industry has been significantly higher than in manufacturing, so that the relative expansion of manufacturing has not had such an obvious stimulating effect on incomes. This also touches on a special form of external diseconomy of growth not emphasized in the literature. Arndt, illustrating a general point, gives an example where the establishment of the last shoe manufacturer justifies the establishment of a specialized shoe-machinery manufacturer, so that all shoe producers benefit from lower priced machinery.[73] But in Australia all might suffer: the effect could be to replace imports with local production requiring tariff protection.

[71] Ibid., Ch. VII.

[72] Entry is also assisted by standardized demand. It could be argued that in Australia (as in the US) tastes were relatively standardized because of egalitarian attitudes and relatively small class and income differences. But the Australian demand had previously been met by imports (especially from Britain), and people may have become accustomed to exercising a wide choice; this was certainly so, for example, with structural steel (see later).

[73] *Economic Record*, XXXI, p. 211.

Not only did special problems arise in the course of obtaining external economies, but the scope for these economies has continuously enlarged. Interdependence between 'industries' changes radically with increasing specialization.[74] Consider Robinson's conclusions:

> . . . in almost all the larger economies the general specialization of firms extended to the specialization of service industries, with additional opportunities for producers to narrow, so far as they might wish, the range of processes for which they made themselves responsible and to extend, with advantage to themselves, their dependence on the services of these specialist firms to the greatest possible extent. There were marked differences in this respect again not only between the very small nations and those of around 50 million, but also between the latter and the United States, as an example of the very big.[75]

Similar views were expressed by Gates and Linden when they examined the reasons for labour productivity being higher in American factories at home than in branches abroad. Their general conclusion was that 'the greater size and maturity of the domestic economy afford a substantial "hidden productivity" factor in prices and availability of both primary materials and intermediate products'.[76] More specifically:

> . . . in the United States, where a diverse and enormous scale of activity has generated a vast network of specialized suppliers ready to produce the specific needs of large and small users, domestic manufacturers can with rare exception readily obtain materials in the quality and specifications required for their most efficient use.[77]

By contrast, in the Australian shipbuilding industry, one of the main factors reducing efficiency at the end of the 1950s was thought to be: 'The restricted availability of specialized sub-contractors and manufacturers specializing in the production of shipbuilding

[74] At this point the distinction between internal and external economies is difficult to maintain. One firm's external economies are another's internal economies, but the internal economies may be obtained outside the manufacturing sector.

[75] *Economic Consequences*, p. xviii..

[76] *Cost and Competition*, Summary (no page number).

[77] Ibid., p. 40.

requisites which forces the local builders to fabricate more of their own requirements.'[78] More generally, this seems to be the heart of the matter, especially when specialization is extended to the fields of finance and labour, transport and marketing.

(c) *The Steel Industry and Economies of Scale*

The development of the steel industry by BHP is regarded as one of the outstanding success stories in Australian industrialization. Steel is at the core of heavy industry and the growth in its production has symbolized the maturity of Australian manufacturing. Not only has the scale of the undertaking been outstanding—BHP has long been the largest manufacturing company in Australia—but production is reputed to have been carried on in a most efficient manner. This industry is unusual in Australia, because at least since about the mid-1930s the price of Australian steel has been lower than that of duty-free imports. What will be examined here is not whether BHP has been efficient within the technology suitable for the Australian market, but whether the size of the market has placed constraints upon the technology which can be applied. It is difficult enough to estimate the value of economies of scale at any given time, let alone over a long period during which considerable changes in technology have taken place. All that can be attempted here is an indication of the limits which the size of the market placed on production processes within the industry, and a general assessment as to whether these were likely to have important effects on costs. Certainly Essington Lewis, the General Manager of BHP, suggested in 1938 that failure to achieve economies of scale was affecting the industry: 'Against this richness of natural resources, an offsetting factor is the smallness of the home market. The most economical unit of iron and steel production is normally very large—the Australian demand is relatively small.'[79]

Whilst it is generally accepted that economies of scale in iron and steel production are important, there are few estimates of their actual dimensions. J. S. Bain's estimates in 1950 are surprisingly modest. On the basis of questionnaires, he suggests that an optimum

[78] *Tariff Board's Report on Shipbuilding Industry*, 1959, p. 10. Similarly, in the production of tractors, an 'important disability arises from the wide dispersion of sub-contractors in Australia compared with Britain'. *Tariff Board's Report on Agricultural Tractors*, Interim Report, 1966, p. 7.

[79] E. Lewis, 'The Economics of the Australian Iron and Steel Industry', *BHP Review*, XV, No. 4, p. 7. Helen Hughes indicates the importance of rich raw materials in Australia in the 1950s. *The Australian Iron and Steel Industry 1848–1962*, Melbourne University Press, 1964, pp. 154–5.

size for a fully integrated steel mill in the United States would be a capacity of 1 to 2·5 million ingot tons, and that unit costs would increase some 5 per cent at the 0·5 million ton capacity.[80] It is not clear how extensive a range of products such mills would produce. More detailed engineering estimates of costs have been made by Pratten and Dean for Britain in the early 1960s (see Table 3.16).

TABLE 3.16. *Production Costs and Scale for an Integrated Steel Works*[a] *(Unit cost per ton for a plant with a capacity of 250,000 tons = 100)*

	Output—000 tons per annum					
	100	250	500	1,000	2,000	4,000
Blast furnaces	120	100	94	89	85	82
Steel furnaces	125	100	90	82	78	75
Finishing	137	100	82	68	56	47
Total	128	100	89	79	72	67

[a] Raw materials are included at the stage of steel making when they are introduced, e.g. iron ore is included as a cost for blast-furnaces and steel scrap as a cost of steel-furnaces, but the costs exclude the costs of materials transferred from the preceding process, e.g. the costs for steel-furnaces exclude the costs of pig iron.

Source: Pratten and Dean, *Economies of Large-scale Production*, p. 80.

On their calculations there are very substantial economies of scale and they appear to be most important at the finishing stage. As they point out: 'The extent of the economies of scale clearly depend on the type of finishing processes used. If a wide hot strip mill is included a capacity of at least 3 million tons . . . is required in order to utilize the full potential of the most modern and efficient equipment.'[81] These estimates relate to a company producing sheet steel, but apparently only a limited range of products.[82] In Britain the large companies, with a few exceptions, tend 'to specialize in making a general category of finished steel products such as sheet

[80] J. S. Bain, *Industrial Organization*, New York, 1959, pp. 256–7.
[81] Pratten and Dean, *Economies of Large-scale Production*, pp. 80–1.
[82] Ibid., p. 79.
[83] Ibid., p. 63.

and strip, or pipes and tubes, or heavy plates and sections or wire rods and bars'.[83] In Australia BHP, although attempting specialization by plants, produces all the general categories of steel products.

In what ways is there scope for economics of scale in steel production? In the production of pig iron, raw materials make up a large proportion of cost. Around 1948–9 (and in 1937) they amounted to 80–85 per cent in Britain and the United States. Similarly in the conversion of pig iron to steel, raw materials (including pig iron) were 75–80 per cent of cost. These figures suggest that an important field for economies of scale could lie in the effect of scale on the quantity of raw materials per unit of output. As steel is further processed (rolled), raw material costs become less important, so that they totalled in 1937 some 50 per cent (US 43 per cent, UK 57 per cent) of the value of all finished steel products. Thus 'the importance of labour costs increases rapidly for rolled steel; it is also at this stage that the degree of labour skill and technological advance is more particularly felt'.[84] Within the category of rolled products, there is great variation in the amount of value added needed to produce the various types of products. Thus in 1935 the US Bureau of Labor Statistics made this calculation of cumulative labour costs for a hypothetical plant:[85]

Number of Integrated Working-hours per ton of Product

Pig iron (inc. labour in raw materials)	12
Steel (inc. labour in raw materials)	17
Weighted average all rolled products	53

The weighted average is composed of the following products

Semi-finished products	29·0
Structural shapes	34·0
Rails	38·5
Strip	42·0
Wire	51·0
Sheet	58·0
Tube	62·7
Tin plate	80·6

Again it must be emphasized that with changing technology and

[84] United Nations Economic Commission for Europe, *European Steel Trends in the Setting of the World Market*, Geneva, 1949, p. 57.
[85] Ibid., p. 58.

costs, figures like those above for a particular date are of only limited use over a period. However, they do illustrate several points which have been of continuing importance: the magnitude of raw material costs in pig iron and steel ingot production; the increasing proportion that value added bears in rolled products; the difference between various rolled products in the amount of value added. With these considerations in mind, what can be said concerning economies of scale in the Australian steel industry in the twentieth century?

One of the most important aspects of increasing blast-furnace productivity in this century has been the increase in furnace size.[86] Early in the century it was the Americans who set the pace: 'The first and foremost article of creed of the American blastfurnaceman is, there is no better divisor for all fixed charges than a large output. . . '.[87] This was achieved through larger furnaces and harder driving. In 1901 it was claimed that the 'typical American blastfurnace' could produce about 500 tons of iron a day,[88] and Lewis writes that in 'the early years of the twentieth century' about 600 tons of pig iron a day was the American maximum.[89] By 1929 the maximum had reached around 1,000 tons, 1945 1,600 tons, 1960 more than 2,000 tons and furnaces are now reported as being built in the USSR with a capacity of 4,000–5,000 tons. In Australia, blast-furnaces have increased in size in similar fashion, but at least initially in Newcastle they were behind best practices overseas. BHP's first furnace in 1915 had a capacity of 350 tons, its second in 1918 450 tons and its third in 1921 600 tons. In 1928 the new furnace at Port Kembla had a capacity of 800 tons, and this was followed in 1937 by one of 1,175 tons, described as 'one of the largest in the world'.[90] Since then market size does not appear to have been a disadvantage. Thus the main steelworks at Newcastle was established on blast-furnaces below optimum size, while the operation of only one blast-furnace at Port Kembla between 1928 and 1937 was a decided disadvantage. No comments are offered here on steel-furnaces: it is thought that they probably obtained economies along the lines of blast-furnaces.

More important, we have seen earlier that the real opportunities

[86] United Nations Economic Commission for Europe, *Long-Term Trends and Problems of the European Steel Industry*, Geneva, 1959, p. 90.

[87] J. C. Carr and W. Taplin, *History of the British Steel Industry*, Harvard University Press, Cambridge, Mass., 1962, p. 205.

[88] Ibid., p. 208.

[89] E. Lewis, 'Iron and Steel Industry in Australia', *Journal of the Institution of Engineers, Australia*, 1929, p. 136.

[90] Hughes, *Australian Iron and Steel Industry*, p. 118.

to obtain economies of scale in the production of steel products come in the rolling processes. In general, a large demand permits the continuous production of standardized products. In turn, cost reductions follow for a variety of reasons, but basically because of the continuous use of equipment which can often be more specialized and efficient. The Americans had made considerable strides in this field well before the First World War. Carr and Taplin consider specialization to have been 'the great feature of American rolling practice';[91] and this stemmed from 'America's advantages in the size and rate of home market growth [which] enabled a degree of specialization by high-capacity mills impossible under European conditions. Consequently American works were organized on a completely different basis. . . '.[92] American production also benefited from moves to standardize demand which began earlier than in other countries, and in this respect Australian manufacturers were at a particular disadvantage. This can be seen in the production of structural steel, where the Inter-State Commission in 1916 noted the advantages if Australian consumers would reduce variety in their demand, 'but, while they have had all the markets of the world to draw from, the inducement to thus standardize has not been great'.[93] In fact the trend towards the use of continuous and semi-continuous mills has been the most important development in the rolling of steel products over the last fifty years or so. What has happened in Australia?

Diseconomies arising from inability to specialize must have been considerable. A description of BHP's merchant mills in the late 1920s, shows that the 18-inch, 12-inch and 8-inch mills each produced an enormous variety of products; moreover, in the 12-inch and 8-inch mills all rolling was done by hand.[94] Similarly, the rail mill produced billets, rails and structural sections.[95] For this variety of output, one commentator remarked: 'it could readily be seen that an enormous stock of rolls were carried'.[96] The problem faced by BHP can be seen clearly in the production of structural steel when, in 1926, the sales manager promised that the company would try to produce a greater range of shapes, make more frequent rollings and

[91] *History of the British Steel Industry*, p. 206.

[92] Ibid., p. 224.

[93] *Inter-State Commission of Australia, Tariff Investigation Report, Iron and Steel*, 1916, p. 25.

[94] T. Hale, 'Through the Merchant Mills: Newcastle Steel Works', *BHP Review*, IV, No. 6, pp. 8–9.

[95] J. Harris, 'Through the Bloom and Rail Mills', ibid., V, No. 8, p. 21.

[96] Hale, 'The Merchant Mills', ibid., V, No. 6, p. 4.

carry larger stocks.[97] Again, when Stewarts and Lloyds and BHP began pipe manufacture in the early 1930s, demand was insufficient to warrant the establishment of a mill for the production of skelp alone.[98] As for the pipe plant itself, it was claimed that it was equal to any in the world, but it also had a capacity 'considerably more than the entire requirements of Australia'.[99] In the late 1930s growing demand at Port Kembla 'made necessary the installation of a continuous sheet bar and billet mill';[100] the first such mill was established in the United States in 1892.[101] However, the really outstanding developments in rolling techniques in this century have been in the field of sheet production, where there has been a great increase in output to meet the growing demand for consumer durables and tinplate. In Australia the demand for flat products increased from 29 per cent of steel output in 1946 to 43 per cent in 1959.[102] Within the field of sheet production the basic innovation has been the continuous wide hot-strip mill, and following from it the continuous cold-rolled mill and the electrolytic tinning line.

The first continuous wide strip mill was established in the United States in 1924, and by 1939 there were twenty-eight in that country but only two in Europe. BHP considered the possibilities of this type of mill at the end of the 1930s, but recognized that the minimum capacity of such a mill of 30,000 to 60,000 tons per month far exceeded the Australian market of around 200,000 tons per annum.[103] In fact a plate and hot-strip mill was not completed until 1955, and it then had a capacity of 'more than 1,000,000 tons'.[104] The economies obtained by this new mill are suggested by an examination of how sheet for galvanizing (the main market) was previously produced. Rolling was carried out by Lysaght whose plant was designed to supply 'small, but diverse markets'.[105] In its modern form this simply meant applying mechanical handling methods to the nineteenth-century standard two-high sheet mill. Even so, in 1939 only

[97] A. Bailey, 'Sales and Salesmanship', ibid., VI, No. 2, p. 7; and generally see Forster, *Industrial Development*, pp. 160–1.

[98] 'Combination Mill-Merchant, Strip and Skelp', *BHP Review*, XI, No. 2, p. 1.

[99] J. A. B. Reid, 'The Romance of Tube Making', ibid., XIII, No. 5, p. 11.

[100] 'Continuous Sheet Bar and Billet Mill installed at A.I. & S. Ltd Kembla Works', ibid., XVI, No. 2, p. 8.

[101] Carr and Taplin, *History of the British Steel Industry*, p. 224.

[102] *Seventy-Five Years of BHP Development in Industry*, pp. 56 and 158.

[103] *Tariff Board's Report on Tinplate*, 1939, pp. 4–6.

[104] Department of Trade, *The Australian Steel Industry*, Melbourne 1958, p. 8.

[105] J. C. F. Lysaght, 'Sheet Rolling in Australia', *BHP Review*, XVI, No. 3, p. 10.

one-third of the production came from these mills, and the remaining two-thirds from old manual mills. It was concluded that 'mills of this type are still of great value in Australia, where the market for steel sheets calls for a wide range of products, but where the tonnage needed is restricted'.[106]

Much the same can be said of continuous cold-strip production, and it was again 1955 when Lysaght established a continuous cold-reduction mill at Port Kembla with a capacity of 570,000 tons.[107] The most modern equipment of this type in pre-war Australia began production in 1939. Its capacity was only 30,000 tons and was described as 'an entirely new type of equipment. It is an adaption of the continuous type cold reduction to a single stand'![108] The war prevented Australia from embarking on tinplate production, which did not begin until 1957, and even then it seems that the size of the market was one consideration inducing BHP to establish a technically inferior plant. The superior electrolytic plant did not come into operation until 1962.[109]

The general conclusion must be that with the growth in demand, production in Australia has become more specialized. But for years the industry has suffered from the inability to apply large-scale technology which, moreover, is not stagnant and on balance is probably favouring increasing scale. Even though BHP has been able to obtain some specialization between its plants at Newcastle and Port Kembla, the Department of Trade could still conclude in 1958 that 'many of the Australian rolling mills are not single purpose mills'.[110] The position in Australia may still be analogous to that of Canada in the mid-1950s when it was thought that 'the limited size of the Canadian market affects both the type of equipment in Canadian steel mills and the way it is operated'.[111] Examples illustrate this point and the final conclusion is reached:

> How much all this decreases productivity it is difficult to say. But certainly per-man-hour productivity, which as has been suggested

[106] Ibid., p. 13. See also Forster, *Industrial Development*, pp. 153–7. Some idea of cost changes can be obtained from United Nations ECE, *Long-Term Trends and Problems*, p. 110.

[107] Dept of Trade, *Australian Steel Industry*, p. 8.

[108] 'The Manufacture of High Quality Steel Sheet at the Commonwealth Rolling Mills Pty Ltd Port Kembla', *BHP Review*, XVII, No. 1, p. 5.

[109] Hughes, *Australian Iron and Steel Industry*, pp. 158–9.

[110] *Australian Steel Industry*, pp. 13–14.

[111] L. Morgan, *The Canadian Primary Iron and Steel Industry*, Royal Commission on Canada's Economic Prospects, 1956, p. 18.

is probably nearly as good at the blast-furnace and open-hearth stages as in the US industry, is lower than in the US industry at the rolling mill level, probably by a fair margin.[112]

Turning to the problems of external economies, these can be seen most clearly at the time of the foundation of the steelworks. We have seen that the Australian economy was not organized to provide finance for new manufacturing industries, but BHP was in a unique position. It came to manufacturing as a large company, with great prestige obtained from mining and with large financial reserves, and it was thus able to turn successfully to the public for very large share and debenture issues. Even so, it was assisted by the newly formed Commonwealth Bank which underwrote the first few issues, a move which caused the *Argus* to comment: 'Such association with an industrial venture is not usual among Australian banks.'[113] For trained labour BHP had to look overseas, and for the first few years all the key workmen were Americans. Similarly, wire netting and galvanized sheet manufacture were begun with English labour. Moreover, the general organization of the work force in such a large industrial complex posed novel problems for Australia.[114] The local company began to use specialized construction firms only after the Second World War.[115] Company officers had to be sent overseas to obtain experience, and for ordinary skilled workers the Newcastle Technical College remained quite inadequate at least into the 1930s.[116] Probably the basic external diseconomy faced by BHP was the inadequate provision of market industries. The small demand made these difficult to establish, and they came slowly, mainly through BHP's own efforts. This was the problem that plagued BHP all through the 1920s, and it was not until after the mid-1930s that primary steel capacity could be fully used. It is true that some degree of vertical integration exists in most steel industries, but the small size of the Australian economy made a large degree necessary and also made its fulfilment a long costly process.

It can be concluded that during its history BHP has obtained significant internal and external economies of scale only gradually. Its reputation for cheap steel gained in the late 1930s arose because some other factors outweighed the lack of economies of scale, the

[112] Ibid., p. 19.

[113] Quoted in N. R. Wills, *Economic Development of the Australian Iron and Steel Industry*, Sydney, 1948, p. 102.

[114] Hughes, *Australian Iron and Steel Industry*, p. 77.

[115] Ibid., p. 156.

[116] Forster, *Industrial Development*, p. 188.

main ones being only partly within the company's control: cheap raw materials, good location, full use of capacity and the general movement of Australian costs and exchange rates. These factors carry less weight as the steel products pass through the rolling mills, and internal economies of scale become more important and more difficult to obtain.

CONCLUSION

Something has been done to illustrate the continuing, though changing, importance of economies of scale in Australian manufacturing. It is perhaps labouring the point to emphasize that for a considerable period economies of scale have been *the* problem. This situation arose as a result of the isolated position of the economy and the small and dispersed population, combined with the attempt to industrialize and establish a modern range of industries. The problem remains today: to a considerable degree perpetuated by an economic policy which has permitted the establishment of plants beyond the optimum number and/or insufficiently specialized. To attempt a quantitative measure of the diseconomies experienced by Australia is beyond the scope of this study, but they would seem to have been an important factor restricting the level and growth of productivity in the first fifty years of this century. Equally, the growth of productivity since the beginning of the 1950s has been connected with the reduction of these diseconomies: the experience of the steel industry has been described in this chapter, and it could easily be extended, especially to new industries like motor vehicles. However, diseconomies still remain heavy compared with some other countries. The effect of these international differences in scale is difficult to measure because there are usually very great differences in total environment between countries, but the problem can be reduced if a comparison is made between the United States and Canada, where scale does seem to be the most important single difference. J. H. Young, looking at these economies in the mid-1950s, wrote that 'American firms with American management and what in many cases is in effect the equivalent of an American working force, producing for a market which in many cases has American tastes, find that highly mechanized production methods which are economical and profitable in America are not profitable in Canada';[117] and

[117] J. H. Young, 'Comparative Economic Development: Canada and the United States', *American Economic Review*, XLV, 1955, p. 91.

he concluded that 'it could be argued with some validity that (the size of the market) appears to be the most important single factor' in explaining their substantial differences in productivity.[118] And Canada is not as badly off as other similar-sized economies because of its ability to use American repairs, parts, training, etc.[119] In their detailed industrial study for the Canadian Royal Commission, Fullerton and Hampson are prepared to go further than Young and risk a quantitative estimate of Canada's disadvantage. They observe that output per man hour in Canadian secondary industry in 1957 was some 35 per cent to 40 per cent below that of the United States, and conclude that 'it is obviously impossible to measure precisely the effects of smaller scale and less specialized operations on the gap. . . . However, in our judgement these factors account for not less than three-quarters of this difference'.[120] Such considerations as these suggest that very substantial economies of scale are still to be obtained in Australian manufacturing.

Economies of scale are dynamic, not just because they operate through time and make difficult the attainment of static equilibrium positions, but because they themselves are the product of a constantly changing technology. Their effect on manufacturing depends not only on various aspects of size, but on the state of technology and the composition of manufacturing output. It thus seems possible that the range of simple industries existing in Australia in the first decade of this century obtained economies of scale nearer the optimum than those obtained by a wider range of industries at a later date. The benefits from the expansion of the market were being outweighed by the establishment of new industries, in which economies of scale became increasingly important and more difficult to obtain. It is also possible that developments in technology in the twentieth century may have worked against the small market and the small economy: certainly change has not been all one way, but changes within industries like chemicals, steel and aircraft have strongly favoured increased scale. How technology will influence economies of scale in the future is unknown, but it is clear that although market growth is giving Australia increased economies, the optimum itself is changing. Future changes in technology may

[118] J. H. Young dissertation, quoted in Balassa, *Theory of Economic Integration*, p. 112.

[119] G. Rosenbluth as cited in ibid., p. 130.

[120] Fullerton and Hampson, *Canadian Secondary Manufacturing*, p. 93. It is, of course, not simply the size of the Canadian market that is relevant here, but also the number of firms sharing the market.

worsen Australia's relative position. In the foreseeable future, of much more importance will be the economic policy adopted to cope with a domestic market which will be small by international standards. Canada's experience makes plain that a population of twenty million provides no automatic solution. There is great scope and need for innovations in economic policy, and given Australia's circumstances, the example of other countries will be of limited use only.

Chapter 4

THE MARKET STRUCTURE OF AUSTRALIAN MANUFACTURING INDUSTRY, 1914 to 1963–4[1]

Pat Brown and Helen Hughes

The conviction that the ownership of Australian manufacturing industry is highly concentrated is almost as old as manufacturing itself. Colonial legislatures began to concern themselves with monopolies and monopolistic practices when the depression of the 1890s made monopoly a focus for moral indignation and political prescription, and by the 1920s federal parliamentary enquiries had added impressive volumes of evidence. Tariff Board reports, albeit incidentally, continued the accumulation of data, and systematic academic studies concerned with the economic rather than the political and social implications of concentration began in the 1950s.[2]

The economic significance of concentration lies in the presumption that pure competition is impaired when the concentration of ownership of industry is high. The allocation of factors of production is then not optimized, prices are distorted, and the rate of industrial growth may fall below that which could have been achieved under

[1] This chapter was read in an early version as a paper at the 40th meeting of the Australian and New Zealand Association for the Advancement of Science at Christchurch, New Zealand, in January 1968. We are indebted to Noel Butlin and Colin Forster for critical comments.

[2] A visiting economist, Edith T. Penrose, drew attention to concentration in Australia in 'Towards a Theory of Industrial Concentration', *Economic Record*, XXXII, 1956, pp. 64–77, and 'Foreign Investment and the Growth of the Firm', *Economic Journal*, LXVI, 1956, pp. 222–3. In March 1961 A. Hunter published 'Restrictive Practices and Monopolies in Australia', *Economic Record*, XXXVII, 1961, pp. 25–52, and in 1962 M. Brunt's calculation of concentration in manufacturing appeared in P. H. Karmel and Maureen Brunt, *The Structure of the Australian Economy*, Cheshire, Melbourne, 1962. This work has been taken further by Kyoko Sheridan in 'An Estimate of the Business Concentration of Australian Manufacturing Industries', *Economic Record*, 44, 1968, pp. 26–41.

competitive conditions. There is no simple correlation between concentration and competition; the degree of concentration merely establishes the framework within which various forms of competition operate. This chapter seeks to analyse the trends in concentration during the period of industrial growth since federation, to relate them to the principal factors which have made Australian industry relatively highly concentrated, to examine trends in competition in the light of the structure of markets for manufactured products, and to consider the implications that such trends have for economic policy.

PROBLEMS OF MEASURING CONCENTRATION

Concentration can be measured by the degree to which a small number of firms accounts for a given proportion of the output of an industry or of its sectors. The best measure of concentration is value added in production, but appropriate value added figures are not available for a comprehensive range of industrial groups in company reports, and they are not available in sufficient detail in official production statistics. Public company reports do provide a great deal of information about paid up capital and capital assets which would appear to be the next best measure of concentration, but it is usually impossible to break these down into relevant industries and subgroups. Holding companies rarely divulge details of their subsidiaries' assets, and information about unincorporated businesses which still produce a substantial proportion of Australian manufacturing output, dates back only to 1961.[3] Official production statistics do not give breakdowns of capital values by industrial sub-groups. The Commonwealth Bureau of Census and Statistics' annual *Production Bulletin, Secondary Industries*, covers all industries and gives the number of plants and average employment figures. These are broken down into seven categories from 'less than four persons (where power is used)' to 'more than 100 persons', so that it is possible to calculate the approximate number of factories required to account

[3] Under the 1961–62 Companies Act, NSW No. 71 of 1961; Vic. No. 6839 of 1961; Qld No. 55 of 1961; SA No. 56 of 1962; WA No. 82 of 1961–2; Tas. 1962 holding companies can either return a separate profit and loss account for each subsidiary or a consolidated account eliminating all intercompany transactions. Only the name and place of incorporation of each subsidiary need be stated if the second alternative is chosen. (Ninth Schedule, 4.) 'Companies not having a share capital' must lodge an annual return with the Registrar of Companies (Section 159) and include a copy of last audited balance sheet and profit and loss account in English (Form 49).

for a given percentage of employment in each sub-group.[4] Some plants may contribute more to total value added than to employment in an industrial sub-group, and average employment figures are not a good basis for comparison in seasonal industries, but close correlation has been found in other countries among indexes of concentration based on average employment and those based on the contribution to value added and capital employed where data for all three are available.[5] A concentration index based on employment therefore seems to be the best approach to a study covering Australian industry since the beginning of the century.

The index is, of course, very imperfect. The Commonwealth Statistician's industrial sub-group classifications, mainly selected on the basis of the similarity of the physical characteristics of inputs, are not well suited to measuring concentration. Although there is some correlation with the cross elasticity of supply, many of the sub-groups include a variety of industrial products which are not substitutes in use, and which should therefore be split up for the measurement of concentration. Other products which are close substitutes are included in a number of separate sub-groups. Apparently oddly assorted industries have to be grouped together to avoid the revelation of the identity of individual units, and a miscellaneous 'other' sub-group is included in twelve of the sixteen principal industrial groups. Since statistics are not normally published under specific sub-group headings unless there are at least three returning units, the 'other' sub-groups generally include monopolies and in some cases duopolies. Repairers are classified together with manufacturers, and this makes for particular difficulties in motor vehicles in early years, and in the machinery and engineering sub-groups where a great deal of competition in repairing exists side by side with considerable concentration in manufacturing. There has been almost continuous minor re-classification, and there was a major break and re-classification in 1930–1. But while there is no doubt that many of the sub-groups should be re-classified according to the cross elasticities of supply and demand, the re-classification of all returning units

[4] The method of calculating a concentration index from grouped employment data was developed by G. Rosenbluth, *Concentration in Canadian Manufacturing Industries*, Princeton University Press, Princeton, 1957, see pp. 11–12, and Appendix B, pp. 140–6.

[5] G. Rosenbluth, 'Measures of Concentration', in National Bureau of Economic Research, *Business Concentration and Price Policy*, Princeton University Press, Princeton, 1955, pp. 89–92, and Rosenbluth, *Concentration in Candian Manufacturing*, pp. 12 and 13.

over a period of some sixty years was too formidable a task, and it required access to confidential individual statistical returns. The major official classifications have therefore been retained, although an attempt has been made to relate sub-groups through the re-classification of 1930–1. Government, municipal and private sectors have been amalgamated where necessary. Because of these changes only 160 of the 167 classifications of 1963–4 have been used.

The main limitation of the index is due to the fact that the Commonwealth Statistician's figures are for plants and not for firms. This of course underestimates the extent of concentration to the degree to which firms own more than one plant in an industrial sub-group. The ownership of a number of plants by one firm is common, and it is not unusual for a firm to have a plant in several of the six states. Some firms have several plants in one state.[6] But it was found that it was possible to identify firms as well as plants from company reports and other sources of information only for large-scale plants and for recent years, and this would have precluded the measurement of concentration in the whole manufacturing sector and over the years since federation. The measurement of concentration by plants therefore became the only practicable choice.

The level of concentration at which competition can be said to be impaired varies from industry to industry, as well as from country to country, since the size of the market as well as the nature of the production technique influences the number of firms which can effectively operate in an industry or sub-group. Under the United Kingdom restrictive practices legislation a firm controlling a third of the product of an industrial sector is liable to investigation by the Monopolies Commission, and this level of concentration is frequently also used as an indicator of financial control of an industry, but the employment of a third of the work force of an industry appears to be too low to indicate a level of concentration seriously impairing competition. A 50 per cent contribution to output or employment is more commonly used as an indicator of concentration and therefore enables some comparisons with concentration in the United King-

[6] Felt and Textiles of Australia Limited in 1952 operated twenty-three factories making footwear through ten subsidiary companies. There were six companies and fourteen plants in Victoria, three companies and six plants in New South Wales and one company and three plants in Western Australia. Commonwealth of Australia, Department of National Development, Division of Industrial Development, *The Structure and Capacity of Australian Manufacturing Industries*, Melbourne, 1952, pp. 404–5.

dom and the United States as well as with Australian studies of concentration by firms,[7] and a 50 per cent index was therefore calculated for Australian manufacturing for 1926–7 and 1963–4. It seemed particularly useful for the analysis of individual sub-groups, eliminating the problems of small units such as repairers in engineering and thus directing attention to effective control. At 80 per cent of employment, however, there could be no doubt of effective control, and this was the index calculated for 1914, 1926–7, 1948–9 and 1963–4. These years were chosen for their comparative stability, and 1963–4 was the most recent year for which figures were available when the calculations were made.[8] This index also enables a comparison to be made with concentration in Canadian industry.

To compensate for the measurement of concentration by plants rather than by firms it was assumed that firms owned two to five plants, and industries in which ten or less plants accounted for 80 per cent of employment were regarded as highly concentrated. Industries with eleven to thirty plants accounting for 80 per cent were regarded as concentrated, those with thirty-one to 200 plants as unconcentrated, and those with more than 200 plants as very unconcentrated.[9]

All concentration indexes have built-in biases in the sense that the number of units in an industry influences the index. An industry containing few units will have a low concentration index although it may be relatively less concentrated than a large industry containing a large number of units. The number of plants in each industrial sub-group has therefore been included in all the principal tables. Concentration indexes have a further drawback that the numerical index is related inversely to the level of concentration: a high numerical index number means that the level of concentration is low; a low numerical index number means that the level of concentration is high. To avoid confusion, all text references are to the actual level of concentration, not to the index number.

[7] In Karmel and Brunt, *Structure*, a 50 per cent concentration concept for firms for 1957–8 is used.

[8] Sheridan, *Economic Record*, 44, uses an 80 per cent concentration index, calculated on Rosenbluth's lines, for concentration by firms in 1961–2.

[9] In Karmel and Brunt, *Structure*, p. 78, Brunt classifies as 'highly concentrated', 'fairly concentrated' or 'slightly concentrated', industries in which the first four, eight or twenty firms respectively account for 50 per cent of total employment in industry. Sheridan, *Economic Record*, 44, p. 41, allocates industries according to the number of firms accounting for 80 per cent of employment and/or gross output as follows—oligopolistic: high 3–5, moderate 6–10, low 11–21; unconcentrated 22–50; competitive 51–200; high-competitive more than 220 firms.

TRENDS IN CONCENTRATION

Industrial growth and development dominate the changes in concentration in Australian manufacturing since 1914. The manufacturing sector has grown from 15,427 plants and an average employment of 331,579 in 1914, to 59,375 and 1,217,520 respectively in 1963–4. The number of plants with more than a hundred employees grew from 554 to 1,946 over the same period. Manufacturing has become more capital intensive and complex, inter-industry linkages are more important, and sophisticated services such as advertising play a much more considerable role in the production of a greatly enlarged array of products.

Between 1914 and 1963–4 there was a slight increase in the proportion of the work force employed in highly concentrated industries (with ten plants and under accounting for 80 per cent of employment), and some decrease in the proportion of the work force employed in very unconcentrated industries (with over 200 plants accounting for 80 per cent of employment). If the group in which eleven to thirty plants account for 80 per cent of employment is added to the highly concentrated group, then there is almost no change at all in the concentration level between 1914 and 1963–4 (see Table 4.1).

Because of the changing composition of industrial output it is very difficult to follow concentration changes in individual industries. The Commonwealth Statistician's number of industrial sub-groups increased from 102 in 1914 to 167 in 1963–4. Of these only fifty-one can be isolated over the entire period, and a further twenty-six can be followed since 1926–7, making a total of seventy-seven. The fifty-one sub-groups consist mainly of industries which were well established by the 1900s, and the twenty-six largely of those which began producing in the 1920s, and generalizations based on them have limited application.

From 1914 to 1963–4, a period of expansion in manufacturing, twenty-one sub-groups showed a change in concentration of less than ten units with an almost equal number of increases and decreases, and twenty sub-groups actually showed an increase in concentration. From 1926–7 to 1963–4 sub-groups with decreased concentration outnumbered those with increased concentration by nineteen to seven, but changes were less than ten in one-third of the sub-groups (see Table 4.2).

The constancy of concentration levels was, indeed, partly due to diverging trends. There are two clearly discernible tendencies in maintaining or increasing a high degree of concentration between

TABLE 4.1. *Concentration at 80 per cent level by Sub-groups, Plants and Employees, 1914, 1926–7, 1948–9 and 1963–4*

Concentration index[a]	Sub-groups		Plants		Employees		Cumulative percentage of employees
	Number	Per cent	Number	Per cent	Number	Per cent	
10 and under							
1914	28	28·6	502	3·3	26,114	7·9	8
1926–27	31	26·3	658	3·0	39,190	8·4	8
1948–49	44	27·0	904	2·3	94,899	10·6	11
1963–64	40	25·0	937	1·6	151,336	12·4	12
11 to 30							
1914	35	35·7	1,768	11·5	73,129	22·1	30
1926–27	41	34·7	2,719	12·6	127,704	27·3	36
1948–49	42	25·8	3,010	7·5	168,380	18·8	29
1963–64	43	26·9	3,702	6·2	195,487	16·1	29
31 to 200							
1914	23	23·5	3,855	25·0	80,994	24·4	54
1926–27	34	28·8	6,805	31·5	159,580	34·1	70
1948–49	65	39·9	15,778	39·3	379,561	42·3	72
1963–64	59	36·9	13,723	23·1	375,479	30·8	59
Over 200							
1914	12	12·2	9,302	60·3	151,342	45·6	100
1926–27	12	10·2	11,397	52·8	140,773	30·1	100
1948–49	12	7·4	20,378	50·8	254,963	28·4	100
1963–64	18	11·3	41,013	69·0	495,218	40·7	100

[a] A measure of the number of plants accounting for 80 per cent of an industry's employment. Where necessary the number of plants has been rounded to the nearest unit.

Source: Calculated from Table 1, H. Hughes and P. Brown, *The Market Structure of Australian Manufacturing Industry 1914 to 1963-4*, 40th ANZAAS Congress paper, 1968.

1914 (or 1926–7) and 1963–4. A relatively unimportant movement is in industries which have become obsolete and declined in relative and even in absolute importance. In these industries an increase in concentration has come about as a result of the contraction in the number of plants and it has generally been accompanied by a fall in the number of employees per plant. Thus changes in transport have led to very large concentration increases in saddlery and harness making, in horse-drawn vehicle manufacture, and in chaff cutting. The decline in handcraft industries has given rise to higher concentration in cooperage and basketware, whereas changes in taste have meant increased concentration in hats and caps, umbrellas and

TABLE 4.2. *Changes in Concentration Index at 80 per cent level 1914, or 1926–7, to 1963–4*

Change in concentration index	Number of sub-groups with: Increased concentration	Decreased concentration	Total
1914 to 1963–64			
Less than 10	11	10	21
10–19	2	6	8
20–29	2	2	4
30–39	0	3	3
40–49	1	2	3
50–99	1	3	4
100 and over	3	5	8
Total	20	31	51
1926–27 to 1963–64			
Less than 10	5	4	9
10–19	1	5	6
20–29	1	2	3
30–49	0	0	0
50–99	0	4	4
100 and over	0	4	4
Total	7	19	26

Source: As for Table 4.1.

walking sticks, and in picture-frame making. But concentration has also been maintained or increased in a number of industries which have grown in importance. In two of these industries, matches and gasworks, total employment fell between 1926–7 and 1963–4 although employment per plant grew. (See Appendix A for details of sub-groups in which both total employment and employment per plant increased without any decrease in concentration.)

The trend towards decreased concentration was also composed of two separate tendencies. In nineteen sub-groups, the average employment per plant increased as concentration decreased, suggesting a rise in the size and number of plants required to account for 80 per cent of employment. In twenty-five other sub-groups, however, average employment per plant did not increase with decreased concentration, suggesting a marginal proliferation of small plants, and this is borne out by the nature of many of the industries in this category (see Appendix A).

Between 1948–9 and 1963–4, 152 sub-groups can be traced, and in these concentration increased in seventy-two and decreased in seventy (see Table 4.3). In 1963–4 the seventy-two sub-groups with increased concentration employed 37 per cent of the work force of the 152 groups traced, and those with decreased concentration, 57 per cent. Although many of the increases and decreases came in industries which showed a consistent tendency in one or the other direction

TABLE 4.3. *Changes in Concentration Index at 80 per cent level 1948–9 to 1963–4*

Change in concentration index	Number of sub-groups with: Increased concentration	Decreased concentration	Total
Less than 5	28	18	46
5–9	15	14	29
10–19	12	15	27
20–29	3	7	10
30–39	4	1	5
40–49	3	1	4
50–99	4	3	7
100 and over	3	11	14
Total	72	70	142

Source: As for Table 4.1.

over the whole period 1914 to 1963–4, there were many exceptions. In the post-war years, concentration increased in particular in food and clothing industries and fell in building materials and paints, ferrous metals and rubber goods. Within the new industries which expanded greatly in the 1940s and 1950s there were also two opposed trends. There was increased concentration in industries such as

TABLE 4.4. *Changes in Concentration at 80 per cent level by Main Industrial Groups, 1948–9 to 1963–4*

Industrial group	Sub-groups with increased concentration		Sub-groups with decreased concentration	
	Number	Employment in 1963–64	Number	Employment in 1963–64
Mining and quarry products	2	3,453	5	18,283
Bricks, pottery, glass	1	10,799	3	11,044
Chemicals, dyes etc.	7	22,571	3	10,898
Industrial metals, engineering	6	33,702	20	456,662
Precious metals	1	2,849	0	0
Textiles	4	48,380	5	17,482
Skins and leather	5	12,144	1	128
Clothing	9	98,988	5	7,050
Food, drink and tobacco	20	75,805	7	56,747
Sawmills, joinery	7	34,547	4	24,135
Furniture, bedding	1	16,068	4	6,653
Paper, stationery printing	2	47,759	7	31,062
Rubber products	0	0	2	20,382
Musical instruments	1	64	2	720
Miscellaneous products	4	6,785	2	5,488
Heat, light and power	2	15,676	0	0
Total	72	429,590	70	666,734

Source: As for Table 4.1.

chemical fertilizers, pharmaceuticals and toilet preparations, and oils, and decreased concentrations in the rapidly expanding electrical, engineering and consumer durable industries (see Table 4.4).

The 50 per cent concentration index throws further light on the principal trends. Firstly, it highlights industries which have been concentrated since 1926–7 or their inception, and which have remained so. Secondly, the 50 per cent concentration index sharply reduces the percentage of sub-groups and employees in unconcentrated industries. In 1963–4, seventy-seven of the 160 sub-groups, accounting for 72 per cent of the total work force, had more than thirty plants employing 80 per cent of the work force in each sub-group. Only thirty-four of the 160 sub-groups had more than thirty plants employing 50 per cent of the work force of each sub-group, and these thirty-four sub-groups accounted for only 49 per cent of the total work force (see Table 4.5). In nineteen of these thirty-four

TABLE 4.5. *Concentration at 50 per cent level by Sub-groups and Employees, 1963–4*

Concentration index	Sub-groups		Employees	
	Number	Per cent	Number	Per cent
10 and under	90	56·25	401,250	33·0
11 to 30	36	22·5	218,448	17·9
31 to 200	26	16·25	405,831	33·3
Over 200	8	5·0	191,991	15·8

Source: As for Table 4.1.

sub-groups, and in sixteen others, a large difference between the 80 per cent and 50 per cent index suggests a pattern of industrial structure in which a small number of plants produce the bulk of output (probably considerably higher a proportion than the 50 per cent of the work force they employ), while a large number of smaller plants on their periphery serve specialized markets and, in the case of metals and engineering, do repair rather than manufacturing work. This is true not only for such large and capital-intensive industries as motor bodies and agricultural machinery, but it appears to be becoming increasingly important in traditionally unconcentrated industries such as tanning and clothing manufacture.

Much work remains to be done on concentration indexes, and conclusions at this stage must be tentative, but some can be drawn. First, the overall level of concentration by plants has remained fairly constant between 1914 and 1963–4 (see Table 4.1). Second, a number of industries which were highly concentrated from 1914 or their inception remained so throughout the period. These were relatively capital-intensive industries, but not all capital-intensive industries behaved in this fashion: some were not highly concentrated at their inception, while others such as non-ferrous metal refining, building materials and tobacco became more unconcentrated with time. Third, the overall picture of almost constant concentration ratios results from compensatory changes within industries. Some industries became more concentrated while the concentration in others declined, and some industries moved towards greater or lesser concentration and back again within the period. Leaving aside the declining industries which showed increased concentration as their relative importance decreased and industries which render services rather than manufacture such as dry cleaning and motor-vehicle repair, there does seem to be a discernible wave pattern in the changes in concentration. As an industry grows in importance, the number of plants increases, particularly if growth is occurring in a period of general economic prosperity. With a depression or even a recession there appears to be a rationalization and consolidation in the number of plants which, however, may expand in the course of another period of general prosperity. The wave pattern varies from industry to industry because technological changes and changes in taste for the products also influence an industry's rate of growth. To some extent this wave pattern is a reflection of the weakness of the index in which the number of plants itself influences the level of concentration, but it also appears to describe a genuine causal relationship between the rate of overall industrial growth and changes in concentration.[10]

Studies of concentration by firms confirm that industries which were concentrated by plants in the 1950s and 1960s were even more highly concentrated by firms.[11] The re-classification of industries in these studies from the Commonwealth Statistician's grouping into economically more meaningful categories also reveals some highly concentrated industries such as ready-mix concrete, electric wires and cables, milk products, glass and glass products and sugar refining

[10] J. A. Bushnell, *Australian Company Mergers, 1946–59*, Melbourne University Press, 1961, pp. 88–99, suggests that recession impaired merger activity, but while this is true for the immediate timing of mergers, recessions nevertheless give the impetus to many mergers which are only consummated some years later.

[11] Karmel and Brunt, *Structure*, pp. 82–3; Sheridan, *Economic Record*, 44; and E. L. Wheelwright and J. Miskelly, *Anatomy of Australian Manufacturing Industry*, Law Book Co., Sydney, 1967, pp. 105, 121 and 142.

which do not emerge as highly concentrated either in the 80 per cent index or in the 50 per cent index, because in the official statistics they are either grouped with other industries or because they are placed in 'other' at the end of an industrial group. Another aspect of concentration studies, the concentration of ownership of industry, suggests that there is also a strong tendency towards vertical integration, horizontal cross ownership of industries, and an overlap between the ownership of manufacturing and other, notably service, firms,[12] all supported by interlocking directorships.[13] This too might be expected to restrict the mobility of factors of production by distorting the competitive mechanism.

Overall it is doubtful whether trends in concentration by firms and in the competitive framework have differed markedly from trends in concentration by plants, although at first sight there appears to be some evidence in favour of increased concentration and a less competitive structure. The sheer size of the very large corporations, the newsworthiness of mergers, and the very weight of studies of concentration suggests that the manufacturing sector has become less competitive over the years. But there is evidence to the contrary. Large corporations towered above their contemporaries in the relatively small markets of the 1900s and 1920s. Mergers have always been a feature of industrial growth and they have frequently led to more vigorous competition. In industries such as non-ferrous metals, an increase in the number of plants has been an accurate indication of an increase in competition between firms. Technological change has kept entry open and competition in existence within such important industries as chemicals where an increase in the number of plants has also been indicative of increased competition among firms. Technological change has also enabled a new dimension of competition across traditional industry divisions. The competition between glass and tinplate containers has brought two great corporations, Australian Consolidated Industries and the Broken Hill Proprietary, into competition. Copper wire producers compete with aluminium wire, copper producers are faced with increasing competition from synthetic materials, and aluminium is vying with coated steels in some markets. It is also important to remember that while there has been some decline in the weight of the very unconcentrated industries (those with 200 or more plants), they still employed in 1963–4 41 per cent of the manufacturing work force (see Table 4.1). Thus Australian manufacturing industry still has, as it did in the 1900s, a large uncon-

[12] Wheelwright and Miskelly, *Anatomy*, passim.
[13] H. Rolfe, *The Controllers*, Cheshire, Melbourne, 1967, pp. 77 and passim.

centrated sector where relatively small firms, usually with one plant only, predominate.

REASONS FOR CONCENTRATION

The smallness of the Australian market, and its geographical isolation, are without question the principal reasons for the concentration of manufacturing industry. On the eve of federation the total population of the Australian colonies was 3·8 million, of which New South Wales accounted for 1·4 million, Victoria 1·2 million and Queensland 500,000 people. It was not surprising, therefore, that manufacturers were among the strongest supporters of federation in the 1890s, and the quickened pace of industrial growth in the 1900s was to some extent at least a response to the increased opportunities of wider markets.[14]

Federation and the First World War stimulated the establishment of a number of capital-intensive, heavy industries, but in spite of their raw material advantages the Australian market did not become large enough to enable iron and steel and non-ferrous metal products to be produced at internationally competitive prices until the 1930s. Even then economies of scale could only be reaped under monopoly conditions.

The iron and steel industry, and the steel-products industries which grew around it, were unable to compete with imports throughout the 1920s, and many steel products continued to be at a disadvantage until the Second World War because of the smallness of the local market and the lack of opportunity for exports. The problems of heavy iron and steel were, however, solved in the mid-1930s when the total market grew to the equivalent of one million tons of ingot steel a year and the Broken Hill Proprietary Company Limited, by taking over the Australian Iron and Steel Company, was able to rationalize its production for the national market.[15] Raw material advantage still played a part in the technical competitiveness of the steel industry, and in that of non-ferrous metals which also became competitive during the 1930s.

After the Second World War the minimum efficient scale of steel production moved up to about two and a half million tons of ingot steel a year. Australian demand reached towards five million tons of

[14] H. Hughes, 'Federalism and Industrial Development in Australia', *Australian Journal of Politics and History*, X, 1964, pp. 323–8.

[15] H. Hughes, *The Australian Iron and Steel Industry, 1848–1962*, Melbourne University Press, 1964, pp. 109–18.

ingot steel equivalent a year and there were good opportunities for exports. It appeared for a time that there would be room for two steel producers in Australia. This was the case in copper refining and manufacturing, and a new firm came into production. But even relatively specialized steelworks are now moving to capacities of five million to seven million tons of ingot steel a year, and at this level it is not possible to benefit from the external economies of scale in research and development which steel producing countries with large domestic markets enjoy, so that the capture of new export markets would be extremely difficult. The Australian iron and steel industry is, moreover, losing its raw material advantage since iron pellet prices at the blast-furnace will not, with the use of very large bulk carriers, vary greatly with distance from the ore fields.[16] Only a specialized steelworks, vertically integrated with its customers, could hope to enter steel production in these circumstances.

Iron and steel, because of the very great economies of scale in production, gives an extreme illustration of the limitations of a small market, but the technical requirements of relatively large-scale production extend far beyond heavy industries.[17]

The Australian market is not only small, it is, in spite of the concentration of the population in the larger cities of the south-eastern states, widely dispersed over the continent. At the turn of the century communications were slow, and internal freight charges, predominantly by sea, were high. In 1906 freight costs were higher between Melbourne and Adelaide than between Melbourne and London.[18] This meant a very fragmented market with a consequent opportunity for local monopolies for bulky goods and for those difficult to transport. Building materials, food processing and brewing are examples of industries which enjoyed considerable local monopoly in the 1900s and retained it into the 1920s and 1930s. But in the last thirty years a continuation of the tendency towards an increased concentration of the population in the south-eastern states together with a great improvement in the efficiency of communications[19] have

[16] H. Hughes and P. Brown, 'Question Marks over the Iron Ore Bonanza', 'Japan Sets the Pace in Steel' and 'Exporting Steel', *Australian Financial Review*, March 23–25, 1966; and 'The World Outlook for Steel', 'Marketing Australian Ore' and 'A Second Steel Industry for Australia', *Australian Financial Review*, May 9–11, 1967.

[17] For further discussion of economies of scale, see Chapter 3.

[18] Report from the Royal Commission on Ocean Shipping Service; together with Proceedings, Minutes of Evidence, and Appendices, *Parliamentary Papers*, 1906, III, pp. 1044–5.

[19] This does not necessarily mean that the relative cost of transport has fallen

tended to create a national market for many products previously concentrated on a state or even regional basis. Thus some relatively capital-intensive industries have become more concentrated, while others such as sugar refining, which might have become less concentrated with the absolute growth of concentration in the outlying states, have remained concentrated. This is not to say that advantages of production and monopoly on a state basis have disappeared. Considerable state encouragement of industrial development includes direct assistance, for example in the provision of low-cost electric power, and such measures as preference in state government contracts. Gentlemen's agreements to remain within given territorial spheres have also tended to preserve state monopolies. Nevertheless, concentration on a state basis is being constantly eroded as communications improve and the optimum technical scale of production grows.

Transport improvements have also led to increased concentration in industries processing rural products, but while this may have reduced competition, it has also reduced the extent of local monopsony which rural processing firms enjoyed in early years. As flour milling became more capital intensive it became more centralized at ports with a decline in the number of plants and firms, and particularly of those in rural areas. In vegetable and fruit canning the advantages of large-scale production were, until the early 1950s, offset by the difficulties of transporting fresh fruit and vegetables over long distances. The difficulty was overcome by fast and refrigerated road transport, and a number of food-canning works have moved from country to urban centres, reducing the number of plants, but also reducing each plant's monopsony position. Industries such as brewing, fruit and vegetable canning and flour milling have moved to large urban centres not only to take advantage of increased internal economies of scale but also to take advantage of the many external economies of agglomeration. The importance of these latter economies has grown as plants have tended to produce a greater variety of products and to cater for national markets and for exports, and hence become more dependent on a number of industrial and commercial services. Agricultural producers have benefited from increasingly competitive bidding for their products, and competition has replaced the tight marketing cartels of the 1900s.

---

but the scattered data available suggests that there probably has been such a fall. See Inter-State Commission, Prices Investigations Report No. 3, *Parliamentary Papers*, 1917–18–19, V, p. 118, for pre-1914 marketing costs.

In recent years improvements in transport have even led to the creation of national markets for such products as cement, which until the 1950s were thought of as having principally regional markets.[20] Among perishable goods, biscuits and ice cream have shown a similar trend, with a corresponding increase in plant concentration.

The existing firm in an industry naturally enjoys advantages in manufacture and sales over potential rivals, and the growth of internal and external economies of scale with the growth of the market has in many cases strengthened its monopoly position in industry. The exploitation of state markets by the multiplication of plants in glass, paper and steel as soon as they became ready for development, and often ahead of the demand to ensure an existing firm's predominance has been common. Although such expansion has been frequently obtained at the cost of national efficiency, the firms themselves are hardly to blame for acceding to state threats and requests.[21] Nor is it likely that this maintenance of firms' monopolies is less efficient than the multiplication of firms as well as plants, which, given state attitudes, would have been the alternative. Some of the minor monopolies such as salt and matches, and tight oligopolies such as paints, have over the years shown an ability to retain their position by marketing manoeuvres. Industries somewhat less prone to the advantages of large-scale production have been at an advantage if, as a result of vertical integration, their raw material supplier was the only one in Australia. This has been true for a large range of steel, non-ferrous metal and chemical products.

On the other hand it would be easy to exaggerate the importance of the existing firm as a barrier to entry. The years have seen the break up of monopoly, duopoly and tight oligopoly throughout manufacturing industry. Most frequently the initiative has come from large international companies which not only have the resources to compete with existing firms, but what is more important at times, the will to do so. The entry of a large number of foreign corporations, many of them of United States origin, into Australia from the 1950s served to loosen up concentration in a wide range of capital-intensive industries with a particularly strong impact in differentiated products

[20] L. J. Vincent, 'Politics Move in on Cement Supply Deal', *Australian Financial Review*, September 5, 1967.

[21] The establishment of steelworks in South Australia and Western Australia when Victoria would have been a much more economic location was due to state pressures. Hughes, *The Australian Iron and Steel Industry*, pp. 118–20 and 187.

(and associated goods) in which international corporations tend to operate. A decline of concentration of ownership by firms could thus be regarded as one of the benefits of foreign investment, but it is doubtful, given the conjunction of oligopolistic international corporations and Australian tariff making, whether the overall gains of an increased number of firms which has accompanied the increase in entry have lowered overall costs or improved the structure of Australian industry.[22]

The entry of new firms, whether local or foreign, has been stimulated in Australia since the 1920s by the presence and prospects of tariffs. Once an industry was established, Australia's made-to-measure tariff system ensured that the tariff would be pitched at the point where the marginal firm in an industry could just make a profit, leaving a substantial profit for the intra-marginal producer. By emphasizing economic efficiency through price competition within Australia, and by placing a high value on consumer sovereignty in terms of a wide choice of products, this policy has from the beginning of the Tariff Board's activities tended to ignore the needs of technical efficiency in an internationally competitive sense.

Already in the 1920s hosiery manufacturers were protesting against tariff increases on the grounds that this would allow excessive entry into the industry and render it more uncompetitive with imports by allowing small manufacturing units and excess capacity to be created. Their pleas were ignored, tariffs rose, and so did entry into the industry.[23] A similar pattern was established in a number of consumer durable goods such as electrical appliances and in producer goods in the engineering industry which accordingly had very high costs compared with foreign large-scale producers. After the Second World War the virtual prohibition of imports by import licensing encouraged local, and particularly foreign firms, to enter production very freely. Entry was further encouraged by the government policies which clearly annunciated that production should not only be Australian, but within Australia, competitive.

These policies affected many producer goods such as agricultural

[22] D. T. Brash, *American Investment in Australian Industry*, ANUP, Canberra, 1966, concludes that on the whole the availability of American parent-company technical knowledge leads to reduced costs in Australia directly (pp. 173–5) and indirectly (pp. 193–202). This is undoubtedly so, but if the structure of industry was not determined by unrestricted entry of oligopolistic overseas (and local) firms in conjunction with tariffs, costs might be lower still. To this point Brash gives but small attention (pp. 269–71).

[23] K. Sheridan, 'A History of Lincoln Mills (Australia) Ltd 1922–1962' unpublished M.Econ. thesis, ANU, 1966, pp. 28–31.

and earth-moving machinery and many engineering products, but their effect was most pervasive in the development of heavy chemicals and, more recently, of aluminium refining. Three aluminium smelters, two of 40,000 ton capacity and one of 72,000 ton capacity, have been built in Australia by three large international corporations.[24] It has been estimated that with given raw material and other input costs, the cost of production in aluminium smelting falls from $US492 per ton of output for a 30,000 ton plant to $US463 a ton for a 60,000 ton plant and $US450 a ton for a 100,000 ton plant.[25] By 1970 the average smelter capacity in North America will be about 135,000 tons per unit per year and twenty individual plants will have an output exceeding Australia's total estimated demand for one year.[26] The Australian aluminium industry will need heavy protection to enable it to survive. It is estimated that total demand in Australia will reach 110,000 tons per annum by 1970.[27] New plants are now above 200,000 tons a year capacity and still growing in size for reasons of technical efficiency. There can be no illusions about the time it will take for demand to reach a point at which three plants can operate competitively in an international context.

In consumer durable industries import licensing first led to entry by local firms. Some of these came in to supply state markets, expanding to national markets as their production grew. In almost every case initial market saturation was accompanied by a proliferation of firms and plants in the late 1940s and early 1950s, but many of these industries became more concentrated as the first demand surge became satisfied and marginal firms went to the wall. The entry of overseas firms was also stimulated, particularly in motor-vehicle manufacture. By the late 1950s the Australian domestic market for passenger cars was about 400,000 a year. The economics of engine block production are such that 200,000 to 250,000 units a year have to be produced for economies of scale to begin to be reached. In 1954 Bain concluded that in motor vehicles the United States could only afford to have a small number of producers if technical efficiency was to be achieved;[28] the number of new passenger-car registrations

[24] R. Dowie, *Industry in Australia, Aluminium*, Longmans, Adelaide, 1967, pp. 22–4.

[25] United Nations, Department of Economic and Social Affairs, *Pre-investment Data for the Aluminium Industry*, 1966, p. 10.

[26] Alcoa of Australia Proprietory Limited, *Aluminium Industry Protection Proposals*, 1965, pp. iv–vi.

[27] Dowie, *Aluminium*, p. 26.

[28] J. S. Bain, 'Economies of Scale, Concentration and Entry' *American Economic Review*, 44, 1954, p. 32.

was then already approaching six million annually.[29] In Australia, taking into account some export possibilities for an all-Australian car, there would either be room for two moderately efficient plants, each producing a limited range of vehicles, or alternatively for one firm and completely free entry from overseas to maintain competition. In the former case, if duopoly proved insufficiently competitive, price control would be possible, in the latter case it would be unnecessary. With six principal car manufacturers the tariff, pitched at the level at which the marginal producers can make a profit, must leave a wide margin to the intra-marginal producer, and competition can be largely spurious.

The conjunction of made-to-measure tariffs with industrial concentration also appears to allow, in the folds of the intra-marginal firms, an unnecessary multiplication of plants. The most striking feature of the Australian industrial pattern is the large number of plants responsible for total production. Calculations of concentration by firms clearly suggest a much greater concentration by firms than by plants. Brunt found that in 1957–8 industries in which the first eight firms accounted for 50 per cent or more of national sales employed at least 60 per cent of the manufacturing work force.[30] The 50 per cent concentration index for 1963–4 shows that 49 per cent of the manufacturing work force was employed by industrial sub-groups which required at least thirty plants to employ half the work force in each sub-group (see Table 4.5). This implies a narrow firm, but multi-plant structure for manufacturing industry, and it is borne out by an examination of the plant structure of large Australian firms.[31] Population dispersion with concomitant transport costs no doubt contributes to plant dispersion, but there is also an implication that in the shelter of state nationalism and imperfect competition there is an absence of plant rationalization.

THE RELATIONSHIP BETWEEN MARKET STRUCTURE AND COMPETITION

In Australia, as in other countries, there is no simple correlation between concentration and the degree and nature of competition.[32]

[29] US Department of Commerce, Office of Business Economics, *Business Statistics; 1957 Biennial Edition, Supplement to the Survey of Current Business*, Washington, 1957, p. 194.

[30] M. Brunt, 'Legislation in Search of an Objective', *Economic Record*, 41, 1965, p. 371.

[31] Department of National Development, *Structure and Capacity of Australian Manufacturing*, passim.

[32] P. J. McNutty, 'Economic Theory and the Meaning of Competition',

Monopoly, duopoly and oligopoly clearly provide opportunities for impaired competition in pricing, quality, the development of new products and processes, the growth of capacity in relation to the market and the utilization of capacity, the treatment of suppliers and users, and new entry, but there is no direct or simple relationship between the degree of concentration and its effect on any of these. In steel and copper, for example, monopoly and duopoly respectively have kept prices below international levels for the most part, although it is impossible to determine to what extent low prices have been due to a relative advantage in raw materials, technical efficiency comparable to best practice overseas, or a fear of being regarded as a monopoly. Steel monopoly led to quality problems for steel users, to delayed response to market opportunities at home and in exports, and at times to cursory treatment of customers, but these disadvantages were offset for many years by low prices. Apparent monopolies such as glass containers which have become increasingly subject to competition from substitutes such as cans have seen price, quality and service competition in recent years. Some tight oligopolies such as petroleum refineries have established uniform prices with the effective support of two state governments which prescribe petroleum prices, restricting competition to product differentiation through advertisement of quality and service differences. More generally industries in which tight oligopoly prevails have some price competition tied to product differentiation, but where the number of firms is too large for the market and the industry is operating under tariff protection principally for this reason, it is very difficult to establish how far the differences between Australian and overseas prices are due to technical inefficiency and how far they are the result of imperfect competition.

It is generally accepted that Australian industry is particularly prone to restrictive practices in those sectors of industry in which large numbers of firms operate.[33] In the 1963–4 sub-groups in which more than thirty plants are required to account for 80 per cent of the

---

Quarterly Journal of Economics, LXXXII, 1968, pp. 639–56, in exploring the meaning of 'competition' shows that its very existence is by no means self-evident.

[33] Hunter, *Economic Record*, XXXVII; Karmel and Brunt, *Structure*; Brunt, *Economic Record*, 41; and J. Hutton, 'Restrictive Trade Practices Legislation, Trade Associations and Orderly Marketing Schemes in Western Australia', *Economic Record*, 40 (1964). Instances of restrictive practices up to the Second World War were fully documented by L. J. Hume, 'Monopolistic Practices in Australia', unpublished manuscript, 1947.

TABLE 4.6. *Manufacturers' Associations and Restrictive Practices in Unconcentrated Sub-groups*

80 per cent concentration index	Number of sub-groups 1963–64	Sub-groups with at least one manufacturers' association after 1914[a]	Sub-groups with confirmed restrictive practices after 1914[a]
31–50	23	18 (78)	17 (74)
51–100	21	12 (57)	18 (86)
101–200	15	13 (87)	12 (80)
201–500	8	8 (100)	7 (88)
Over 500	10	7 (70)	8 (80)
Total	77	58 (75)	62 (81)

[a] Figures in parentheses are percentages of the line total of sub-groups.

Source: Evidence of associations and restrictive practices before the 1940s from L. J. Hume, 'Monopolistic Practices in Australia', unpublished manuscript, 1947. After that date see Hunter, *Economic Record*, XXXVII; Karmel and Brunt, *Structure*; and Tariff Board Reports.

work force, that is sub-groups employing some 70 per cent of the total work force, trade associations and other price and marketing agreements flourish. They have been noted in all except four of the sub-groups with 80 per cent concentration index over 100 (see Table 4.6).

Trade associations have long been suspected of initiating and maintaining restrictive agreements to further their stated objectives of 'encouraging orderly marketing' and 'promoting and protecting the interests and welfare of the trade or industry'. In many cases they have grown up as a result of opposition to monopoly or import or export rings. Association among grain producers was advocated by the Inter-State Commission in 1915 to combat the control of the local wheat and flour market by combinations of millers.[34] Faced with new conditional leases for hiring machines from the United Shoe Machinery Company in 1913, the members of the Boot and

[34] Inter-State Commission, Tariff Investigation Report, Grain and Pulse, *Parliamentary Papers*, 1914–15–16–17, VI, p. 1319.

Shoe Manufacturers' Association looked to their price setting procedures.[35] Not all trade associations are responsible for trade practices,[36] and a variety of restrictive practices exists outside their organization (see Table 4.6). Collusive tendering which includes the sharing of tendering costs, level tendering with common prices and collusive bidding, and agreements not to bid, are all common. Price agreements, moreover, lead to exclusive dealing, withholding of supplies by collective boycott, and resale price maintenance resulting in withholding of supplies if prices are cut by the retailer or wholesaler. But not all restrictive agreements can be effectively policed,[37] and this results in tied distribution channels, full-line forcing, and price concessions. Manufacturers of electrical products, for example, failed in their efforts to maintain minimum selling prices for domestic appliances in 1967 because they 'failed to pull together'.[38]

Restrictive measures not only vary in content and the degree to which they are policed, but also in the area of application. Restrictive practices can be nationwide, statewide or regional. Markets can be regionally divided as in bread, beer, biscuits and cement, and quotas can be operated in times of short supply. In many products imports are included in market arrangements, so that the lowering of tariffs would be unlikely to affect prices. A price ring of agricultural-machinery producers and importers operated successfully in the 1890s. When it temporarily broke up in the 1900s the Australian producers turned to tariff protection in a sequence of events which eventually led to the Harvester wage award and the establishment of the basic wage.[39] Restrictive practices and price leadership have included imported agricultural products behind the tariff since the 1900s. The manufacturers of ceramic tiles have been tied in with tile

[35] Inter-State Commission, Tariff Investigation Report, Boots and Shoes, *Parliamentary Papers*, 1914–15–16–17, VI, pp. 273 and 358; and Inter-State Commission, Prices Investigation Report No. 9, Boots and Shoes, *Parliamentary Papers*, 1917–18–19, V, p. 325.

[36] R. D. Freeman, 'Trade Associations in the Australian Economy', *Public Administration*, New Series, 24, 1965, showed that there is no simple correlation between the existence of trade associations and restrictive practices, pp. 339–43. In 1968 the Trade Practices Commissioner reported that of 1,058 restrictive practices registered in manufacturing, only 375 were Trade Association Agreements.

[37] Freeman, ibid., p. 342.

[38] 'Appliance Trade Price Moves Fail', *Australian Financial Review*, July 14, 1967.

[39] Royal Commission on Customs and Excise Tariffs, Progress Report No. 5, Agricultural Machinery and Implements, *Parliamentary Papers*, 1906, IV, pp. 94–6.

importers in tight price agreements in an industry where restrictive practices were operating during the First World War.[40]

Restrictive practices are as much in the Australian tradition as monopolies and oligopolies. In some industries a broadening out of the number of plants and firms has led from oligopoly to monopolistic competition; in others, such as bakeries and dry cleaners, where a growing need for economies of scale has led to a consolidation of plants and firms, the tendency has been in the other direction from restrictive practice agreements through trade associations to informal price agreements. Price agreements for food products have sometimes been bolstered by state fixing of maximum prices. Such prices, of course, immediately became the only prices.

A business climate in which orderly marketing has enveloped agricultural product after agricultural product until wool is the only major one not yet subject to government regulation is conducive to marketing controls throughout the economy: uniform wage determination through the arbitration system probably helps to nurture attitudes of uniformity; and the procedures of the Tariff Board which seek to prevent only undue profiteering do nothing to deter them.

In the absence of detailed evidence about the extent of price and other agreements and the degree to which they are observed, it is impossible to draw conclusions about the extent to which competition in the unconcentrated sectors of industry is impaired. On the other hand it seems safe to conclude on the evidence available (see Table 4.6) that workable competition is frequently absent, with consequent technical inefficiency, the lack of a progressive outlook and lost growth opportunities.[41] Restrictive practices thus possibly contribute as much to the inefficiencies and rigidities of the Australian economy, to the downward inflexibility of prices, and towards inflationary tendencies, as monopolies, duopolies and oligopolies.

Whatever the objective of the current restrictive practices legislation turns out to be,[42] if it is at all successful in improving attitudes in the

[40] *Tariff-Board's Report on Ceramic Tiles and Tile Blanks*, 1961; and Inter-State Commission, Prices Investigation Report No. 12, Rents, *Parliamentary Papers*, 1917–18–19, V, pp. 473–4.

[41] Karmel and Brunt, *Structure*, defines workable competition in these terms, pp. 100–2.

[42] Although the passing of the Trade Practices Act in 1965, fifty-nine years after Australia's last national attempt at dealing with restricted competition with an Industries Preservation Act, was a landmark, it is still far from clear what the effects of the act will be. See 'The Trade Practices Bill', *Economic Record*, 41, 1965, pp. 341–411.

direction of competitive vigour, it will be the marginal firms which can be expected to suffer and the inefficient plants which will have to be eliminated. The overall effect is likely to be a movement towards increased concentration. There would then be increased possibilities of technical efficiency.

AUSTRALIA, CANADA AND DEVELOPING COUNTRIES

Hunter shows that while in Australia the four largest firms control the whole market in a number of Australian industries, in the United Kingdom and the United States the four largest firms control only a portion of the market of the same industries.[43] Brunt has calculated that whereas in Australia industries in which the first eight firms accounted for 50 per cent or more of national sales employed at least 60 per cent of the industrial work force, in the United States industries in which the first eight firms accounted for at least 50 per cent of national sales employed only 30 per cent of the industrial work force.[44] Given the relative size of markets, this is only to be expected, and comparisons with large West European countries would probably show similar results. Comparisons with Canada, however, do not show very great differences in manufacturing concentration by firms. There are not as many monopolies in Canada as there are in Australia, but Canadian industry is much more highly concentrated than United States industry,[45] and concentration by firms seems to be parallel to Australian experience.[46]

By plants, however, Australian industry is much less concentrated than Canadian industry, and this is accompanied by a generally smaller average size of plant in Australia than in Canada. Appendix B compares the 80 per cent concentration index, the total number of plants and average employment per plant for 1948 for Canada with 1948–9 and 1963–4 for Australia.[47] The forty-six sub-groups which

[43] Hunter, *Economic Record*, XXXVII.

[44] Brunt, *Economic Record*, 41, p. 371.

[45] Rosenbluth, *Concentration in Canandian Manufacturing*, pp. 80–3, and Joe S. Bain, *International Differences in Industrial Structure*, Yale University Press, Newhaven, 1966, pp. 103–6.

[46] This judgement is based on a comparison of 80 per cent concentration index by firms as calculated by Sheridan, *Economic Record*, 44, and by Rosenbluth, *Concentration in Canadian Manufacturing*. Karmel and Brunt, *Structure*, claim not only that Canada has fewer pure monopolies, but also that it has fewer tight oligopolies, pp. 87–8, but see Bain, *International Differences*, pp. 104–5.

[47] In Canada in 1948, 1,156,000 were employed in manufacturing, and in Australia in 1963–4, 1,219, 520.

could be compared employed 504,200 people in Canada in 1948, 324,500 people in Australia in 1948–9, and 407,500 people in Australia in 1963–4. Five sub-groups, employing 33,900 people in Canada in 1948 and approximately the same number in Australia in 1963–4, had a markedly lower employment per plant in Canada than in Australia. They included industries such as cigarettes, matches and breweries in which concentration in Australia is particularly high. Three sub-groups with large-scale production in both countries, showed approximately the same average employment per plant in the two countries. These were coke, glass and biscuits, all highly concentrated industries in Australia. In twenty of the sub-groups, employing 219,500 people in Canada and 195,500 people in Australia in 1963–4, employment per plant was markedly lower in Australia than in Canada.

These comparisons suggest that Canadian technical practice has been closely influenced by the proximity to the United States and that it is therefore probably closer to best practice than Australian plant organizations. Canada provides particularly valuable plant concentration and size comparisons for Australia because of the similarity of population dispersal. The Canadian federal system allows more state rights than the Australian, but the disparity shown by the comparison suggests that population dispersion and federalism are probably not as important in the multiplication of plants as would appear from a consideration of the Australian situation alone.

While Canada and Australia have highly concentrated industries compared with the United Kingdom and the United States, this industrial structure is typical of many countries which have industrialized at a late date or which are still in the process of industrializing, and this is particularly so if the domestic market is small and scattered, and if the country is far from other industrialized markets. The South African industrial structure is closely parallel to the Australian even to the point of a number of monopoly-dominated industries covering the same fields of production as Australia. Thus in South Africa steel production, sugar refining and glass container production are all pure monopolies, while tobacco, pulp and paper, and newspaper printing are duopolies, or tight oligopolies. A tight oligopoly structure behind high tariffs is characteristic of consumer durables, and particularly of motor-vehicle manufacture.[48] It is not

[48] Da Gama Publications Ltd, *Industrial Profile, Republic of South Africa*, Johannesburg, no date, and O.P.F. Harwood and John R. Burrows, 'The South African Economy', in C. B. Hoover, ed., *Economic Systems of the Commonwealth*, Duke University Press, Durham NC, 1962, pp. 485–8.

surprising that several Australian manufacturers venturing abroad have gone to South Africa where they have found the industrial climate familiar and congenial. Another major group of countries with a very similar and highly concentrated industrial structure are those of Latin America, and this is particularly true of Brazil, where the import replacement policy of the 1950s led to an industrial structure closely resembling Australia's.[49] Finally, and closer to home, the smaller industrializing countries of South East Asia—Malaysia, Thailand and the Philippines—are showing a very similar pattern of industrial development with emphasis on tight oligopoly behind tariffs.

LOOKING AHEAD

A high level of industrial concentration appears to have remained stable throughout Australia's industrial development. Since the principal reasons for industrial concentration arise out of the large size of the technically efficient plants in relation to the market, it would seem that the Australian market, in spite of overall growth and internal changes, has not grown faster than the rate at which technical advances have increased the requirements for large-scale production. There are no indications that the rate of growth of the size of plants is slackening, nor is it likely to be slower than the rate of Australian population growth in the future. Even with the increased exports of manufactured goods a high level of industrial concentration is therefore inevitable in the foreseeable future if Australian industry is to be technically efficient.

In many sectors Australia has an unnecessarily cumbersome industrial structure characterized by a relatively large number of plants, each employing a relatively small number of workers. In some of these industries the total number of firms is small, and in some of them restrictive practices are common. As a result economic competition may not be very effective and lack of competition is probably the principal cause of the uneconomically large number of plants. But although the industrial structure is basically the result of the smallness of market, its inefficiencies have been exaggerated by the policies of a number of government instrumentalities and depart-

[49] L. Gordon and E. L. Grommers, *United States Manufacturing Investment in Brazil: the Impact of Brazilian Government Policies, 1946–1960*, Harvard University Press, Boston, 1962, pp. 35–7 and N. H. Leff, *The Brazilian Capital Goods Industry: Economic Policy and Economic Development*, Cambridge, Mass., 1966.

ments acting without adequate information and in isolation from each other.

Australia is a very small country in terms of markets, it has limited employment opportunities in agriculture and associated service industries, and geographical isolation impairs its trading ability. It is improbable that the manufacturing sector could have been built up without strongly protectionist policies in the past, and unlikely that they can be greatly modified in the near future without a concerted effort to restructure manufacturing industry. The free entry of foreign investors has made a valuable contribution to the development of manufacturing industry as well as contributing to the unnecessary duplication of plants and the impairment of competition. State and regional nationalism with their contribution to the multiplication of plants are likely to be with us for many years to come. Policy has to be formulated in the light of political economy, but co-ordinated state and federal policies, taking into account the problems of technical as well as economic efficiency, could make for a much more productive industrial structure in Australia in the future.

APPENDIX A. *Sub-group Classifications Relating to Concentration and Employment 1914, or 1926–7, to 1963–4*

	Year	Employment Total	Employment Average per plant	Total number of plants	80 per cent concentration index[a]
A. Sub-groups in which concentration at 80 per cent level was maintained or increased and in which both total employment and average employment per plant have increased.					
Soap and candles	1914	1,861	25	75	18
	1963–64	3,297	27	122	15
Stoves, ovens and ranges	1914	863	22	40	13
	1963–64	3,373	75	45	10
Woolscouring and fellmongering	1914	2,298	21	108	44
	1963–64	2,598	48	54	20
Tanneries	1914	3,091	19	166	46
Tanning, currying, leather dressing	1963–64	4,321	42	102	35
Flour milling	1914	2,833	14	208	101
	1963–64	4,612	40	114	56
Biscuits	1914	3,554	99	36	10
	1963–64	6,290	119	53	9
Bacon curing	1914	1,129	15	73	24
	1963–64	4,872	57	85	23
Butterine and margarine	1914	116	13	9	6
Margarine	1963–64	1,505	56	27	5

APPENDIX A.—*continued*

	Year	Employment Total	Employment Average per plant	Total number of plants	80 per cent concentration index[a]
Aerated waters	1914	4,295	7	637	280
	1963–64	5,204	10	509	188
Breweries	1914	3,535	37	95	32
	1963–64	5,744	239	24	11
Malting	1914	378	11	36	21
	1963–64	629	33	19	11
Tobacco, cigars, cigarettes	1914	3,658	102	36	6
	1963–64	4,537	302	15	3
Perambulators	1914	175	16	11	6
	1963–64	449	21	21	6
Electric light and power	1914	3,298	14	233	39
	1963–64	12,227	45	269	28
Coke works	1926–27	943	73	13	5
	1963–64	1,883	269	7	1
Bricks and tiles	1926–27	7,989	23	344	136
	1963–64	10,799	39	279	112
Chemical fertilisers	1926–27	2,320	70	33	15
	1963–64	4,483	93	48	14
Rope and cordage	1926–27	1,344	56	24	7
	1963–64	2,444	98	25	5
Dried fruits	1926–27	628	13	47	26
Dehydrated fruits and vegetables	1963–64	767	26	29	12

	Year	Employment Total	Employment Average per plant	Total number of plants	80 per cent concentration index[a]
B. Sub-groups in which concentration at 80 per cent level decreased and total employment and average employment per plant remained the same or increased.					
Paints and varnishes	1914	243	11	22	10
Whitelead, paints and varnish	1963–64	5,368	29	184	40
Boiling down, tallow refining	1914	862	10	84	40
	1963–64	2,233	19	118	45
Electrical apparatus	1914	714	24	64	28
Electrical machinery, apparatus and cables	1963–64	59,524	41	1,438	224
Galvanised ironwork and tin smithing	1914	5,087	16	313	136
Sheet metal working	1963–64	29,610	25	1,181	283
Electroplating	1914	359	8	45	25
	1963–64	2,849	10	285	131
Boots and shoes	1914	13,192	37	357	95
Boots and shoes (not rubber)	1963–64	21,135	54	393	132
Cornflour, oatmeal and starch	1914	1,297	25	52	17
Cereal foods	1963–64	3,622	45	80	29
Confectionery	1914	4,163	37	114	26
	1963–64	8,125	43	189	27
Sausage skins	1914	310	22	14	7
Sausage casings	1963–64	1,222	34	36	13

APPENDIX A.—*continued*

	Year	Employment Total	Employment Average per plant	Total number of plants	80 per cent concentration index[a]
Woodturning	1914	541	7	82	36
Woodturning, woodcarving, etc.	1963–64	1,954	7	264	108
Window blinds	1914	120	7	18	11
Blinds	1963–64	1,774	10	176	62
Photo engraving and lithography	1914	337	13	26	14
Process and photo engraving	1963–64	1,808	25	71	37
Rubber goods	1914	1,790	64	28	4
	1963–64	17,070	143	119	21
Brooms and brushes	1914	824	16	52	23
	1963–64	1,991	20	102	28
Inks and polishes	1926–27	861	13	65	28
	1963–64	2,182	16	140	44
Cotton mills	1926–27	744	107	7	1
Cotton spinning and weaving	1963–64	9,911	117	85	23
Knitting factories	1926–27	10,020	39	255	77
Hosiery and other knitted goods	1963–64	25,684	42	607	159
Jam, fruit and vegetable canning	1926–27	4,679	56	83	20
	1963–64	11,139	93	120	32
Pickles, sauces and vinegar	1926–27	812	24	34	14
	1963–64	1,435	31	47	15

	Year	Employment Total	Employment Average per plant	Total number of plants	80 per cent concentration index[a]
C. Sub-groups in which concentration at 80 per cent level decreased but in which average employment remained the same or fell in spite of an increase in total employment.					
Marble, slate	1914	1,030	12	86	44
	1963–64	1,570	8	206	85
Railway carriages, railway and tramway workshops	1914	21,745	290	75	12
Tramcars and railway rolling stock	1963–64	36,489	272	134	24
Agricultural implements	1914	3,865	25	154	40
Agricultural machinery and implements	1963–64	13,843	25	556	76
Lead mills and shot works	1914	174	25	7	3
Lead mills	1963–64	71	12	6	4
Tents, tarpaulins, and sail making	1914	820	16	51	20
Canvas goods, tents, tarpaulins, etc.	1963–64	1,689	11	150	54
Furriers	1914	282	10	27	20
Furriers and fur dressing	1963–64	697	7	106	48
Waterproofs and oilskins	1914	351	39	9	4
	1963–64	1,465	39	38	11
Dyeworks and cleaning	1914	321	12	26	13
	1963–64	10,403	8	1,367	701
Meat and fish preserving	1914	8,094	176	46	20
	1963–64	10,707	65	164	32

APPENDIX A—*continued*

	Year	Employment Total	Employment Average per plant	Total number of plants	80 per cent concentration index[a]
Condiments, coffee and spices	1914	1,029	24	43	16
	1963–64	5,440	23	238	71
Ice and refrigerating	1914	2,130	12	182	54
	1963–64	3,953	10	381	96
Sawmills	1914	18,990	19	1,009	383
	1963–64	29,069	12	2,345	954
Ship and boat building and repairing	1926–27	5,244	72	88	9
	1963–64	14,283	41	346	22
Motor body building and repairing	1926–27	9,283	60	156	28
Motor bodies	1963–64	33,888	15	2,291	410
Sewing machines	1926–27	98	16	6	2
	1963–64	549	14	40	7
Woollen and tweed mills	1926–27	11,068	209	55	27
Wool, carding, spinning and weaving	1963–64	20,078	156	129	45
Bags and sacks	1926–27	926	24	38	13
	1963–64	1,270	14	91	29
Boot repairing	1926–27	1,967	2	931	409
Boot and shoe repairs	1963–64	3,509	2	1,922	1,314
Animal and poultry foods	1926–27	187	19	10	5
Animal and bird foods	1963–64	1,749	10	174	68
Bottling	1926–27	392	20	20	10
	1963–64	1,427	16	92	39

	Year	Employment Total	Employment Average per plant	Total number of plants	80 per cent concentration index[a]
Joinery	1926–27	10,186	12	828	300
	1963–64	17,857	8	2,239	811
Boxes and cases	1926–27	1,610	12	139	59
	1963–64	2,559	9	300	128
Furnishing drapery	1926–27	501	17	29	12
	1963–64	1,821	11	170	72
Printing and binding	1926–27	26,873	21	1,289	353
	1963–64	31,698	18	1,780	534
Electrotyping and stereotyping	1926–27	186	10	18	11
	1963–64	491	16	30	17

[a] Number of plants rounded to nearest unit.

Source: Table 1, H. Hughes and P. Brown, ANZAAS Paper, 1968 and Commonwealth Bureau of Census and Statistics, *Production Bulletins*, *Secondary Industries*.

APPENDIX B. *Comparison Relating to Concentration and Employment Canada 1948 and Australia 1948–9 and 1963–4*

Sub-group		Year	Employment Total	Employment Average per plant	Total number of plants	80 per cent concentration index[a]
A. Same average employment per plant:[b]						
Coke products	Canada	1948	3,241	270	12	7
Coke works	Australia	1948–49	1,243	155	8	2
		1963–64	1,883	269	7	1
Glass	Canada	1948	4,002	572	7	3
Glass bottles	Australia	1948–49	2,486	355	7	2
		1963–64	4,014	572	7	2
Biscuits	Canada	1948	5,671	116	49	18
	Australia	1948–49	4,320	71	61	13
		1963–64	6,290	119	53	9
B. Markedly lower average employment per plant in Canada:[c]						
Asbestos products	Canada	1948	1,020	68	15	5
Asbestos cement sheets, etc.	Australia	1948–49	1,969	151	13	5
		1963–64	2,994	187	16	7
Matches	Canada	1948	738	74	10	4
	Australia	1948–49	1,035	207	5	2
		1963–64	512	171	3	2
Woollen yarn	Canada	1948	4,840	83	58	17

Sub-group		Year	Employment Total	Employment Average per plant	Total number of plants	80 per cent concentration index[a]
Woollen cloth			9,895	110	90	28
Wool	Australia	1948–49	24,930	163	153	46
		1963–64	20,078	156	129	45
Breweries	Canada	1948	8,407	138	61	27
	Australia	1948–49	5,016	157	32	12
		1963–64	5,744	239	24	11
Cigarettes, etc.	Canada	1948	8,959	144	62	7
	Australia	1948–49	5,279	143	37	9
		1963–64	4,537	302	15	2
C. Average employment per plant in Canada more than double that in Australia:[d]						
Vegetable oils	Canada	1948	819	68	16	9
	Australia	1948–49	637	25	25	9
		1963–64	780	23	34	9
Petroleum products	Canada	1948	8,245	250	33	11
Mineral oils	Australia	1948–49	1,644	32	52	12
		1963–64	5,296	65	82	10
Railway rolling stock	Canada	1948	31,371	826	38	13
Tramcars and railway rolling stock	Australia	1948–49	40,012	292	137	18
		1963–64	36,489	272	134	24

APPENDIX B.—*continued*

Sub-group		Year	Employment Total	Employment Average per plant	Total number of plants	80 per cent concentration index[a]
Automobiles	Canada	1948	24,703	2,246	11	2
Motor vehicles	Australia	1948–49	9,069	146	62	14
		1963–64	24,327	566	43	9
Aircraft	Canada	1948	8,049	732	11	3
	Australia	1948–49	10,799	240	45	9
		1963–64	12,678	155	82	9
Bicycles	Canada	1948	795	66	12	3
Cycles	Australia	1948–49	1,374	12	118	30
		1963–64	480	4	130	59
Agricultural implements	Canada	1948	19,111	277	69	6
Agricultural machines and implements	Australia	1948–49	9,633	49	196	20
		1963–64	13,843	25	556	76
Hosiery	Canada	1948	27,634	102	271	76
	Australia	1948–49	21,172	46	465	171
		1963–64	25,684	42	607	160
Synthetics	Canada	1948	16,097	358	45	14
	Australia	1948–49	1,356	136	10	2
		1963–64	4,527	105	43	13
Cotton, jute bags	Canada	1948	1,360	39	35	18
Bags, sacks	Australia	1948–49	737	15	50	21
		1963–64	1,270	14	91	29

Sub-group		Year	Employment Total	Employment Average per plant	Total number of plants	80 per cent concentration index[a]
Plywood and veneer	Canada	1948	6,335	144	44	15
	Australia	1948–49	2,306	49	47	20
		1963–64	3,832	50	76	32

[a] Number of plants rounded to nearest unit.

[b] The difference in average employment per plant in cement products, medicinal and pharmaceutical preparations, animal foods, bakeries, soft drinks, and sawmills, was small (±5).

[c] The average employment per plant in flour milling establishments was lower in Canada (32) than in Australia in 1963–4 (40) but not in 1948–9 (29).

[d] Industries with markedly lower average employment per plant in Australia were soaps, rope and cordage, textile dyeing and finishing, tanning, corsets, boots and shoes, malting, furniture, and paper boxes. In cement, paints, cotton, furs, umbrellas, confectionery, and paper, average employment per plant was slightly lower in Australia. In the iron and steel industry and in milk products there are classification difficulties.

Source: Extracted from Table 3, Hughes and Brown, ANZAAS paper, 1968.

Chapter 5

THE SERVICE ENSEMBLE

J. A. Dowie

In 1890 the six Australian colonies, besides having possibly the highest standard of living in the Western world and displaying the greatest degree of urbanization, also employed the highest proportion of workers in 'tertiary' and 'service' industries. Three-quarters of a century later, long since united, they had yielded their pre-eminence in measured living standards and almost certainly been surpassed in the race to the cities. Moreover, despite their early lead in this area, they had only just followed the United States and Canada across the 'service economy' threshold and reached the point where only a minority of the work force was employed on commodity production. By implication the modal Australian worker of the last hundred years has been not the farm-hand or factory worker, but the service-man. And it also follows that the 'service revolution' has taken place at a significantly slower rate in Australia this century than in the most comparable developed economies.

This essay has three limited objectives. The central aim is to document the changing dimension of the service sector in Australia between 1891 and 1961 in terms of familiar criteria—share of income generated, share of real product and share of employment. Explanation of the observed changes is attempted only within the confines of the data pertaining to these measures, though since they permit some inferences concerning both relative price and productivity trends the restriction is less onerous than it might seem initially. I would, of course, be the first to admit the need for future work to delve behind these first-order determinants into the more precise behavioural and institutional origins of change. Such work will surely have the added attraction for readers of dealing with people and places rather than the arid abstractions encountered in the present paper.

The second purpose is to raise constructive doubts concerning the merits of the preceding analysis, conducted as it is within the boundaries of conventional social accounting procedures and on the basis of sector and industry groupings. The limitations and occasional arbitrariness of both are not emphasized for their own sake, but in relation to the question of deciding on the most meaningful level of treatment for components of an economy. The major doubts expressed here about use of the sector concept, particularly but not exclusively in relation to services, concern both aggregation involved (the question of homogeneity of components) and the usefulness of broad demarcations in an economy characterized by extensive specialization (the question of interdependence manifested in input-output transactions). Discussion of these doubts leads on to a plea for a fully disaggregated investigation of individual service areas derived from meaningful economic and institutional criteria.

Thirdly, the essay aims to provide some background to Australian study from previous writing, particularly that seeking to relate services to the broad structural changes which accompany, and partly define, economic development. Neither the selection of writings nor the reports on their contents are intended to be in any way comprehensive and no personal comments on the arguments or conclusions are made at this stage. The selection does, however, serve to give limited international perspective to the material presented on the Australian experience in section two and to raise most of the issues taken up in the final section. This is the task pursued first.

SELECTED WRITINGS ON SERVICES

The service industries in fact have a highly respectable place in the economic historiography of Australasia. Conceived as the third, or tertiary, component of the industrial structure, they may even be said to have been born in the minds of two economists with close Australasian associations, Allen G. B. Fisher and Colin Clark. Early explorers of the relationship between income growth and structural change, these two were in the 1930s the foremost advocates of the need to pay greater attention to the economic significance of activities other than rural industries and manufacturing. In particular they decried what they saw as an all too prevalent tendency to regard service activities as 'unproductive'.

FISHER,[1] much less interested in quantitative investigations than

[1] Allen G. B. Fisher, 'Capital and the Growth of Knowledge', *Economic Journal*, XLIII, 1933, pp. 379–89; *The Clash of Progress and Security*, Macmillan, London, 1935; 'Production, Primary, Secondary and Tertiary', *Economic*

Clark, was reluctant to set down a rigid definition of what constituted tertiary production, although he always insisted that it was something more than a residual rag-bag after primary and secondary activity had been defined. He found the 'hard core of meaning' in the concept of tertiary products primarily in their demand characteristics: they were those products for which, after 'modest' income levels had been reached, demand rose most rapidly as income continued to rise. The technical criterion of tangibility and the associated service character of most tertiary products he found much less useful; strawberries and mushrooms would be excluded by such a definition, whereas he felt they probably should be included. He was not, however, prepared to approve an entirely mechanical delineation in terms of income elasticities, or to exclude all supply conditions, such as a negligible or zero rate of technical progress, as criteria for some purposes. This imprecise and catholic view—'Different definitions and classifications may serve different but equally useful purposes'—left him open to criticism in the early 1950s when interest in all aspects of economic growth and development, including its relationship with structural change, burgeoned.[2] But the virtues of imprecision—or rather the vices of precision—have undoubtedly reasserted themselves since.

CLARK provided a much less elusive target than Fisher.[3] His statistical inclinations required more precise boundary drawing, and in addition he was generally less guarded in his assertions about the economic forces responsible for empirically observed trends. The trends which he was particularly interested in establishing and

Record, XV, 1939, pp. 24–38; *Economic Progress and Social Security*, Macmillan, London, 1945, pp. 5–6; 'A Note on Tertiary Production', *Economic Journal*, LXII, 1952, pp. 820–34; 'Marketing Structure and Economic Development: Comment', *Quarterly Journal of Economics*, LXVIII, 1954, pp. 151–4.

[2] Four of the main responses were P. T. Bauer and B. S. Yamey, 'Economic Progress and Occupational Distribution', *Economic Journal*, LXI, 1951, pp. 741–55; S. G. Triantis, 'Economic Progress, Occupational Redistribution and International Terms of Trade', *Economic Journal*, LXIII, 1953, pp. 627–37; A. L. Minks, 'Statistical Evidence and the Concept of Tertiary Industry', *Economic Development and Cultural Change*, III, 1955, pp. 366–73; and Nelson N. Foote and Paul K. Hatt, 'Social Mobility and Economic Advancement', *American Economic Review*, XLIII, 1953, pp. 364–78.

[3] Colin Clark, *National Income and Outlay*, Macmillan, London, 1938, Ch. XI; 'Australian Economic Progress against a World Background', Jospeh Fisher Lecture in Commerce, Hassell, Adelaide, 1938; *The Conditions of Economic Progress*, Macmillan, London, 1940, 1951 and 1957; *The Economics of 1960*, Macmillan, London, 1943, Ch. III; with R. H. Fields, 'Tertiary Industries in the Economy', in C. Hartley Grattan, ed., *Australia*, University of California Press, 1947, pp. 213–25 (mainly a description of the relevant 1933 census data).

explaining were those in the industrial distribution of the work force during economic progress. While later revisions saw qualifications introduced, the original Clark claim was that:

> Studying economic progress in relation to the economic structure of different countries, we find a very firmly established generalization that a high average level of real income per head is always associated with a high proportion of the working population engaged in tertiary industries. . . .
>
> When we examine the trend through time [within countries], we find a similar result. In every case we find the proportion engaged in primary industry declining and in tertiary industry increasing. The proportion of the working population engaged in secondary industry appears in every country to rise to a maximum and then to begin falling, apparently indicating that each country reaches a stage of maximum industrialization beyond which industry begins to decline relative to tertiary production.[4]

The explanation of the observed trends lay, according to Clark, in both the demand and supply characteristics of the three types of product. Defining tertiary products by their intangible, service nature, Clark was able to use a high income elasticity of demand as part of the explanation of the observed trend. (Fisher's definition was of a substantially *ex post* character, not really telling us what tertiary products are until growth has occurred). But of equal importance and inseparable from this demand characteristic was the typical supply condition of tertiary production: the difficulty of increasing labour productivity as rapidly in the production of services as in the other sectors. Even if tertiary output were to grow as rapidly as primary and secondary output (in real terms) it would, under this condition, have to absorb an increasing share of the work force. A slow rate of productivity improvement in the service area was not only a statistical phenomenon to Clark—the result of unsatisfactory output measurement—although he was not blind to the probable importance of biases at this level; slow productivity improvement was *built into* many services.

Despite later criticism on both empirical and theoretical grounds the thinking of Fisher and Clark has retained its influence. Indeed, their 'model' has been recently resurrected in only slightly modified form by W. J. Baumol.[5] The equations, the terminology and the

[4] Clark, *The Conditions*, 1940, pp. 6–7.

[5] W. J. Baumol, 'Macroeconomics of Unbalanced Growth: the Anatomy of Urban Crisis', *American Economic Review*, LVII, 1967, pp. 415–26. See also the

examples betray the passing of a generation but the message is essentially the same.

BAUMOL argues that there is a clear distinction in advanced economies between the 'progressive' sector and the 'non-progressive' one. In the former (labour) productivity rises cumulatively because of innovation, capital accumulation and economies of scale. In the non-progressive sector, however, labour rather than being an incidental input is 'for all practical purposes . . . itself the end product';[6] productivity rises slowly, if at all, because of the small opportunity for any of its three sources to operate. Baumol admits that the distinction is a relative rather than absolute one, but is firm in declaring it to be both sizeable and the result of the 'inherent technological structure' of activities rather than simple arithmetical division or historical accident. His polar examples are manufacturing ('When someone purchases an air conditioner he neither knows nor cares how much labor went into it') and live artistic performance ('A half hour horn quintet calls for the expenditure of 2½ man hours in its performance, and any attempt to increase productivity here is likely to be viewed with concern by critics and audience alike').[7] But he argues that technological non-progression also characterizes education, health, law and public order, municipal government, *haute cuisine* restaurants, hand-made objects of many sorts (pottery, glassware, clothes, furniture) and stately homes. From the inclusion of the latter items it is clear that the division does not conceptually parallel a goods-service one but it is also obvious that the resemblance must be fairly close quantitatively.

The detailed consequences of such an unbalanced technological structure depend on demand as well as supply influences, and on the extent to which markets, including factor ones, operate freely. Baumol assumes that in the long run labour is mobile between the sectors and that wage rates will accordingly move in similar fashion in both. This assumption generates the 'progressive and cumulative increase' in the *real* costs of supplying non-progressive services which leads to their slow demise if they are in fairly elastic demand over the relevant price ranges, or their absorption of an ever-increasing share of the work force (with more and more adverse effects on global productivity) if demand is significantly inelastic. Income

series of replies (and Baumol's rejoinder) in the September 1968 issue, especially that by Carolyn Shaw Bell which represents an intelligent—and readable—appraisal of some of the main changes in service *activities* over the years and their implications for output measurement based on *industrial* classifications.

[6] Ibid., p. 416. [7] Ibid.

effects or market intervention by government may, of course, weaken or intensify these trends. Baumol's normative concern is with those areas where government intervention is 'required' because the community's price and income elasticities 'should' be lower and higher respectively than revealed preferences indicate.

If Baumol tends to be more in the tradition of Fisher, Kuznets and Fuchs represent the main academic descendants of Clark. These two, with some recent support from Temin, and Chenery and Taylor, have in their individual ways produced the most significant empirical studies of broad structural change since the war. Some acquaintance with the approaches and conclusions of these writers is a desirable preliminary to an examination of the Australian services picture. In the case of Kuznets this also means some direct introduction to the Australian experience, since he includes it among his observations and, indeed, lists Australia as an exception not only to his relevant labour force generalization (it is one of a few countries in which the 'share of the services sector . . . was constant or changed little') but also to his product generalization ('In Sweden and Australia the share of the services sector declined').[8]

KUZNETS' arena is characteristically all developed economies for which figures exist over long periods. The relevant study in his monumental series of quantitative investigations is largely an expanded version of Clark.[9] And while his recent synthesizing work represents his more considered views, it is informative to record the approach and interpretation of the earlier study.

Using both time series for individual countries and cross-section data, Kuznets originally compared the shares of national product and labour force of the three main sectors with levels of *per capita* product. He found (by inspection) no significant relationship between share of *product* and level of *per capita* product, but confirmed the essence of the Fisher–Clark position by asserting a positive correlation between share of *labour force* and level of development (as approximated by *per capita* product). However, the international and intertemporal studies threw up different suggestions as to the exact strength of the service response. The cross-section data implied that falls in the number of primary workers as *per capita* income rose were offset mainly by rises in secondary numbers, with services

[8] Kuznets, *Modern Economic Growth: Rate, Structure, and Spread*, Yale University Press, New Haven and London, 1966, pp. 97 and 111.

[9] Simon Kuznets, 'Quantitative Aspects of the Economic Growth of Nations: II. Industrial Distribution of National Product and Labor Force', *Economic Development and Cultural Change*, V, 1957, Supplement.

attracting a minority share of those displaced. On the other hand, the time series analysis suggested that the service response was greater than the industrial. Kuznets' speculative resolution of the conflict in 1957 was a two-stage growth process (akin to that proposed by Clark) in which the tendency for labour to move largely from primary to secondary would be reversed when increasing productivity in the latter and a shift in the structure of consumer wants made possible, and called for, a greater flow into tertiary activities.

The conflict was abolished in *Modern Economic Growth*—and the need for a two-stage process eliminated—as a result of Kuznets' disenchantment with cross-section analysis. Changes in technology and taste through time could not, he now argued, usually be captured in cross-section study. Since their impact was often different in direction and magnitude to the effects of *per capita* product changes, completely erroneous inferences were possible from interspatial analysis. The growing use of hypothetical examples also suggested diminishing confidence in the underlying data. Nevertheless, the negligible income response of the service *product* share (now minus transport and communication) was confirmed: 'by and large the downward trend in the share of the agriculture sector was offset by the upward trend in the share of the industry sector—leaving no marked trend in the share of the residual services sector in total product'.[10] The positive response of the service *labour* share was also confirmed but with greater prominence now given to the exceptions—those countries where the share had changed little rather than actually fallen.

Kuznets' explanations of the found trends also differ in his more recent work, though since these must inevitably be couched in fairly broad hypothetical terms, the scope for change is really confined to emphasis. Unchanged is his reluctance to attribute too much importance to 'an invariant structure of human wants' in explaining the relatively unchanging service share of production. A constant income elasticity for service products in general *is* possible, but Kuznets is aware of the heterogeneity of this sector and of the range of consumption patterns it embodies. And since his product data are restricted to current prices, he can draw no direct inferences about income elasticities anyway. Relative price changes and shifts in 'tastes' rank as other conventional factors on the demand side and differential technical progress is mentioned as the obvious leading probability on the supply side.

If there is a personal emphasis to be discerned in Kuznets' analysis

[10] Kuznets, *Modern Economic Growth*, p. 97.

it is that placed on the importance of trade on structure. Most services, whether purchased as final products by households or as intermediate inputs by firms or government, are produced and consumed almost instantaneously. Very high transport costs, often supplemented by cultural or political sanctions, give the domestic producer of services a high degree of protection against imports. Based on and working through the demand and supply forces listed above, this protection, Kuznets would argue, tends to produce a higher minimum share of product for services internationally than for either of the 'trading' sectors. On the other hand, he argues that there is a lower ceiling to the service share as well as a higher floor, since to benefit from its comparative advantages a country must have a substantial sector (primary and secondary) whatever its income level.

It has already been noted that Kuznets finds much contrast between the Australian experience and the 'typical' one, both in output and work force terms. The atypicality of Australasian growth features more prominently in the early work than in the recent one. In 1957 Kuznets performed a third set of comparisons, between relative product per worker in each sector and the level of *per capita* product. A declining *relative* product per worker in services, reasonably to be expected in view of the earlier result, was found for most countries in the 'second stage' of growth. But among the deviants were Australia and New Zealand, where Kuznets found the relative productivity of workers in primary activity *declining* through time while that in services *increased*. This he attributed to the fact that 'the initial relative levels of product per worker in the A-sector [agriculture, forestry, fishing] were quite high, an atypical condition'.[11] In a later calculation of the contribution of structural change to the rate of growth of *per capita* product Australia and New Zealand again stood out. They were the only ones where the contribution of structural change was negative, tending in fact to depress the overall rate of growth. In other words the net direction of structural movement in the Australasian work forces was from sectors in which (average) productivity was higher to ones in which it was lower. Although it is not intended to engage in extensive criticism here, it should be observed that this interpretation depends on the assumed equation of average productivity measures with marginal products. Since we must question this equation we must clearly question the conclusion.

More formally econometric essays which incorporate use of time series (as distinct from numerous cross-sectional studies) have emerged recently to supplement and extend the work of Kuznets;

[11] Kuznets, *Economic Development and Cultural Change*, V, p. 47.

the notable ones are those by Temin, and Chenery and Taylor.[12]

TEMIN is, unfortunately for us, concerned only with relating changes in the (current-price) shares of the A (agriculture, forestry, fishing) and M (manufacturing, mining, construction) sectors to changes in real income per head. Australia is one of the nine advanced economies he uses, with observations for 1870, 1890, 1910, 1930 and 1950. He finds no significant relationship between the A share and level of real income per head 'in any but the most general and long-run of senses'. The M share, on the other hand, is found to have an elasticity of about 0·3, though the explanatory power of the relation is not high. Obviously no implications for service shares emerge.

CHENERY AND TAYLOR'S is a much more ambitious exercise, attempting to 'explain' the changing structure of product in terms of three factors: (*a*) the average effect of universal factors as indicated by intercountry variation in shares; (*b*) the systematic effect of changes in technology and other universal factors as indicated by changes in the cross-country patterns over time; and (*c*) individual differences arising from varying resources, trading opportunities, etc. Unfortunately for us, attention is concentrated on the post-war period, with only a brief attempt to compare modified Temin data for the past century with the post-war relationships. One modification is the substitution of Norway for Australia and with, again, no explicit attention to services the substantial implications for the present study are small. The main long-term claim raising out of the comparison is that the post-war cross-section regression would explain about 80 per cent of the 1860–1960 fall in the primary shares. The unexplained elimination of Australia (as an unwelcome deviant?) is perhaps the most interesting feature of the exercise.

FUCHS has been the central figure in recent attempts to redress the previous neglect of services, both in general and in particular, in applied economic studies.[13] Juxtaposition of *The Service Economy*

[12] Peter Temin, 'A Time-series Test of Patterns of Industrial Growth', *Economic Development and Cultural Change*, XV, 1967, pp. 174–82, and Hollis B. Chenery and Lance Taylor, 'Development Patterns: Among Countries and Over Time', *Review of Economics and Statistics*, L, 1968, pp. 391–416.

[13] Victor R. Fuchs, assisted by Irving F. Leveson, *The Service Economy*, Columbia University Press, New York and London, 1968. Many of the points of substance have been communicated in earlier publications: *Productivity Trends in the Goods and Service Sectors, 1929–61: a Preliminary Survey*, NBER Occasional Paper 89, Columbia University Press, New York, 1964; *The Growing Importance of the Service Industries*, NBER Occasional Paper 96, Columbia University Press, New York, 1965; and with Jean Alexander Milburn, *Productivity Differences Within the Service Sector*, NBER Occasional Paper 102, Columbia University Press, New York, 1967. See also Fuchs, ed., *Production*

with Kuznets' *Modern Economic Growth* illustrates well the alternative levels at which applied economic history can be written, reflecting differences in focus, depth and, in the end, temperament.

Fuchs' prime aim in his major work is the now familar one. After establishing its magnitude and composition, he seeks to explain a dramatic shift towards service employment in the United States in recent decades and examine the implications for economic life, policy and analysis of continuation of this trend. He concentrates on the post-1929 period but casts a fleeting glance at longer-run trends, tracing the movement towards services as far back as 1870. Gallman and Weiss have recently attempted to establish the trend from the second quarter of the nineteenth century (like Fuchs, they rely on prior work by Fabricant and Lebergott) and their implied estimates for Fuchs' service sector are included in Table 5.1.[14] Despite the thoroughness with which Gallman and Weiss have exploited the available sources, admiration must be tinged with doubt concerning the realism of extending twentieth-century concepts into a period in which the extent of specialization within the market area and the boundaries of market activity must both have differed substantially.

It can be seen that movement from a 'gainful worker' to a 'persons engaged' concept (excluding unpaid helpers and unemployed) adds something of the order of 5–7 per cent to the service share. Fortunately the *trends* are reasonably consistent and we should not be far wrong in suggesting that the 1839 'persons employed' share for the United States would be approximately one quarter. The magnitude of the redistribution of United States employment over the century and a quarter, with all its implications in geographical and social as well as economic terms, is therefore apparent. Equally clear is the acceleration of the process through time. The service share took all but five or ten years of the 125 to double, but the first half of this was accomplished in something like eighty-five years (by the mid-twenties), the second half in only approximately thirty years (by the mid-fifties). The significance of the twenties as a turning point is enhanced when the complementary agriculture and industry shares available from 1870 are examined. Until the twenties the movement out of agriculture was split between industry and services, with industry taking the major share; after the twenties, services account for the full extent of the shift, the industry share in 1965

and Productivity in the Service Industries, NBER Studies in Income and Wealth, 34, New York, 1969.

[14] Robert F. Gallman and Thomas J. Weiss, 'The Service Industries in the Nineteenth Century', in Fuchs, ed., *Production and Productivity*, pp. 287–381.

TABLE 5.1. *Distribution of Employment by Sector, United States, Selected Years, 1839–1965*
(per cent)

	Agriculture	Industry	Services	Fuchs	Services[b] Gallman–Weiss
1839	—	—	—	—	19
1849	—	—	—	—	21
1859	—	—	—	—	22
1869	—	—	—	—	21
1870	47·3	27·1	25·6	19·2	—
1879	—	—	—	—	21
1880	47·1	27·1	25·8	19·3	—
1889	—	—	—	—	25
1890	39·7	31·2	29·2	22·1	—
1899	—	—	—	—	26
1900	34·7	33·7	31·7	24·1	—
1910	28·4	37·8	33·8	—	—
1920	23·8	41·4	34·8	—	—
1930[a]	21·9	35·8	42·3	—	—
1930[a]	20·4	38·1	41·5	—	—
1937	18·8	36·3	44·9	—	—
1947	12·1	42·1	45·8	—	—
1956	8·3	42·0	49·7	—	—
1960	7·2	40·2	52·7	—	—
1965	5·7	39·6	54·8	—	—

[a] Alternatives for 1930 indicate different sources for series before and after this date.

[b] 'Gainful worker' rather than 'persons employed' concept. Sector components: industry = mining, construction, manufacturing, transport, communication and public utilities, government enterprise; services = wholesale and retail trade, finance and insurance, professional, personal, business and repair services, real estate, households and institutions, general government (including armed forces).

Source: Fuchs, *The Service Economy*, Tables 2 and 4; Gallman and Weiss, 'The Service Industries', in Fuchs' ed., *Production and Productivity*, Tables 6 and A-12 (transportation and public utilities deducted from their service sector).

remaining at its 1929 level while services absorbed the fifteen percentage points disgorged from agriculture. Obvious analogies with the Clark and Kuznets analyses may be proposed.

No brief summary can do justice to Fuchs' discussion of the reasons for the recent dramatic shift towards service employment in the United States and of the implications of a continued trend in this direction. Ideally all readers should make some acquaintance with the work itself, particularly the initial summary chapter. A short précis is, however, desirable in order to place the references in later sections in a more coherent setting. All empirical assertions relate to the 1929–65 period and all differentials referred to are service-*industry* ones (rather than service-goods, where the latter includes agriculture).

The evidence, admittedly indirect but impressive in overall impact, overwhelmingly favours a slower growth of output per man in services, rather than a faster growth of service output (implying a higher income elasticity of demand), as the explanation of the employment shift. The small amount of support which does exist for the latter explanation draws its strength from the growth of intermediate demand (for services as inputs) rather than from the growth of final demand (for services as final goods). Just under half of the difference in the rate of increase of output per man cannot be 'explained' and remains as a 'technical progress plus economies of scale residual'. Of the adjustments which account for slightly over half the differential the most important seems to be the slower growth of labour quality in services (as manifested in age and sex composition and levels of educational attainment). Mix factors aside, the other contributing factors are a more rapid decline of hours worked per man in services (confirming the weakness of the per man formulation even as a partial productivity measure) and a slower growth of fixed capital per man than in industry. Downward bias in the measurement of service output, usually thought of as major part of the explanation for such a differential, is regarded as only of similar dimension to these latter adjustments.

Output per man has not only grown more slowly in services (though relatively more quickly than usually thought and certainly not at a near zero rate); it has also displayed a greater cyclical instability than that in industry, says Fuchs. This instability of output per man is, however, consistent with greater stability in both output and employment compared with industry. The relative stability of *output* reflects essentially the intangible character of service product and the consequent inability to accumulate inventories; to the extent that short-term fluctuations in the economy are the product of the building up and running down of stocks there is less scope for variation in service industries than in good ones. The stability of *employment* in services partly reflects the stability of output, but goes beyond this as is implied in the greater instability of output per man. Three characteristics of the service work force are relevant here. First, a greater proportion is salaried and enjoys security of employment and earnings almost irrespective of output. Second, a higher number of service workers are self-employed. And third, a larger role is played by workers who are in effect on 'flexible wages' because of the role of tips, commissions or piecework payments in their earnings. In the second and third cases both output and earnings fluctuate, while in the first earnings are potentially much more stable than output. (Present measurement techniques in areas such as government may in fact eliminate much of the potential gap.)

Many of the implications of a continued shift of employment towards service industries can be already inferred, e.g. a slowing down of aggregate productivity growth and a greater short-term stability of employment. (One must be very careful, however, in drawing any policy conclusions from these prospects. Neither rapid productivity growth in terms of the prices or weights of a given year nor stability of employment, where employment is innocent of all productivity content, are necessarily relevant—or consistent—goals.) Fuchs' studies do however bring out other implications, especially for market structure and industrial relations.

If the present 'average' position in each sector remains applicable, then continued expansion of services can be expected to bring a further increase in the number of small, owner-operated, non-corporate enterprises in the 'profit-oriented' area of the economy. But it can also be expected to bring a further growth in the role of 'non-profit' institutions, and since these are usually reasonably large the overall effect is likely to be a greater reduction in the 'corporateness' of the economy than in the average size of its components. In terms of the age and sex structure of the work force, continued service growth can be expected to both permit, and call forth, increased participation by women, older workers and part-time workers in general. Both the lesser physical demands of most services and the uneven incidence of demand through time (e.g. for personal services) underlies these tendencies. Also, with present service industries much less unionized than their industrial counterparts, either a decline in union influence or, more likely, a significant change in union structure and behaviour, is implied. Finally, Fuchs suggests that the advent of the 'service economy' may involve a reduction in 'alienation' of the worker from his work usually thought to be attributable to the change from craftsmanship to mass production in the course of 'industrialization'.

SERVICE TRENDS IN AUSTRALIA 1890–1960

While simple international comparisons are undoubtedly of more limited use than is usually implied, real interest lies in the relationship between the American and Australian experiences of structural change. The relationship is not, however, pursued at any length here because the sectoral boundaries employed for the detailed study of the Australian experience do not fully accord with those used by Fuchs in America. A serious comparative study might be expected to grapple much more extensively with the compatibility of industry and sector definitions. Nevertheless, a brief look, at least at the

TABLE 5.2. *Distribution of Employment by Sector, United States and Australia, Selected Years, 1890–1960*
(per cent; Fuchs sector definitions)

	Agriculture		Industry		Services	
	US	Australia	US	Australia	US	Australia
1890	39·7	24·6	31·2	41·1	29·2	34·3
1900	34·7	24·0	33·7	39·3	31·7	36·7
1910	28·4	24·0	37·8	41·1	33·8	34·9
1920	23·8	23·1	41·4	40·4	34·8	36·5
1929	19·9	21·5	39·7	42·7	40·4	35·8
1937	18·8	21·2	36·3	42·9	44·9	35·9
1947	12·1	16·3	42·1	46·4	45·8	37·2
1956	8·3	12·8	42·0	49·0	49·7	38·2
1960	7·2	11·2	40·2	48·9	52·7	39·9
1965	5·7	—	39·6	—	54·8	—

Sector components. US: as for Table 5.1; Australia: agriculture = rural, forestry, etc; industry = mining, construction, manufacturing, transport and communication, gas, electricity and water; services = commerce, finance and property, community and business services, public administration and defence, other services.

Source: US: as for Table 5.1; Australia: see Appendix.
(N.B. Australian figures are for years beginning July 1 of stated year).

differing employment trends, is appropriate in the process of transferring from the overseas to the local scene.

Let us look first at the three-sector level as seen by Fuchs. At this level sizeable contrasts between the Australian and American long-term pictures are clear from Table 5.2.

The higher levels of both non-agricultural sectors in Australia in the late nineteenth century appear to have exerted considerable influence on the nature of succeeding development. Firstly, in producing a slower overall pace of structural change in Australia: a negligible shift between 1890 and the 1930s and a slower rate relative to America since then. Approximated very crudely by the relative rate of movement out of agriculture, America underwent more than two and a half times as much structural change in employment as Australia during these seven decades. And secondly, in generating a temporal lag of perhaps three decades between the completion of the 'industrialization' process in the two countries, as evidenced, again very crudely, by the reduction of the growth rate of industrial employment to the average for the economy. Whereas the United States industry share ceases to rise from the mid-twenties, the Australian share rises until the fifties.

As far as services are concerned, the Australian story is thus far from the dramatic one Fuchs finds in the United States. Indeed, the series go a long way towards reinforcing the suggestion, most explicit in Kuznets' work, of an atypicality in the Australian experience. Only since just before the Second World War has there been anything like a decisive increase in the share of employment accounted for by service activities. Even if, as Fuchs has established in the United States, the industrial trend understates the occupational one (towards service-type *jobs*), there seems little likelihood that Australia has yet crossed the 'service economy' threshold (50 per cent of employment) by his definition of services.[15] (As we shall soon see, it almost certainly did so, sometime in the early sixties, when transport and communications are included in services.) By implication it has been industrial activity that has absorbed the major part of the *net* twentieth-century out-movement from agriculture in Australia, though the net requires some emphasis because the generalization is by no means true of all periods. The post-war trends, however, suggest that Australia is now moving firmly along the line followed by the American economy since the 1920s, so that the main contrast is to be found in the decades immediately before the equivalent turning points.

[15] Fuchs, *The Service Economy*, p. 1.

It would be reasonable to suggest on the basis of these figures that the Australia of the second half of the nineteenth century already had a comparatively high proportion of its employment engaged in service activities, reflecting *inter alia* its isolation, the high relative productivity of its primary sector, and the strong inducement to urban growth implied by the land and resource-intensive production functions of the main rural industries. The same factors were also responsible for an above-average industrial work force; mining, it will be recalled, being included in 'industry' by this definition. It seems unlikely that Australian agriculture absorbed the American employment share of 1870 (nearly half) even in the middle decades of the nineteenth century, though little weight should be attached to the fact that the censuses of 1860, 1870 and 1880 in the eastern states yield proportions around the 30 per cent mark. The figures are close to being meaningless. The allocation of mining to the industry sector almost certainly means that the latter's share would rise only slowly in Australia during these thirty years, and we are left with the probability that the services share also changed little. Decline in the sixties, a slight rise in the seventies and a more significant rise in the prosperous eighties may be the most sensible guesses.[16] On this interpretation there seems little chance that the Australian service share was significantly closer to the American one at any time during the nineteenth century that it was at the end of it.

When we turn to a somewhat more disaggregated description, the dangers of possible inconsistency in definition between the countries almost certainly grow. The attempt is made in Table 5.3, though it is restricted to the 1929–65 period. There must be particular reservations about the comparability of the treatment of government in the two sets of employment estimates, and since it is the general government (including defence) component which accounts for the bulk of United States service expansion over the period (9·5 out of the 14·4 percentage points increase), this must be of some concern. It seems most unlikely, however, that it is simply data deficiencies which produce the outstanding contrasts and similarities of the table. Thus it can be claimed with some confidence that the relatively low service share in Australia in recent decades, and its relatively slow expansion, both reflect in a proximate sense the behaviour of three components. Firstly, agriculture, where not dissimilar shares

[16] Clark's tertiary sector shares for 1871 and 1881 are 29·6 per cent and 31·6 per cent respectively. Since his 1891 and 1901 figures are virtually identical with our later labour input ones (despite obvious differences in concept), similar extrapolation may be reasonably acceptable. Clark, *The Conditions*, 1957, p. 510.

TABLE 5.3. *Distribution of Employment, by Industry, United States and Australia, Selected Years*, 1929–65

(per cent)

	Agriculture		Mining		Construction		Manufacturing		Transport and utilities		Trade		Finance and property		Community and business services		Public administration and defence		Other services	
	A	USA	A	USA	A	USA	A	USA	A	USA	A	USA	A	USA	A	USA	A	USA	A	USA
1929	21·5	19·9	1·8	2·2	10·9	5·0	21·0	22·8	8·9	9·7	15·5	16·7	2·1	3·4	6·3	7·3	2·1	6·0	9·8	7·0
1937	21·2	18·8	2·5	2·1	9·4	3·7	23·2	22·7	7·7	7·8	15·7	16·8	2·1	3·2	6·6	7·6	2·1	10·7	9·3	6·5
1947	16·3	12·1	1·7	1·7	7·1	5·2	28·2	26·7	9·5	8·6	14·6	18·4	2·4	3·2	6·3	8·3	6·5	10·6	7·4	5·2
1956	12·8	8·3	1·6	1·4	9·2	5·6	28·3	27·1	9·9	8·0	16·1	18·2	2·9	3·9	7·9	7·8	5·3	13·7	6·1	6·1
1960	11·2	—	1·3	—	9·5	—	28·3	—	9·7	—	16·4	—	3·5	—	9·3	—	4·8	—	5·9	—
1965	—	5·7	—	0·9	—	5·6	—	25·9	—	7·2	—	18·4	—	4·3	—	9·4	—	15·5	—	7·1

Source: USA: Fuchs, *The Service Economy*, Table 2; Australia. See Appendix.

in the twenties had become very different by the sixties, with the American by then roughly half the Australian. (The similarity of the twenties was a temporary conjunction as the American share continued the rapid decline which dates from the late nineteenth century.) Secondly, general government, where, whatever the accuracy of the comparative *levels*, we can be fairly sure that the Australian trend has lagged considerably behind that in the United States. Differential defence expansion almost certainly plays a major part in the deviation. And thirdly, construction, where the Australian share is roughly double that of the American, though the gap shows some tendency to narrow. Again there is a reasonably high probability of inconsistent boundaries. The sources of these differential trends and levels in terms of levels of capital intensity, technological progressiveness or market structure are not even speculated on here. The points which require emphasis are that the manufacturing shares are very similar (contrary to the implication of the 'industrial' figures) and that, on the service side, the differences are very much reduced if we set aside the public administration and defence components.

As already intimated the third (tertiary) sector employed in subsequent description of the Australian experience is a much wider one than Fuchs' 'services', reflecting a preference for a purely manufacturing intermediate sector. As such it would almost certainly not come within the category of 'reasonable change' in sector boundaries and we would not necessarily expect Fuchs' conclusions to hold for it. However, the service sub-sector of tertiary differs only in the inclusion of transport and communication and Fuchs explicitly asserts that none of his conclusions would be altered significantly by such a change.[17] A brief outline of the reasons for the boundaries adopted now precedes examination of the changing shares of the various sectors in Australian employment, output and income. It is appropriate to remind the reader that he is being asked to go along with the sector approach at this stage, bearing in mind that doubts about its usefulness are to be raised in the final section.

The maximum disaggregation compatible with interrelated discussion of Australian employment, income and output trends since 1890 leaves us with eight industries:[18]

(i) rural (agricultural, pastoral, dairying, forestry, fishing, hunting, etc.)
(ii) mining and quarrying

[17] Fuchs, *The Service Economy*, p. 17.
[18] For basic data and sources, see Appendix.

(iii) manufacturing
(iv) gas, electricity, and water supply (the 'utilities')
(v) building and construction
(vi) trade and transport (distribution/commerce, transport, communications, storage)
(vii) finance and property
(viii) other services (public administration, defence, community and business services, other services).

Livestock accumulation and house rents (whether the latter arise from market operations or from imputation in the case of owner-occupied dwellings) are excluded from both aggregates and relevant components in the following. No extended justification is called for in either case; with familiar arguments giving no decisive verdict, statistical convenience (continuity with the post-war estimates which exclude livestock accumulation) and analytical usefulness (there is no practical employment equivalent to the ownership of dwellings product) prevailed.

Even at the eight industry level we cannot be certain that product and employment boundaries are consistent in concept or definition. In some cases there is no marketed labour input exactly matching product (especially in construction); some labour input has no measured product equivalent (especially in agriculture). And there must remain considerable doubt about the mutual consistency of the product and work force boundaries particularly in manufacturing, commerce and 'other services'. This necessarily carries over to the sector estimates. A fuller treatment of some of the issues can be found elsewhere.[19]

How the eight industries may be combined into a smaller number of sectors could be discussed at length, but the only realistic conclusion is that the validity of the sector definitions adopted is primarily a function of the economy being studied and the questions being posed. The sector breakdown employed here—seen as pertinent to the particular economy and questions in which we are interested—is a modified three-fold one. It is impossible, in the Australian context, to rely on a simple three-sector breakdown in discussion of both domestic trends and the external implications (and origins) of structural change. While the present purpose is essentially descriptive, provision of alternative data seems desirable.

The primary sector poses little difficulty. It consists of the rural

[19] N. G. Butlin and J. A. Dowie, 'Estimates of Australian Workforce and Employment 1861–1961', *Australian Economic History Review*, IX, 1969.

and mining industries. Many—including Fuchs—would include mining with the more 'industrial' industries, but in Australia the correct allocation in terms of both geography and technology is with agriculture rather than industry if a choice must be made. The alternative breakdowns arise solely from the allocation of the utilities and construction. In discussion of domestic trends it is advantageous to define a service component as those industries producing an intangible output (trade and transport, finance and property, other services). On the other hand, where international considerations arise, and they arise much more forcefully in the Australian than in the United States' case, a sector which best approximates a 'non-traded' one is desirable. This means the addition of construction and the utilities to services and the formation of the tertiary sector. Manufacturing is consequently raised, by itself, to sector status and, abstracting from the complexities arising from input-output relationships (discussed in the concluding section), the primary sector may be viewed as historically the main source of 'exportables' and the manufacturing sector as the main source of 'importables'. These two can be conceived of as collectively making up the 'traded goods' segment of the economy. The tertiary sector represents largely 'non-traded' production, mainly though not exclusively services which are produced and consumed instantaneously, and hence tend to be a domestic preserve because of high transport costs.

STRUCTURAL SHIFTS IN EMPLOYMENT

Subsequent charts and tables reaffirm that services and tertiary activities have not been the consistently rapid absorbers of labour they have been in America in the last three-quarters of a century. There are obvious reservations about the representativeness of the single observations for 1890–1 and 1900–1, particularly for the tertiary sector, where the phasing of the medium-run 'building cycle' exerts a clear influence on the employment level. Nevertheless there seems little doubt that services have grown at only slightly above the average rate during the seventy years. Surprisingly, the two crude steps which have been taken towards a labour input measure (weighting females at two-thirds of a male and helpers as half of their appropriate sex) make almost no difference to the sector rates of growth over the whole period. Other desirable adjustments to the employment measure (desirable for productivity calculations in particular) may disturb this symmetry, but at the present stage it is possible to discuss the employment and crude labour input estimates simultaneously.

Between 1890–1 and 1960–1 the service share of employment rose from 40 to 48 per cent, and its share of crude labour inputs from 37 to 46 per cent (Table 5.4). Both reflect compound rates of growth of 1·9 per cent per annum compared with the average for the whole economy of 1·7. Primary employment, which grew negligibly after the first war though it did not reach its peak in absolute terms until 1937–8, had an overall growth rate of 0·4 per cent, while manufacturing inputs grew at 2·7 per cent per annum. These are quite distinctly different patterns of growth. Manufacturing absorbed the majority of the out-migration from primary—13 of the 19 percentage points. Tertiary by definition absorbed the other 6, and the fact that services rose by 8 points implies that construction and utilities collectively lost ground slightly.

In order to discover whether these long-term trends mask divergent

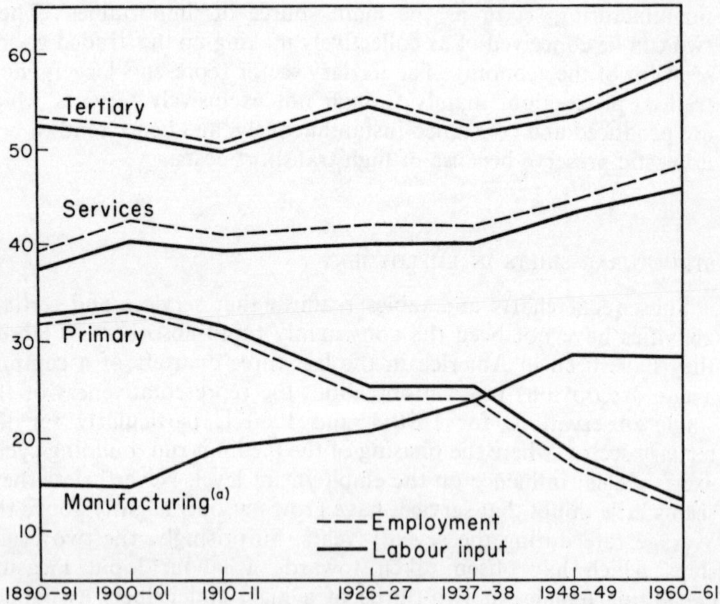

Chart 5.1 Shares of Employment and Labour Input by Sector, Selected Years, 1890–91 to 1960–61

(a) Employment and Labour Input virtually indistinguishable.

Source: See Appendix.

shorter-term movements (in primary it has already been implied that they do), an appropriate periodization must be produced. Since the choice of periods carries through all subsequent description—of product, income, productivity, etc.—a brief formal note is called for. Ideally we seek points which will represent the Australian economy operating at similar levels of capacity utilization; strictly when it is in long-term equilibrium. As a minimum practical requirement, this can be taken to imply a similar degree of labour under-utilization; in fact, trade cycle peaks, whatever the absolute unemployment rate, have normally to suffice. In a longer-term sense it might be desirable to have points at which the 'allocative efficiency' (or degree of misallocation) of the economy was of a similar order. This would imply that the effects of the elimination of structural inefficiencies would be excluded from 'true' productivity measures calculated between the selected points. We have little alternative but to leave such effects in the results.

Four major periods are defined (1890–1 to 1910–11, 1910–11 to

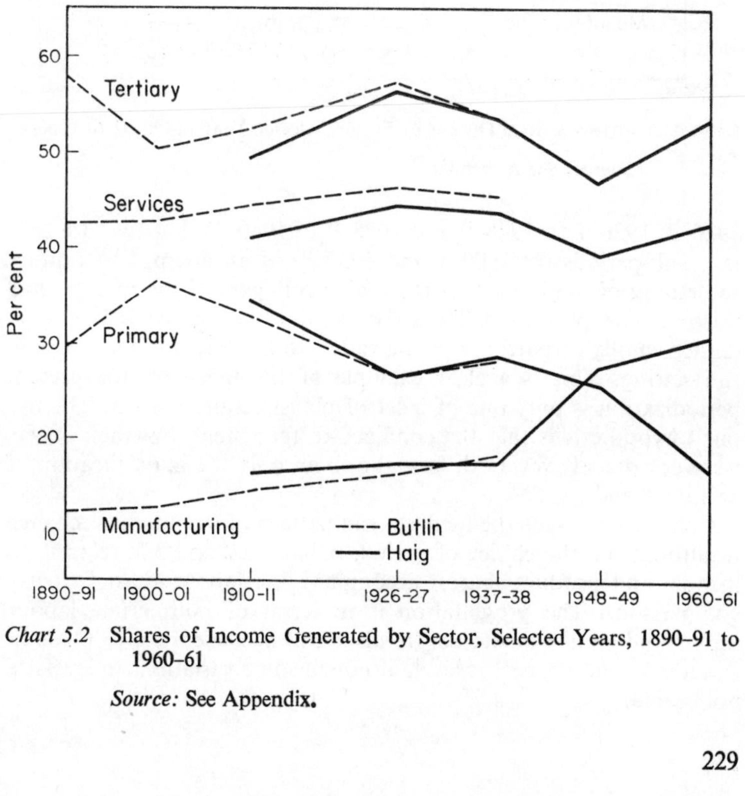

Chart 5.2 Shares of Income Generated by Sector, Selected Years, 1890–91 to 1960–61

Source: See Appendix.

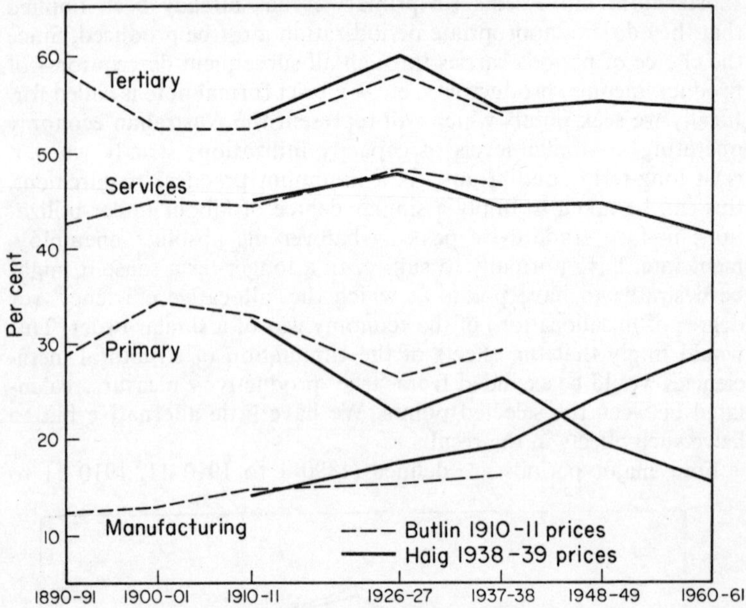

Chart 5.3 Shares of Real Output by Sector, Selected Years, 1890–91 to 1960–61

Source: See Appendix.

1926–7, 1926–7 to 1948–9 and 1948–9 to 1960–1), but two are split into sub-periods (at 1900–1 and 1937–8) in an attempt to capture something of the impact of the major collapses of the nineties and thirties. The periods deliberately avoid isolating the major wars (either wholly or partly), seeking rather to place them in a medium-run setting. This is a clear example of the fact that the present periodization is only one of a set of plausible alternatives. The implicit hypothesis is that the conflicts, to the extent that their effects were not quickly reversed, brought about only the intensification of existing trends.

Chart 5.1 presents the medium-run pattern of employment change resulting from the choice of period. (Charts 5.2 and 5.3, relating to income and product shares, accompany the labour chart for easy comparison.) The presentation is in terms of both crude labour inputs and employment; the trends are almost identical to those in employment at the sector level, although some variations in level are noticeable.

TABLE 5.4. *Shares of Employment and Labour Input by Sector, Selected Years, 1890–1 to 1960–1*
(per cent)

	Primary	Manufacturing	Tertiary Services	All
EMPLOYMENT				
1890–91	31·5	15·0	39·6	53·6
1900–01	33·0	14·7	42·3	52·3
1910–11	30·5	18·8	41·1	50·7
1926–27	24·0	20·5	42·0	55·5
1937–38	23·9	23·5	42·0	52·6
1948–49	17·0	28·6	44·8	54·4
1960–61	12·6	28·2	48·0	59·2
LABOUR INPUT				
1890–91	32·4	15·1	37·3	52·5
1900–01	33·6	15·0	40·4	51·4
1910–11	31·4	18·7	39·5	49·9
1926–27	25·1	20·3	40·1	54·6
1937–38	25·1	23·3	40·1	51·6
1948–49	17·9	28·5	43·2	53·5
1960–61	13·2	28·5	46·1	58·3

Source: See Appendix.

The halving of the primary share of labour inputs over the whole period was accomplished by a consistent decline, with the exception of the nineties and the 1926–7 to 1937–8 period, when the rural industries and mining both benefited from depressed conditions in urban labour markets. Even so the interruptions were little more than holding operations, especially in the thirties. Manufacturing employment lost some ground in the readjustments of the nineties but, in contrast, during those of the thirties it continued to display the above average growth which it experienced from about 1900. In many ways manufacturing employment seems to have benefited more from the second depression than the primary industries. 'Artificial' influences such as the interim expansion of the tariff would clearly have to be introduced alongside 'natural' developments to explain the contrasting experience of manufacturing in the two depression periods. Accelerated growth in manufacturing in the decade which embraces the second war took its share of employment to the 28 per cent level and obviously of considerable significance is the constancy of this fraction during the remaining period to 1960.

While there appear to be fairly persistent tendencies for the trading sectors to either grow or decline relatively, the pictures on the tertiary and service sides are more ambiguous. The medium-run volatility of the building and construction industry, superimposed on a service share which is virtually stationary for the first four decades of this century, gives a wave-like character to the tertiary share. (This would appear to have particular importance for external questions and be closely relevant to suggestions concerning the existence of 'long swings' in the growth process.) Only in the post-Second World War period has the services sector displayed a rate of growth of labour inputs greater than that in manufacturing. However, while it only became the fastest—indeed *only*—grower in the post-war period, the beginning of its relative growth after several decades of average expansion is certainly to be found in the late thirties and early forties.

Since it is not possible to assess the normality (or abnormality) of the trends in the 1890s with much confidence, the aim as far as work force trends are concerned must be explanation of (*a*) the constant medium-run service share (42 per cent of employment, 40 per cent of labour inputs) which seems to have existed between the late nineties and late thirties, and (*b*) the growing service share which characterized the subsequent period (raising the shares to 48 and 46 per cent respectively).

INCOME AND PRODUCT SHARES

The apparent simplicity of employment shares is illusory, the adjustments in search of a 'labour input' measure giving some small indication of the true complexity of quantification of the economic —as against human—concept involved. The difficulties come to the surface in moving to consideration of income and product shares. Here it is necessary to cope not only with minor statistical differences in alternative current price series but, more important, with both the statistical and conceptual variations between alternative estimates of real product by sector.

In the case of the unpublished Haig estimates running from 1910–11 to 1960–1 and providing the crucial—and previously unavailable—link between 1938–9 and 1948–9, it is not yet possible to gather any clear picture of possible biases. However, the series represent a major contribution to a consistent picture of the twentieth-century Australian economy and I am most grateful for the opportunity to extract some of their implications at this stage. For present purposes I propose to assume that a considerable part of the differences in the real output trends shown by the Haig estimates and the established series of Butlin (in the overlapping periods) may be directly explicable in terms of the different base years employed. Different deflation techniques are regarded as possible sizeable contributors, but ones which may not distort prohibitively at the sector level. In fact, as far as the broad trends in services are concerned, the differences between the series can be handled without too much difficulty. Nevertheless, it is imperative to remember that there is no such thing as *the* change in the service (or any) share of real output, and if this unpleasant fact is not made too obtrusive in the following discussion, the alternative series in charts and tables should provide frequent reminders.

Inspection of Charts 5.2 and 5.3, and Table 5.5 suggests that over the seven decades *as a whole* the proportion of income and product originating in the service sub-sector changed only slightly. The terminal current price shares of services are identical (though the alternative series differ slightly in between) and, comparing the strictly incomparable, the constant price share was almost exactly the same in 1960–1 (1938–9 prices) as it was in 1890–1 (1910–11 prices). However, even when concern is essentially with medium to long-run trends, the charts suggest there is clear merit in splitting the period in half. Both price bases yield identical shares for 1926–7 and, taken in conjunction with the similar terminal shares, provide some foundation for the hypothesis that the service share expanded relatively in output terms until the middle or late twenties, but from then until 1960 underwent an equivalent reversal. The rise and fall were both of the order of six percentage points and are accordingly comparable in scale with the extent of the employment share rise between 1937–8 and 1960–1. The pattern also shows up in the current price series, although here the difference in levels between the series is a little more substantial. Still, the picture is surprisingly clear in both cases and has the comforting implication that overseas studies, including those given some space above, are both relevant to, and less than fully informative on, the Australian story. Neither in the case of labour inputs or of output and income can we talk in terms of a one-directional long-run trend in Australia since 1890.

While the implications of the alternative series are gratifyingly similar for services, the contrasts in the associated changes in other sectors are of substance. The rates of growth contained in Table 5.6 (see also Chart 5.4) show that Haig's 1938–9 based series yields an aggregate rate of growth 50 per cent higher for the 1910–11 to 1926–7 period than Butlin's 1910–11 based one (2·7 per cent per annum against 1·8). Arithmetically this is the result of a manufacturing rate which is almost double that of Butlin's (4·0 against 2·2) and of a substantially higher rate of growth of service output (3·1 against 2·3).

TABLE 5.5. *Shares of Income and Product by Sector, Selected Years, 1890–1 to 1960–1*
(per cent)

	Primary		Manufacturing		Tertiary			
					Services		All	
	Butlin	Haig	Butlin	Haig	Butlin	Haig	Butlin	Haig
GDP in current prices								
1890–91	29·9		12·2		42·8		57·9	
1900–01	36·6		12·9		42·9		50·5	
1910–11	32·9	34·4	14·5	16·3	44·4	41·0	52·6	49·3
1926–27	26·4	26·5	16·4	16·9	46·6	44·1	57·3	56·7
1937–38	28·2	28·4	18·0	17·7	45·5	43·6	53·8	53·9
1948–49		25·8		27·3		39·2		46·9
1960–61		16·2		30·5		42·4		53·3
GDP in constant prices (Butlin 1910–11, Haig 1938–9)								
1890–91	28·9		12·3		42·7		58·8	
1900–01	34·4		13·0		44·9		52·6	
1910–11	32·9	32·3	14·5	14·2	44·4	44·7	52·6	53·5
1926–27	26·4	22·2	15·5	17·4	48·0	47·7	58·1	60·4
1937–38	29·4	26·3	16·5	19·3	46·2	44·3	54·0	54·4
1948–49		19·5		24·4		45·7		56·1
1960–61		15·6		29·0		42·3		55·4

Source: See Appendix.

Note: A belated official entry into the field, *Estimates of Gross Product by Industry at Current and Constant Prices 1959–60 to 1965–66* (Supplement to Australian National Accounts, National Income and Expenditure, 1953–4 to 1966–7) yields the shares below. The differing 1960–1 current price shares warn the reader of classification differences as well as differences in deflation procedures (and base years). But no revisions in the argument seem called for.

	Primary	Manufacturing	Tertiary Services	All
Current Prices				
1960–61	14·6	31·3	43·4	54·0
1965–66	12·8	54·0	43·7	55·7
1959–60 Prices				
1960–61	15·6	31·9	42·1	52·5
1965–66	13·4	33·6	41·7	53·0

In *relative* terms, as we have already seen, the service sector is not affected, so that the faster relative manufacturing growth in Haig is reflected in, and reflects, faster relative primary contraction.

Before considering the productivity implications of the alternative

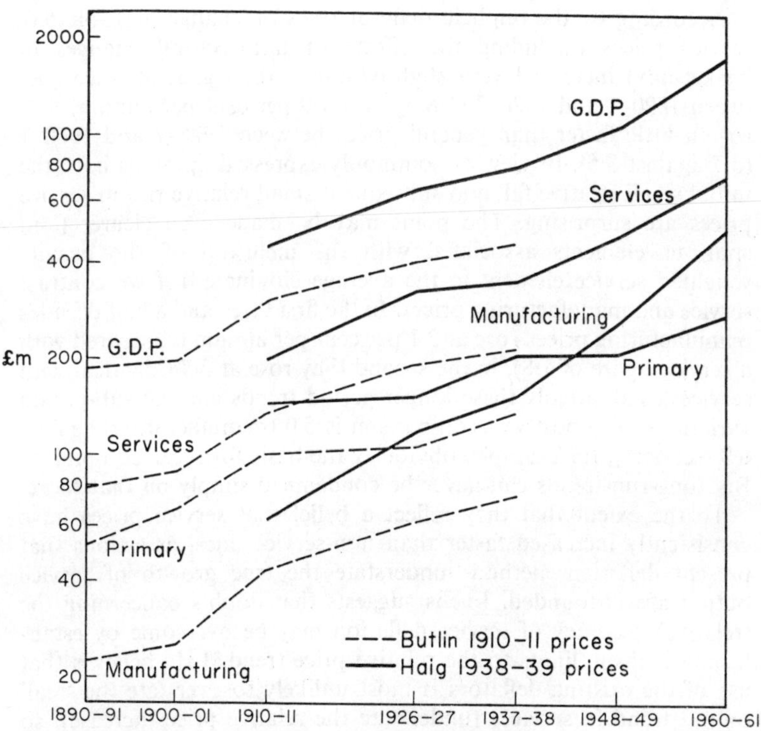

Chart 5.4 Real Output by Sector (1910–11 and 1938–39 Prices) Selected Years, 1890–91 to 1960–61

Source: See Appendix

series we may ask what light the income and product figures throw on the found trend in twentieth-century service employment (average growth for four decades, above average in the subsequent two). It is, of course, conventional to postulate that any given input trend can be interpreted initially as the result of either the relevant output trend or of a change in the output-input relationship (or some combination of the two). A rising service share of labour inputs indicates a rising service share of output and/or a below average rate of increase in labour productivity in services. The above estimates give little support to the hypothesis that service product (value added) has a *consistently* above-average income elasticity of demand. On the contrary in fact, they provide some grounds for believing that the response was positive for the first half of the period but became negative for the second half.

According to the implicit deflator rates of change in Table 5.6, service prices (including the effects of intrasectoral changes in basket-mix) increased very slightly slower than general prices between 1890–1 and 1926–7 (1·8 against 1·9 per cent per annum), but rose a little faster than general prices between 1926–7 and 1960–1 (3·7 against 3·5). In view of commonly expressed opinions both the initial small relative fall and subsequent small relative rise in service prices are surprising. The point may be made even clearer (and spurious elements associated with the inclusion of the heavily weighted service element in the average eliminated) if we contrast service and manufacturing prices. In the first three and a half decades manufacturing prices rose at 2·1 per cent per annum (compared with a service figure of 1·8), in the second they rose at 3·7 (identical with services). Admittedly these longer-period trends conceal sub-period variations. The post-war comparison is 5·0 (manufacturing) against 6·9 (services), for example, obviously the basis for received opinion. But long-run trends can never be condemned simply on that score.

To the extent that they reflect a belief that service prices have consistently increased faster than non-service ones, assertions that present deflation methods understate the true growth of service output are ill-founded. Fuchs suggests that doubts concerning the (relative) accuracy of service deflation may be overcome by establishing realistic limits to the relative price trend.[20] He believes that use of the existing deflators is most unlikely to overstate the 'real' output trend in services (understate the relative price increase), so that this gives a lower limit. (Retail trade is noted as a possible exception within the service sector.) The upper limit is taken to be

[20] Fuchs, *The Service Economy*, pp. 35–7.

TABLE 5.6. *Rates of Growth of Income, Output and Implicit Prices, by Sector, Selected Periods, 1890–1 to 1960–1*

(per cent per annum; alternative series B = Butlin, H = Haig)

	Primary		Manufacturing		Tertiary				Total	
					Services		All			
	B	H	B	H	B	H	B	H	B	H
GDP at current prices										
1890–91 to 1900–01	2·5		1·1		0·5		−0·9		0·5	
1900–01 to 1910–11	4·1		6·4		5·6		5·6		5·2	
1910–11 to 1926–27	4·3	4·3	6·6	6·3	6·1	6·6	6·4	6·9	5·8	6·1
1926–27 to 1937–38	1·2	1·2	1·4	1·0	0·4	0·4	−0·1	0·1	0·5	0·5
1937–38 to 1948–49		7·7		13·0		7·6		7·3		8·6
1948–49 to 1960–61		6·0		11·2		10·9		11·4		10·2
1890–91 to 1926–27	3·8		5·0		4·4		4·1		4·1	
1926–27 to 1960–61		4·9		8·3		6·3		6·3		6·5
GDP at constant prices (B = 1910–11 base; H = 1938–9 base)										
1890–91 to 1900–01	2·4		1·2		1·2		−0·5		0·6	
1900–01 to 1910–11	3·9		5·5		4·2		4·4		4·4	
1910–11 to 1926–27	0·4	0·4	2·2	4·0	2·3	3·1	2·4	3·5	1·8	2·7
1926–27 to 1937–38	2·3	2·9	1·9	2·4	1·0	0·7	0·7	0·4	1·3	1·4
1937–38 to 1948–49		−0·0		4·9		3·0		3·0		2·7
1948–49 to 1960–61		2·5		5·9		3·7		4·3		4·4
1890–91 to 1926–27	1·9		2·8		2·5		2·2		2·2	
1926–27 to 1960–61		1·8		4·4		2·5		2·6		2·9
Implicit price deflator (B = 1910–11 base; H = 1938–9 base)										

TABLE 5.6.—*continued*

	Primary		Manufac-turing		Tertiary Services		All		Total	
	B	H	B	H	B	H	B	H	B	H
1890–91 to 1900–01	0·1		−0·1		−0·6		−0·4		−0·2	
1900–01 to 1910–11	0·2		0·9		1·3		1·2		0·8	
1910–11 to 1926–27	3·9	4·0	4·3	2·2	3·7	3·3	3·8	3·4	3·9	3·3
1926–27 to 2937–38	−1·2	−1·7	−0·5	−1·4	−0·6	−0·3	−0·7	−0·4	−0·8	−0·8
1937–38 to 1948–49		7·7		7·7		4·4		4·1		5·8
1948–49 to 1960–61		3·5		5·0		6·9		6·8		5·5
1890–91 to 1927–27	1·8		2·1		1·8		1·9		1·9	
1926–27 to 1960–61		3·1		3·7		3·7		3·6		3·5

Source: See Appendix.

Note: Official estimates recently available (see note to Table 5.5) yield following rates of growth for 1960–1 to 1965–6 period:

Current prices	4·2	7·1	7·1	7·6	7·0
1959–60 prices	1·7	5·8	4·5	4·9	4·7
Implicit deflator	2·5	1·3	2·6	2·7	2·3

the rate of output growth which would result if service prices had really changed at the same rate as all prices, that is at the same rate as the aggregate implicit deflator. In terms of the later of our two main sub-periods this would mean setting the service price trends 0·2 per cent per annum lower and real output (and productivity) measures roughly the same amount higher. However, Fuchs had clearly not considered as a realistic possibility a situation where measured service prices increased *slower* than the aggregate index. Application of the technique would, in the case of our first sub-period, produce an 'upper' limit which was lower than the lower limit. Unless we believe that the possible bias in measurement may work in different directions in different periods, the procedure consequently holds little promise for Australia.

Because of the small measured changes in relative service prices, it would be desirable to have an independent check on the present conclusion regarding the income elasticity of demand for service product. In practice, of course, the income elasticity concept is usually phrased in expenditure rather than product terms, with the coefficients referring to the final output of (say) services rather than to the value added by that sector. Strictly, calculated elasticities would only be similar in the two cases if the relative proportions of intermediate inputs into each sector's output remained unchanged over the relevant period. The input-output table discussed in the final section indicates the variations in these proportions at one point of time and it would be reasonable to expect shifts in them through time. Nevertheless, in our present state of knowledge, evidence from expenditure data which suggested that the income response of service demand was not far removed from the average (unity) would be welcomed. Welcomed at least as far as the whole seventy-year period is concerned, that is. The first half period service product response is apparently of the order of 1·20, the largely offsetting one for the second half of the order of 0·85.

Fuchs reports the results of two experiments in the United States which do suggest a service elasticity only marginally higher than unity. One, utilizing time series data by state for the 1939–58 period yielded an elasticity for retail sales of goods of 0·97, for personal services of 1·12 and for total state and local government expenditures of 1·07. Another investigation, relying on a 160-region breakdown of 1960–1 United States consumer expenditures, yielded a service elasticity of 1·12 compared with 0·93 for goods. In fact, when 'at home food' and tobacco were excluded from goods, the later figure rose to 1·05. (Incidentally, the study also suggested that demand for services was positively related to education and age, but negatively related to family size.)

Some preliminary analysis of the results if a large-scale Australian consumption study for the 1920–1 to 1965–6 period yields the elasticities shown in Table 5.7.[21] Estimates have been made with and without a time trend extracted and for the interwar and post-war periods (as defined in this paper), as well as for the second half of the overall period which incorporates them. (The latter, overall estimates, however, include only one observation beyond those of the two individual periods.) While the longer-run (1926–7 to 1960–1) income elasticities for services can be regarded as reasonably consistent—at 0·7—with the implications of the output figures, the outstanding feature of the table is undoubtedly the massive difference between the interwar and post-war coefficients for services; a value (0·4) less than that for food comes to exceed goods (excluding food) by 1·8 to 1·6. In fact, there must be grave doubts about the present

[21] B. D. Haig and Jennifer Finlayson, 'Consumption Expenditure and Living Standards, 1920/21 to 1965/66', in preparation.

TABLE 5.7. *Demand Elasticities for Food, Goods and Services,*[a] *Selected Periods, 1926–7 to 1960–1*
(regression coefficient, standard error in parentheses, t ratio; adjusted R^2, F test)

	1926–7 to 1937–8			1948–9 to 1960–1			1926–7 to 1960–1		
	Food	Goods	Services	Food	Goods	Services	Food	Goods	Services
A. *Income and Price*									
Income	0·696	1·937	0·420	0·231	1·623	1·757	0·343	1·889	0·714
	(0·075)	(0·108)	(0·034)	(0·050)	(0·177)	(0·249)	(0·039)	(0·026)	(0·110)
	9·2	17·9	12·4	4·7	9·2	7·1	8·9	71·8	6·5
Price	−0·621	−0·578	0·338	−0·516	−0·181	−0·654	−0·462	−0·238	−0·529
	(0·156)	(0·246)	(0·347)	(0·049)	(0·160)	(0·245)	(0·136)	(0·098)	(0·149)
	−4·0	−2·3	1·0	−10·4	−1·1	−2·7	−3·4	−2·4	−3·5
Adj. R^2	0·900	0·989	0·944	0·912	0·972	0·825	0·783	0·995	0·946
F (D.F.)	44·9	453·0	83·5	56·7	186·5	26·1	43·8	2,593·5	208·7
	(2, 9)			(2, 10)			(2, 23)		
B. *Income, Price and Time*[b]									
Income	0·627	2·184	0·422	0·054	1·681	1·728	0·167	2·279	0·702
	(0·114)	(0·136)	(0·036)	(0·110)	(0·173)	(0·140)	(0·070)	(0·050)	(0·103)
	5·5	16·1	11·7	0·5	9·7	12·3	2·4	45·7	6·8
Price	−0·383	0·177	0·255	−0·590	−0·634	−0·649	−0·373	0·047	−0·512
	(0·332)	(0·375)	(0·433)	(0·065)	(0·442)	(0·069)	(0·115)	(0·078)	(0·140)
	−1·2	0·5	0·6	−9·1	−1·4	−9·4	−3·2	0·6	− 3·6
Time[b]	0·003	−0·007	0·000	0·003	0·007	0·000	0·003	0·007	0·000
	(0·003)	(0·003)	(0·001)	(0·002)	(0·006)	(0·002)	(0·001)	(0·001)	(0·002)
	0·8	−2·4	0·4	1·8	−1·1	0·2	2·8	−8·5	0·2
Adj. R^2	0·897	0·993	0·939	0·911	0·976	0·988	0·855	0·998	0·968
F (D.F.)	29·0	460·2	50·3	37·3	144·4	292·6	47·6	3,306·8	240·9
	(3, 8)			(3, 9)			(3, 22)		

[a] Including Net Expenditure Abroad.
[b] Time trend extracted throughout is that for 1926–7 to 1937–8.

Source: B. D. Haig and Jennifer Finlayson, 'Consumption Expenditure and Living Standards, 1920/21 to 1965/66', in preparation. I am most grateful to the authors for access to their preliminary estimates and for arranging a run tailored to my requirements.

interwar coefficient. It seems inevitable that there is currently some understatement of the growth of real expenditures on services, reflecting itself in both the very low income elasticity and the positive and insignificant price elasticity. But we can perhaps speculate that future revisions will not eliminate the significant contrast in the income elasticities for services in the two periods, though they will probably narrow the gap and bring the overall coefficient much closer to unity. Of course, quite dramatic contrary *short*-term movements might in some sense be expected (because of swings in consumer durable consumption, for example), but in general I would

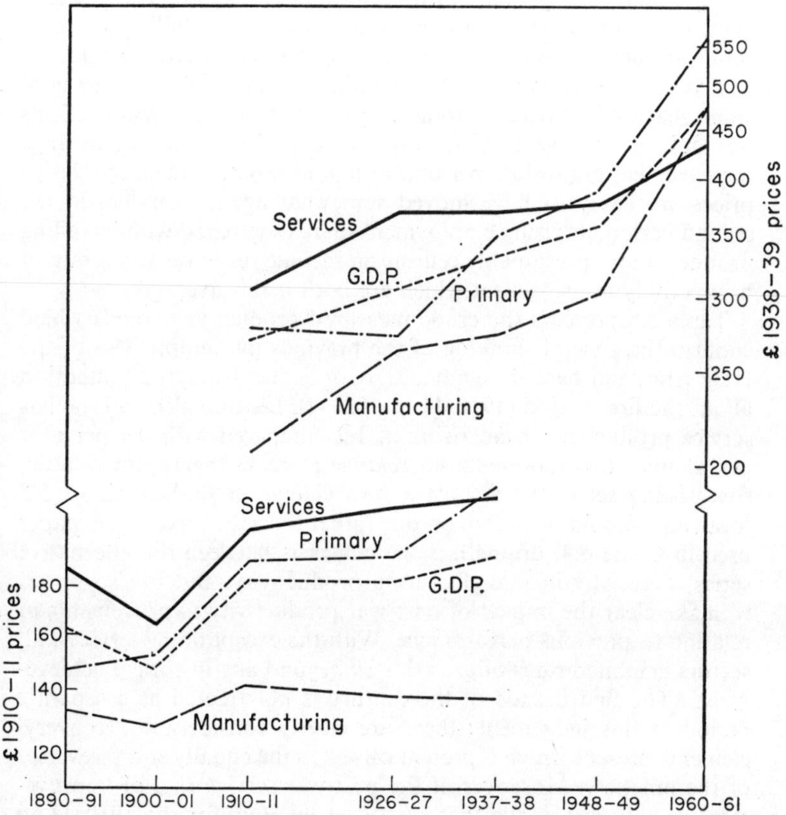

Chart 5.5 Product per Unit of Labour Input by Sector (1910–11 and 1938–39 Prices) Selected Years, 1890–91 to 1960–61

Source: See Appendix.

take this analysis to constitute a further warning against confident proclamations concerning the consistency of service trends.

Viewing the seventy years as a whole, then, it is possible to be fairly confident that in Australia, as in America, it is a slower rate of growth of product per labour input in services, rather than a faster growth of service product, that accounts for shifts towards service employment. But within the period trends in product and employment are distinctive enough to make the overall conclusion of dubious interest. From about 1900 to the middle and late twenties a constant service share of labour inputs is generating a constant or rising (mainly rising) share of total production; subsequently a constant or rising share of labour inputs generates a falling share of total product. Since relative prices look to have moved very slightly in favour of services in the first period, it is probable that the constant share of services in total employment in these years reflects not only a positive income response but also an above average improvement in product per unit of labour input. And since relative prices are likely to have moved somewhat against services in the second period, its rising employment share (compared with its falling product share) presumably reflects an income response and a rate of productivity improvement which are both below average.

Table 5.8 presents the crude measured productivity trends which confirm the general thinking of the previous paragraph. Use of the Haig series and base does not add to, or deduct from, the contention about the first period (1910–11 to 1926–7), because although he has service product per head rising at 1·2 compared with 0·4 per cent per annum, this represents no *relative* increase (aggregate productivity being set at 0·8 against a zero change in Butlin). Chart 5.5 (drawn, it should be noted, on one rather than the three, cycle paper used in Chart 5.4) dramatizes the contrasts between the alternative series, especially in manufacturing productivity. But it also serves to make clear the impact of post-war productivity improvements in relation to previous performance. With the exception of services, all sectors exhibited rates of growth *well* beyond any historical achievement. (The first decade of the century is not treated as a separate period in this judgement; there are clearly considerable 'recovery' elements present which represent offsets to the equally sharp reverses of the nineties.) Moreover, if the post-war service rate of improvement is only just above that suggested by Haig for the 1910–11 to 1926–7 period, it is interesting to note that, at 1·3 per cent per annum, it still exceeds that achieved in either primary or manufacturing for most of the overall period. There is certainly no ground for

TABLE 5.8. *Rates of Growth of Employment, Labour Input, and Product per Unit of Labour Input, by Sector, Selected Periods, 1890–1 to 1960–1*

(per cent per annum; alternative product series B = Butlin, H = Haig)

	Primary		Manufac-turing		Tertiary Services		Tertiary All		Total	
Employment and labour input	E	LI	E	LI	E	LI	E	LI	E	LI
1890–91 to 1900–01	2·3	2·1	1·6	1·6	2·5	2·5	1·6	1·5	1·8	1·7
1900–01 to 1910–11	1·3	1·5	4·6	4·4	1·8	1·9	1·8	1·9	2·1	2·2
1910–11 to 1926–27	0·3	0·4	2·4	2·4	2·0	1·9	2·4	2·4	1·8	1·8
1926–27 to 1937–38	0·8	0·7	2·0	2·0	0·8	0·7	0·3	0·2	0·8	0·7
1937–38 to 1948–49	−1·0	−1·0	3·9	4·0	2·7	2·8	2·4	2·4	2·1	2·1
1948–49 to 1960–61	−0·7	−0·7	1·8	1·9	2·5	2·4	2·6	2·6	1·9	1·9
1890–91 to 1926–27	1·1	1·2	2·8	2·7	2·1	2·1	2·0	2·0	1·9	1·9
1926–27 to 1960–61	−0·3	−0·3	2·6	2·6	2·0	2·0	1·8	1·8	1·6	1·6
Real product per unit of labour input	B	H	B	H	B	H	B	H	B	H
1890–91 to 1900–01	0·4		−0·5		−1·3		−1·9		−1·0	
1900–01 to 1910–11	2·4		1·0		2·2		2·4		2·2	
1910–11 to 1926–27	0·0	−0·1	−0·1	1·6	0·4	1·2	0·0	1·0	−0·0	0·9
1926–27 to 1937–38	1·6	2·2	−0·0	0·4	0·3	−0·0	0·5	0·2	0·6	0·6
1937–38 to 1948–49		1·0		0·9		0·2		0·5		0·6
1948–49 to 1960–61		3·2		4·0		1·3		1·7		2·5
1890–91 to 1926–27	0·8		0·1		0·4		0·2		0·3	
1926–27 to 1960–61		2·1		1·8		0·5		0·8		1·3

Source: See Appendix.

suggesting that productivity is *static* in services *as a whole*. In any event the lessons of the (thankfully) expiring 'growth rate' debate of recent years should certainly have made all of us aware of the vastness of the problem of deciding on the relevant yardstick—inter-area (i.e. intersectoral in this case), intertemporal, or some assessed potential—when seeking to affix the designations 'fast' and 'slow', 'high' and 'low'. If I appear to remain agnostic on productivity at the sector level, resisting all but the most mechanical of judgements, it is for very good reasons.

What are the likely results of further refinement of the input measures, including consideration of capital inputs, and of the development of superior output indexes? Here it is necessary to rely mainly on speculation and the possible relevance of American experience, by far the best documented. The existence of disaggregated information for that country has enabled the homogeneity of the service sector to be tested with regard to a number of indicators, and studies in depth of particular service areas have thrown up suggestions about the impact of such varied developments as changing hours, rising capital per worker, technical innovation, increasing consumer participation in the productive process, growth of unionization, and changing quality of the work force (approximated by age and sex composition and educational attainment). Fuchs' reported assessments, noted briefly above, might be expected to be most relevant to the 1926–7 to 1960–1 period in Australia, when the sectoral patterns of change in the two countries are more comparable, but naturally no strict applicability to the Australian economy could be proposed.

Fuchs' *industry*-service differential over the 1929–65 period was about 1·1 per cent per annum; the present *manufacturing*-service differential for 1926–7 to 1960–1 is 1·3. Fuchs believes that the 1·1 comprises, as rough orders of magnitude:

0·1 or 0·2 *net* understatement of the growth rate of real output in services. (The net is emphasized because of the probability of some downward bias in the construction component of industry and of possible *upward* bias in retail trade);

about 0·1 faster decline of hours worked per man in services;

about 0·3 slower rise in the 'quality of labour' in services. (Calculated as the net result of about 0·5 slower rise in compensation per man, and about 0·2 reflecting faster decline in hours and slower rate of unionization);

about 0·1 or 0·2 slower rise of capital inputs per worker in services; and, as a residual,

about 0·4 or 0·5 attributable to general influences such as a slower rate of technological change in services and/or a slower realization of economies of scale.[22]

This 'total factor' productivity difference of just under one-half of 1 per cent per annum is also that suggested by reference to the implicit price trend differential. Under the (heroic) assumption that the price of a composite, standardized unit of factor input *changes* at the same rate in each sector through the period—irrespective of relative sector initial or terminal prices—the relative change in total factor compensation in a sector is equal to the relative change in total factor inputs in that sector. Since the relative change in total factor compensation is given by the relative change in product at *current* prices, it is possible to arrive at the relative rate of change of resources-use efficiency in a sector by estimating the relative rate of change in its (implicit) price. The industry-service price differential in the United States, 1929–65, was 0·4 per cent per annum, equivalent to the observed residual.

Data limitations make it impossible to attempt seriously any of the direct adjustments of the input measure for Australia, but the result of making the necessary assumption about factor compensa-

TABLE 5.9. *Differential Rates of Change in Labour Productivity and Implicit Prices, Selected Periods, 1890–1 to 1960–1*
(per cent per annum; B = Butlin, H = Haig)

	Labour productivity (manufacturing-service)		Implicit price (service-manufacturing)	
	B	H	B	H
1890–91 to 1900–01	0·8	—	–0·5	—
1900–01 to 1910–11	–1·2	—	0·4	—
1910–11 to 1926–27	–0·5	0·4	–0·6	1·1
1926–27 to 1937–38	–0·3	0·4	–0·1	1·1
1937–38 to 1948–49	—	0·7	—	–3·3
1948–49 to 1960–61	—	2·7	—	1·9
1890–91 to 1926–27	–0·3	—	–0·3	—
1926–27 to 1960–61	—	1·3	—	0·0

Source: See Tables 5.6 and 5.8.

[22] Fuchs, *The Service Economy*, pp. 75–6.

tion trends can be noted. The differentials between the trends in manufacturing and service *labour* (not total) productivity and prices are set out in Table 5.9 (the differentials being reversed for easy comparison).

The outstanding feature is clearly the similarity of the Butlin differentials in all but one period compared with the consistent dissimilarity of the Haig ones. Naturally no implications about the relative accuracy of the underlying data flow directly from this contrast. There are two good sets of reasons for differences arising between these sets of figures.

Firstly, the assumption that the rates of change in factor rewards (adjusted for differential changes in hours, conditions, skill, quality, etc.) were the same in both sectors may *not* hold, fully or partly. In the absence of other reasons, the 1·3 *difference* in the 1926–7 to 1960–1 period (1·3 minus 0·0) might be explained, for example, by manufacturing unions being more successful in wage negotiations than their less numerous and more constrained service equivalents. Alternatively, the prevalence of salary scales and self employment in large areas of services may build in some lag. On the capital side one might hazard a guess that equity capital is a less important part of total investment in services relative to that in manufacturing, while the greater role of small-scale working proprietor enterprises could also help produce a slower growth of measured rewards to capital in the former.

Secondly, the standard adjustments to the crude labour productivity measure necessary in order to produce a true total factor input (and productivity) figure may account for the difference. Allowance for differential sector changes in hours worked, quality of labour and, particularly, capital per worker might, hypothetically, see the relative manufacturing input growth rate raised, and its productivity rate reduced to that in services. Capital is unlikely to provide anything like a complete explanation, however, because weighting it at one-third in both sectors, the necessary *differential* in capital stock growth in favour of manufacturing would have to be over 4·0 per cent per annum in order to close the gap. In the post-war period I have previously guesstimated that the *goods* capital stock grew about 1·5 per cent per annum faster than that in services.[23] This would narrow the 1·3 gap to about 0·8, if it is applicable to the longer period and to *manufacturing*. In fact, since it is likely that the manufacturing stock grew somewhat faster than the average for all goods, it would

[23] J. A. Dowie, 'Productivity Growth in Goods and Services: Australia, USA, UK', *Economic Record*, 42, 1966, p. 549.

probably be realistic to regard the capital adjustment as halving the difference.

It would be a shattering blow to many articles of local faith if the remaining six or seven points were to fall to the challenge of simple adjustments to the labour input measure. Admittedly, the widespread reliance on tariff protection during the era almost certainly resulted in the persistent introduction of small-scale and (relative to overseas best practice) technically-backward firms. But surely the technical stimuli of war and subsequent large-scale foreign investment in local manufacturing, *plus* the maturing of earlier decades of 'developmental' efforts, yielded a total productivity *advance* in this sector at least 1·0 per cent per annum better than that in the amalgam of service industries? We are well into the realm of hunch now, but my inclination would be in this case to support the local faith, not because of any firm conviction about manufacturing progress but because it seems not improbable to me that hours have been falling *more slowly* in services, and the quality of the work force rising *more quickly* in services (*vis à vis* manufacturing) in recent decades in Australia. In both these cases the initial sector *levels* (e.g. extent of graduate employment) are likely to have been quite different in Australia in the 1920s from what they were in America, opening up corresponding possibilities for growth rate divergence. These adjustments might accordingly tend to widen the gap in Australia rather than reduce it as in America.

The implication of accepting something like a 1·0 per cent residual differential would be, of course, an unwillingness to accept the necessary assumptions regarding competition in factor markets. Some reasons for reluctance in this direction have already been outlined. Resolution of data doubts, which represent a much more fundamental level of concern regarding the whole exercise, must await the promised presentation of the sources and methods underlying the Haig series.

INTERDEPENDENCE, AGGREGATION AND FUTURE WORK

In terms of Stigler's picturesque characterization we have tasted only *tout ensemble*, and that in a fairly mechanical way.[24] Promiscuity awaits, but it is no intention of this essay to satisfy desires

[24] '. . . the promiscuous ensemble of service industries'; George J. Stigler, *Trends in Employment in the Service Industries*, Princeton University Press, 1956, p. 166.

which may be held in that direction. It is possible to provide some information for a number of service components, reasonably comprehensive in work force terms, very restricted in systematic terms as far as income and product are concerned. Such information shows either that the service sector is, statistically, reasonably homogeneous—the dispersal of behaviour around its average trend is small as far as a given indicator (employment, output, productivity, etc.) is concerned—or that there is a considerable variety of experience contained within the sector, such that the sector average has statistically little significance. To proceed to such study in a limited way, and on the basis of existing data, would be largely profitless in my view. Indeed, the merits of even a comprehensive analysis of this sort, based on good data, can be questioned. In brief, the wisdom and necessity of decomposed study of *all* sectors is taken as self-evident, irrespective of the homogeneity or heterogeneity they exhibit according to statistical analysis of industrially-defined components. More particularly, the resolution of the above question for its own sake could well be regarded as basically uninteresting and likely to involve unproductive diversion from the individual study in depth of particular—meaningfully delimited—service areas. Clearly, faith in the service sector as an operational concept either in economic analysis or policy terms must be wavering at best. To that extent the central section of this essay is self-destructive: I would not expect many to think of the service sector as more than a yardstick construct, helpful in opening out questions without burying the searcher in data, but functional in only the most limited of senses.

The objections to use of the sector concept—at their clearest in the case of services but by no means unique to them—are simply stated in terms of the resulting lack of emphasis on interdependence and the familiar perils of aggregation. The question of interdependence may usefully be considered in the context of the earlier characterization of the primary and manufacturing sectors as producing 'traded goods' and the tertiary as producing 'non-traded goods'. Discussion focusing on other breakdowns of demand would be equally pertinent to the point, but the one chosen here is particularly relevant to the Australian case.

It is easy to point to the general complexities of discussing the changing structure of production in an economy in which specialization is highly developed and inter-industry transactions ubiquitous. But in Australia only very limited formal insight is possible through examination of the official 1958–9 input-output table and its inversions. The average relationships emerging from a single input-output

TABLE 5.10. *Sectoral Input-Output Table, 1958–9*
(£m, producers' prices, imports allocated directly)

	Inputs into				Final demands		
Outputs of	Primary	Manufacturing	Construction, utilities	Services	Exports	Other	Total output
Primary	—	372·2	51·9	8·9	422·8	392·8	1,248·6
Manufacturing	155·5	—	404·9	410·9	294·7	1,853·4	3,119·4
Construction and utilities	39·4	70·2	—	135·2	0·5	982·1	1,227·4
Services	75·8	370·4	142·4	—	205·7	2,474·8	3,269·1
Unallocated	−9·8	−84·0	11·4	135·0	5·3	−2·2	55·7
Sub-total	260·9	728·8	610·6	690·0	929·0	5,700·9	8,920·2
Factor payments (GDP)	930·0	1,612·7	555·8	2,210·5	—	—	5,309·0
Net indirect taxes	42·7	284·6	20·5	250·1	49·5	45·8	693·2
Imports	15·0	493·3	40·5	118·5	1·6	312·4	981·3
Total input	1,248·6	3,119·4	1,227·4	3,269·1	980·1	6,059·1	15,903·7

Note: To move to the three-sector (primary, manufacturing, tertiary) table sum construction and utilities and services in both rows and columns, but eliminate their internal transactions. These sum to 277·6 so that both tertiary and total output/input are less by this amount than in the above table.

Source: Commonwealth Bureau of Census and Statistics, *Input-Output Tables 1958–9*, Table 1 (dwelling rent has been eliminated and factor payments brought into line with the 1964–5 *National Accounts* by adjusting the unallocated items).

study do not, of course, reveal anything about the more relevant marginal ones and in historical terms there is no way of knowing how the 1958–9 coefficients compare with those of thirty, sixty, or even ten years earlier. Since the essence of the developmental process might well be regarded as the transformation of the input-output relationships of the economy—including the relative importance of service inputs into goods and goods inputs into services—it would be hazardous to regard the information below as more than a useful half loaf. Fuchs, with tables available for 1947 and 1958, indeed found the intermediate demand for service output growing faster than the final demand, though neither enough to account for a significant fraction of service employment expansion.

The results of combining the thirty-four industries of the Australian 1958–9 table into four sectors are shown in Table 5.10. (Construction and utilities are presented as a separate sector in order to be able to refer to services directly, but also derive tertiary without difficulty.) *Reading across* the rows we ascertain the immediate destination of the final output of each sector—the amounts which went as inputs into other sectors' production, those which were purchased directly by consumers (public and private) at home, and those which were sold abroad. For instance, of the £3,269·1m. total output emerging from the service sector, 18·0 per cent was purchased by other sectors (2·3 by primary, 11·3 by manufacturing and 4·4 by the non-service component of tertiary), 6·3 per cent was sold abroad, and 75·7 per cent was purchased by households, firms and governments at home for either consumption or investment purposes. *Reading down* the columns we locate the immediate origin of the inputs used by each sector in generating its output. Again taking services as the example, 24·9 per cent of the inputs took the form of purchases from other sectors (0·7 from primary, 13·2 from manufacturing, 11·0 from construction and utilities). Direct import requirements made up 3·6 per cent and two-thirds (67·6 per cent) of the inputs took the form of payments to productive factors. The valuation of output at market prices and statistical deficiences mean that we also have, as 'inputs', net indirect taxes (7·7 per cent) and unallocated (4·1 per cent).

As might be expected, the table confirms that there is a considerable volume of intersector transactions (not to mention the vast amount of intersector trade which has been netted out) and that there are sizeable variations in the relative importance of the intermediate home, final home and export markets among sectors. However, the value of the table in this form is limited by the fact that the inputs and destinations are immediate rather than ultimate. While 18 per cent of service output went directly as intermediate input into other sectors, we also know that a quarter of the inputs generating this output came from these other sectors. To elicit the true extent of each sector's demand on, and contribution to, every other one, requires inversion of the table and calculation of ultimate requirements and ultimate destinations.[25] Subsequent tables detail the

TABLE 5.11. *Requirements per £100 of Sector Output and Product*

	Primary	Manu-facturing	Construction and utilities	Services
In terms of output				
Primary	102	13	9	2
Manufacturing	15	104	37	15
Construction and utilities	4	3	102	5
Services	8	14	17	102
Imports	4	17	10	2
Net indirect taxes	6	11	7	9
In terms of product (value added)				
Primary	76	10	7	1
Manufacturing	8	54	19	8
Construction and utilities	2	1	46	2
Services	5	9	11	69
Imports	4	17	10	6
Net indirect taxes	6	11	7	9
Discrepancy	–1	–2	—	5
	100	100	100	100

Source: Inversion of *Input-Output Tables 1958–59* (see Table 5.10).

[25] The assumptions required by the inversion—that there are no lags, that the average coefficients apply to all elements of final demand, and that the failure to exclude stock appreciation or eliminate the statistical discrepancy does not seriously affect interpretation—are discussed briefly in B. D. Haig, 'Input-output Relationships, 1958–59', *Economic Record*, 41, 1965, pp. 118–23. This note presents the results of inverting an eleven-industry condensation of the original table. I am indebted to Bryan Haig for assistance with the current inversion.

ultimate requirements per £100 of sector output and product, the sector composition of final demand and the distribution of sector output between exports and other final demands.

In terms of the three-sector breakdown we can see from Table 5.11 that each sector draws roughly equally on the other two taken together. Within this rough equality, primary draws slightly more from manufacturing than from tertiary, and manufacturing slightly more from tertiary than primary, but in neither case is the split great. The purchases of tertiary are, however, very much biased towards manufacturing with only negligible demands on primary product. Breaking tertiary into its service and non-service components reveals that service demands on primary are even lower than those for the combined sector and separation shows clearly the much above-average intersectoral demands of construction and the utilities, particularly on manufacturing. Services are, conversely, somewhat below average in this respect, though still drawing mainly on manufacturing. In their turn, service inputs are ultimately as important contributors to manufacturing product as primary ones, but as inputs into primary they are only half as important as manufacturing ones.

TABLE 5.12. *Sector Composition of Final Expenditure*
(per cent)

	Exports	Other final demands	Total final expenditure
Primary	38	10	14
Manufacturing	23	25	25
Construction and utilities	2	9	8
Services	21	35	33
Imports	9	10	10
Net indirect taxes	8	9	9
Discrepancy	—	1	1
	100	100	100

Source: As for Table 5.11.

None of the tables provides a thorough test of any external characterization of the various sectors, which in any event must be significantly counterfactual and not amenable to direct testing. The major point of interest thrown up by the exercise is clearly the fact

TABLE 5.13. *Distribution of Sector Output to Export and Other Categories of Final Expenditure*
(per cent)

	Exports			Other			
	Final	Inter-mediate	Total	Final	Inter-mediate	Total	Total
Primary	34	4	38	31	31	62	100
Manufacturing	9	4	13	59	28	87	100
Construction and utilities	—	3	3	82	15	97	100
Services	6	2	9	76	15	19	100

Source: As for Table 5.11.

that one-fifth of exports in 1958–9 was accounted for by service product (Table 5.12). (Manufacturing also contributes nearly a quarter of exports.) Table 5.13 shows that this represented only 9 per cent of total service product (6 per cent being exported directly e.g. as airline seat sales, 3 per cent as intermediate content of other exports), and many people would undoubtedly be happy to regard this as insignificant. But there are really no absolute criteria for significance in this sort of question, and concern about interdependence overlaps considerably with concern about aggregation at this point.

Conflicting pressures to generalize and particularize are ever present in the social sciences. Perhaps the most common response of economic analysts is to argue that greater than the danger of consistently falling prey to one extreme, is the danger of thinking that some intermediate point on the scale of aggregation (running, say, between establishment and economy) is optimal for all questions. If the following remarks have any overall thrust it is towards questioning this response and suggesting that the meaningful level of analysis cannot be treated largely as an *ad hoc* matter, using the term in its literal and non-pejorative sense.

What constitutes the meaningful level of analysis? It is clearly not the level where interdependence is minimal or non-existent. The concern expressed above about the sector approach was couched in terms of the resulting lack of *emphasis* on interdependence, not on any supposed denial of interdependence. Obviously, in order to minimise interdependence we would move to the entire economy where only external transactions remain as a 'complication'. Conversely, the degree of interdependence almost certainly tends to grow as we disaggregate—the smaller the unit the more likely is value added to form a smaller proportion of output. No, the search for a meaningful level means, so far as the question of interdependence is concerned, attempting to arrive at an area where the forms and channels of interaction can be construed in an operational way. The dangers of aggregation reflect in this case, not primarily the possible summation of distinctly different time trends but the amalgamation of patterns of interaction which have little, if anything, in common. The possibilities are dramatized most effectively when activities whose output is destined almost entirely for household (or other final) consumption are coupled with those whose outputs are absorbed almost completely by other enterprises. But this example in terms of destination is merely one form of the problem (and the most easily dealt with perhaps). It cuts across others which reflect both 'real' economic forces, pre-eminently demand and supply functions, and the surrounding framework of market, extra-market and non-market institutions. It is against this background of multifarious interaction that aggregation of industries (even sub-industries), defined primarily in terms of the physical characteristics of product, needs to be evaluated. On any reasonable adjudication the criterion of physical intangibility—that which above all generates a service sector—seems shaky ground for aggregation on which it is hoped to base analysis of any substantial predictive or explanatory power.

The main point is not, then, that statistical analysis may reveal a wide diversity of trends within an aggregate. That the latter is likely in the case of services is plain. Fuchs, surveying eighteen service components which accounted for 30 per cent of US service employment in 1963, found a 'tremendous diversity' of experience in output, employment and output per man growth rates.[26] And the Australian data, such as it is, tends to confirm the picture of a considerable variety of growth patterns. Table 5.3 has already suggested something of this sort in abbreviated form, and Table 5.14 reinforces this in terms of changing shares of employment, by sex, for seven service divisions. (I do not propose to discuss the import of the latter table in any serious way because with the possible—and almost entirely useless—exception of defence, none of the component industries of the service sector constitute, in my view, a meaningful entity for analysis.) However, once a meaningful level of analysis has been reached, the question of statistical heterogeneity becomes largely irrelevant. The superficial characteristic of a meaningful level might

[26] Fuchs, *The Service Economy*, p. 86.

TABLE 5.14. *Shares of Male, Female and Total Employment by Sector and Tertiary Component, Census Years, 1890–1 to 1960–1*
(per cent)

	1890–91	1900–01	1910–11	1920–21	1932–33	1946–47	1953–54	1960–61
				Males				
PRIMARY	37·5	39·5	36·9	32·3	34·4	22·6	19·2	15·5
MANUFACTURING	14·8	14·4	17·4	18·7	17·9	27·6	27·9	28·9
TERTIARY	47·7	46·1	45·7	49·0	47·7	49·8	52·9	55·6
Electricity, gas and water	0·6	0·7	1·0	1·5	1·2	1·4	1·7	2·1
Building and construction	16·8	11·7	10·9	11·7	10·5	9·1	11·5	12·5
SERVICES	30·3	33·7	33·8	35·8	36·0	39·3	39·7	41·0
Transport and communications	6·6	7·1	7·9	8·7	9·1	9·5	9·9	9·5
Commerce	12·1	13·9	14·7	14·3	14·0	13·1	13·7	14·4
Public administration	1·3	1·3	2·3	3·1	1·9	3·8	3·7	3·8
Defence	0·3	0·5	0·3	0·6	0·3	3·4	2·2	1·5
Community and business services	3·7	3·7	3·3	3·3	4·3	3·4	4·2	5·2
Finance and property	1·2	1·4	1·5	1·7	2·4	2·1	2·3	2·9
Other services	5·1	5·8	3·8	4·1	4·0	4·0	3·7	3·7
				Females				
PRIMARY	6·5	5·5	4·4	2·3	3·9	4·1	4·1	4·0
MANUFACTURING	15·6	15·8	24·3	22·7	23·4	29·9	28·1	26·2
TERTIARY	77·9	78·7	71·3	75·0	72·7	66·0	67·8	69·8
Electricity, gas and water	—	—	0·1	0·3	0·2	0·4	0·5	0·6
Building and construction	0·1	—	—	—	0·1	0·2	0·4	0·6
SERVICES	77·8	78·7	71·2	74·7	72·4	65·4	66·9	68·6
Transport and communications	1·1	1·2	1·3	1·3	2·1	4·0	3·8	3·5
Commerce	20·4	14·7	14·7	17·1	16·8	19·3	22·0	22·3
Public administration	—	0·1	0·2	1·2	1·0	3·8	3·4	3·4
Defence	—	—	—	0·1	—	0·6	0·2	0·2
Community and business services	10·6	13·4	13·5	16·7	16·3	15·8	18·3	21·3

TABLE 5.14 (*continued*)

	1890–91	1900 01–	1910 –11	1920 –21	1932 –33	1946 –47	1953 –54	1960 –61
				Females (*continued*)				
Finance and property	—	0·2	0·4	1·4	1·9	3·2	4·2	5·5
Other services	45·7	49·1	41·1	36·9	34·3	18·7	15·0	12·4
				Persons				
PRIMARY	31·6	33·1	30·8	26·5	27·5	18·3	15·7	12·6
MANUFACTURING	14·9	14·7	18·6	19·5	19·1	28·2	27·9	28·2
TERTIARY	53·5	52·2	50·6	54·0	53·4	53·5	56·4	59·2
Electricity, gas & water	0·5	0·6	0·8	1·2	1·0	1·2	1·4	1·7
Building and construction	13·5	9·4	8·7	9·4	8·1	7·0	8·9	9·5
SERVICES	39·5	42·2	41·1	43·4	44·3	45·3	46·1	48·0
Transport and communications	5·4	5·8	6·5	7·2	7·5	8·2	8·5	8·0
Commerce	13·7	14·1	14·7	14·9	14·7	14·5	15·7	16·5
Public administration	1·1	1·1	1·9	2·7	1·7	3·8	3·6	3·7
Defence	0·2	0·4	0·3	0·5	0·2	2·7	1·8	1·1
Community and business services	5·1	5·6	5·3	5·9	7·0	6·3	7·4	9·3
Finance and property	1·0	1·2	1·3	1·6	2·3	2·4	2·8	3·5
Other services	13·0	14·0	11·1	10·6	10·9	7·4	6·3	5·9

Source: See Appendix.

indeed be that it permits, even compels, the summation of diametrically-opposed component trends.

'Community and business services' can be taken as a far from extreme example for discussion purposes and I can think of no better way of introducing the argument than to record verbatim the three digit components of the Australian employment classification for this group ('broadly' the classification also used in the official national product by industry breakdown).

COMMUNITY AND BUSINESS SERVICES

Sub-Group 1—Law, Order and Public Safety

680 Police
681 Prisons and reformatory institutions (other than industrial schools), excluding inmates

682 Legal profession (private practice)
683 Fire Brigades
689 Other

Sub-Group 2—Religion and Social Welfare

690 Social service and welfare organizations (other than governmental)
691 Religion
692 Missions for aboriginals (staff only)
693 Benevolent institutions (other than hospitals) excluding inmates
699 Other

Sub-Group 3—Health, Hospitals, etc.

700 Hospitals (other than mental)
710 Mental hospitals
720 Medicine (private practice)
721 Dentistry (private practice)
722 Vetinary surgery (private practice)
723 Private nursing and midwifery
724 Baby health centres
725 Ambulance services
729 Other

Sub-Group 4—Education

730 Kindergarten, primary and secondary schools and teachers' colleges
731 Technical colleges
732 Agricultural colleges
733 Universities
734 Other schools and private teaching
735 Libraries and reading rooms
739 Other

Sub-Group 5—Other Community and Business Services (including Professional

740 Consultant engineering and surveying
741 Architecture
742 Accountancy and auditing
743 Musical composition, literature, painting and sculpture
744 Industrial and trade associations

745 Advertising
746 Typewriting and copying services
749 Other

It seems intuitively obvious to me that, within this 'industry', it is only at the sub-group level that we are remotely approaching areas where coherent pictures of a consumer demand and producer supply situation can be constructed and given institutional meaning; where the problem of simply defining exactly what the product concerned is takes on an air of reality, and where we can begin to conceive of a discrete set of interdependencies (in the mechanical sense, input-output relationships) that can be regarded as having a recognizable existence. Even then the operational significance of a group denoted 'health' has its limitations, encompassing as it does a variety of products subject to very different demand conditions and produced within greatly varying institutional settings. In the case of other sub-groups, especially the residual one, descent to the component level would seem imperative.

These remarks should not be interpreted as nihilistic in intent. They are directed particularly at the nature of future research into the economics of service activities (but by implication have relevance to research in 'manufacturing' and 'primary sector'). Such work should, according to the present viewpoint, take the form of a series of studies—undertaken for their own sake and not as 'case' studies—in carefully delimited areas such as health, education, law enforcement, entertainment, charity and so on (still confining ourselves to the previous example). As suggested, it is not even a settled question that these groups would necessarily represent optimal levels, but delimitation is itself part of the future task and no capsuled answers are offered here.[27] It can, however be asserted that there is no necessary reason for the individual areas selected to be rigidly exclusive in a social accounting sense. In many cases the costs of a unique and consistent breakdown will outweigh the benefits of a guaranteed consistency and absence of double-counting. The latter can be dealt with at other stages of a study besides the first one.

Subsequent juxtaposition of the results of individual studies drawn from the service area would hopefully be rejected in favour of a general comparison across the whole economy. In other words,

[27] Reports of the results of early attempts to undertake study of the required depth in relation to medical care, retail trade, barber and beauty shops and banking are reported in Fuchs, *The Service Economy*, Ch. 5 and Fuchs, ed., *Production and Productivity*, Papers 3–5.

the main functions of the yardstick construct (the 'service sector')—drawing attention to those areas which have suffered (in a bibliographical sense) from producing an intangible output and throwing up some reference points for individual studies—should by then have been achieved. And the core of this essay should have served its very limited purpose.

APPENDIX. *Basic Data by Sector, Selected Years, 1890–1 to 1960–1*
(B = Butlin, H = Haig)

	Primary[a]		Manufacturing		Tertiary[b] Services		Tertiary[b] All		Total[b]	
	B	H	B	H	B	H	B	H	B	H
A. *GDP at current prices* (£m)										
1890–91	51·6		21·0		73·8		100·0		172·6	
1900–01	66·1		23·4		77·6		91·2		180·7	
1910–11	99·0	99·0	43·5	46·8	133·3	117·9	158·0	141·9	300·5	287·7
1926–27	195·1	195·1	121·1	124·5	343·5	325·5	424·2	418·0	740·4	737·6
1937–38	221·3	221·3	141·0	138·4	357·1	340·1	422·0	420·5	784·3	780·2
1948–49		498·3		528·6		758·0		908·1		1,935·0
1960–61		1,002·8		1,884·5		2,620·5		3,300·2		6,187·5
B. *GDP at constant prices* (£m) (B = 1910–11 base, H = 1938–9 base)										
1890–91	53·1		22·7		78·6		108·1		183·9	
1900–01	67·5		25·5		88·1		103·1		196·1	
1910–11	99·0	142·9	43·5	63·0	133·3	197·9	158·0	236·9	300·5	442·8
1926–27	105·8	151·1	62·0	118·2	191·9	324·3	232·3	410·1	400·1	679·4
1937–38	136·2	207·5	76·5	152·6	213·9	349·5	249·9	429·0	462·6	789·1
1948–49		206·9		258·3		484·0		594·1		1,059·3
1960–61		276·6		513·9		749·9		983·3		1,773·8

	Primary[a]		Manufacturing		Tertiary[b] Services		Tertiary[b] All		Total[b]	

C. *Employment and crude labour inputs* ('000)

	E	L.I.	E	L.I.	E	L.I.	E	L.I.	E	L.I.
1890–91	383·8	363·8	182·4	169·4	482·7	418·3	653·8	589·1	1,220·0	1,122·3
1900–01	482·2	446·7	214·3	199·0	617·5	536·0	764·1	681·9	1,460·6	1,327·6
1910–11	547·8	516·6	336·4	306·9	737·8	649·8	909·8	821·4	1,794·0	1,644·9
1926–27	573·9	552·5	491·3	447·5	1,003·9	881·7	1,326·5	1,200·4	2,391·7	2,200·4
1937–38	622·4	598·3	610·3	554·3	1,093·2	954·0	1,368·6	1,228·1	2,601·3	2,380·7
1948–49	556·6	536·1	933·1	852·9	1,463·2	1,290·3	1,774·6	1,599·9	3,264·3	2,988·9
1960–61	514·8	493·9	1,155·5	1,062·5	1,962·9	1,717·2	2,421·6	2,171·6	4,091·9	3,728·0

D. *Products per unit of labour input, at current prices* (£)

	B	H	B	H	B	H	B	H	B	H
1890–91	141·8		124·0		176·4		169·8		153·8	
1900–01	148·0		117·6		144·8		133·7		136·1	
1910–11	191·6	191·6	141·7	152·5	205·1	181·4	192·4	172·8	182·7	174·9
1926–27	353·1	353·1	270·6	278·2	389·6	369·2	353·4	339·9	336·5	335·2
1937–38	369·9	369·9	254·4	249·7	374·3	356·5	343·6	342·4	329·4	327·7
1948–49		929·5		619·8		587·5		567·6		647·4
1960–61		2,030·4		1,773·6		1,526·0		1,519·7		1,659·7

APPENDIX—*continued*

	Primary[a]		Manufacturing		Tertiary[b] Services		Tertiary[b] All		Total[b]	
	E. Relative products per unit of labour input, at current prices (£)									
	B	H	B	H	B	H	B	H	B	H
1890–91	92·2		80·6		114·7		110·4		100	
1900–01	108·7		86·4		106·4		98·2		100	
1910–11	104·9	109·5	77·6	87·2	112·3	103·7	105·3	98·8	100	100
1926–27	104·9	105·3	80·4	83·0	115·8	110·1	105·0	101·4	100	100
1937–38	112·3	112·9	77·2	76·2	113·6	108·8	104·3	104·5	100	100
1948–49		143·6		95·7		90·7		87·7		100
1960–61		122·3		106·9		91·9		91·6		100
	F. Products per unit of labour input, at constant prices (£)									
1890–91	146·0		134·0		187·9		183·5		163·9	
1900–01	151·1		128·1		164·4		151·2		147·7	
1910–11	191·6	276·6	141·7	205·3	205·1	304·6	192·4	288·4	182·7	269·2
1926–27	191·5	273·5	138·5	264·1	217·6	367·8	193·5	341·6	181·8	308·8
1937–38	227·6	346·8	138·0	275·3	224·2	366·4	203·5	349·3	194·3	331·4
1948–49		385·9		302·8		375·1		371·3		354·4
1960–61		560·0		483·7		436·7		452·8		475·8

	Primary[a]		Manufacturing		Tertiary[b] Services		Tertiary[b] All		Total[b]	
	G. *Relative products per unit of labour input, at constant prices*									
	B	H	B	H	B	H	B	H	B	H
1890–91	89·1		81·8		114·6		112·0		100	
1900–01	102·3		86·7		111·3		102·4		100	
1910–11	104·9	102·7	77·6	76·3	112·3	113·2	105·3	107·1	100	100
1926–27	105·3	88·6	76·2	85·5	119·7	119·1	106·4	110·6	100	100
1937–38	117·1	104·6	71·0	83·1	115·4	110·6	104·7	105·4	100	100
1948–49		108·9		85·4		105·8		104·8		100
1960–61		117·7		101·7		91·8		95·2		100
	H. *Implicit prices* (B = 1910–11 base, H = 1938–9 base)									
1890–91	97·2		92·5		93·9		92·5		93·9	
1900–01	97·9		91·8		88·1		88·5		92·1	
1910–11[c]	100·0	69·3	100·0	74·3	100·0	59·6	100·0	59·9	100·0	65·0
1926–27	184·4	129·1	195·3	105·3	179·0	100·4	182·6	101·9	185·1	108·6
1937–38	162·5	106·7	184·3	90·7	166·9	97·3	168·9	98·0	169·5	98·9
1948–49		240·8		204·6		156·6		152·9		182·7
1960–61		362·5		366·7		349·4		335·6		348·8

APPENDIX—*continued*

I. *Relative prices*

	Primary[a]		Manufacturing		Tertiary[b] Services		Tertiary[b] All		Total[b]	
	B	H	B	H	B	H	B	H	B	H
1890–91	103·5		98·5		100·0		98·5		100	
1900–01	106·3		99·7		95·7		96·1		100	
1910–11[c]	100·0	106·6	100·0	114·3	100·0	91·7	100·0	92·2	100	100
1926–27	99·6	118·9	105·5	97·0	96·7	92·4	98·6	93·8	100	100
1937–38	95·9	107·9	108·7	91·7	98·5	98·4	99·6	99·1	100	100
1948–49		131·8		112·0		85·7		83·7		100
1960–61		103·9		105·1		100·2		96·2		100

[a] Excludes livestock accumulation.
[b] Excludes dwelling rents.
[c] Identical values in Butlin series reflect assumption of competitive equilibrium in base year.

Source: For all Australian data in paper:
Employment: Michael Keating, *The Growth and Composition of the Australian Work Force, 1910–11 to 1960–61*, Ph.D. thesis, ANU, 1967, and 'Australian Work Force and Employment 1910–11 to 1960–61', *Australian Economic History Review*, VII, 1967, pp. 150–71; N. G. Butlin and J. A. Dowie, 'Estimates of Australian Workforce and Employment 1861–1961', *Australian Economic History*, IX, 1969.

Income and product: N. G. Butlin, *Australian Domestic Product, Investment and Foreign Borrowing 1861–1938/39*, Cambridge University Press, 1964; *Australian National Accounts*; B. D. Haig, unpublished estimates for eight industry subdivisions from 1910–11 to 1960–1 at 1938–9 prices, based partly on shifting weight quantum indexes. For some details of Haig's 1938–9 to 1948–9 link see his '1938/39 National Income Estimates', *Australian Economic History Review*, VII, 1967, pp. 172–86 and for the post-war series based at 1953–4 see 'Estimates of Australian Real Product by Industry', *Australian Economic Papers*, 5, 1966, pp. 230–50.

Chapter 6

SOME PERSPECTIVES OF AUSTRALIAN ECONOMIC DEVELOPMENT, 1890–1965

N. G. Butlin

LONG-TERM TRENDS OF BROAD AGGREGATES

Had the Australian rate of growth of *per capita* real product over the past seventy-five years attained the 'typical' Western trend growth rate (a compound rate of the order of 1·5 per cent per annum), our present-day *per capita* real product would probably have been in excess of that of the United States, now easily the wealthiest country in the world. A comment of this type might well attract critical reaction. The end result is intrinsically improbable; the conditions in which the counterfactual performance might be attained are unspecified; the simplest of aggregate indexes of growth performance are adopted; and the most elusive form of highly questionable international comparison is required. Yet critics of Australian performance over the past three generations appear to believe that Australia could well have been expected to sustain a growth rate higher than this approximate level and very much higher than the rate actually achieved; and imply that this simple indicator, *per capita* real product, is the appropriate criterion of success. Criticism of Australian development unwittingly depends on implicit assessment of the type spelled out here.

Despite misgivings on aggregate and comparative trend measures, it is useful to explore briefly the limited light they might cast on Australian trend performance. Disregarding the conceptual and measurement problems in this context, the central feature of Australian economic development since 1890 that appears is, indeed, that our *per capita* growth rate was not only less than, but far below, the approximate Western trend growth rate.[1] In historical perspective,

[1] I make no apologies for this fiction. It is the approximate rate frequently used

there appear to be impelling reasons why this should have been the case. But to appreciate the reasons and the character of the experience, it is of some value to view them in a larger context, say of the past century, and in a selective comparative setting.

We cannot put very much faith in the long-term social accounting measures that have been developed for a large number of countries over the past century. Performance in Britain and the United States provides orders of magnitude with which to assess Australian achievement in general terms. In simple aggregative measures, Table 6.1 shows the century comparisons in average rates of growth per decade.

Leaving aside the idiosyncrasies of different regions, Britain and the United States display the general characteristics of two differing sets of circumstances, each common in certain types of Western countries. In the former, a relatively wealthy country expanded

TABLE 6.1. *Secular Growth Rates per Decade: United Kingdom, United States and Australia*
(per cent)

	Real product	Population	*Per capita* real product
United Kingdom	21·1	6·1	14·1
United States	42·5	21·6	17·2
Australia	34·1	24·2	8·0

Source: Kuznets, *Modern Economic Growth.*

relatively slowly in aggregate real product. But population increased very much more slowly with *per capita* product growing somewhat more slowly than many other Western countries, but not far below the mean performance. In the United States, by contrast, real product grew much faster—twice as fast as the United Kingdom—but population rose well over three times as fast. The net effect was to leave a *per capita* growth rate better than that in Britain but not very greatly different from mean Western performance.

in discussions of long-term growth. The approximate level suggested derives from the mass of social accounting data presented in S. Kuznets, *Modern Economic Growth: Rate, Structure, and Spread,* Yale University Press, New Haven, 1966. Basically, it is adopted here as a convenient reference point to avoid excessive reference to detailed overseas experience.

Australian aggregate product expanded less rapidly than United States, but clearly very much faster than that in Britain (or, indeed, in most Western countries). But Australian population grew four times as fast as Britain's. Indeed, only a few South American countries might have challenged Australia as the most rapidly growing population nucleus over the century. So close did population press on real product that a very small growth rate of real product *per capita* was attained. At 8 per cent per decade, the achieved growth rate was little better than half the Western mean.

This was a very poor performance indeed, or so it would appear. Yet, despite this relatively very low *per capita* growth rate, most rankings of present-day Australian *levels* of *per capita* real product would place Australia among the high income countries of the world. We would appear to have learned a special secret: how to be wealthy without (or almost without) a *per capita* growth rate Obviously, if we accept the general orders of magnitude, one inference is unavoidable, given that growth rates have not accelerated in recent decades beyond Western growth rates: conditions in Australia in the second half of the nineteenth century, relative to the rest of the world, must have been peculiar and peculiarly advantageous. Whether this position was, in fact, only precariously advantageous or not, it would also follow that we failed to sustain it.

If we search for parallels in long-term *per capita* performance, it is possible that some countries of southern Europe achieved a slower *per capita* growth. The most direct parallel, southern Ireland, yields a *per capita* growth rate over the century almost exactly the same as Australia, at 8 per cent per decade. Here was an economy beset with economic and social problems, relatively unresponsive to structural, technological and institutional change; and with an 'end-product' of *per capita* income levels far inferior to those of Australia. Have we then to expect, in Australia, a poor performance also in terms of increased efficiency of resource use and of quality of inputs as an explanation of the trend pattern?

It would be advantageous, even at the aggregative level, if we could attempt to provide orders of magnitude of trends in the rate of growth of factor inputs and of changes in the level of output per unit of input. Unfortunately, we lack one key item, measures of capital stock. Nevertheless, it may be of some value to explore, aggregatively, the question whether the rate of growth of output per unit of input in Australia was likely to have been as bad relative to the other developing Western countries as was the achievement in real product per head.

CENTURY-LONG INPUT TRENDS AND THE 'RESIDUAL' GROWTH RATE

Chart 6.1 displays the unsmoothed estimates of some major aggregates covering the century 1861–1960–1. It will be seen that the Australian economy expanded enormously. Population increased almost tenfold, labour inputs (full-time male equivalent employment) rose approximately seven times the 1861 level, and gross real domestic product expanded to a figure of almost twenty-four times the product of 1861. Expansion in this sense is an interesting and important question. Perhaps, particularly in Australian conditions, the increasing scale of domestic markets, of work force and labour inputs or of capital stock may have had significant implications for the efficiency of resource utilization, for technological development, for the ability to achieve qualitative changes in (improve the quality of both) of inputs and outputs or to introduce organizational methods, all of which, direct or indirectly, may have affected the rate at which output per unit of input (in general terms, the overall 'efficiency' index) increased. In turn, the rate of increase of efficiency has a vital bearing on the essentially welfare measure, the rate of growth of real product or real consumption per head of population, depending on the relative rates of growth of population and inputs.

For this reason, if for no other, we should not confine our attention to *per capita* or per unit measures. From the data contained in Chart 6.1, we may calculate simple century-long trend growth rates as broad indicators of the behaviour of these aggregates. The chart contains only a sketchy suggestion of capital inputs; and it omits the adjustment (contained in the calculations) of labour inputs to man-hour inputs, full-time male equivalents adjusted for reduced hours of work and increased holidays and vacations over the century. We will endeavour to deal with the question of capital stock later. In the summary tabulation of trend rates of Table 6.2 we include a rough approximation of a man-hours input growth rate. This is based on an assumed decline in the length of the working year over the century of one-third the 1861 level (note that we beg the question, here, of the timing of this increase in leisure).[2]

[2] The estimated decline is based on the propositions that (*a*) the 48-hours movement in Australia had, in the early 1860s, achieved only very limited sucess and average hours were almost certainly in excess of 55 per week; (*b*) hours of work had fallen a century later to approximately 40; (*c*) public holidays and vacations, rare in 1861, increased substantially and were generally available to the work force by 1960.

The consequential decline in the length of the work-year is approximately one-third. This conforms quite closely to the average decline in west European

From the general compounding formula

$$t \log (1+r) = \log x - \log a$$

where t = 100 years and x and a the 1961 and 1861 values respectively, we can calculate compound growth rates (r) over the century. In Table 6.3 the first column records aggregate growth rates of each series and the second column (derived crudely but adequately as the difference between each relevant growth rate and that of GDP) shows the rates of growth of real product per unit (labour, population, etc.).

In conventional factor contribution analysis (based on a two-factor Cobb–Douglas production function with *constant* returns to scale and factors paid their marginal products) the rates of growth of the various labour measures are weighted by the share of wages and salaries (including incomes of working proprietors) in gross product. We lack adequate data on Australian income distribution, but it is improbable that the appropriate weight diverges radically from 0·75, an approximation to average Western experience. The figures in brackets indicate the consequences of using a weight of 0·67 as a probable lower limit. As we shall see in discussing the possible limits of the direct 'contribution' of capital inputs, the alternative weights have little importance for the outcome.

It is of some significance to convert the measures in Table 6.2 to the concept with which we began, the rate of growth of real product *per capita*. Table 6.3 is, then, merely a rearrangement to determine,

TABLE 6.2. *Century-trend Compound Growth Rates*
(per cent per annum)

	Aggre-gates	GDP per unit	Weighted growth rates of aggregates	Partial residual growth rates per unit
GDP	3·1			
Population	2·3	0·8		
Work force (benchmarks)	2·0	1·1	1·5 (1·3)	1·6 (1·8)
Labour inputs	2·1	1·0	1·6 (1·4)	1·5 (1·7)
Man-hour inputs	1·6	1·5	1·2 (1·1)	1·9 (2·0)

countries over the century. Note, however, that the substantial reductions in hours between 1860 and 1890 were seriously affected by the depression of the nineties, and it is probable that average hours per week at the beginning of the twentieth century were once more in excess of 48.

TABLE 6.3. *Century-trend Compound Growth Rates per Head of Population*

(per cent per annum)

	Growth rates	Weighted growth rates	Partial residual growth rates per head of population
GDP *per capita*	0·8		
Work force *per capita*	—0·3	—0·2 (—0·2)	1·0
Labour inputs *per capita*	—0·2	—0·2 (—0·2)	1·0
Man hours *per capita*	—0·7	—0·5 (—0·5)	1·3

Source: Butlin.

in this conventional procedure, the implications for rates of growth of *per capita* (not aggregate) real product of the rates of growth of the various labour measures per head.

This formulation has some interest in that, at this level, the apparently poor Australian performance in terms of rates of growth of real product per head appears significantly improved when we adjust for the rate of growth of the labour measures per head. Australian experience may not be quite unique, but certainly is exceptional in Western economic history in the slower rate of growth of work force than of population over the century. In contrast with almost every other Western country, the proportion of population occupied *fell* in Australia between 1861 and 1961, averaged at a compound rate of 0·3 per cent per annum. Work force inputs per head accounted *not for an increase* in *per capita* real product *but for a decline*. It is doubtful if any other Western country of significance behaved in the same way. The mean Western experience suggests a significant *increase* in the proportion of population occupied and hence a significant positive contribution to *per capita* growth rates from the trend rate of increase of *work force*. Nevertheless, all Western countries achieved very substantially increased leisure and, typically, though not invariably, this increase in leisure (reduction in man-hours per year) more than offset the increase in work force as a proportion of the total population. On an average, therefore, labour inputs per head, adjusted for man-hours, accounted for a *decline*, of approximately 0·2 per cent per annum compounded, in real product per head in Western Europe.

The Australian rate of *decline* of man-hours per head of population was very much more severe than this approximate mean experience. Labour inputs, as defined, declined at 0·2 per cent per annum and man-hours per head fell at the relatively very high rate of 0·7 per cent per annum. Using the same weights as in Table 6.2 (0·75 in column 2 and 0·67 in brackets), we can measure the weighted rate of decline and in column 3 derive the rate of increase of a preliminary partial residual (rate of increase of real product per unit of labour measure per head of population). Given the weighted *decline* of man-hours per head at 0·5 (with both sets of weights) we have a rate of increase in the residual per head of 1·3 per cent per annum. If we similarly weight the approximate Western mean rate of decline of 0·2 per cent, the weighted rate of 0·15 per cent, given a rate of increase of real product per head, on an average, at 1·5 per cent per annum, implies a comparable Western mean residual growth rate per head of between 1·6 and 1·7 per cent per annum.

The differentials in Australian and mean Western experience appear then greatly narrowed in these partial residual growth rate terms. At 0·8 per cent per annum growth rate of real product per head, Australian performance was 0·7 percentage points per annum less than (very slightly over half) the Western mean rate of growth of real product per head. Adjusted for weighted rates of *decline* of man-hours per head in both cases, the Australian residual growth rate per head at 1·3 per cent per annum was only 0·3 to 0·4 percentage points below (almost 80 per cent of) the mean Western residual growth rate per head. If our rate of growth of real product per head was relatively poor, our rate of increase of 'efficiency' in the use of labour inputs appears to be much more akin to Western experience.

LABOUR INPUTS PER HEAD

It is convenient to pause to examine some of the outstanding characteristics of the trend behaviour of Australian work force, labour inputs and man-hours per head. Even given serious reservations about the accuracy of these measures, it would appear that some exceptional demographic and/or work force participation conditions applied in Australia. Table 6.4 presents some simple measures that help to convey some of the changes that occurred. Some estimates for the United Kingdom are included to give a comparative relevance to Australian experience.

Table 6.4 is confined to censal and intercensal measures and conceals some significant variations in the short run. The first special feature in Australia is the constancy of the share of work force in total population at approximately 40 per cent between 1881 and 1961. This contrasts with the 4·5 percentage point increase in the United Kingdom over the same period, conforming broadly with general Western experience. But during these eighty years the Australian work force proportion failed to attain the British percentage level, so that by 1961 the British share was 7·6 percentage points higher than that in Australia.

In 1861, however, these relationships were reversed. The proportion of the Australian population occupied, at 50·6 per cent, was exceptionally high. This represented a peculiarly advantageous demographic condition, tending, other things being equal, to create an exceptionally high level of *per capita* real product that was abnormal and untenable. The long-run consequences of this exceptionally high work force share in population cannot be traced effectively here. It should be noted from Table 6.4 that it derives from the exceptionally high proportion of males in the work force ages in total population and the exceptionally high masculinity of the total population of work force ages as shown in Table 6.4. These conditions do not derive merely from the high proportion of adult male immigrants during the fifties. This influx merely accentuated the masculinity and special age composition established before gold, particularly due to the transportation system and the age and sex (adult male) composition of unassisted immigration before (and during) the gold decade. The primary offsets to this masculinity and age composition were in the supplements to population through natural increase and the emphasis on female immigrants in the assisted immigration schemes. But, in turn, the character of the assisted immigration programmes also gave a specially advantageous temporary twist by significantly raising the specific age work force participation by newly-arrived unmarried women.

Most of this special demographic advantage was lost quite quickly, a process that was speeded by re-migration of adult males to New Zealand in the sixties. Nevertheless, it was a significant factor affecting the *per capita* real product levels of the 1860s and limiting the ability to sustain higher *per capita* growth rates. Indeed, these peculiar, and in the long run untenable features, make the relatively high *per capita* growth rates of the three decades after 1860 all the more impressive.

The circumstances of the shift from the relatively high share of population occupied in Australia in 1861 to the relatively low share by comparison with the United Kingdom in 1961 cannot be discussed here. But given the divergent behaviour, three important

TABLE 6.4. *Work Force and Demographic Ratios*
(per cent)

	Australia: United Kingdom comparisons						Australia						
	Occupied persons/total population		Male/female aged 15–64		Males: 15–64/total population		Participation rates[a]			Intercensal growth rates			Intercensal migration contribution
	Australia	UK	Australia	UK	Australia	UK	Males	Females	Persons	Population	Work force	Labour inputs	
1851	(46·1)[b]	44·2	185[c]	93	66·0[c]	59·1							
1861	50·6	45·1	202	93	67·4	59·3	104	34	78	11·3			76·6
1871	38·5?	44·6	136	93	59·1	58·0	101	26	68	3·7	0·9	1·0	26·8
1881	40·4	43·3	126	93	60·9	58·1	99	27	66	3·0	3·5	4·0	31·4
1891	40·9	44·1	122	94	62·0	59·5	96	28	66	3·5	3·7	2·9	41·5
1901	40·9	44·1	113	90	61·8	62·2	99	26	65	1·7	1·7	1·8	—
1911	42·3	44·6	111	94	64·8	63·2	98	26	64	1·6	2·0	2·1	1·2
1921	40·5	44·8	108	94	63·9	65·1	91	23	58	2·0	1·5	1·6	20·7
1931 (33)	40·8	45·4	103	?	66·1	67·7	93	27	61	1·6	1·7	0·4	26·1
1951 (47)	42·2	48·1	100	93	67·1	66·5	95	28	62	0·9	1·1	2·5	4·2
1961	40·2	47·8	100	97	62·2	65·9	93	33	64	2·5	2·0	2·0	38·0

[a] Occupied persons as percentage of numbers aged 14–65.
[b] Victoria only.
[c] Victoria, New South Wales (incl. present Queensland) only.

Source: Calculated from Australian and United Kingdom censuses.

implications should be noted. First, a high *per capita* real product in Australia in the 1860s does not necessarily imply a *comparably* high real output per member of the work force. If we were to assume, hypothetically, that real product *per worker* in 1861 was the same in both countries, real product *per head* in Australia would have been about 12 per cent higher than in the United Kingdom. Secondly, taking merely end-point comparisons, the reversal of the relative share positions could account for a major part of the differential *per capita* real product growth rates in the United Kingdom and Australia. Assuming, hypothetically, the same output per worker in both countries in 1961, Australian real product per head would have been 18 per cent *lower* than in the United Kingdom. A *decline* from a level 12 per cent higher to one 18 per cent lower would mean that the relative shifts in work force shares in the United Kingdom and Australia accounted for a rate of growth of real product per head in Australia of 0·3 percentage points *lower* than in the United Kingdom. But the United Kingdom *per capita* real product growth rate was approximately 1·4 per cent per annum, or 0·6 percentage points higher than that in Australia. It is possible, therefore, that the relative changes in work force shares could account for half the difference in rates of growth of *per capita* output over the century.

The third point arises from the fact that our task here is to try to understand some of the major characteristics of Australian economic development, specifically since 1890. These demographic characteristics of 1861 are not by any means irrelevant to this problem. Nevertheless, the relative demographic advantage in Australia had been largely dissipated by 1891 (most of it by 1871) and, indeed, the work force share was then significantly lower than in the United Kingdom. The available social accounting measures suggest that, although the United Kingdom economy suffered some retardation in the late nineteenth and early twentieth centuries, over the whole period from 1890 to date its trend growth rate in *per capita* and per worker terms did not fall greatly. Chart 6.1 implies a much more severe and prolonged retardation in Australia. Relative trends in work force shares contribute part, but a significantly smaller part, of the explanation after 1891. Given the relative shares of population occupied at 1891 and 1933, these changes are irrelevant to an explanation of differentials in growth rates between the United Kingdom and Australia; between 1891 and 1961, changes in relative work force shares would account for roughly 0·1 percentage points in a differential *per capita* growth rate of approximately 1·0 percentage points per annum.

This third consideration is important in that if we are comparing century-long trend experience in Australia and other Western countries, we do not have to place nearly so much weight in explanation on relative labour productivity trends; *but by far the major part of the explanation, it would appear, must be found in relative labour productivities if our departure point is in 1891.* It follows that if special conditions existed in the later part of the nineteenth century in Australia, tending to limit the prospect of rapid gains in real product per head, they must be sought in productivity, efficiency, structural or qualitative terms, not primarily in demographic or work force participation characteristics. But we will suggest later that Australian demographic characteristics between 1861 and 1891 may have had a significant, if less direct, bearing on levels of real product per worker or per unit of labour input attained by the 1880s and hence on the ability to sustain *per capita* growth rates.

THE PROBLEM OF CAPITAL INPUTS

There is no merit in pursuing the conventional production function approach to the limits of a meaningless numbers game, least of all when one has many reservations on the value of the concepts and measures necessary to play it. No adequate data on total or reproducible capital in the nineteenth century exist for Australia. A few approximations are available between 1903 and 1956, and are contained in Chart 6.1; and a number of attempts to estimate one component, manufacturing capital stock, have been made. To complete the measurement of the contribution of factor inputs to aggregate and *per capita* growth rates, we are compelled largely into speculation. In part, this speculation is imposed because of the suggestions that have been made elsewhere that the slow rate of growth of capital per head in Australia is a major factor in the relatively slow rate of growth of real product per head. This does not seem to be a tenable explanation, though it might appear likely that capital contributed less to Australian growth rates than it did elsewhere.

Assuming a two-factor Cobb–Douglas production function, given the allocation of a weight of 0·75 (0·67) to labour inputs, the weight to be attached to capital inputs is 0·25 (0·33) in order to sum the combined inputs into a total factor input growth rate. In adopting weights at these levels, it is implied that we are dealing with total, not reproducible capital. Given this weight, we might approach the problem of capital inputs by posing two hypothetical questions. In doing so, we should bear in mind that we are at this stage merely attempting to guage the scale of the *direct* contribution of capital to Australian growth rates. First, how fast would capital per head or the capital/output ratio be required to grow over the century to offset the decline in man-hours per head? Alternatively, what rate of change would have been required in the capital/output ratio to equate the Australian residual growth rate with the Western mean? [For those willing to accept the following technical discussion on trust, the essential conclusion is presented in the paragraphs of this section following Table 6.5.]

These are hypothetical questions, representing forms of extremes. The answer to the first question, given that the change in the share of population occupied and decline in man-hours combined accounted for a decline in real product per head of 0·5 per cent per annum, weighted, is that capital per head would have had to increase at 2·0 per cent per annum unweighted (0·5 per cent per annum weighted). It is the unweighted growth rate that we need to consider here. We can of course translate the problem into capital/output ratio terms. Given a compound rate of population increase of 2·3 per cent per annum, this implies a rate of increase of capital stock of 4·3 per cent per annum. Since gross domestic product was rising 0·8 percentage points per annum faster than population, it follows that the total capital/output ratio would need to have *risen* at the very impressive rate of 1·2 per cent per annum. Under these conditions, and this is the reason for imposing the hypothetical conditions, the Australian residual growth rate (rate of increase of output per unit of input) would have been no better than the poor *per capita* real product growth rate.

Before commenting on the credibility of this condition, let us consider the other alternative. Here we have first to calculate, approximately, the residual Western growth rate after allowance for both labour and capital inputs. Allowing for a weighted labour man-hours input per head, we have suggested a preliminary partial residual growth rate of approximately 1·6 to 1·7 per cent per annum. Kuznets has suggested that the Western total capital/output ratio over the century generally may be taken as *declining* by a figure of the order of 25 per cent. Given a mean *per capita* real product growth rate of 1·5 per cent per annum and a similar mean rate of growth of population at 1·5 per cent, gross product is assumed to have risen at approximately 3 per cent per annum. At this growth rate, gross product would increase twenty-fold in a century; with the total capital/output ratio declining 25 per cent over the century, total capital stock would have risen fifteen-fold. This would imply a compound growth rate of 2·7 per cent per annum for total capital. Hence capital per head would rise by 1·2 per cent per annum. Weighted by 0·25, this would imply a direct capital input per head positive contribution to the mean Western growth rate of 0·3 percentage points per annum. Adding this weighted total capital per head *positive* contribution of 0·3 per cent to the man-hours per head weighted *decline* of 0·15 per cent, we have the Western residual growth rate, as an approximate average, reduced to 1·4 per cent per annum—very slightly *below* the rate of growth of real product per head.

We have, from the preceding section, a preliminary partial residual growth rate per head for Australia, after allowing for declining man-hours per head, of 1·3 per cent per annum. The mean Western residual growth of 1·4 per cent is, then, of the order of 0·1 percentage point higher. To *raise* the Australian residual growth rate to 1·4 per cent would require that capital per head, weighted at 0·25, should fall at the rate of 0·1 per cent per annum. Hence, before weighting, capital per head would need to fall at 0·4 per cent per annum. But population was growing, in trend terms, at 2·3 per cent per annum. It follows that total capital would need to grow less rapidly over the century, at the rate of only 1·9 per cent per annum. Given a rate of growth of real product at 3·1 per cent per annum, the capital/output ratio would then be expected to *fall* at the rate of 1·2 per cent per annum. This would imply a century-long decline in the Australian capital/output ratio of nearly twice the mean Western decline. Under these conditions the rate of growth of real product per unit of total factor inputs would have been the same in Australia as in the mean Western experience.

Summarizing, we have, then:

(*a*) Australian residual growth rate equals rate of growth of Australian real product per head: total capital rises at 4·3 per cent per annum;
(*b*) Australian residual growth rate equals Western mean residual: Australian total capital rises at the rate of 1·9 per cent per annum.

The first possibility can be dismissed out of hand. No Western country recorded a rise in total capital/output ratios over the century and an Australian increase at this rate is out of the question. There is no possibility that the Australian rate of increase of output per unit of factor input approximated a level as low as the rate of growth of real product per head. It must be assumed that the Australian rate of increase of 'efficiency' (as the residual is sometimes loosely described) was significantly more akin to mean Western 'efficiency' performance.

The issue narrows down to the feasibility of Australia attaining the Western mean. Total capital in Australia almost certainly grew much more slowly than it did in most Western countries. Given the scale of natural resources and the paucity of fixed assets in the 1860s, non-reproducible capital dominated the total in Australia far more than elsewhere. The rate of increase depended on the respective sizes of reproducible and non-reproducible capital and the rate of net investment. These dimensions were such that Australian total capital almost certainly grew significantly more slowly than in mean Western experience. But had Australian capital grown as fast as it did in the West, at about 2·7 per cent per annum, it would have exceeded population growth by only 0·4 per cent per annum. Weighted at 0·25, this would imply a *positive* contribution to the Australian total factor input per head of 0·1 per cent. Hence, on this basis, the Australian residual growth rate would have been reduced from 1·3 to 1·2 per cent per annum, or 85 per cent of the Western mean.

But Australian capital cannot have grown so fast. Its trend share of gross product invested was not significantly above average Western performance, and this alone would have reduced the rate of growth of Australian capital below the Western rate, given the relatively large component of non-reproducible capital. Unfortunately, we cannot rely on the accuracy or comparability of the few scattered estimates of capital stock that have been made. For what they are

TABLE 6.5. *Australian Capital Stock Estimates, 1936/7 Prices* (£m.)

	Reproducible capital	Reproducible capital per head
1903	1,800	460
1915	2,300	470
1929	3,400	530
1947	2,981	395
1956	4,504	475

Source: J. M. Garland and R. W. Goldsmith, 'The National Wealth of Australia', Ch. 12 in R. W. Goldsmith and C. Saunders, eds, *The Measurement of National Wealth*, Income and Wealth Series VIII, London, 1959.

worth, they are consistent with the view that capital grew relatively slowly. Assembled by Garland and Goldsmith, we have the rough calculations of *reproducible* capital in total and per head from 1903 to 1956 (see Table 6.5).

Almost no trend change in reproducible capital per head is shown in this tabulation. Given a substantial component of non-reproducible capital, it would be implied that total capital per head fell over this period, i.e. total capital grew more slowly than the rate of growth, 2·3 per cent per annum, of population. This would mean that capital per head contributed not an increase *but a very small decline* in the Australian *per capita* growth rate and raised the residual growth rate very slightly above 1·3 per cent per annum.

Given the weight to be attached to capital inputs, it seems to be unlikely that the Australian residual growth rate per head should be fully equated with the Western mean. This is even more the case if we were to transfer attention to reproducible capital alone. Here the trend growth rates were generally significantly different from the behaviour of total capital. But the rent component in total surpluses in Australia was so large that only a very small weight should be attached to reproducible capital. In these circumstances, its *direct* effect on the residual growth rate would be too small to warrant serious attention, leaving the Australian residual growth rate at about 90 per cent of the mean Western performance.

This speculative discussion has not been undertaken as preamble to a detailed arithmetical dissection of the residual growth rate into possible components of structural change, quality of inputs, organizational change, technical change, etc. I have little sympathy with the mechanistic attitude underlying this type of decomposition. It is, however, significant for less 'precise' analytical purposes to appreciate the possible combination of contributions to the residual and this may help to give shape, if no arithmetical content, to subsequent discussion. Clearly, too, the general 'conclusion' so far suggested is by no means unambiguous or certain. The purpose of the discussion to this point is to suggest an important hypothesis. It is implied that, despite the relatively low rate of growth of real product per head over the whole century since 1861, the Australian rate of increase in real product per unit of input may not have been very markedly different from that generally experienced in the West. The significance of this hypothesis emerges when we turn directly to the period after 1890. This relative similarity in residual growth rates may have existed over the full century 1861–1961. But there is no possibility that the Australian residual growth rate could have remotely approximated typical Western performance during most of the period after 1890, perhaps for as long as half a century before the Second World War. It would follow that during either or both of the sub-periods 1861–90 and 1939 to date, residual growth rates were relatively very high indeed. To appreciate the contrast, let us turn to the variations in Australian growth rates and to the identification of approximate sub-periods with significantly different sub-period trend growth rates.

VARIATIONS IN THE RATE OF GROWTH

Since the Second World War, variations in the growth rate have attracted attention as a business cycle phenomenon because of current policy objectives of external and internal stability. The fluctuations have been slight compared to the interruptions that occurred between 1890 and 1939. One of the major characteristics of Australian development during these fifty years has been its relatively high degree of instability. Within the limits of 1890–1939, but not necessarily or directly part of the explanation of our slow *long-term trend* growth rate, the Australian economy has been subjected to major fluctuations more severe in terms of both amplitude and duration than most other Western countries.

Leaving aside minor trade cycle variations, there were, as can be seen in Chart 6.1, three major disturbances after 1890, only one of which affected other Western countries comparably. The depression of the 1930s, the beginning of which might be dated in Australia as early as 1926/7, reached a trough in 1932. This was a world phenomenon of major proportions, not unique to Australia. Prior to this, a combination of cyclical, structural and exogenous disturbances imposed drastic restraints on growth. The years 1889–91 mark, approximately, the peak of the late nineteenth-century boom in Australia. While most Western countries grew relatively steadily until the First World War, the Australian economy suffered a succession of checks until 1903. A deep trade cycle trough was reached in 1894. Some recovery was initiated by the stimuli particularly of gold production (especially in Western Australia) and the renewed rise in world primary product prices. But while the latter influence encouraged high boom conditions until the First World War in such comparable areas as Canada and the Argentine, the early recovery stimulus in Australia was attenuated because of the scale of capacity established at the peak of 1889–91, the disruption of the financial system, the physical effects of overstocking in the pastoral industry and a long-term reduction in key areas in rainfall. The latter restraint reached catastrophic proportions in 1902–3 when severe drought conditions decimated Australian livestock populations.

After the drought, recovery was very rapid and the economy moved into boom conditions by 1909, activity remaining high until 1913. Then the early signs of a cyclical downturn were submerged by the disruptive effects of the First World War. Isolation and severe shipping shortage left Australia largely cut off from world markets, for both exports and imports, and the manpower loss due to movement of troops to Europe brought activity down further in the first half of the war.

Disregarding minor trade cycle fluctuations, the net effects on *per capita* real product due to these major variations in the growth rate represented severe limitations on growth on a scale not approximated elsewhere. It was not until 1904 that the 1890 aggregate real product was surpassed and only by 1907 that the level of *per capita* real income attained in 1890 was restored. Similarly, the restoration of the pre-1914 peak of *per capita* real product was delayed until 1920. Finally, the peak levels of the 1920s, achieved in 1926/7, may not have been restored until as late as 1937/8. It was only from that date that sustained growth occurred, with a degree of stability and a speed of growth paralleled most closely by the period 1860–90. Hence, for perhaps as many as thirty-three years of the total since 1890, the Australian growth rate was either negative or rising only to achieve, as a recovery process, the *per capita* real product of the preceding boom. In other works, growth *beyond* previously established peaks was achieved in brief periods of intermittent 'booms', totalling fewer than seventeen of the years between 1890 and 1939. No other Western country operated under a handicap of this dimension, despite the restrictions and comparative stagnation of the interwar years.

The implications for the trend pattern of Australian growth arising from these disturbances are by no means clear. Approximate trade cycle peaks can be identified at 1889, 1910, 1926/7 and 1936/7. These represented the closest approximations to full capacity utilization achieved between 1890 and the Second World War. In the movement between each successive peak, structural, technological and institutional changes had occurred, the product of a confused process of recovery and growth. We cannot reach any very clear conclusion that the trend growth rate in Australia would have been increased had these major disturbances and restraints been avoided. On the one hand, it appears that depressed conditions encouraged and accelerated some structural and technological change. On the other hand, the failure to utilize capacity implied the loss of output, of capital accumulation and replacement outlays, and of opportunity to introduce some technological change that may have reduced the long-term trend growth rate. It has been suggested elsewhere that the relatively very slow growth of capital per head in Australia, partly a product of prolonged periods of relatively low *per capita* incomes and savings, may help in an explanation of our slow growth rate after 1890. It is possible that the successive peaks of 1889, 1910, 1926/7 and 1936/7 contained progressively larger proportions of unused resources, limiting the comparability of each boom. But it is an open question whether the high growth rate *since* the Second World War would have been experienced, or might have been achieved at an earlier point in time, had there been a greater degree of stability *before* the war. The feasibility of an acceleration of the type depends, in part, on the character of technological and structural change that was attempted or induced in the whole period 1890–1965 and on the detailed structural characteristics of successive booms. But any discussion of these issues depends on the analysis of much more highly disaggregated data and the conditions in which structural and technological change was possible.

SUB-PERIOD GROWTH RATES

The retardation of growth rates after 1890 emerges more definitely when we turn to shorter periods of economic development. In Table 6.6 trend growth rates are shown for a number of indicators in five separate periods. Extension of these shorter periods back to as early as 1830 increases the likely errors but enlarges our perspective of the past seventy-five years. There are some other advantages in this approximate subdivision. The character of the period before 1890, as we have already suggested, may have some important implications for post-1890 change. Structural and technological change, in particular after 1890, acquires more meaning as a movement away from the pattern preceding 1890. Some long-lagged relationships will later need to be identified extending across these sub-periods and, particularly, originating before 1890. It should be appreciated that from 1891–1961, the sub-period trends are derived by comparing rates from peak to peak (or approximately so) representing growth between points that approached full capacity utilization.

During 1830–60 the figures, other than for population, are informed guesstimates, but it is improbable that more careful estimation would alter the general appearance of relatively *very* rapid

TABLE. 6.6 *Sub-period Compound Growth Rates.* (per cent per annum)

	Population	GDP	GDP/cap.	Work force	Labour inputs	GDP per member of work force	GDP per unit of labour input
1830–60	11·2	(14·0)	(2·8)	(10·0)	(10·0)	(4·0)	(4·0)
1861–90	3·5	4·7	1·2	2·7	2·7	2·0	2·7
1891–1913	2·0	2·4	0·4	1·8	1·9	0·6	0·5
1914–39	1·2	1·2	—	1·6	1·3	−0·4	−0·1
1939–61	2·5	4·6	2·1	1·5	2·0	2·6	2·0

development. A sordid, predominantly convict and ex-convict society of 1830 was transformed out of all recognition by pastoral expansion and gold to such an extent that it appears to have attained the world pinnacle of *per capita* real product in 1860. Subsequent development to 1890 represented prodigious effective effort to achieve control of a new continent, converting a primeval wilderness into a capital-intensive and highly productive economy. Despite the pioneering character of this expansion, with attendant inefficiencies, *per capita* growth rates in Australia were reasonably close to the long-term trend growth rates in the Western world.

But during the two sub-periods, 1891–1913 and 1913–39, a drastic retardation occurred. It is important to note that this was much less marked in terms of population, work force and labour inputs. Indeed, these grew much faster in Australia than elsewhere in the West; it is of some significance that, in these terms, Australian *expansion* was relatively better sustained, and this raises the question whether Australian policy, pursuing expansion and increased scale of the economy, should not properly be judged on its own terms of aggregate rather than *per capita* growth. The retardation of gross product, however, was more severe than in the cases of population and work force, leaving little room for improvement in *per capita* real product (over the whole period 1890–1939, the compound growth rate was perhaps between 0·3 and 0·6 per cent per annum). If the figures are to be treated literally, output per worker and per unit of labour input may even have fallen in the interwar period but, at best, appears to have risen very slowly. The figures should not, of course, be taken too literally. Nevertheless, it would appear probable that adjustments for very large errors indeed would still allow only a very slow rise in these measures during the whole fifty years. This is in marked contrast with, at all events, several significant Western countries, including Britain and the United States, where *per capita* and per worker growth rates tend to follow reasonably closely along the long-term trend (subject only to one major fluctuation). In the Australian case this simple tabulation conceals some brief spurts of relatively rapid growth. These were not sustained and, in considerable measure, represented recovery from preceding down-swings of activity.

It was not until the latter part of the thirties (possibly not until after the Second World War) that the *per capita* and per worker growth rates were sustained at or above the levels achieved by the pioneering activities of the later nineteenth century. Criticism of Australian performance after the Second World War has been frequent, based partly on comparison with the historically short-term achievements of some Western economies (and the spectacular Japanese success). In the light of historical perspective, in contrast with current international comparison, Australian growth rates in the past quarter century have been high.

The dominant phenomenon of the past seventy-five years in Australian economic growth appears then, in trend terms, to be the prolonged period of relative *per capita* and per worker stagnation, with only intermittent spurts of growth, in the first fifty years. If attention were confined to the years 1890–1939, this stagnation might well be the appropriate focus. But it would be misleading to disregard behaviour before 1890 and after 1939. Given the relatively high growth rates surrounding the fifty years after 1890, the general contours appear in the form of a deep and prolonged trough in trend growth rates into which the economy moved from the nineteenth century and from which it appears to have emerged.

Trend growth rates in many Western countries were relatively low in the interwar years. None of these economies matched the severity and the duration of Australian stagnation. With only one economy has some broad similarity been identified, though the timing has been significantly different. In Argentina, growth rates until the late 1920s appear to have been sustained in a predominantly agricultural economy at relatively high rates from as far back as the 1850s. A severe and prolonged retardation occurred in this case and has persisted over the past forty years during the period when Australian growth rates recovered. But it would appear—and the comparison acquires more direct relevance later—that the Argentine economy since 1930 has been experiencing a form of transition comparable to that initiated in Australia in the early years of the twentieth century. Given the general similarity of resource and product patterns of the two economies, it may be fruitful to explore some of the common elements in their experience.

TABLE 6.7. *Sub-period Residual Growth Rates, 1861–1961*
(per cent per annum)

	1861–1891	1891–1914	1914–1939	1939–1961
	A. Aggregate growth rates			
GROSS AGGREGATES				
GPD	4·7	2·4	1·2	4·6
Population	3·5	2·0	1·2	2·0
Work force	2·7	1·8	1·6	1·5
Labour inputs	2·7	1·9	1·3	2·0
Man-hour inputs	2·5	1·9	1·2	1·8
Capital inputs	?	2·0	0·8	2·8
GROSS PRODUCT PER UNIT				
Population	1·2	0·4	0·0	2·6
Work force	2·0	0·6	−0·4	3·1
Labour inputs	2·0	0·5	−0·1	2·6
Man-hour inputs	2·2	0·5	0·0	2·8
Capital inputs	?	0·4	0·4	1·8
WEIGHTED INPUTS				
Work force	2·0 (1·8)	1·4 (1·2)	1·2 (1·1)	1·1 (1·0)
Labour inputs	2·0 (1·8)	1·4 (1·3)	1·0 (0·9)	1·5 (1·3)
Man-hour inputs	1·9 (1·7)	1·4 (1·3)	0·9 (0·8)	1·4 (1·2)
Capital inputs	?	0·5 (0·7)	0·2 (0·3)	0·7 (0·9)
Total inputs	?	2·0 (1·9)	1·1 (1·1)	2·1 (2·1)
RESIDUAL GROWTH RATES				
Work force	2·7 (2·9)	1·0 (1·2)	0·0 (0·1)	3·5 (3·6)
Labour inputs	2·7 (2·9)	1·0 (1·1)	0·2 (0·3)	3·1 (3·3)
Man-hour inputs	2·8 (3·0)	1·0 (1·1)	0·3 (0·4)	3·2 (3·4)
Capital inputs	?	1·9 (1·7)	1·0 (0·9)	3·9 (3·7)
Total inputs	?	0·4 (0·5)	0·1 (0·1)	2·5 (2·5)
	B. *Per capita* growth rates			
PER CAPITA GROSS MEASURES				
GPD per head	1·2	0·4	0·0	2·6
Work force per head	−0·8	−0·2	+0·4	−0·5
Labour inputs per head	−0·8	−0·1	+0·1	0·0
Man-hours per head	−1·0	−0·1	0·0	−0·2
Capital per head	?	0·0	−0·4	0·8
PER CAPITA WEIGHTED INPUTS				
Work force per head	−0·6 (−0·5)	−0·2 (−0·1)	+0·3 (+0·3)	−0·4 (0·3)
Labour inputs per head	−0·6 (−0·5)	−0·1 (−0·1)	+0·1 (+0·1)	0·0 (0·0)
Man-hours per head	−0·8 (−0·7)	−0·1 (−0·1)	0·0 (0·0)	−0·2 (−0·1)
Capital per head	?	0·0 (. .)	−0·1 (−0·1)	+0·2 (+0·3)
Total inputs per head	?	−0·1 (−0·1)	−0·1 (−0·1)	0·0 (+0·2)
RESIDUAL GROWTH RATES PER HEAD				
Work force per head	1·8 (1·7)	0·6 (0·5)	−0·3 (−0·3)	3·0 (2·9)
Labour inputs per head	1·8 (1·7)	0·5 (0·5)	−0·1 (−0·1)	2·6 (2·6)
Man-hours per head	2·0 (1·9)	0·5 (0·5)	0·0 (0·0)	2·8 (2·7)
Capital per head	?	0·4 (0·4)	0·1 (0·1)	2·4 (2·3)
Total inputs per head	?	0·5 (0·5)	0·1 (0·1)	2·6 (2·4)

The risk of error in attempting to measure different factor contributions in sub-periods is much greater than for the century as a whole. Table 6.7 should not be taken very literally. It gives some support to the hypothesis of severe retardation in both *per capita* and residual growth rates during 1890/1–1913/14 and in the interwar years. The table has, perhaps, some value in accentuating the proposition that, in so far as the Australian residual growth rate may not have been far short of 'typical' Western experience *over the whole century since 1861*, this long-term achievement may have been due almost entirely to the very much higher growth rates before 1891 and since 1939—perhaps particularly the latter period. We may reject the decomposition of the residual growth rate as the mechanical product of a complex sum of component factors due to qualitative changes of output and inputs, structural change, change in organization, technological change, changes in the terms of trade, and (peace be to the Cobb–Douglas production function!) the effects of economies of scale. But Table 6.7 suggests that we should consider whether the period 1890–1939 displayed a process of transformation in which either very little change occurred in these conditions of growth or there were offsetting adjustments as between these factors; and whether the appearance of a dramatic improvement in the scale of the positive contributions of these conditions after 1939 can be substantiated.

Residual growth rates have been derived roughly by simple deduction of growth rates; this procedure does not offset the main implication of the table. The weights adopted are those used earlier. The capital stock estimates cannot be taken very seriously and they have been included with some adjustments from the Garland and Goldsmith calculations for illustrative purposes rather than with any expectation that very firm conclusions can be based on them. For what they are worth, the aggregate and *per capita* residual growth rates in Table 6.7 do not suggest any marked deviation from the contrast displayed in Table 6.2 in the severe retardation in the interwar period and the quite dramatic recovery since 1939.

SUMMARY DATA OF AUSTRALIAN ECONOMIC TRANSFORMATION

Tables 6.8–6.11 present, for the period 1861–1965, some of the characteristics of the transformation of the Australian economy: some aggregate relationships in Table 6.8; Table 6.9 includes the composition of gross product by eight industrial subdivisions; Table 6.10 is limited to labour inputs for the same subdivisions for the period 1891–1961; Table 6.11 shows the shares of some categories of capital formation. It is not intended to manipulate all these interrelated changes nor, on the other hand, to confine comment merely to data as aggregated as these. These tables present a form of summary as decade averages that can yield only an approximate indication of change over time. All calculations, other than obvious volume measures, are based on current prices. For this reason, decade averages are taken as averages of annual percentages, not percentages of decade sums. Chart 6.2 gives continuous unsmoothed series of shares of product in both current and constant prices to indicate differences in behaviour of these series and shares of labour inputs; Chart 6.3 shows the ratios of export and total trade to gross product and Chart 6.4 shares in capital formation.

From the data of Tables 6.9 and 6.10, and Chart 6.2, inferences of certain sorts can be drawn. Equation of product and labour input shares in any subdivision implies equality of subdivision and overall average product per unit of labour. More generally, the percentage excess (deficiency) of product shares over input shares measures the extent to which the subdivision exceeds (falls short of) overall average labour productivity. Secondly, the ratio of the product: labour input shares of any two subdivisions measures their relative labour productivities. Thirdly, by simple summation of shares, relative productivities of any combinations can be similarly compared with each other. Fourthly, by comparing percentage point changes over time in product and labour input shares, we can determine the rate of growth of labour productivity of any subdivision relative to the overall average or to performance by any other subdivision.

It is essential, however, to recognize a limitation that is too often ignored in policy discussion. The measures of labour productivity implicit in these data are measures of *average* labour productivity. They do not convey relative levels and movements in *marginal* productivity. These measures help us to obtain some perspective on the *ex post* arithmetic of growth and do not indicate in themselves deviations from or approximations to maximizing behaviour. Other conditions must be introduced to throw light on these issues.

Traditionally, the explanation of Western economic growth has been found predominantly in terms of acceleration due to structural change, particularly in the large-scale shift from agriculture to manufacturing; improved quality of inputs, both capital and labour; changes in economic and business organization; economies of scale due to the progressive expansion of markets, industries, firms and

TABLE 6.8. *Aggregate Relationships*
(per cent)

	Net immigration: population increase 1	Current account balance: GDP[a] 2	Capital imports: GDCF 3	GNCF: GDP 4	GDCF: GDP 5	Total net wealth: GNP 6	Net foreign obligations: total wealth 7	Exports: GPD 8	Exports plus imports: GDP 9
1861–1870	26·8	−5·7	41·9	6·0	11·7			26·8	54·9
1871–1880	31·4	−1·7	9·0	13·3	15·0			23·0	43·8
1881–1890	41·5	−8·7	50·5	9·4	18·8			15·9	36·4
1891–1900	—	−2·5	23·4	9·6	12·2			24·2	43·6
1901–1910[b]	1·2	+1·7	—	13·7	13·1	4·6[c]	24·4[c]	21·9	42·8
1911–1920	20·7	−2·6	29·9	11·7	15·3			20·4	38·4
1921–1930	26·1	−4·3	27·5	14·4	18·0			19·0	38·4
1931–1940	4·2 (bracketed)	−1·6	13·6	12·8	13·5			19·4	30·7
1941–1950	4·2 (bracketed)	+0·6	?	?	11·3			?	?
1951–1960	38·2	−2·4	10·0	18·5	23·9	4·4[d]	5·4[d]	19·0	38·0
1961–1965	?	−3·0 (?)	12·2	21·6	24·6			16·1	32·3

[a] Minus equals net capital outflow.
[b] Financial years from beginning of twentieth century; for 1901 read 1900/1, etc.
[c] 1903.
[d] 1906.

Source: Col. 1, Commonwealth of Australia, *Demography Bulletin.*
Col. 2, See Chapter 2.
Cols. 3, 4, 5, 8, 9, Butlin, *Australian Domestic Product.*
Cols. 6, 7, Garland and Goldsmith, 'National Wealth of Australia', Ch. 12 in Goldsmith and Saunders eds. *Measurement of National Wealth.*

TABLE 6.9. *Subdivision Shares in GDP, Excluding Rents*
(current prices, per cent)

	Rural	Mining	Manufacturing	Gas, electricity and water	Building and construction	Trade and transport	Finance and property	Other
1861–1870	26·5	14·2	6·4 (Manufacturing and gas, electricity and water combined)		9·4	18·8	4·5	19·2
1871–1880	30·1	8·2	10·5		12·7	18·3	4·6	15·6
1881–1890	25·8	5·1	12·5		15·7	19·9	4·6	16·4
1891–1900	25·2	9·0	13·3		9·3	19·5	2·5	21·1
1901–1910	28·1	9·7	12·6		7·0	22·6	2·0	18·0
1911–1920	27·2	5·4	14·4	1·4	7·9	23·2	1·9	18·8
1921–1930	24·6	2·4	16·0	1·7	8·4	26·1	2·2	18·1
1931–1940	25·2	2·9	17·6	1·5	6·8	24·0	2·4	17·7
1941–1950	?	?	?	?	?	?	?	?
1951–1960	18·4	2·2	28·4	2·5	7·6	23·7	3·0	14·4
1961–1966	13·1	1·8	29·5	3·6	8·4	23·8	3·7	16·1

Note: Calendar years to 1900. Thereafter financial years—for 1901 read 1900/1, etc.

Source: Butlin, *Australian Domestic Product*.

TABLE 6.10. *Subdivision Shares in Work Force*
(per cent)

	Rural	Mining	Manufac-turing	Gas, electricity and water	Building and construction	Trade and transport	Finance and property	Other
1890/91	25·9	6·5	15·1	0·5	14·7	19·3	1·1	16·9
1900/01	25·3	8·3	15·0	0·6	10·4	20·7	1·3	18·4
1910/11–1919/20	23·8	4·2	17·8	1·1	10·3	21·5	1·5	20·0
1920/21–1929/30	23·8	2·5	19·9	1·3	12·1	22·5	2·0	15·9
1930/31–1939/40	24·3	2·7	21·1	1·4	9·2	22·7	2·3	16·7
1940/41–1949/50	16·4	1·8	26·3	1·1	6·5	20·4	2·0	25·6
1950/51–1959/60	13·9	1·7	28·1	1·6	10·1	24·1	2·8	17·8

Source: Butlin and Dowie, *Australian Economic History Review*, IX.

TABLE 6.11. *Percentage Shares of Industrial Subdivisions in GDCF* (current prices)

	Primary	Mining	Manufacturing	Trade	Transport	Electricity and water	Residential	Local authorities	Other
1861–1870	16·0	2·1	6·8	4·6	23·4	1·7	32·2	7·6	5·5
1871–1880	29·4	1·0	6·7	4·0	22·2	1·4	23·8	6·6	5·0
1881–1890	21·8	1·0	4·6	6·2	27·3	2·8	24·8	6·8	4·6
1891–1900	16·6	2·8	4·0	3·8	31·9	4·5	16·6	14·0	5·8
1900/01–1909/10	12·9	6·1	8·1	7·2	26·7	4·3	21·3	9·4	4·1
1910/11–1919/20	13·4	2·2	10·3	6·0	28·1	5·0	18·8	9·7	6·4
1920/21–1929/30	10·9	1·2	10·5	7·9	23·6	6·6	22·4	12·8	4·2
1930/31–1938/39	10·0	4·0	8·3	7·7	17·6	7·9	18·6	21·6	4·3

Source: Calculated from Butlin, *Australian Domestic Product*.

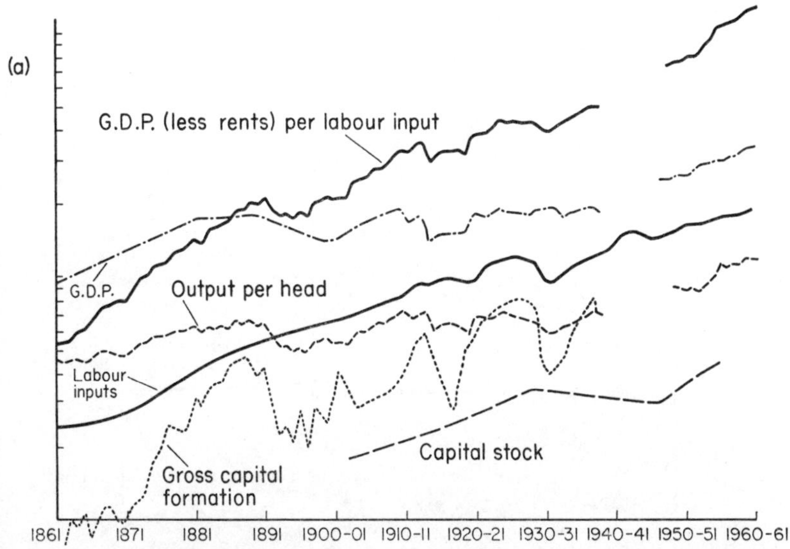

Chart 6.1 Aggregate Indicators
(a) Each graph has own scale; compare slope of lines.

Source: N. G. Butlin, *Australian Domestic Product, Investment and Foreign Borrowing, 1861–1938/39*, Cambridge University Press, 1962; J. M. Garland and R. W. Goldsmith 'The National Wealth of Australia', Ch. 12 in R. W. Goldsmith and C. Saunders eds, *The Measurement of National Wealth*, Income and Wealth Series VIII, London, 1959; N. G. Butlin and J. A. Dowie, 'Estimates of Australian Workforce and Employment 1861–1961', *Australian Economic History Review*, IX, 1969.

plants (note the inconsistency with the Cobb–Douglas production function); changes in tastes; and technological change. Other, sociological, conditions that have been suggested are left aside in this chapter. Development over long periods has typically been investigated in terms of a national economy, for many of which advantages aiding high growth rates have been found in terms of 'backwardness', expressed in relatively low *per capita* income, low savings rates and low rates of capital formation, predominance of agriculture, obsolete techniques, etc.

Perhaps the most interesting feature of Australian economic growth over the past seventy-five years is in the fact that most of these considerations appear to have had very limited opportunity to accelerate growth rates; and curiously enough, they all became

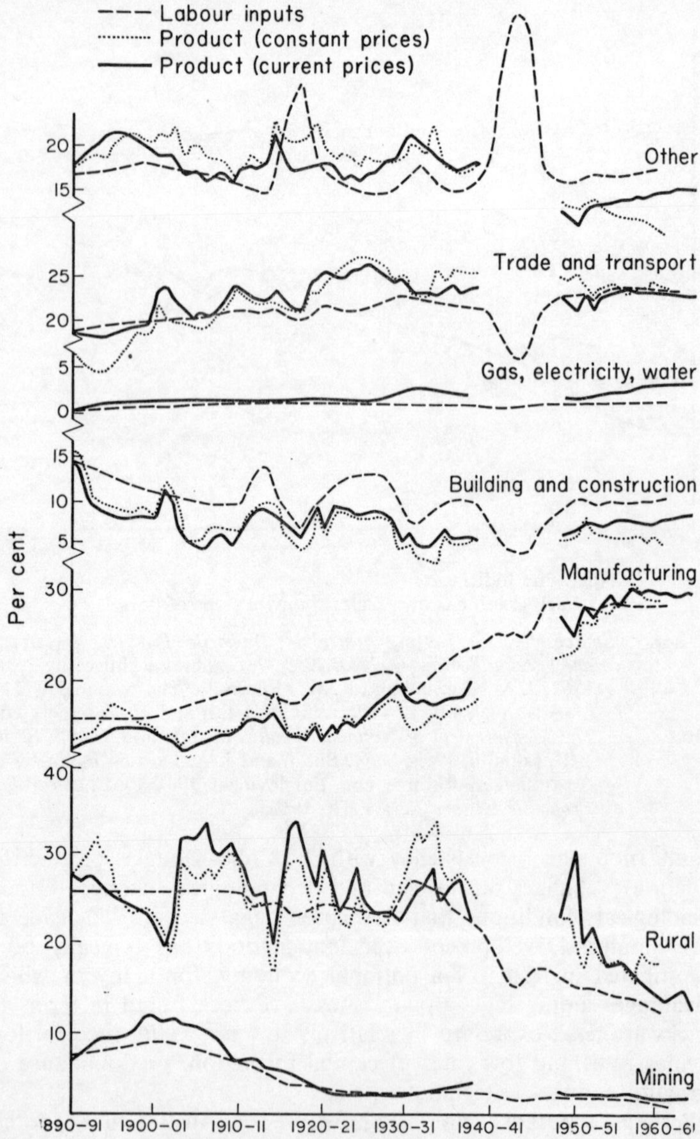

Chart 6.2 Shares of Industrial Subdivisions

Source: See Tables 6.10 and 6.11

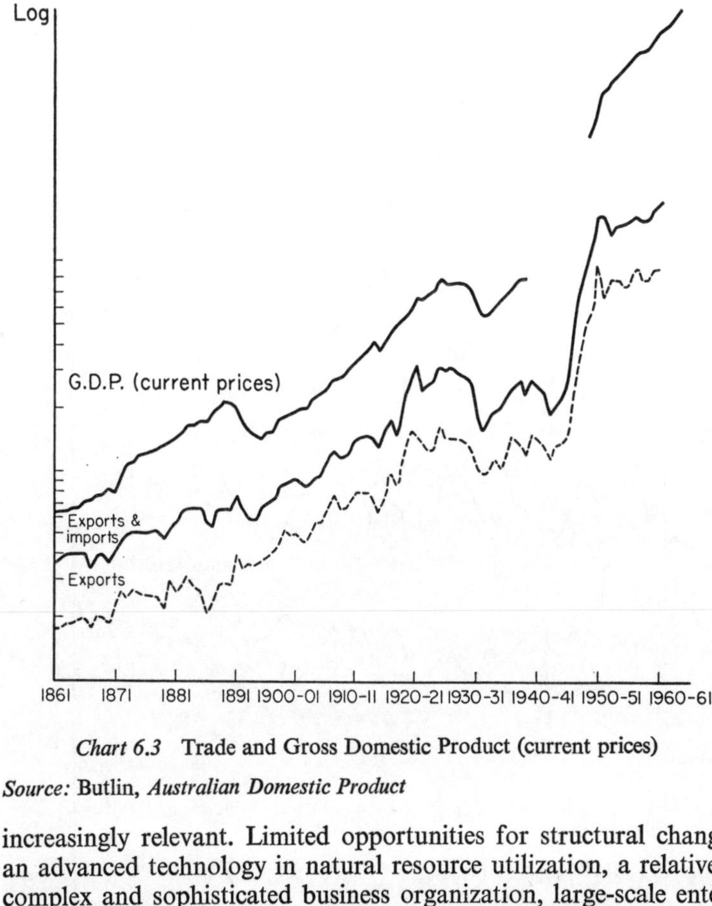

Chart 6.3 Trade and Gross Domestic Product (current prices)

Source: Butlin, *Australian Domestic Product*

increasingly relevant. Limited opportunities for structural change, an advanced technology in natural resource utilization, a relatively complex and sophisticated business organization, large-scale enterprises in major sectors of the economy, a very high level of *per capita* real product, a high rate of capital formation: these are the conditions from which a study of Australian growth since 1890 begins. We cannot comprehend post-1890 development without some attention to some selective characteristics before 1890.

PRE-HISTORY, 1861–90

In the early 1860s, Australians were the beneficiaries of a natural resource bonanza. A literal exchange rate conversion of Australian

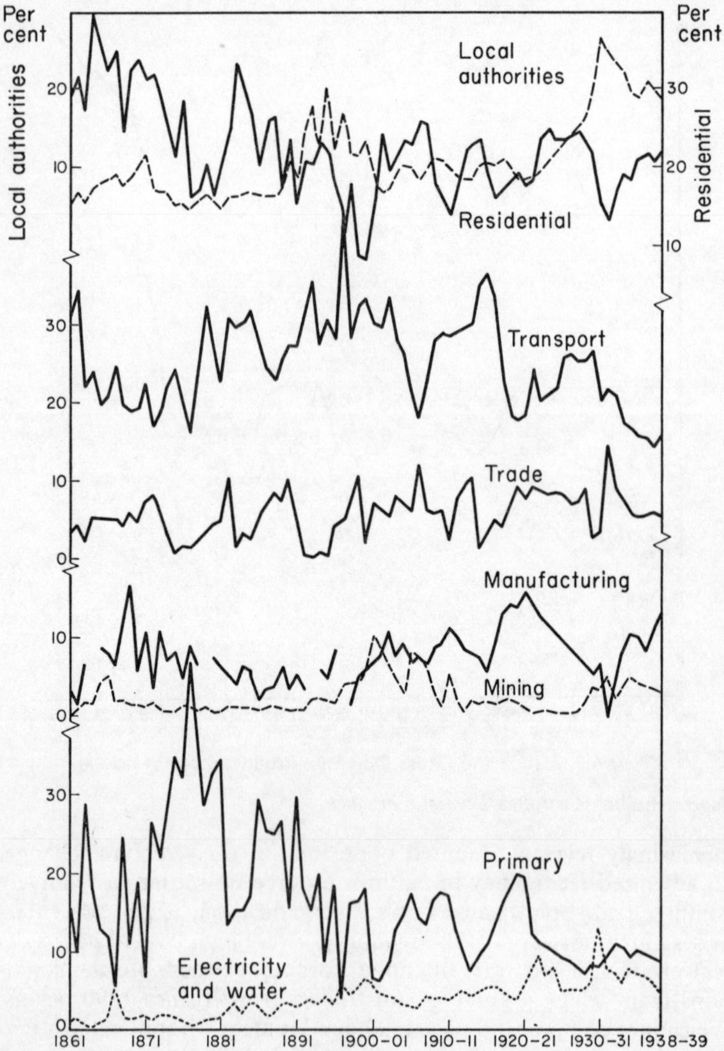

Chart 6.4 Percentage Shares of Industrial Subdivisions in G.D.C.F. (current Prices)

Source: Butlin, *Australian Domestic Product*

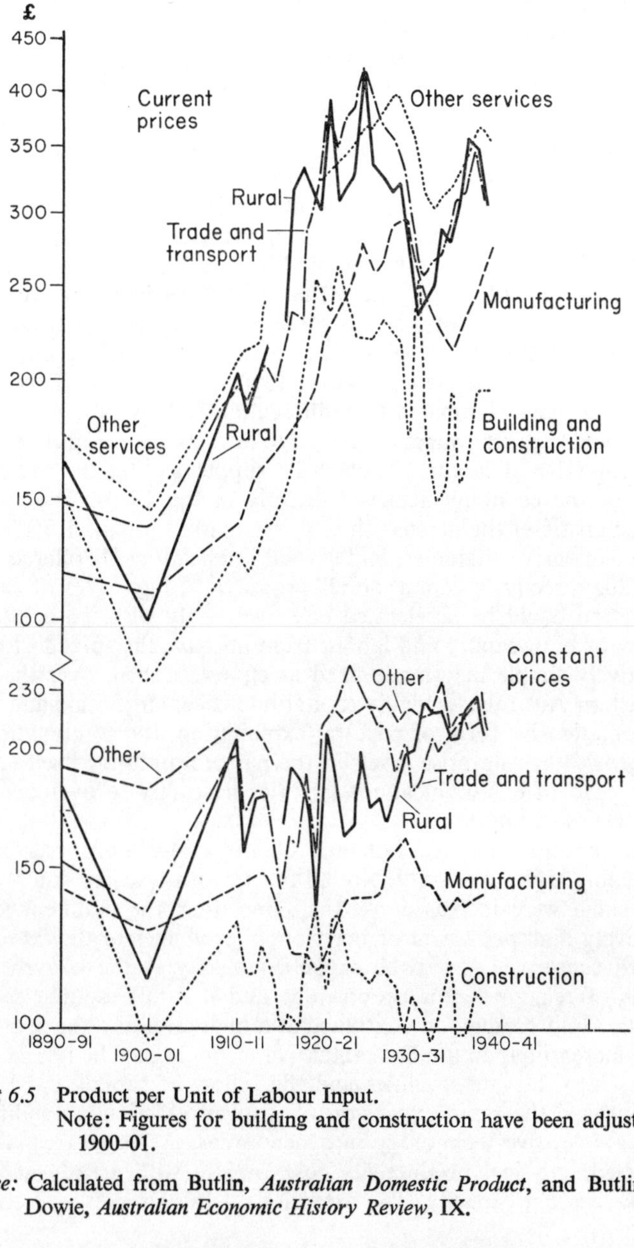

Chart 6.5 Product per Unit of Labour Input.
Note: Figures for building and construction have been adjusted in 1900–01.

Source: Calculated from Butlin, *Australian Domestic Product*, and Butlin and Dowie, *Australian Economic History Review*, IX.

per capita product is rightly suspect, particularly for remote dates, and it would be misleading to suggest definite relativities. It would appear, however, that this conversion would yield an Australian *per capita* real product in the early 1860s far above the level of the United Kingdom, then one of the wealthiest countries in the world. Making generous allowances for likely differences in relative prices, composition of expenditures and different qualities of goods and services, we appear to be left with a substantial Australian superiority. Demographic differences, as we suggested, might account for a significant part of this differential. Making this additional adjustment, it would still appear likely that output per worker or per unit of labour input in Australia was significantly higher than in Britain.

Modern Australian development began with the disadvantage of being wealthy. Subsequent growth to 1890 appears to have narrowed, but not to have eliminated this differential. Relatively high rates of return and high real wages continued to attract a large influx of overseas capital and labour (Table 6.8), supplementing the increased scale of the economy achieved directly in the 1850s. The special characteristic of the nineteenth-century capital formation, its highly labour-intensive character, had several implications. It offered little stimulus directly to capital goods production; high rates of capital formation could be accelerated effectively only with the combined inflow of both capital and labour from abroad; the spread of comparatively simple man-made fixed assets established, over the face of eastern Australia, a highly capital-intensive, large-scale and non-labour intensive form of pastoral exploitation, the combination of the growth of enterprise assetsi n the pastoral industry itself and in the spread of communications facilities necessary to overcome the obstacle of distance.

The natural resource bonanza of the mid-century created an untenably high superiority. Not all the advantages were quickly lost and some were increased. At the same time, the maintenance of relatively high *per capita* or per worker product into the late nineteenth century is not to be explained merely in the conventional terms of relative factor proportions and natural resource endowments. Gold production continued at a high level into the seventies, with increasingly non-labour intensive technology. The rise in wool prices into the late seventies and the inflow of capital and labour encouraged the rapid expansion of wool production, extending its capital-intensive technology into new areas. As price trends were reversed, physical productivity rose rapidly with greatly enlarged stock-carrying capacity. The extension of this process into the beginning of the nineties depended on more than the mere availability of internal resources on a continental scale and the repetitive application of capital-intensive technology. This was the first experimental use of a continent, the constraints on the use of which were only dimly perceived. Pastoral expansion and productivity gains depended on both the use and progressive wasting of natural assets through the largely unwitting denudation of vast areas of vegetation. It depended, too, on the formation of artificial water supplies which freed both sheep and other competitors for grassland from their dependence on natural water. In 1890, some of these hidden costs were beginning to emerge. But they had not yet had significant effect in any tendency to lower real product per head or per worker.

One of the implications of an increasingly non-labour intensive form of natural resource use, in a new economy in which population and work force were growing rapidly, was to encourage a progressive structural change in inputs and outputs. The reorientation was, however, the product of a variety of consequential changes and appears in various forms. It derived partly from the rising rates of capital formation encouraging the relatively very rapid growth of construction output and inputs. A major part of the reorientation of output, in particular, followed from the fact that one important activity, mining, depended on a wasting, non-replaceable asset. High *per capita* income, the preference systems of migrant populations newly arrived from and possessing the built-in tastes of an advanced society, coupled with isolation and high transport costs, encouraged the development of local manufacturing. Preference of many migrants for urban life may have given a differential advantage to the ability of manufacturing to attract a growing work force. One major area, services, appears to have been at an exceptionally high level in the sixties and did not keep pace with the rate of growth of gross product.

The reorientation can be seen, in part, in the more aggregative form, in terms of the declining ratio of traded to non-traded goods. These rather shadowy concepts are less revealing than the more conventional structural changes in inputs and outputs in industrial subdivisions. The thirty years before 1890 display quite marked structural adjustment, summarized in terms of product shares (we cannot make meaningful estimates of corresponding labour input) in current and constant prices. (See table on page 300.)

In this transition, the relative expansion of manufacturing needs some comment. It does not, by any means, follow from the natural resources advantage of Australia that the shift to manufacturing implied a movement to a markedly low productivity sector. Indeed,

Percentage Point Changes in Product Shares, 1861–3 to 1890/1

	Current prices	Constant prices
Rural	+2·7	+8·0
Mining	–11·2	–10·9
Manufacturing	+7·4	+6·9
Building and construction	+4·0	+4·3
Trade and transport	+0·6	+2·4
Finance and property	+0·1	–0·9
'Other' services	–3·4	–9·5

Chart 6.2 would imply that the *average* labour productivity in manufacturing in 1891 may have been as much as three-quarters that of the rural industries. Manufacturing in the nineteenth century was closely related to the rise of urban populations, growing from about 40 per cent to over 60 per cent of total population. An important component of manufacturing lay in the construction demands, particularly building materials for housing as this urbanization developed. Much of this activity depended on the relatively simple (in technological terms) processing of local materials. This type of processing, extending to food and drink, clothing and textiles, appears to have accounted for the major part of manufacturing. In addition, manufacturing activity was substantially enlarged by repair and replacement demands. It would be impossible in the present stage of knowledge to be very confident on productivity conditions. However, it seems unlikely that, in the nineteenth century, there were many opportunities for marked economies of scale over very wide areas of manufacturing, least of all in the types of activities that predominated in Australia. In any event, increasing concentration in a small number of large urban centres established large and increasing markets for these products—forming, on international standards, large groups of localized, accessible consumers.

The other major feature of structural adjustment is the tendency for the relative importance of rural industries to increase. This was contrary to typical Western experience, including that in the United States. But this increase is less significant than the fact that, even in 1891, the share of output of the rural industries was little more than a quarter of gross domestic product. The relatively low share limited the opportunities for a subsequent transition from rural to manufacturing activity on the scale that played so important a part in structural change elsewhere. This limitation was significantly increased by the high proportion of services and the rise in the share of manufacturing to the level attained in 1891.

A final comment on pre-history should be made. The tendency to a more highly urbanized society in the nineteenth century did not exert a substantial effective demand for utilities and amenities of urban life. Apart from housing, social overhead assets in Australian towns and cities were quite primitive in 1890. Housing, factory and commercial assets represented the dominant capital requirements, the latter two contributing directly to enterprise inputs. As in pastoral expansion, the full costs of urban concentration had not, in 1890, been fully recognized as investment in low-yield assets was largely avoided, creating a large potential back-log that was to have a long-lagged effect in retarding subsequent growth.

STRUCTURAL CHANGE, 1891–1939

Special events have played such an important role in the 'success' of Australian economic development that reason may be submerged in a Micawber-like reliance on 'turning up' a succession of gold discoveries in Western Australia, a Second World War, a myxomatosis virus and, most recently, another mineral bonanza. The stimulus of these events makes it difficult to evaluate the direction of growth after 1890 or the extent to which policies pursued were optimal or maximizing. From many points of view, leaving these incidents aside, conditions in 1890 were not obviously propitious for the maintenance of high growth rates, substantial structural change or a high rate of technical advance. The economy of 1890 was, at once, so advantageous in terms of *per capita* product and contained such substantial weaknesses as almost to impose some retardation on *per capita* growth rates. That the Australian economy emerged from the difficulties of the years 1891–1903, with a policy aimed still at pursuing accelerated population expansion, committed it largely to slow structural change, limited opportunities for technical advance and slow *per capita* growth rates. These limitations were accentuated by the long-lagged costs of nineteenth-century growth that became apparent in the twentieth century and were heightened by restraint imposed artificially on world markets in the interwar years. Hypothetical history becomes exceedingly complex at this level, and of doubtful value. Nevertheless, we cannot evade it completely if we wish to try to deal with one of the more interesting questions of Australian development during 1890–1939, whether artificially accelerated population growth, continued expansion in the scale of the economy, limited structural change artificially induced, accompanied by severe retardation of *per capita* growth rates was, or was not, in the long run, the appropriate optimal policy for Australia and a necessary path to pursue in order to attain greater *per capita* gains in the long run.

At the aggregative level, the signs of retardation are ubiquitous during 1890–1914 and in the interwar years. Given the greatly reduced rate of growth of real product to 1914 and the more severe retardation in the interwar years, the stable ratio of exports to gross product implied a greatly diminished stimulus to growth from the export industries. This reflected, particularly after 1914, the slackened expansion of world trade and the difficulties, in the context of interwar retraints, of sustained expansion of export industries in primary producing countries. The similar approximate constancy of the ratio, at a lower level than during 1861–90, of imports to gross product was not merely to be taken as the counterpart of export earnings. Capital inflow which had been a major supplement to local resources before 1890 was much less significant (the flow actually reversed for a time); moreover, it was channelled predominantly into government activity, both before and after the First World War. Partly offsetting this reduced capital inflow, domestic savings rates rose, though they remained low by comparison with many Western countries. The proportion of capital formation to gross product varied greatly but tended to be significantly less than the ratio attained before 1890. At the same time, the rate of growth of the work force slackened greatly. Retardation was even more severe in terms of labour inputs as the proportion of the total work force unemployed tended, over the long run, to rise. Of all these indicators, it appears that migration, variable though it was, tended to maintain its earlier dimension relative to population increase. This reflected, in part, the strength of government policy to sustain population growth. Nevertheless, the rate of population growth fell in the pre-1914 period to about 60 per cent the 1861–90 growth and slackened even further to about one-third the 1861–90 level in the interwar years. On the other hand, this slackened rate of population growth (and of work force) was very considerably above Western population increase over this period.

These are very general indicators of the slackened *expansion* after 1890. They tell us little of the factors that might enlighten the processes that yielded such drastically reduced *per capita* and per worker *growth rates*. The eight industrial subdivisions in Tables 6.9 and 6.10, used to define the structure of gross product and labour inputs, conceal much of the readjustment of the Australian economy. So far as they go, they suggest an extremely limited structural adjustment in product shares or in labour input shares between 1890 and 1939. In some cases, some substantial short-term changes occurred but these tended to be quite quickly reversed in most cases. The more persistent increases in product and labour input shares are shown in the limited rise in the proportion of manufacturing from approximately one-eighth to one-fifth of gross product and the less sustained increase in the share of trade and transport, whose share of product rose to a peak in the mid-twenties and dropped to a lower plateau which persisted (apart from war years) into the 1960s. In this half-century of structural stolidity, the most definite decline in relative importance was in mining, particularly from its peak in 1899/1900. The share of rural industries in gross product (but not in labour inputs) was highly unstable, making the trend more difficult to determine; but there is little evidence of any marked change in their relative importance to 1938/9. After its fall in relative importance in the nineties, building and construction tended to drift downwards slowly in product and labour input shares. One major sector, 'other' services, changed comparatively little. The set of adjustments is shown in percentage point changes in shares at beginning and end points in Table 6.12.

TABLE 6.12. *Percentage Point Changes in Product and Labour Input Shares*

	1890/91–1913/14			1913/14–1938/39		
	Gross product			Gross product		
	Current prices	Constant prices	Labour inputs	Current prices	Constant prices	Labour inputs
Rural	−1·2	−2·7	−2·1	−4·2	+0·2	−1·9
Mining	−0·3	+0·3	−1·8	−2·0	−3·1	−2·0
Manufacturing	+4·0	+4·3	+3·2	+5·7	+2·4	+5·5
Gas, electricity, water	[a]	[a]	[a]	+0·8	+0·4	+0·1
Building and construction	−5·0	−5·9	−0·7	−3·5	−4·2	−4·0
Trade and transport	+3·3	+6·2	+2·6	+2·0	+3·1	+0·5
Finance and property	−2·7	−2·9	+0·3	+0·9	+1·0	+0·8
'Other' services	+1·8	+0·7	−1·4	+0·2	+0·1	+1·1

[a] Included in manufacturing.

There was extremely little scope in this very restricted set of adjustments for a contribution from mix effects (at this level of disaggregation) to accelerate growth rates in either period. Although one sustained shift to manufacturing appears, the limited structural adjustment was not offset, as in 'traditional' experience, by matching decline of rural industries. Nor did the relative percentage point changes in product and labour input shares suggest that manufacturing provided much, if any, acceleration of the very low rate of change of labour productivity; it is possible that, in the interwar years, this expanding subdivision served to retard the rate of growth of real product per worker and per head. But in this respect manufacturing was not exceptional. There appears, on the evidence of these figures, to be a remarkable lack of leadership in productivity in every area of the economy, a characteristic that becomes more pronounced as we move into the conditions of the interwar years. If we accept, not necessarily the literal measurement, but the more general appearance of very slow increase in labour productivity in the economy as a whole, this tabulation implies that all subdivisions were subject to severe retardation, with manufacturing performing on constant price indicators rather worse than most of the major sectors. Slight relative productivity gains ahead of the poor economy-wide average experience were largely confined to trade and transport and, in the pre-1914 period, to construction.

It would be wrong to conclude, however, that no significant structural change occurred. These subdivisions conceal reorientation not only by inadequate disaggregation. They cannot be treated as merely arithmetic components. If we attempt to do so, they also conceal structural change in terms of the shifts in functional relations between different areas of activity. It is more interesting at this stage, to shift our attention from statistical manipulations to some more detailed structural adjustments and to the more important forms of functional changes. These seem more rewarding, at this stage, despite inadequate knowledge of many areas, in helping to understand the structural stolidity of these eight subdivisions and contributing, even if only tentatively, to an explanation of their apparently poor productivity performance.

SOME CONDITIONS OF LIMITED STRUCTURAL AND PRODUCTIVITY CHANGE

In shifting our emphasis, we are no longer limited to the comparison of comparable boom points, but need to trace some shorter-term characteristics. Within the scope of this chapter only highly selective comments can be made. More detailed discussion can be found in chapters on international trade, manufacturing, services and capital formation. Here attention is directed primarily to the complex of rural, manufacturing and construction industries, with more observations on the development of service components. Explanation must deal with (a) retardation of rates of expansion of product by comparison with the nineteenth century; (b) changes in each period in relative growth rates, with some activities accelerating and others decelerating relative to the slowly growing economy and (c) similar retardation and relative shifts in rates of growth of labour productivity.

(a) *Rural industries*

A combination of reduced rates of capital inputs, limited technical opportunities, slackened rates of growth and shifts in demand, and some policy measures combined to reduce greatly the rate of growth of pastoral product. Technical limitations restricting supply elasticities and slackening demand appear to have had a progressively retarding influence, lowering rates of product expansion and of labour productivity more severely in the interwar years.

Some long-lagged effects of the nineteenth-century expansion emerged clearly by the end of the century, following the reduction in output induced by the depression, reduced capital inflow into the industry and financial reconstruction which drastically reduced new investment and replacement of industry assets. Overstocking by the late nineties had denuded large areas of natural vegetation, a problem aggravated by poor rainfall experience which ended in the severe drought of 1902/3. The drastically reduced livestock was regenerated quickly by improved climatic conditions. But vast semi-arid areas had suffered long-term damage and the industry contracted geographically. To this physical withdrawal was added another indirect effect of the nineteenth-century capital formation: artificial water and paddocking that had freed sheep from natural pastures had similarly permitted rabbits to multiply over the face of eastern Australia. By the early twentieth century, their competition for pastures had become a serious problem which, from want of effective control measures, increased progressively throughout the period to the Second World War. That rabbit skins and carcases became a significant source of rural diversification was only a partial offset to their opportunity cost in terms of sheep. By their methods of nineteenth-century expansion, pastoralists were confronted, particularly in the interwar years, with a physical obstacle to further growth: the shortage of natural grassland. Technical knowledge (which existed in the nineteenth century) of artificial pastures had limited value where a prime beneficiary was the rabbit population.

In these conditions, the upward trend in primary product prices, including wool, does not appear to have encouraged much additional growth of sheep population or increase in pastoral assets. The industry appears to have pursued a path of technical change until the First World War, greatly increasing the use of heavy-fleeced, meat-producing sheep. In part, this readjustment represented a shift to meat. Primarily it was a technical experiment that led pastoralists into directions from which they eventually withdrew: rising fleece weights per sheep were a function primarily of increased dirt, burrs and grease, the product of inappropriate breeds. The reversion to merino which followed was distorted by the First World War and as it again induced temporarily cross-bred production, it also established large surplus stocks. Intervention by controlled disposal under government control sustained output until the mid-twenties. But from this point, the opportunities for further expansion of output were severely limited by physical obstacles to expanding pastures, by slackened European demand for wool and by the imposition of higher artificial restraints on imports into foreign countries. Despite the short-run stimulus to expansion due to exchange depreciation in 1931/2, by the latter half of the thirties the pastoral industry had lost its role as a 'growth' industry. Opportunities for expansion and for rising productivity depended essentially on the elimination of the pasture constraint.

The slackened rate of expansion and of technical improvement in the pastoral industry was offset, until possibly as late as the mid-twenties, by the diversification of the rural industries and the more rapid expansion of grains, dairy produce and miscellaneous rural output. That the rural industries failed, as a whole, to grow more rapidly in the period from 1896–1914 (when primary product prices rose) was due primarily to physical limitations and climatic uncertainties that prevented Australia from sharing in the agricultural boom that supported so strongly the growth, for instance, of the Canadian economy. Some restraint on grain expansion may have been imposed by the degree of control of land use by pastoralists. But it appears to have been inappropriate wheat strains, transport constraints and, above all, climatic conditions that limited grain expansion and created an extremely unstable output performance. These constraints were progressively reduced and the instability lessened throughout the period into the mid-twenties. Wheat breeding, in the first instance and for most of the years to the First World War, coped with some technical problems but exposed wheat production to less and less secure climatic conditions. The spread of output to progressively more arid conditions set a very low limit on opportunities for increase in labour productivity. Reducing marginal yields per acre depended on rising capital outlay to avoid an actual fall in labour productivity, and increasing capital inputs in the form of additions to farm machinery primarily acted to allow the industry to spread to lower yield areas.

The expansion of grain production depended also on the resumption of relatively heavy public capital outlays on branch railways, amplifying the nineteenth-century trunk system, in wheat areas. These outlays, made primarily before the First World War and continued into the twenties, had exerted their chief stimulus by the late twenties. Public support reflected an assumption of policy that rural industries continued to offer a major opportunity for economic development and increase in rural land settlement. Despite its instability before 1914, agricultural development could plausibly be expected to offer a limited source of accelerated product and employment. But the basic inconsistency lay in the rising levels of capital stock implicit in the rate of machinery investment and the life expectancy of farm equipment. Rising machinery inputs, a related increase in farm size and spread to lower yield areas tended towards a situation in which population per acre fell without corresponding increase in production of grain per man.

Perhaps the vision of increased rural land settlement had faded after the soldier settlement fiasco following the First World War. But by then, the rural industries had diversified far beyond meats and grains and had been stimulated further by the British war contracts of 1915–18. The rise in output of grain and other primary products during and immediately after the war created a situation comparable with the surplus pastoral stocks. But even more than in the case of wool, non-pastoral agricultural exports were exposed in the interwar years to restrictive trade practices in the world markets. The impact on Australia was lessened or made less direct to the extent to which exports were oriented to Britain. But Britain's very slow rate of expansion of real product and expenditure in the interwar years limited Australian rates of expansion of rural industries. The critical policy problem in the interwar years was to provide artificial restraints and stimuli to sustain the rural industries rather than to accelerate their growth. Export subsidies, import duties on primary products, marketing controls operated increasingly to sustain low-yield enterprises by two-price systems, dumping, concealed freight concessions and the like. Limited attempts to diversify export markets made little impact on this unfavourable world environment.

Increasing primacy protection and, in the depression, devaluation, induced a short-run expansion in rural activity. The consequence was to sustain and to expand output in progressively less productive or efficient activities, accentuating the retardation of productivity growth throughout the interwar years. It appears to have been in the less advantageous small-scale activities such as dairying, sugar, dried fruits, etc. that the most substantial artificial support was provided and in these, through inefficiency, that the main growth of farm population and work force was so well maintained. If the purpose of these policy measures was to support the artificially high rate of growth of population due to migration, regardless of costs in terms of productivity and output per man or per head, these policies should be taken to be successful. Certainly the rural industries substantially maintained their share of labour inputs up to the Second World War.

(b) *Construction*

The rural sector, beginning as an above-average productivity sector, did not diverge significantly from the rate of expansion of the whole economy and its relative labour productivity superiority dwindled. Some of the major features of the behaviour of construction stemmed directly from rural performance and the conditions of rural growth. Construction, typically well below average labour productivity (Chart 6.2), fell sharply in relative importance in the nineties and continued to decline slowly relatively to the economy as a whole.

It is in this subdivision, perhaps above all, that the risks of treating industry groups of this type as monoliths emerge. Not only did construction products and inputs change, but the functional relationship with the other sectors of the Australian economy was altered in the twentieth century. In the nineteenth century, construction and capital formation were closely related through the predominance of simple man-made capital, produced primarily as on-site construction products. The relative decline of construction activity in the twentieth century was partly a response to lower rates of capital formation. But more than proportional decline of construction derived from changing composition of capital equipment and the increasing significance of finished *manufactured* capital goods, particularly in rural and manufacturing activity.

The associated fall in the share of construction and capital formation has been represented by Kuznets as explicable in terms of low Australian savings rates. It is doubtful if the behaviour of savings rates was a major factor. As capital inflow ceased in the nineties and an outflow occurred until 1908, local savings rates rose and continued to grow into the twenties despite the resumption (on a more restricted scale than in the nineteenth century) of capital inflow. The dominant factors in the reduced share of construction were (a) the greatly lessened capital requirements of the pastoral industry, dwindling to negligible proportions at the turn of the century and remaining slight until the Second World War and (b) the partially compensating increase in agriculture and manufacturing investment, with their high proportion of capital expenditures on non-contruction finished capital goods.

Agricultural construction did not remotely offset the drastically reduced pastoral construction. From these points of view, one would expect to find a quite profound tendency for construction to decline throughout the pre-1914 and interwar years, despite the increasing diversification of the rural sector. Though one would need to introduce more sophisticated considerations, the declining rate of increase of population tended to slacken the rate of expansion of construction by the slower rate of increase in demand for housing, particularly in the interwar years. To some extent, this factor was offset by relocation of the population in large cities. That construction tended to grow at only a slightly less pace than the slowly-expanding economy was due to the relatively rapid shift in the direction of investment expenditures and associated construction towards urban, especially metropolitan, development. Additional factors included the resumption of railway building by government (though this tapered off in the interwar years). The latter activity was primarily the consequence of government commitment to increased rural settlement, though even here new railway building in metropolitan areas became an increasing component of railway outlays in the twenties.

The offsetting rise in relative importance of non-pastoral capital outlays had another implication bearing on the apparently poor (less than average) labour productivity of construction. The shift to manufacturing and commercial investment was accompanied by some significant technological changes that became increasingly important in the interwar years (use of cement, reinforced concrete and increase in scale of structures) and tended to raise construction productivity relative to the average. This throws into greater relief the sequence of events elsewhere, tending to restrain severely the rate of growth of productivity of construction as a whole and possibly to reduce this rate of growth progressively into the interwar years. Much of this arose from the changing character and increased relative importance of government capital outlays.

The resumption of capital inflow before the First World War and during the twenties, though on a relatively smaller scale than in the nineteenth century, was concentrated in government activities. The private rural sector had largely lost its attraction for foreign capital. Some limited new private activities—mining, particularly gold, in the early years of the century; some direct manufacturing investment in the early twenties—offered a very restricted scope for foreign investment in private activity. The concentration of foreign capital in public activities raised the relative significance of public capital outlays in total capital formation (to approximately half compared with an average of about one-third during 1861–90) and enlarged relatively the area of capital outlays in which short-run maximization could be, and apparently was, disregarded in favour of the pursuit of other goals.

These goals were, partly, the increase in land settlement as part of the rationale of migration. From this objective followed the recovery, in the pre-1914 period, of branch-line building. A more substantial factor was the long-lagged consequence of the very limited social overhead capital in towns and cities, a lag that attained progressively increasing importance as the proportion of population in urban areas rose in the decade before the First World War and in the interwar years. It is not possible to separate urban and non-urban public construction with any great accuracy even when the distinction is made in simple geographical terms. Nevertheless, outlays on public utilities, transport services and urban roads, particularly in the main metropolitan areas, rose strongly during the decade before 1914 and even more rapidly into the late twenties. These projects had much more in common with nineteenth-century technology than did the rising twentieth-century agricultural and industrial capital outlays. Water and sewerage, gas and electricity supplies, roads and even the more complex metropolitan railways were highly labour-intensive, with a high derived demand for on-site unskilled labour. A rough approximation of the shift in public capital outlays suggests that from the late eighties to the boom of the twenties, these components of gross capital outlays rose from rather more than one-third of total capital formation to probably more than three-quarters.

But another factor operated to increase the proportion of highly labour-intensive construction in total public outlays, particularly in the interwar years. Relatively high unemployment rates appear to have been sustained throughout the 1920s, and persisted even after recovery from the severe unemployment levels of the depression in the thirties. Not only the placement of migrants but also the limitation of unemployment became an increasing factor in determining the level of public construction activity. In the outlays underlying Table 6.11, explicitly general relief expenditures are excluded. Nevertheless, the multiplication of projects, part of whose purpose was to provide employment, clearly affected the rise in local and semi-government expenditures in the late twenties and throughout the whole of the thirties. As partially work-creation projects, these outlays tended to be undertaken without regard for rates of return and, on the contrary, were designed as deliberately labour-intensive.

(c) *Manufacturing*

The orientation of construction activity was part of the conditions of the one sustained increase in product and input shares in the pre-1914 and the interwar years—the growth of manufacturing. In addition, until the latter part of the twenties, there was also a sustained shift to trade and transport. These two subdivisions, primarily urban in terms of the location of the enterprises concerned, were rising somewhat faster than the rest of the economy. But the increase was much more restrained than the rise that occurred in the shares of these subdivisions in other countries such as the United States and Canada (Australian manufacturing product +9·7 percentage points in current prices and +6·7 in constant prices; trade and transport respectively +5·3 and +9·3).

For present purposes, three major characteristics of late nineteenth-century manufacturing should be noted. A significant component, largely local processing, provided construction inputs through production of building materials. A much larger group, supplying consumer goods, was based similarly on the limited processing of local materials for the production of food and drink. Probably the largest component, the 'metals and machinery' group, contained an imprecisely known but clearly large component of repair activity, a 'service' function of so-called manufacturing that recurred also in other groups such as vehicles and leather working.

The relative importance of these types of activities does not appear to have changed much by the early years of the twentieth century. The main relative gains made up to the First World War were also in food and drink, and metals and machinery complexes. Important though these activities were, they offered, in themselves, no easy route to rapid industrialization.

The development of a large manufacturing sector, from the Australian base of 1890, was a far more complex process than can be easily categorized by text-book concepts. The conditions of successful industrialization were more than merely in the form of expanding demands, increasing inputs or the adoption of new technical methods. The development of skills, the complex interrelationships of a large variety of skills, better education, specific and appropriately designed training institutions, forms of business organization, the emergence of financial institutions geared to industrial financing, the increase in entrepreneurial skills adequately illustrate the conditions of development behind the façade of changing consumption and input levels and components. Industrialization from relatively primitive beginnings depends on the emergence of highly complex interrelated institutions, including social values, the achievement of which is likely to be a long drawn out process.

Until the First World War, policy in relation to manufacturing was ambivalent. The early gains in food, drink and metals linked the manufacturing sector more firmly with the diversifying rural sector, the growth of which appears to have been the prior policy consideration. The preservation of this link until the First World War may have helped to preserve manufacturing productivity and to have sustained an accelerated rate of expansion of product and inputs. In addition, the local customs union, due to federation and the application of moderate but still definitely protective tariffs in the beginning of the century, enlarged local opportunities, particularly for the Victorian and New South Wales industrial complex. It is probable that, for most of these activities, few potential economies of scale existed, the limited processing required not very advanced technology or skills and in these areas Australian productivity may not have suffered greatly by comparison with similar activities in Western countries. Nevertheless, before the First World War the limited expansion of manufacturing appears already to have encountered serious problems of shortage of skilled labour.

The disruption of the First World War prompted the attempts to introduce a large variety of new products, the supply of which had been cut off by war and made the encouragement of manufacturing over wider and more complex ranges of activity a prime consideration. In the fifteen years after the end of the war, Australian tariff levels rose rapidly to enlarge the share of the local market for Australian manufacturers, attract direct industrial investment and to provide artificial conditions raising factor rewards in manufacturing relatively to other areas of the economy. Closely linked with tariff policy, a wages policy that increasingly recognized margins for skill increased the attractions of labour training and the addition of higher skills in industry.

Tariff levels doubled between 1907 and 1928/9 and then doubled again by 1932, the whole increase occurring almost entirely after 1919. The slight decline in the level of the tariff after 1932 is deceptive since it needs to be read in the light of the much more substantial devaluation. Although there were counterbalancing movements in world prices of manufactured goods, it would appear that protective measures as a whole were very much higher after 1932 than before it. But the added encouragement to local manufacturing through devaluation was shared by the encouragement to rural export industries. Chart 6.5 is merely a crude representation of the difference in movement of current price and constant price product per unit of labour input. Though this difference compounds a number of factors, the chart does help to suggest the strength of artificial distortions that yielded a relative advantage to manufacturing, in particular in the 1920s.

In the event it appears probable that it was the 'old' industries of food, drink, clothing, that gained most from the opportunities for import substitution. As these enterprises expanded to meet demands previously serviced by imports, they were exposed to inducements to provide more complex or sophisticated products, to increase product differentiation and to commit themselves to enlarged plants which were inefficiently used because of the variety of outputs (and probably lack of adequate skill). It is possible that the smallness of the Australian market imposed diseconomies of scale on these enterprises. But the grounds for any conclusion along these lines seem highly dubious. It seems probable that tariff policy, not combined with effective restraint on entry into protected industries in these areas, represented a combination of action and non-action that enlarged total markets for Australian firms and ensured their division between an increasing number of firms, the efficiency of all of which was adversely affected by inadequate policy measures.

The newer industries—steel, steel products, electrical products, rubber, chemicals, etc.—demanded a scale of activity, a sophistication of equipment and a supply of more complex skills that the Australian economy was not readily equipped to supply. Moreover, they depended for successful development on the existence of interrelated manufacturing production that was only feasible gradually by conscious artificial intervention. Direct investment of foreign, especially British firms, in the early 1920s gave an initial stimulus to the necessary new technology. Employment and investment, for a time, rose very quickly until skill limitations and the emergence of excess capacity in many areas emerged to plague most of these new enterprises until the Second World War. Relying to a large extent on British technology, entrepreneurial and managerial skills and, more generally, on the importation of British mechanical equipment, Australian manufacturing in any event tended to follow British industrial practice. Given the interwar lag in British technology behind the best practice elsewhere, it seems probable that this new Australian industry began similarly committed to backward technique.

Undoubtedly, a gradual evolutionary advance was occurring in the interwar years. Educational standards were rising steadily; provisions for technical training were widening; public company organization was replacing private firms; entrepreneurial and managerial skills developed. It would be difficult in any circumstances to determine the quantitative significance of these gradual changes. But one could not, at this stage, reach any conclusion on the issue of whether, before the Second World War, these infant industries were growing up. This would be a major enquiry that would be of central importance to an understanding of the success of Australian manufacturing development in the interwar years. In the Australian economy, in which policy was committed to accelerated population increase, it would seem that this acceleration depended on the expansion of labour-intensive activities, including labour-intensive manufacturing. Whether the actual process was optimal is more than merely a sixty-four dollar question.

(d) *Services*

Since services are given detailed attention elsewhere, only a few comments are made here. As we have seen, services attained a very high share of gross product and total work force in the nineteenth century. It has been suggested that this high share at about 1890 might be explicable basically in terms of high *per capita* incomes, British-formed preference systems and isolation. Other considerations could be added in the high demand for transport and services to overcome the obstacle of distance or the widely scattered nature of primary export activity, with its dependence on transport services. To attempt an effective study of services after 1890, we would need a more effective method of valuing service output than has so far been contrived and, most importantly, a much greater degree of disaggregation needs to be achieved. At this stage, a few general observations may help to indicate some of the broad characteristics.

First, it should be noted that neither current nor constant price productivity per unit of labour input in services appears to have been inferior to the countrywide average labour productivity with two exceptions. First, in the depression of the nineties and into the first few years of this century, the estimates suggest that transport performed less well than the economy as a whole. Secondly, in the two war episodes, it appears probable that services productivity shrank considerably, reflecting the conventional pricing of the services of the armed forces. Trade and transport productivity did tend to improve in the long run, at least until the depression of the thirties and to rise quite substantially in the twenties. For the rest, 'other' services largely kept pace with the very slow overall rate of growth of labour productivity.

The behaviour of trade and transport may appear, then, to warrant some special attention as a better-than-average performer. In general, there do appear to be some major changes occurring in the Australian economy that would support this view. The basic consideration that may be suggested is the greatly increased institutional specialization that occurred after 1890, partly the product of depression, partly the result of the expansion and diversification of the economy. In the nineteenth century, lack of specialization reflected the relatively underdeveloped state of particular components of activity and the shortage of skills. The many-sided entrepreneur, the institutional combination of manufacturing, trade and transport functions, the confusion of rural production, construction, transport and selling activities were by no means unique to or uncommon in Australia. The gradual separation of these functions does not merely imply a statistical trick. It was a basic feature of pre-1914 and interwar growth from which a separately measurable, because separately conducted, trade and transport emerged more clearly. More sophisticated separation, particularly promoting 'other' services, appeared more definitely after the Second World War. But prior to then, increasing specialization appears to have promoted trade and transport. *A priori*, one might expect that increased specialization in these areas might enlarge opportunities for increased efficiency.

To this general institutional influence, a major policy consideraton was added affecting particularly the transport sector. Not only did public outlays expand to provide for more effective transport systems in main urban centres but the growth of city populations, in particular, enhanced the demand for this type of utility. But reinforcing this stimulus, the intervention of the tariff provided substantial opportunities, perhaps particularly in the area of transport, to substitute locally provided public services for imports. This cross-influence from tariff policy, designed to encourage import substitution, is not commonly appreciated, the assumption being typically that replacement of imported goods is achieved by locally produced goods. In practice, transport goods (especially motor vehicles) did not become objects of mass consumption until after the Second World War. In so far as it was protective, it appears that the tariff provided a substantial economy measure to maximize the use of transport equipment in socially-used and often publicly provided transport services. This substitution was, perhaps, encouraged by the relative complexity of motor-vehicle manufacture and the importance of economies of scale (the disadvantages of small scale) in vehicle production and assembly. Concentrating increasingly on relatively rapidly growing metropolitan centres, the opportunities for increased labour productivity in these areas may have been enhanced.

Public policy did not provide merely a stimulus to transport development. Protective tariffs offered a trade-off for other services in some areas, particularly where other than merely separate individual consumption of goods was possible. Illustrations could include entertainment (the development of cinemas in the twenties and thirties) or even the (not unimportant) economy achieved in laundering clothes in circumstances in which the relative prices of new clothing rose due to tariffs. But public activity had a more direct bearing on the growth of services. Of all service activities, the most rapid expansion after the turn of the century appears to have been concentrated on public enterprise utility functions, the non-enterprise public service development and, perhaps most significantly, in the growth of publicly provided education.

With the first we need to be little concerned. Already reference has been made, in the section on construction, to the growth of metropolitan utilities in the twentieth century. The increased prominence of government services reflected partly the more complicated government structure under federation but perhaps most importantly the increasing complexity of government intervention in the economy and society. The depression of the nineties greatly enlarged government commitment to problems of stability of economic and social activity, and increasingly interest in stabilization functions spread from labour relations to problems of farm incomes, prices and marketing arrangements, social welfare, banking and monetary conditions, etc. Given the method of measurement, there was little scope for a significant productivity increase to be recorded in this area, in contrast with the potential gains in the conduct of public enterprises in the provision of utilities.

The significance of education services changed greatly after the turn of the century and the educational work force rose rapidly. This expansion appears to have been concentrated on the higher levels of education, beyond elementary primary levels. Particularly secondary education and to a less extent, though still substantially, technical education, expanded under the growing demands for skill and higher educational qualifications. These two segments appear to have dominated the faster growth of education services and it is almost certain that, properly measured, more significant increases in productivity would be recorded than is implied by our calculations.

Closely related to these changes, some important occupational shifts can be detected. Amongst the more highly trained professionals, the more technical groups such as engineers, surveyors, etc., appear to have expanded quite rapidly only until the First World War and then to have experienced severe retardation. By constrast, the improving provision of health services appears to have largely followed the First World War and to have risen relatively rapidly throughout until World War II. Relatively rapidly expanding medical services were matched by increasing numbers forming legal enterprises, the two representing the main areas of rapid growth among the more specialized and highly trained sector of 'other' services.

Reinforcing productivity gains through mix-effects due to increases in more highly trained service personnel, the numbers engaged in domestic service largely stagnated until the depression of the thirties. Then a special stimulus was offered particularly to women to seek supplementary earnings and numbers rose fitfully until the Second World War. The long-run influence was, however, significantly to reduce the importance of this relatively very low productivity group in the total work force. The decline in *relative* importance of domestic service may be explicable largely in comparatively straightforward terms of the comparative stagnation of income levels, though we would need to know more of changes in income distribution before we could be very confident of this. Certainly, during the years before the Second World War, consumer durables in households offered little scope for economizing on domestic service. The growth of mass consumption of these articles appears to have begun to rise very sharply indeed in the year or two before the war. After 1945, the very rapid increase in durable consumer goods in households was a major factor in the drastic decline of domestic service in Australia.

A recitation of these types of changes may be of some value. Unfortunately, the elementary bar to meaningful interpretation lies in the difficulty of measuring services productivity. It would appear in general that a sequence of conflicting shifts in service consumption may have been important in preserving the relative stability of recorded productivity of 'other' services over the long period to 1939. In addition, the substantial absence of new factor combinations, the failure to introduce capital equipment and embodied technical change, appears to have been an important factor retarding improvement in this sector. Given its importance in the economy as a whole, this stagnation had major implications for overall economic performance.

ACCELERATED GROWTH SINCE 1939

It was essentially in the period since 1939 that the 'traditional' offsetting adjustment away from rural activities and towards manufacturing occurred in Australia. Table 6.13 shows the change in product shares and input shares for the whole period 1891–1961 and for the limited period 1939–1961.

TABLE 6.13. *Percentage Point Changes in Shares of Subdivisions*

	1890–1961			1939–61		
	Product shares			Product shares		
	Current prices	Constant prices	Labour inputs	Current prices	Constant prices	Labour inputs
Rural	−13·2	−10·0	−14·0	−7·8	−7·5	−10·0
Mining	−4·1	−2·6	−2·6	−1·8	+0·2	−0·7
Manufacturing	+21·4	+19·2	+13·5	+9·7	+11·3	+5·3
Gas, electricity, water	[a]	[a]	[a]	+1·2	+0·6	+0·6
Building and construction	−6·5	−10·2	−4·4	+2·0	−0·1	+0·3
Trade and transport	+4·7	+7·5	+5·0	−0·6	−2·8	+1·9
Finance and property	−1·1	+2·0	+2·3	+0·7	+3·9	+1·3
'Other' services	−1·4	−6·9	+1·5	−3·4	−7·7	+1·8

[a] Included in manufacturing.

Perhaps the most significant feature of this table, given the division of the offsetting changes in rural industries and manufacturing (over half the structural shift of product to manufacturing and a considerably larger fraction of the total shift from rural industries occurred since 1939) is in the fact that both subdivisions contributed a significant acceleration of the rate of growth of labour productivity. This was the one period in Australian economic development in which a rapid increase in the productivity of both sectors occurred simultaneously. Manufacturing share of product rose to account (including gas, electricity and water supply) for about one-third of gross product. During the sixties, Australia had moved to a degree of industrialization comparable in these terms to the United States and Canada. Given the export orientation of the rural industries, their share has not yet fallen to the very low American level.

The Second World War makes a critical break in Australian economic development, though its contribution to subsequent economic growth was often indirect and, to some extent, fortuitous, depending on the related effects of other exogenous events. The severe control on civilian consumption, combined with detailed war planning, restrained output in areas of manufacturing that had formed the mass of pre-war activity, contributed to a widespread rationalization of essential civilian production and led to drastic deterioration of plant and equipment by the end of the war. By contrast, a major opportunity was offered in war production, leading to the formation of new plants and the installation of new equipment in areas of activity that formed the basis of post-war growth industries—in chemicals and explosives, rubber and metal working, arms and munition, basic steel production, etc. Under wartime control a high degree of rationalization and concentration of these newly-expanded industries was achieved. To service this wartime manufacturing, measures to dilute the skilled work force by removal of trade union barriers to entry and, at the same time, to provide for training in industrial processes, had the fundamental effect by the end of the war of greatly extending the basic skills in, and familiarity with, manufacturing techniques. Perhaps, most importantly, the entry of women into wartime manufacturing tapped a source of labour and opened up a flow of women into the work force of major significance for post-war development. The technology of war itself enlarged the mechanical skills of servicemen and post-war retraining added further to the stock of skilled labour.

The outstanding change in the post-war years, in contrast with the interwar period, was the sustained high level of activity throughout the trading world, a high prosperity in which Australia shared. Post-war reconstruction expenditures, domestic full employment policies, cold war outlays, provided part of the foundations for sustained economic development. Within Australia itself, the pursuits of full employment substantially eliminated unemployment as a significant social and economic problem and ensured, with only slight fluctuations, full capacity operation of the economy.

For at least twelve years after the end of the war, the old protective devices of the interwar tariff were largely irrelevant. First intensive post-war shortages throughout the world limited supplies of competing imports into Australia. Subsequently, until the late fifties, quantitative import restrictions determined the extent of potential foreign competition with Australian manufacturing production. For a time, Australia was able to take little advantage of this restrictive situation. Rather, post-war shortages restricted the imported supply of basic equipment needed to restore run-down physical assets. At the same time, Australian foreign exchange resources were limited and subject to restraints imposed by sterling area controls, severely restricting importation of equipment from the one area, the United States capable of supplying needed goods. To these world-wide shortages was added domestic shortage of basic materials, particularly steel and fuel and power supplies. On the other hand, pent-up demands for both consumer and capital goods created a high demand for manufactured products that could not be quickly supplied and which served to create inflationary pressures in the late forties.

There is no space in this chapter to do more than hint at some of the major influences affecting the course of events from this point. The Korean War with its accompanying wool boom transformed, for a time, the foreign exchange situation and helped to remove the post-war restraints on peacetime economic growth. Thereafter, development was interrupted by only comparatively slight variations in rates of growth as a whole, representing a degree of stability at a high level of employment that may have been paralleled during the period 1860–90.

The wool boom provided the immediate incentive to a renewed pastoral expansion, while, at the same time, the accompanying price rise exposed the pastoral industry to intensified competition from artificial fibres. The fears of competition appeared subsequently to be exaggerated. Nevertheless, during the late fifties, the expectation of this competition played a significant part in inducing an increased diversification of rural activity into beef and grain production. At the same time they encouraged shifts that had been occurring in the 1930s towards more diversified export markets, orientating the Australian export industries farther towards Asian countries. This orientation was extended as the grain component of rural production rose and the difficulties of disposing of enlarged output in Western markets increased. Restraints on demand in export markets played an increasing part in restraining the rate of expansion of the major rural industries. The tendency for wool and grain prices to decline relatively, particularly after the mid-fifties, checked the rate of growth of output of the rural industries and progressively reduced the ratio of exports to gross domestic product.

The uncertain export market for these major industries developed at a time when far-reaching technological changes, with accompanying increased demand for capital, had established the physical conditions to permit a rapid expansion of wool and grain production, a more pronounced trend towards capital-intensive and non-labour intensive farming and an economizing in land use. Wool production, in particular, tended increasingly in the 1950s and 1960s to concentrate in the more secure climatic areas, reflecting their comparative advance for the application of the new techniques and more capital-intensive methods. In the 1950s, Australia's rural industries had acquired peculiar advantages of backwardness. Myxomatosis virus, identified and separated sixty years earlier, was introduced as a highly successful act of biological warfare against rabbits, almost but not quite eliminating them as competitors for pastures and grain lands. Artificially seeded pastures with fertilizer applications had been in use in Australia a century earlier and their adoption had quickened from the late twenties. In the 1950s, a war-enlarged chemical industry was able to supply mass quantities of manufactured fertilizer; and former wartime pilots gave a peculiarly important addition of a special skill required for mass seeding and fertilizing. The additional new technology of trace elements enhanced the value of fertilizers in both pasture and grain development. Finally, post-Korean prosperity initiated, and the higher yields from fertilizer stimulated, the greatly increased use of mechanized equipment in both pastoral and grain production, equipment that was now capable of local production on a much larger scale than before the Nazi war.

We are not in the position to do much more, at this stage, than guess at the course of rates of returns from capital outlays in the rural industries. Indeed, the influence of these changes is concealed by the exceptional seasons and bumper yields fortuitously enlarging output at the very end of the forties. Adjusted to normal seasonal performance, productivity in the rural industries rose strongly after 1950. The level of capital formation that had been minimal in the pastoral industry for half a century after 1890 received a powerful stimulus, despite market uncertainties, until the late 1950s. Clearly the gains in labour productivity in the rural industries were achieved by a combination of technological changes, increased capital intensity and an altered product mix. By comparison with earlier experience, particularly that before 1914 and more so before 1890, this demand for rural capital had, however, one important advantage. It was confined almost entirely to enterprise capital, with little demand for social overhead equipment as a condition of expanded output. The gains made in labour productivity in these main industries were restrained by the productivity performance of 'minor' rural activities, particularly dairying, that had been supported as labour-intensive activities since the First World War and to which support continued.

The declining share of labour inputs in the rural industries more than offset the rising share of labour inputs into manufacturing. In common with the rural industries, labour productivity in manufacturing rose considerably. But it appears to have risen significantly faster than in rural activity as the share of gross product due to manufacturing rose much faster than its share of labour inputs. This acceleration of manufacturing labour productivity, accompanying the rapid increase in the output of this major subdivision, is the outstanding feature of post-war development until the early sixties. We cannot, at this stage, pretend to quantify the sources of this productivity change nor can we be very confident that even the 'major' probable contributions to this accelerated expansion and productivity gain can be adequately listed. The significance of the change in simple labour productivity terms is indicated in Chart 6.2. It would appear that in 1948/9, manufacturing labour productivity may have been of the order of 20 per cent below the overall average labour productivity of the economy. By the second half of the fifties, this inferior relationship had disappeared, and in the early sixties manufacturing rose definitely above the economy average.

It is probable that the inferior productivity position in manufacturing at the end of the 1940s was partly due to post-war shortages, including shortage of new plant and equipment, and to the discontinuities in productive activity due to interruptions in basic services, particularly fuel and power. Relaxation of foreign exchange constraints at the beginning of the fifties appears to have marked the start of substantial re-equipment of war-worn plants. As in the rural industries, Australian manufacturing now had a significant 'advantage of being backward'. The rapidly growing population, its growth accelerated by high birth rates and a high level of immigration, full employment with high incomes, now provided a very substantially increased market for industrial products. The pre-war concentration in urban areas was carried further as the two leading metropolitan areas, Sydney and Melbourne, increased rapidly to provide sources of labour supply and consuming centres that were very large on world standards. The lagged effects of wartime shortages continued to provide stimulus to accelerated expansion. Finally, the retention, with some interludes, of quantitative import restrictions assured local industry of rising shares of the local market through import substitution that was carried further than had been possible under the pre-war tariff. The tendency in many areas, particularly in the 'old' industries of food and drink, clothing and textiles, leather products, etc. to approach complete import substitution increased incentives to seek export opportunities. The post-war enlargement of skills and scale of domestic activity provided much greater opportunites for more effective competition in overseas markets and, though they remained small in the fifties and grew slowly, the share of manufactured goods in exports rose steadily to introduce a substantially larger long-term horizon for Australian manufacturing.

It does not necessarily follow that these Australian industries had 'grown up'. One of the more important issues for research in economic structure and policy is in the current effectiveness of the Australian tariff. Re-equipment and expansion of plant in the fifties and sixties provided opportunities for Australian manufacturing to 'catch up' on foreign technology and to utilize the available and increasing skills of the work force. It would be hazardous to judge how far these opportunities were realized, more particularly since improving overseas technology in these areas now offers scope for economies of scale to a degree not common in the 1920s and 1930s.

The major opportunities for catching up occurred, however, in the industrial areas that had been stimulated by the war—electrical goods, chemicals, rubber, vehicles, machinery and metal production. It was in these areas that lack of skills and the small scale of the market kept output and productivity in check before the Second World War and prevented the adoption of mass-production techniques in Australia. The wartime development of scale and assembly-line production provided the technological basis for peacetime adaptation. It was, however, more than merely a growing population and rising income levels that enlarged the post-war market for these products in Australia. Consumer demand 'caught up' with advanced Western countries through the rapidly rising demand for consumer durables which became articles of mass consumption for the first time in Australia during the 1950s. The greater complexity of these consumer durables stimulated the whole range of these 'growth' industries through demands for household electrical goods and, above all, for automobiles.

Whether Australian manufacturers would have introduced mass-production techniques as extensively as they were adopted without external intervention is an intriguing counterfactual question. Equally interesting is whether the introduction of foreign firms and foreign interest in Australian enterprises carried mass-production methods beyond optimum adaptation in Australian conditions. The inflow of foreign, especially American, capital and technology into Australian industry throughout the 1950s and 1960s appears as a major stimulus to increased efficiency. This direct investment was on a scale far above the limited British entry in the 1920s and, as in the 1920s, was induced by Australian trade barriers. It is possible, as discussed in the chapter on manufacturing, that the gradual breakdown of the initial restriction on competition in these products and the increased product differentiation increasingly limited Australia's productivity gains relative to the rest of the world. Partly offsetting these tendencies, the successive merger movements helped to concentrate output, though it is by no means clear from available studies whether a corresponding concentration of plants, the effective production units, was achieved. Some views on this issue are expressed in the chapter by Pat Brown and Helen Hughes. In fact, it is doubtful whether simple comparisons with Australian and overseas technology are very revealing. Amongst other considerations, direct investment in these areas allowed Australia to purchase foreign technology without the very high overheads associated with technological advance.

The relatively rapid expansion of these sectors of manufacturing, together with the growth of plant and machinery in food, drink, textiles, etc. greatly increased the capital intensity of Australian manufacturing. From the point of view of an economy with a rapidly growing work force, accelerated by planned immigration, this was not an unmixed blessing. The rise in labour productivity that followed implied a much less rapid increase in job opportunities in manufacturing and, indeed, the rapidly expanding manufacturing production became progressively less important in absorbing additions to the work force. The pre-war nexus between planned population acceleration and labour-intensive manufacturing had been broken by the post-war success of manufacturing growth. This change in input composition of manufacturing has become one factor suggesting the need for a reappraisal of the policy of sustaining high rates of immigration.

One of the important implications of the foregoing discussion lies in the character of capital inflow into Australia and the composition of capital formation since the Second World War. The interwar dependence on public borrowing overseas was drastically reversed, by far the greater part of foreign capital now entering the private sector and much of it by way of direct investment. This is a novel experience for Australia, raising important political issues. Here we are concerned with some general economic consequences. Concentrated on enterprise capital, foreign funds had an important effect in raising the relative significance of private investment in total capital formation. Public investment fell to approximately one-third compared with one-half of the total in pre-war years. Not only did this capital inflow provide a substantial enlargement of private fixed assets but was increasingly oriented into the major task of determining the resource potential of the continent, particularly in oil and mineral exploration and development.

For most of the period to the mid-sixties, the emphasis was on the growth of physical equipment. Rapidly growing manufacturing and service activities in major cities added a new dimension to the growth of capital. The progressive post-war rearrangement of urban patterns inducing relocation of manufacturing in outer areas may have encouraged the continued demand for conventional residential investment in the traditional urban sprawl. But the enlarged population concentration in the major cities, the rise of vehicular traffic and the increased complexity of city functions created opportunities and imposed increased pressures for large-scale urban redevelopment. These pressures were greatly intensified because of the past lumpiness in city centre development; the preceding major central building boom in Melbourne had occurred some seventy years earlier and in Sydney the central structures had been established during the 1870s and 1880s and in the 1920s. The obsolescence and physical decay of these structures tended to impose a similarly lumpy renewal task leading to a large-scale increase of redevelopment investment and the re-equipment of commercial, office and service activities.

While private enterprise capital expanded rapidly in rural, manufacturing and commercial facilities, the provision of publicly-provided social overhead capital fell, until the early sixties, increasingly behind. While its relative importance in total capital formation declined substantially, public investment changed substantially in composition. Its productivity performance may have gained from the disappearance of unemployment and the absence of work-creation incentives, though the fears of major recession died hard in the booming post-war world and appear to have had still some impact on the structure of public outlays. The public capital outlays of the 1950s and early sixties were directed into avenues more akin to enterprise capital than had been the case before the war. The relative decline in outlays on communications was the major structural change by comparison with pre-1939. This decline developed in contrast with the rapid growth of motor vehicle use both in long-distance carriage and in servicing demands in local, particularly increasingly congested city areas. By the early sixties, the failure to provide facilities for a highly motorized society had become a serious constraint representing one of the major policy shortcomings in post-war development.

The prospect of substantially increased demands for social overhead capital; the limitation of job opportunities in manufacturing; the uncertainty of rural export prospects, particularly in grain disposal; the increasing service orientation of the Australian economy and its greater need for human skills and the quality of performance in improving productivity and *per capita* standards; increasing foreign ownership and control of Australian enterprises—these might have been major problems demanding active solution and may well turn out to be serious problems for the future. They have tended to be partially submerged in the very recent past by other events. It would, perhaps, be inappropriate in local circumstances to say that Australians have a remarkable facility for pulling a rabbit out of the hat. A hat of continental proportions is, in any event, likely to be well stocked. At a time when, in the late 1840s, growth appears to have been seriously retarded, with long-run prospects in doubt for technological reasons, the gold 'discoveries' transformed the scene. At the turn of the century, uncertainly moving out of severe depression and experiencing the long-run effects of mismanagement of natural resources, Western Australian mineral resources were important in lifting the economy out of its difficulties. The Second World War may not have been an unmixed blessing. Nevertheless, it yielded for Australia an asset that perhaps should be the most highly prized: a greatly increased stock of human skills acquired under pressure of war. Now, in the 1960s, the prospects of a new natural resource bonanza are being revealed in the discovery of large and varied mineral resources in process of transforming our relations with the outside world, our export earnings and our domestic economy.

It would be rash to attempt to predict the outcome of this new bonanza. But it would be even rasher to allow the continuing and substantial problems of traditional Australian development to be submerged by visions of opulence. The experience of 1890–1939 should serve as ample warning of the consequences of mismanagement of assets, of too heavily discounting the future and of the reliance on wasting assets. We are now committed, in the foreseeable future, to a highly capital-intensive form of economic activity in both natural resource utilization, manufacturing and transport.

It seems more than doubtful whether a continued accent on accelerated growth of scale of the economy can be sensibly sustained in this light. The implication appears now to be more definitely than ever before in a progressive aggregation of the economy in metropolitan centres, unless positive action is taken to avoid this, and in service activities in those centres. The maintenance of traditional attitudes towards scale and population growth, in present policy conditions, seems likely to aggravate underlying problems of the future, not as was anticipated before 1939, to help to resolve them. Moreover, given the prospect of absorption of labour in services; and given the future dependence of manufacturing development on the entry into overseas markets, the emphasis on quantity of population needs to be adjusted radically to allow for increased quality. This is not to suggest the need merely for increased quality of migrants. Future long-run rates of growth of income per head depend basically on major improvements in the quality of all human capital. Given the immediate prospects of mineral development, the foundations for rapid *per capita* increase exist. But mineral resources represent a wasting asset and are subject to high risks, as past experience demonstrates. The major task is to divert a substantial part of increased affluence into the most enduring and adaptable resource—human capital—at a stage in our development when this can be achieved most easily, rather than to maximize current *per capita* consumption.

INDEX